AF519076

INDIAN LIBRARY AND INFORMATION SCIENCE LITERATURE (1992-1993)

INDIAN LIBRARY AND INFORMATION SCIENCE LITERATURE (1992-1993)

SEWA SINGH
Reader
Department of Library & Information Science
Guru Nanak Dev University
Amritsar

Ess Ess Publications

4837/24, Ansari Road
Daryaganj, New Delhi - 110 002
Phone : - 3260807

First published 1996

ISBN 81-7000-195-1

Rs. Ess Ess Rs.800/-

Published by
Ess Ess Publications
4837/24, Ansari Road,
Daryaganj
New Delhi - 110002.
Phone : 3260807

Composed by :
Academy of Computer Studies
BG-1/42, Paschim Vihar
New Delhi - 110063
Phone : 5580312

Printed By :
Santosh Offset, Delhi-110035

PREFACE

There is greater awareness now than before on the importance of library services in learning, scholarship, knowledge advancement, problem-solving, etc. It is being increasingly recognised that information is an essential input to development process, and libraries as repositories of knowledge and information provide vital support. Information now is regarded as resource of resources. The application of the importance of information will make far better informed users, and their level of expectation will be much higher. This introduces elements of change and role of library and information centres has already changed in the Western society. Due to this favourable environment the role of libraries and information centres has been undergoing a change also in India during the last more than a decade or so.

On looking at the library scene in India, we find all round development in all types of libraries, documentation and information centres. The development of public libraries has been greatly helped by the Raja Rammohun Roy Library Foundation ever since its establishement. Although the exact figures about the census of public libraries are not available, yet it can be concluded from the literature that they constitute the largest library system in the country. At present there are above 200 universities and about 8,000 colleges in the country. The number of various types of schools is in lakhs. Almost all the universities and colleges have set up libraries of various sizes; but unfortunately a large number of schools do not have their libraries.

A large number of special libraries and information centres have been set up in the country in the areas of science and technology, agriculture, defence, medicine, social sciences, arts and humanities. These are developing a sound and balanced collection equipped with tools of modern technology to provide efficient and effective services.

All these libraries have become agents of change and active force in the programmes of instituions, society and nation. They make a significant contributation to the educational advancement, cultural enrichment, scientific and technological development, economic progress, and so on. Correspondingly, the libraries of today have not only to organise the variety of documentary and non-documentary sources of information but also to make available the specific piece of information to the users. For performing these functions, they, today and tomorrow, need essentially to know the new publications, their sources, and the forms in which they are available.

There has also been development in the library and information science (LIS) education in the country. The number of LIS departments at the university level alone has grown tremendously, taking their strength to more than 80 in which are working about 350 teachers. Together, these departments produce about 2,700 first degree holders (ie, B L I Sc), about 400 to 450 with M L I Sc degrees, about 30 to 35 M Phil degree holders, and between 5 to 10 with Ph D degrees every year.

This all round growth has resulted in the growth of professional literature published in about 25 active English language journals; some regional language journals; while some authors publish abroad also. LIS literature is also reported, besides periodicals, in the proceedings of seminars and conferences organised by the various national level associations, state level associations, specialised associations, teaching departments and libraries and information centres.

In addition, the professional literature is also being published in book form by many Indian authors. It is estimated that about 30 books are published in India every year. These books include research books, text books, various festschrift volumes brought out in the honour of the library professionals, books edited for other purposes from time to time, and so on.

Some literature is also brought out in report form by the various government and non-government agencies, such as the University Grant Commission, Planning Commission, Raja Rammohun Roy Library Foundation, The National Library, etc.

This plethora of literature being published in Indian sources is increasing every year, more significantly for the last few years, and has now reached the annual average of about 950 items. It, therefore, requires bibliographical control to have easy access to all the items of published literature, and make the task of literature search in the field of LIS easier.

Efforts are being made at the national level, particularly by the IASLIC by publishing *Indian Library Science Abstracts*, which unfortunately has not been up-to-date. Besides, various bibliographies on LIS literature publisheded in India have been compiled from time to time. The latest bibliography has been complied by Dr Sewa Singh in 1994 for the period 1990-1991. He has earlier complied more such annotated bibliographies covering the period since 1971 to 1980; 1981 to 1985; and 1986 to 1989, thereby making it a continuous effort at bibliographic control in LIS literature published in India.

Some specialised bibliographies in classification and cataloguing, LIS education, Colon Classification, etc have also been compiled from time to time by some of our library professionals. Cumulative indexes have also been published for some of the LIS journals such as the Annals of Library Science and Documentation, Herald of Library Science, Library Science with a slant to Documentation and Information Studies. Some bibliographies for PhD theses and M L I Sc dissertations are also available. This provides, in brief, an overview of the various bibliographical control efforts made from time to time. However, these remain dated, and even the *Indian Library Science Abstracts* is not up-to-date, nor is it fully comprehensive in its coverage because it does not include articles published in books edited for various purposes.

The present work is an attempt at bibliographic control of the publications pertaining to the Indian librarians, library and information science teachers, and other scholars, of different aspects of library and information science. It covers the following:

- Articles published in LIS journals in English language only;

- Literature published in the form of books, monographs, reports, edited books, conference and seminar proceedings, etc;

- Articles by Indian LIS authors published in Indian LIS journals, books, etc.

It does not include in its scope the PhD theses and M L I Sc dissertations. It also excludes 'grey literature', book reviews, notes and news, and the like. This bibliographical work covers the published literature for the two years 1992 and 1993 only.

Thus besides being a useful guide for librarians, this fully annotated bibliography is equally important, rather a sine qua non, for educationists, researchers, students, and administrators alike who want to conduct survey in any branch of Indian library and information science literature.

It avoids any duplicate effort already attempted in other

bibliographical sources, and includes only that professional literature published during the two years of 1992 and 1993.

Although no effort has been spared to scan all the possible sources available in different university libraries at Amritsar, Chandigarh, Delhi, Kurukshetra, Patiala, Ujjain, etc, yet a few of these might have eluded me due to a variety of reasons. One notable reason has been the time lag in the publication of journals, so much so that some of them have not published their completed volumes for 1993. A comprehensive coverage for the years 1992-1993 is, therefore, not claimed, though that has been the cherished goal.

Despite this the total number of contributions has gone up during the last two years when compared with either the first two years of the 1990s, or any two years of the 1980s. The total citations included in Sewa Singh's latest bibliography for 1990-1991 are about 1,400 with an yearly average of about 700 items; while the yearly average for 1986-89 was about 665 items. There has been a regular rise in the total and average contribution to LIS literature in India.

The present volume includes a total of 1992 citations, including about 92 items for 1990 which somehow remained uncovered in the bibliography for 1990-1991. This brings the actual citations for 1992-1993 to about 1900, but at the same time about 90 to 100 contributions for 1993 still remain uncovered in the present volume for the reasons mentioned above. It shows a remarkable increase in the Indian contribution to the body of LIS literature in recent years. This increase speaks volumes of the maturity of Indian librarianship and greater awareness among the library and information professionals, a step in the right direction.

However, the phenomenal rise in the LIS literature for the years 1992 and 1993 could also be attributed to a great event, the celebration of the Birth Centenary Year of the great Indian librarian and library educator, Dr Shiyali Ramamrita Ranganathan in 1992 which overflowed to 1993 also. It witnessed a spurt of literature published by Indian and foreign friends/colleagues, librarians, and others about the life and work of Ranganathan, his contribution to the various aspeccts of LIS field. As was expected, the Birth Centenery Year, 1992, has seen the publication of maximum literature (ie, 1134 items) in form of books as well as the periodical literature; followed by 761 items for 1993.

For the compilation of this volume well recognised national and international practices of bibliographies have closely been followed. Standard abbreviations with minor variations are used for the periodicals covered. To meet the needs of the complexities of LIS literature published in these years, the citations are arranged according to the 20th edition of Dewey Decimal Classification system with extended schedules at various places depending on the requirements of literature. Both the DDC notation and their equivalent subject headings are given for the convenience of the professional users. The citations are arranged alphabetically by author under each subject heading. For the quick and relevant retrieval of citations, all the references are serially numbered.

The full bibliographical information with regard to an item is in this order: Citation number, Author(s), Title of article, Name of the journal (in abbreviated form), Volume number, Issue numbers, Months, Year, particular pages, and annotation or abstract. All the citations included in the bibliographical work are fully annotated. The absracts/annotations are informative to the needy users conducting literature search.

This work is divided into five parts. Part I includes citations on subjects like general knowledge, book, computers, data communications, etc. This grouping is like this because it is based on the organisation of DDC schedule (000-019). Part II covers citations on different aspects of library and information science (020-029); while Part Ill includes citations on other related subjects including library legislation, copyright law, social sciences, etc (030-999). Part IV of this work includes a supplement; and Part V includes two Indexes: Subjects Index in alphabetical order, and Author Index arranged also alphabetically bringing all the contributions of one author together. Both the indexes refer to the citation numbers included in Parts I to IV.

The supplement includes another 25 entries all for 1992, which somehow slipped while preparing the volume. With this the total number of entries goes upto 2017 taking the yearly average to more than one thousand contributions.

The hours of overwork, effort, and sweat involved in the preparation of this volume will mean a time well invested if it is of any help and use to the library administrators, library educators, researchers and students surveying literature and gathering necessary bits of information on various facets of library and information science.

In preparing this bibliographical work I have depended upon a large number of primary and secondary sources. I would like to express my thanks to the personnel of various libraries who allowed me free access to their holdings. Thanks are due to the friends in the profession and outside who helped me in many ways in the collection of relevant data. I would like to record my sincere thanks to Prof P B Mangla, Krishan Kumar, Dr S R Gupta of the University of Delhi; Ms Rekha Mittal of INSDOC, New Delhi; Sh Ashok Kumar of DESIDOC, Delhi; Dr P S Kawatra and Ms Nirmal Malhotra of NCERT, New Delhi; Dr P S G Kumar of the University of Nagpur; Dr B B Shukla, Editor, Indian Journal of Information Library & Society; Sh D R Kalia, Editor, CLIS Observer; Dr M K Stanley, University Librarian and Editor of Indian Journal of Agricultural Library and information Services; the Editor, Granthana; the Editor, College Library; the Editor, Bhavan's Journal. I would also like to record my gratitude to Ms Kalpana Dasgupta, Principal Information Officer of the National Library, now chief Librarian, central Secretariat library, Delhi; Sh G S Dhillon of CSIO, Chandigarh; Dr Jasmer Singh of Punjabi University, Patiala; Dr H R Chopra of the Panjab University, Chandigarh; Sh S K Ghai of Sterling Publishers; Sh Praveen Mittal of B R Publishing Corporation; the managers of Aditya Prakashan; Dr L S Ramaiah of CIEFL, Hyderabad; Dr Suseela Kumar, President, Madras Library Association, Dr B Ramesh Babu of the University of Madras; Sh. Sanjaya Mishra of IGNOU, Patna. My wife Narinder Kaur, and children Serebdeep, Amardeep, and Mahsa Sondeep deserve my appreciation for their patience and cooperation in completing the work in time. For mistakes, if any, the responsibility is entirely mine. I am finally thankful to M/s Ess Ess Publications, New Delhi, for promptly publishing this volume.

Amritsar

Sewa Singh

CONTENTS

ABBREVIATIONS AND THEIR EXPLANATIONS

ALD	Academic Library Development, edited by K Rajasekharan and R Raman Nair, New Delhi: Ess Ess Publications 1991. 92 p.
ALE	Academic Library Effectiveness, edited by R Raman Nair and K Rajasekharan, New Delhi: Ess Ess Publications, 1992. viii, 123 p.
ALIS	Advances in Library And Information Science, edited by D C Ojha and CD Sharma , Jodhapur: Scientific Publishers, 1993-1994. Vols 3-4.
ALR	Academic Libraries: Role in National Development: Festschrift volume in honour of Prof N B Inamdar, edited by Isaac Dorothy, A A N Raju and L S Ramaiah, Madras: T R Publications, 1993. xx, 304 p.
CC	Colon Classification 7th edition: Some Perspectives, edited by M P Satija, New Delhi: Sterling Publishers, 1993. xx, 220 p.
CLA	Chandigarh Librarians' Association Souvenir, Chandigarh: CLA, 1992.
CODE	Collection Development in the Context of Economic Recession: Papers of XIX All India Library Conference, Calcutta: IASLIC, 1993. iv, 174 p.
COP	Cognitive Paradigms in Knowledge Organisation; Second international ISKO conference, edited by A Neelameghan, M A Gopinath, K S Raghavan and P Sankralingam, Bangalore: Sarada Ranganathan Endowment for Library Science, 1992. 466 p.
CRL	Current Research in Library and Information Science: Festschrift to Prof M R Kumbhar, edited by S Seetharama and C R Karisiddappa, Jaipur: R B S A Publishers, 1993. xii, 219 p.
CS	Current Studies in Library and Information science (Felicitation volume of Dr S R Gunjal), edited by C R Karisiddappa, S L Sangam and B S Maheswarappa, Delhi: Manak Publications,

	1993. xii, 354 p.
CTIT	Current Trends in Information Technology: Its Impact on Information Scene in India, edited by Kuldip Chand, New Delhi: Batra Book Service. 1993. viii, 199 p.
DAB	Documentation and Bibliographic Control of the Humanities in India, edited by L S Ramaiah and M Kankachary, New Delhi: Aditya Prakashan, 1992. xv, 349 p.
DL	Dynamics of Librarianship; Felicitation to Luminaries in the Profession: Birth Centenary publication of Dr S R Ranganathan, Annamalainagar : Department of Library & Infromation Science, Annamalai University, 1992. x, 327+ 14 p.
IASLIC	Indian Association of Special Libraries and Information Centres, Calcutta
ILA	Indian Library Association, Delhi
ILS	Institute of Library Science, Hyderabad , Souvenir, edited by S Sudarshan Rao, Hyderabad: Institute of Library Science, 1991.
INFO	A compendium of selected papers on bibliometrics and informetrics, edited by I K Ravichandra Rao, Bangalore: Sarada Ranganathan Endowment for Library Science, 1992. ix, 580 p.
IPLA	Indian Public Library Association, Hyderabad, Souvenir of All India Public Library Conference, Hyderabad: Indian Public Library Association, 1992.
IR	Information Retrieval: Models and Techniques; Papers of 15th National Seminar, 26-29 December, 1992, Annamalai University, Calcutta: IASLIC, 1992. iv, 100 p.
ITAH	Information Technology and Health Science Libraries: Papers presented at the national convention and workshop, edited by S P Gupta, Divya Srivastava, A M Siddiqui, and R P Kumar, New Delhi: Medical Library Association, 1993. x, 279 p.

LID	Librarianship in Developing Countries, edited by N Guruswamy Naidu, New Delhi : Ess Ess Publications 1992. xii, 266 p.
LIM	Workshop on Library and Information Management, August 7-9, 1992, edited by S. Seetharama, Bangalore: DRTC, 1992, various pagings.
LIN	Librarianship in North-east India: A souvenir to commemorate the Silver jubilee celebrations, Dept. of Library and Information Science, Gauhati University, 4-5 July 1992, edited by Bhadra Borah and Bhupen Goswamee, Guwahati : Dept of Library and Information Science, Gauhati University, 1992. xvi, 146 p.
LIS	Library and Information Science: Trends and challenges: Essays in honour of Prof S S Agrawal, edited by A Tejomurty and S Kumar, New Delhi: Indus Publishing Co, 1993. 192 p.
LISI	Library and Iinformation Science in India, edited by P S G Kumar and C P Vashishth, New Delhi: Sterling Publishers, 1992. xii, 220 p.
LIT	Library and Information Technology: In pursuit of excellence; Seminar papers of 38th All India Library Conference, Utkal University, Bhubaneswar, Nov 21-24, 1992, edited by C P Vashishth, O P Sharma, A P Gakhar and Dev Raj Singh, Delhi: ILA, 1992. xii, 318 p.
LM	The Library Movement: A collection of essays by diverse hands, Madras: Madras Library Association, 1929, Reprinted by Government Press, 1992. various pagings.
LT	Library Trends: Agricultural Libraries and Information, edited by Keith W Russell and Maria G Pisa, Jodhpur: Scientific Publishers, 1992. 312 p.
ML	Medical Libraries: Keys to Health Information: Proceedings of the 6th International Congress on Medical librarianship..., New Delhi: Medical Library Association, 1992. 2 Volumes. 794 p.

PLD	Public Library Development, edited by R Raman Nair, New Delhi: Ess Ess Publications, 1993. xi, 178 p.
PP	Petits Petals: A tribute to S R Ranganathan, edited by K Navalani and M P Satija, New Delhi: ABC Publishing House, 1993, xiv, 150 p.
RAT	S R Ranganathan: A tribute, Calcutta: The National Library, 1993. 57p.
RAW	S R Ranganathan and the West, edited by R N Sharma, New Delhi: Sterling Publishers, 1992. xvii, 179 p.
RDAL	Resource Development in Academic Libraries, edited by G Devarajan, P Gopapakrishana Nair, and M Ahmed Kunju, New Delhi: Ess Ess Publications, 1992. xii, 124 p.
SPLS	Seminar on Public Library System at Cross roads, by Andhra Pradesh Library Association, Vijaywada : Andhra Pradesh Library Association, 1992. various pagings.
SRR	S R Ranganathan, 1892-1972, edited by Edward Dudley, New Delhi: Ess Ess Publications, 1992. 39 p. (First Indian reprint; originally published by the Library Association, London, 1973).
STIM	S & T Information Management in India: Papers presented at the 10th Annual Convention & Conference of the Society for Information Science, held at RRL, Trivandrum, during 17-19 Jan 1991, edited by H C Jain and B M Gupta, New Delhi : Aditya Prakashan, 1993. viii, 182 p.
TDF	Two Decades of the Foundation (1972-1992): Souvenir brought out on the occasion of the 20th Anniversary celebrations, by Raja Rammohun Roy Library Foundation, Calcutta : RRRLF, 1993. 87 p.

ABBREVIATIONS OF THE JOURNALS INDEXED

Indian

AGLIS Jl	AGLIS Journal
Ann Lib Sci & Docum	Annals of Library Science & Documentation
CLIS Observer	CLIS Observer
Coll Libs	College Libraries
DESIDOC Bull	DESIDOC Bulletin of Information Technology
Granthana	Granthana; Indian Journal of Library Studies
Her Lib Sci	Herald of Library Science
Iaslic Bull	Iaslic Bulletin
ILA Bull	ILA Bulletin
IJALIS	Indian Journal of Agricultural Libraries and Information Systems
IJILIS	Indian Journal of Information Library & Society
INICAE	International Information Communication & Education
Int Lib Move	International Library Movement
Jl Info Sci	Journal of Information Sciences
Jl Lib & Info Sci	Journal of Library and Information Science
Lib Her	Library Herald
Lib Prog (Int)	Library Progress (International)
Lib Sci slant Docum & Info Std	Library Science with a slant to Documentation and Information Studies
Lib Today	Library Today
Luck Libn	Lucknow Librarian
NISSAT Newsletter	NISSAT Newsletter
Rilisar Bull	Rilisar Bulletin
Siscom	Siscom
Timeless Fellowship	Timeless Fellowship

Foreign

Aslib Proceedings	Aslib Proceedings
IFLA Jl	IFLA Journal
Info Mgmt Rep	Information Management Report
Int Cat & Bib Cont	International Cataloguing & Bibliographic Control
Int Classif	International Classification (now Knowledge Organization)
Int Info Lib Rev	International Information & Library Review
Jl of Docum	Journal of Documentation
Lib Rev	Library Review
Libri	Libri; International Library Review
Lib Times Int	Library Times International
Program	Program
Third World Lib	Third World Libraries

Non- Professional Periodicals

Administrator	Administrator
Aryan Heritage	Aryan Heritage
Bhavan's Jl	Bhavan's Journal
CSIR Newsletter	CSIR Newsletter
Fortnight	Fortnight
Frontline	Forntline
India Mgmt	India Management
India Today	India Today
Inside Outside	Inside Outside
NIRD Newsletter	NIRD Newsletter
Univ News	University News
WII Newsletter	WII Newsletter

Indian Newspapers

The Hindu
Hindustan Times
Indian Express
Patriot
Pioneer
Times of India
The Tribune

PART 1

KNOWLEDGE, COMPUTERS, BIBLIOGRAPHIES, ETC.

PART 1

KNOWLEDGE, COMPUTERS, BIBLIOGRAPHIES, ETC.

001 KNOWLEDGE

BINWAL, J C 1

Mode of formation of subjects : A model for knowledge representation, *Jl Lib & Inf Sci* 17 (1) June 1992 : 82-88.

Discusses the concept of social knowledge. Describes the criterion for distinguising different kinds of social knowledge. Enumerates the attributes of a subject and concept of formation of subjects. Describes empirical study carried out to test the model prepared by Ranganathan. Concludes that this model is a powerful tool for knowledge representation in information retrieval.

BINWAL, J C 2

Ranganathan and the universe of knowledge, *Int Classif* 19 (4) 1992 : 195-200.

States that Ranganathan was the first library and information scientist to recognise the role of developmental and structural studies of subjects in knowledge representation. Mentions structural contribution of Ranganathan.Gives different types of social knowledge. Highlights other structural and developmental attributes of the universe of subjects as propounted by Ranganathan. Points out their relevance and role in information retrieval.

BORAH, MEENA 3

Theory of knowledge of three great legends, *LIN*, 5-9.

Discusses about the Greek philosophers thought as expounded by Socrates, Plato and Aristotle. Gives also the bases of their systems of philosophy which has been improved by one over the other thus making it case of classic contribution to the body of knowledge.

HALDANE, J B S 4

Scientific knowledge problems of dissemination, *Iaslic Bull* 37 (2) June 1992 : 51-54.

Originally written in 1961, discusses four stages of generation of scientific knowledge: Collection of primary data; organisation of data; analysis of results; and publication. Discusses roles of editing, teaching, textbooks, and libraries in growth, transmission and education of scientific knowledge. Discusses desireable process of library upkeeping and book selection. Compares the states of affairs in India and Europe.

PADHI, PITAMBARA 5

Authority centred mode of thinking, *CS*, 17-23.

Defines the term 'authority'. Gives its scope and limitations. Mentions sources of authoritative knowledge. Explains in detail, with examples, the authoritative mode of thinking and its influence on society.

SANGAM, S L 6

Pattern of development of knowledge, *CS*, 5-16.

States the meaning and genesis of knowledge. Describes types of knowledge. Discusses patterns of growth and development of knowledge through the centuries. Mentions mapping of knowledge based on some identified epochs. Highlights spiral of scientific method of S R Ranganathan.

SATIJA, M P 7

Anatomy of the evolution and growth of knowledge, *Int Lib Move* 15 (2) 1993 : 77-86. Also in *Luck Libn* 24 (2) Apr.-June 1992 : 49-57.

Defines knowledge. Discusses the growth of knowledge, natural growth, planned growth, induced growth. Describes three modes of growth, namely, specialisation trends, interdisciplinary growth, and multidisciplinary growth of knowledge. Concludes that new modes may emerge in the future in consonance with the new research trends.

SINGH, SONAL 8

Knowledge and its kinds, *Jl Info Sci* 3 (2) Oct-Dec 1992: 73-80.

Gives definitions and meanings of knowledge which is the outcome of human mind. Describes types of knowledge both on the basis of availability and nature of knowledge. Takes also knowledge as a trinity through tantric symbol in Indian mythology, the emblem of *Shakti*, the ultimate power. Depicts that the knowledge we have today is resultant outcome of our total experiences gained through perception, intellect and intuition.

SRIVASTAVA, A P 9

Knowledge as stock-in-trade of librarians, *Ann Lib Sci & Docum* 39 (3) Sept 1992 : 81-85.

Describes knowledge as power, and that libraries and institutions which deal with utilisation of knowledge and role of librarians is essential in generation and utilisation of knowledge, so that he becomes knowledge broker.

001 (1) HUMANITIES

KAULA, P N 10

The positive aspect of humanistic studies, *DAB*, 23-29.

Defines humanities. Traces the thought of culture of the ancient past. Discusses India's contribution to the development of humanities. Explains that Indian contribution has been highlighted through foreign authors as William Jones, Max Mueller, Grierson, Keith, Cunningham, etc. Discusses methodology on research in humanities. Points out need to introduce indological material in education system and need to establish databanks and networks.

NARASIMHA RAJU, GVSL 11

Humanities - the dilemma of definition, *DAB*, 33-37.

Gives meaning of humanities. Traces history of humanities. Mentions aims of humanities. Discusses the relationship of religion and humanities; and science and humanities. Concludes that justification of humanities lie in its subjectivity besides objectivity

PANIKER, K AYYAPPA 12

Aim and scope of research in humanities, *DAB*, 18-22.

Defines research. Discusses research in humanities as different from research in physical, natural, and social sciences on the basis of aim and nature. Discusses also science of literature and literary scholarship. Describes methodology of research in humanities.

RAMAKRISHNA RAO, K 13

Humanities and the university, *DAB*, 9-17.

Defines education. Explains role of the humanities in the university curriculum. Describes humanities and higher education in India, after independence. States that the value of humanities is recognised by education commissions also. Studies also the relationship between humanities and science and that their studies be offered to students. Describes the teaching of humanities in our universities suffers from many defects.

VISWANATHAN, K 14

A plea for the humanities, *DAB*, 1-8.

Explains art and its importance in human life. States that men only make books. Defines humanism. Discusses the need for humanistic studies as it deals with human problems. Describes the value of humanistic studies which is minimised by our unproductive education system. Makes a plea for the humanisties in this age of technology.

001.4 Research

VISWANATHAN, B 15

Indian scientific reviews-an overview, *Rilisar Bull* 8 (2) Apr-June 1993: 9-15.

Explains the need for good review articles in science. Asessess one of the possible reasons for the low intrinsic quality of Indian scinetific research. Analyses the reasons probably lack of comprehensive information and habit of citing for the low quality.

002 BOOK

KALSEKAR, SATISH 16

Books, *Univ News* 30 (35) Aug 31, 1992: 149.

Highlights the importance of books in our life. States that these are not junk and can not be sold like ornaments. It is translated from Marathi by Shirish Chindhade for the benefit of the English reading public.

NARAYANA KURPA, P 17

The true university - a collection of books, *LM*, 120-121.

Explains the importance of books in making or unmaking a nation of good people. Suggests that every home should have a collection of books and thus create a university there.

SESHADRI, P 18

Among my books, *LM*, 106-108.

Describes that an essential aspect of the library movement should be the instilling of the love of books in every educated person. Concludes that book buying habits should be developed to make the movement successful and establish the libraries everywhere.

TAKING the byte out of books, *Indian Express* 25 Oct 1993, p 6 19

Describes how floppy disks and CD-ROMs are revolutionising the world of books, as was evident at the recent Frankfurt Book Fair. States that electronic publishing, however, is unlikely to banish the printed book unless a totally computer-nurtured generation of children appears.

002 (1) Book Club

NARAYANAN, V 20

The book club, *LM*, 109-110.

Highlights the importance of books and libraries in the lives of people. States that there should be set up Book Clubs where books are always kept ready to welcome us and we could browse through their pages full of wisdom.

004 COMPUTERS

MIRANI, A N 21

Role of CMC for the development and maintenance of computers in India *CTIT*, 133-140.

Discusses the role and activities of the Computer Maintenance Corporation, New Delhi in the development and maintenance of computers in India. Explains maintenance systems developed by the CMC for this purpose.

004 (1) AI & ES

JANAKIRAMAN, V S 22

Foundations of artificial intelligence and Expert Systems, New Delhi : Macmillan, 1993, xvi, 23 p.

Deals with the basics and the fundamental concepts of artificial intelligence (AI), and Expert Systems (ES)as a further development of computers. States the concepts in a simple and lucid language to enable the readers to comprehend the terms and their meanings.

004.03 Computers - Dictionaries

TIWARI, P C 23

A dictionary of abbreviations in computers and information science, 1993. 120 p.

Enumerates all the important abbreviations used frequently in computers as well as in the subject of information science. Gives their meaning also. However, it can not be termed as comprehensive.

004.33 Online Processing

REITT, DAVID 24

16th International online information Meeting, *INICAE* 12 (1) Mar 1993 : 97-100.

Reports about this Meeting held on 8-10 December 1992 at Olympia, London attended by about 8,000 people. Mentions its programme, language sessions, awards presented, satellite events. States that the largest online CD-ROM Information exhibition was held on this occasion.

004.56 CD-ROM

CD-ROM OF ASIAN INFORMATION ON HEALTH AND ENVIRONMENT : 25

First consortium meeting, *NISSAT Newsletter* 12 (4) Oct-Dec 1993: 10-11.

Describes the first consortium meeting of about 30 experts from Asian countries held in New Delhi during 20-23 September 1993 sponsored by IDRC, Canada on the theme of CD-ROM of Asian Information on Health and the Environment. All the sessions were chaired by Mr Shahid Akhtar, Director, Information and Communication System and Networks, IDRC, Canada.

CD-ROM Online Users : Second National Meet, 26

NISSAT Newsletter 12(3) July-Sept 1993: 5-18.

Describes the Second meet organised at the Department of Science and Technology, New Delhi during 15-16 July 1993 by NISSAT in collaboration with Society for Information Science which was attended by about 60 participants. At four sessions 25 presentations were made. These were capped by Panel discussion devoted to issues like acquisitions and custom clearance, etc.

GAYASUDDIN and BUXTON, ANDREW B 27

CD-ROM as an alternate medium of access to biomedical information in developing countries, *ML*, 163-170.

Describes biomedical information as a vital need. States importance of access to biomedical information. Demonstrates that the new CD-ROM technology seems to be one of the best short term and practical alternative for improving biomedical information supply and increasing information self sufficiency in developing countries.

GEETHA, V 28

CD-ROM - an information media, *LIT*, 254-255.

States that in view of the changes in library and information science field, the storage media is also changing. Discusses optical disks and structure of CD-ROM. Describes application of CD-ROM in library and information field. Concludes that it resolves many retrieval issues.

004.6 (1) Computer Networking

NITYANAND, B, KARWANYUN, S N , SRIVASTAVA, S C, and DHAR, B B 29

Layered structure of computer networking for efficient management of a research laboratory, *Ann Lib Sci & Docum* 40 (4) Dec 1993 : 138-145.

Mentions importance of office automation. Suggests layered structure for the application layer for a research laboratory. Suggests Local Area Network (LAN) with different protocols in accordance with the Open System International (OSI).

004.6(1) Communication Technologies

ASHOK KUMAR 30

Advances in communication technology: Tele-conferencing and telepresence, *Desidoc Bull Inf Techn* 13 (5) Sept 1993: 3-5.

States that as a result of the developments in 'Virtual technology' teleconferencing mode of communication may be allowed. Gives advantages of video teleconferencing. Mentions that telepresence is another application made possible by the development in communication technology. Discusses how virtual reality technology enables the user to participate in artificially created worlds, simulated inside a computer.

ASHOK KUMAR and UDAYA SANKAR, L 31

Current communication technologies - an overview, *Desidoc Bull Inf Techn* 12 (3) May 1992: 3-10.

States that like most of the current interdisciplinary technologies, advances in computer and communication are influencing many different areas such as printing, photography and mass communication. Discusses that as a result of these development, in future, one may read newspaper on computer screen using E-mail, high definition or digital TV, filmless cameras, and telecommute to work.

GUIROYE, A DE 32

Policy on telecommunications, *INICAE* 12 (2) Sept 1993: 227-231.

Describes about the community policy in telecommunications developed in three stages. The first stage began with the action programme, the Second with the publication of the Commission's Green Paper on telecommunications service and equipment, and the third stage began with the publication of a report on implementation of objectives. Mentions also the future initiatives in this regards.

RAVAIOLI, PIERO and ZOURABICHVILI, MILLY 33

Directive to operate telecommunications sectors, *INICAE* 12 (2) Sept 1993: 236-239.

Describes the new Directive of the European Council regarding the suppliers and purchasers in the telecommunications sector. Discusses objectives and scope of the Directive with reference to the improved information for suppliers, transparent decision-making, and the international dimension it assumes.

WARNER, FRANCOIS 34

Changes in telecommunication service, *INICAE* 12 (2) Sept 1993: 231-236.

Reviews the bottlenecks in way of telecommunications, and the prospect for its development. Discusses the role of telecommunication industry and the economic consequences. Mentions the proposed four options of the Commission and that it is leading towards liberalisation. Discusses also medium-term priorities, set by the Commission.

004.69 HYPERTEXT. HYPERMEDIA

RAMAISH, C K 35

Hypertext and hypermedia : An overview, *Desidoc Bull Inf Techn* 12 (6) Nov 1992: 3-13.

Provides an overview of the historical development of hypertext (HT), which non-linear text or non-sequential writing, hypermedia (HM) and multimedia; types of HT system; their general characteristics, advantages, disadvantages and limitations. Lists important HT systems and HM products; their shortage and distribution patterns. Discusses problems like disorientation, cognitive overhead, lack of presentation, rhetoric and construction of default paths.

RAMAIAH, C K 36

Is hyper text a more flexible teaching tool for education ?, *Ann Lib Sci & Docum* 39 (1) Mar 1992: 1-8.

Defines hypertext (HT) as nonlinear and nonsequential text. Gives a brief view of HT and its salient features. Describes why HT is required for teaching and what are its strengths and weaknesses for using it as a teaching tool in education. Points out also the important reasons for using HT as teaching tool and its impact on education.

RAMAIAH, C K 37

An overview of hypertext and hypermedia, *INICAE* 11 (1) Mar 1992: 26-42.

Describes historical development of hypertext (HT), hypermedia (HM) and multimedia. Discusses types of HT system, general characteristics, advantages and disadvantages, drawbacks and limitations of HT, HM systems. Outlines detailed overview of HT, introduced to HM and multimedia. Discusses also problems like disorientation, cognitive overhead, lack of presentation, rhetoric, etc.

SINGH, SURYA NATH 38

Hyper media : A flexible tool for medical information system, *ITAH*, 105-118.

Defines hypertext. Differantiates between hypermedia, multimedia, and hypertext. Gives brief historical development. Highlights some of the salient features of HM with advantages and disadvantages. Explains in detail its applications in biomedical information systems. Makes suggestions to create awareness about this new system in India.

SRINATH, MANORAMA and NARAYANAN, A 39

Hypertext and hypermedia: An overview, *IR*, 93.

Discusses about the origin and development of the terms 'hypertext' and 'hypermedia'. Mentions the differences between the two. Provides an overview of the two important electronic forms of the text.

005.3 SOFTWARE. PROGRAMS

JOSE, J M and VISWANATHAN, T 40

Software documentation and standards, *Ann Lib Sci & Docum* 39 (4) Dec 1993: 123-133.

Deals with software documentation and standards which occupy an important place in software engineering process. Discusses the need of a software librarian as a part of software engineering team. Deals with evolving a standardization process for an organization using international standards as guidelines. Presents some quality indicators for software documentation.

MACINTOSH's System 7.0 - MAC's latest system software, 41
Desidoc Bull Inf Techn 12 (1) Jan 1992 : 3-5.
Discusses what is Desk Top Publishing (DTP), and mentions its benefits. Describes about MacIntosh series of DTP systems, particulary the Macintosh System 7.0 which is a step towards ease of use and functionality. Gives the system requirement and mentions need and problem of upgradation of the System.

MIYAZAWA, AKIRA 42
CJK -JRG : International Conference on East Asian character code, *INICAE* 12 (1) Mar 1993: 100-102.

Gives the background of CJK - JRG (Chinna, Japan, Korea - Joint Research Group), and its meeting held in July 1991 in Tokyo to study the creation of a unified character repertoire for ideographic East Asian characters. Mentions the issues discussed. Points out the future outlook.

SOFTWARE SOURCES CATALOGUE, *J1 INF SCI* 3
(3) JAN-MAR 1993: 161-170. 43
Provides a comprehensive guide to specific category of Databses which runs under Microsoft Windows. Arranged in alphabetical order, gives information about software, the equipments required and a few special features.

TSAI, BOR-SHENG 44
Mapping metrics for subject-object coordinated field recognition and representation, *Lib Sci slant Docum & Inf Std* 30 (3) Sept 1993: 91-102.

Gives a sample microcomputer software program, using concise IBM BASICA LOGO language, provides a formula and skelton for micro-networking and mapping the essential objects, a cumulative repository of advantageous learning experience and knowledge.

VENKATASUBRAMANIAN, M 45

Programming without programmers : Over to 4 GLs, *CSI Communication* 17 (3) 1993: 9-11.

Discusses role of end-user programming in the field of IT. Takes stock of the scenario in information system development and addresses its difficulties. Focuses on the fourth general languages (4 GLs), comprehending the concepts, its role in IT, merits and limitations.

VIDONDO, FELIX 46

Galileo : Design language for real time systems, *INICAE* 12 (2) Sept 1993: 172-190.

Discusses the problems of real time software systems and the new language methodology called Galileo. Examines the Galileo project history and characteristics of its language. Describes Galileo building blocks; procedure blocks; process blocks; and the methodological steps used. Presents Galileo design example through a number of illustrations. Gives also some observations on the system.

005.71 DATA COMMUNICATION. DATA TRANSMISSION

GUEST EDITORIAL : Global access to information,

Lib Sci Slant Docum & Inf Std 30 (4) Dec 1993: i-ii. 47

Traces history of communication revolution upto the present when data communication networks are all around. Reports about the data communication technology in India.

SHARMA, JAIDEEP 48

Data transmission techniques, *ILA Bull* 29 (1-2) Apr-Sept 1993: 21-25.

Describes the term telecommunication. Discusses problems in telecommunication. Explains packet switching. Describes briefly various data transmission techniques, and modes of transmission including microwave transmission and digital transmission. Concludes that library networks should be established for exchange of information.

005.74 DATABASES. DATABANKS

MANGROVES ECOSYSTEM INFORMATION SERVICE, *NISSAT Newsletter* 12 (4) Oct-Dec 1993: 11, 17. 49

Describes about the databases package developed on mangroves aimed at helping presentation of global biodiversity and ecological balance. Mangroves Ecosystem Information Service (MEIS) is an integrated package of four databases, namely MANEXP, MANBIB, MANRES and MANKAR.

005.78 Distributed Databases

ARORA, JAGDISH and AHUJA, J P S 50

Distributed databases and micro computer based LAN for a library and information centre, *AGLIS Jl* 9, 1993 (Abstract only).

Tells the concept of distributed databases hosted on microcomputer based LAN for a library and information centre.

015.54 INDIAN NATIONAL BIBLIOGRAPHY

VENKATACHARI, P N 51

Ranganathan's views on Romanisation of Indian scripts for the Indian National Bibliography, *Iaslic Bull* 37 (3) Sept 1992: 183-185.

Traces the early phase of development of INB. Discusses that as INB had to cover publications in Indian languages and in Indian scripts, which are many problems of romanisation were to be solved. Discusses views of Ranganathan in the matter as obtained by the author.

015.5484 Bibliographies-Telugu

VENKATAPPAIAH, V 52

Bibiographical tools in Telugu, *DAB*, 203-208.

Mentions functions of bibliogrpahy. Traces need for a bibliography in Telugu. Mentions about the development of regional language fascicules of INB which serve as bibliographical tools. Gives importance of library catalogues as tools of bibliographical control. Discusses about indexes of periodicals. Enumerates Telugu bibliography in English. Mentions that there is no retrospective bibliography of books in Telugu.

015.5487 Bibliographies-Kannada

NAGAPPA, B and NAGARAJA, S 53

Bibliographical phenomena of Kannada books reprinted during 1977-87, *CS*, 267-283.

Provides statistical details covering annual book production in Kannada during 1977-87. Compares the number of original prints with those of reprints. Identifies subjectwise scattering, average size, price, pagination, etc. with ranks of authors, titles, publishers of 1162 reprintes works. Gives a brief note on printing, publishing and bibliographical activities in Kannada.

PART -II

LIBRARY AND INFORMATION SCIENCE

PART -II

LIBRARY AND INFORMATION SCIENCE

020 LIBRARY AND INFORMATION SCIENCE

AGRAWAL, S P and SHARMA, PUSHPA RANI 54

Communication informatics and librarianship in India; an introductory guide to publications based on a survey of libraries in Capital city of India, New Delhi: Concept Publishing Company, 1992. 479 p.

Enlists in one single sequence the national information resources in communication, information and librarianship of 33 important Delhi libraries. Intends to help the practising librarians, teachers, researchers. Provides subject approach and author approach. Gives added entries to author approach also.

BORAH, BHADRA and GOSWAMEE, BHUPEN, *Eds* 55

Librarianship in North-east India: A souvenir to commemorate the Silver Jubilee celebrations, Department of Library and Information Science, Gauhati University 4-5 July 1992. xvi, 146 p.

Includes 12 articles in English and 8 articles in Assamese on different aspects of library and information science in this Souvenir brought out on the occasion of Silver Jubilee of the Department of Library and Information Science, Gauhati University. It is fondly dedicated to the Dr S R Ranganathan, Father of Library Science in India, and late Dr R L Mittal who served Gauhati University for some time.

BOSE, H 56

Information science: Principles and practice -a treatise on documentation, New Delhi: Sterling Publishers, 1993. xiii, 199 p

Contains good number of chapters on various facets of information science as well as documentation. It is a revised edition of the author's earlier book and facets on documentation have been added in it.

DEVARAI, RAJASHEKHAR and DAMODARAM, T 57

Information for the common man and the future of librarianship: A critical analysis, *IJILIS* 6(1-2) Jan-June 1993: 84-92.

Defines some keywords. Analyses relationship between information needs of common man and future of librarianship.

Hypothesizes that the more the librarianship focuses its attention on the needs of common man, more it will prosper towards professionalisation resulting in higher salary, status, and prestige in society. Presents a critical analysis.

GOPINATH, M A and SUDARSANA REDDY, D 58

Comparative study of the theoretical basic of mass communication and information science, *Lib Sci slant Docum & Inf Std* 30 (4) Dec 1993: 129-138.

Delineates the difference between mass communication and information science. Establishes the theoretical models which present a framework to mass communication. Presents the inter-relationships existing between most communication studies and information science in the form of a table. It is also shown as to how the two can together work for an information conscious society.

GUPTA, PAWAN K 59

The social and professional responsibilities of the profession, In *Papers*, 58th IFLA General Conference, New Delhi, 30 Aug - 5 Sept 1992, pp

Describes the profession, and profession of library and information science. Explains in detail the social as well as the professional responsibilities of the library and information professionals, particularly in the changing environment as a result of the application of new information technology.

GUPTA, PAWAN K and USHA PAWAN 60

The status, expectations and image of library and information profession in India, *AGLIS Jl* 9, 1993 (Abstract only).

Provides useful information about the present state of affairs of the status of librarians and the libraries. Describes about the high and rising users expectations from the profession particularly with the onslaught of the gadgets of new technology such as computers, etc. Concludes that the time has come when library and information professionals must learn to meet the expectations of their alert users, and thus help raise the image of the profession.

GUPTA, S R 61

Institute of Chartered librarian: A conceptual framework, *Jl Lib & Inf Sci* 17 (2) Dec 1992: 143-157.

Justifies the need for professional consultancy for libraries on the basis of observations and findings of a research study of college libraries in India. Distinguishes between instrument of certification and instrument of licensing in a profession. Points out so far only certification is being done by library and information science schools. Argues that licensing is required to prepare library consultants who may be called as Chartered Librarians. Identifies areas in library world for chartered librarian. Proposes a model for an Institute of Chartered Librarians (India).

GUPTA, S R 62

Institute of chartered librarian: A conceptual framework, *AGLIS Jl* 9, 1993 (Abstract only).

Mentions only about the abstract of this article on the need for an Institute of chartered librarians who should be given license to do practice in the form of consultancy work in the new emerging area of information profession. States that LIS schools must not only give certification but also the instrument of licensing for the purpose. Proposes a model for an Institute of Chartered Librarians (India), and identifies areas of their work.

IBRAHIM, ABBAS 63

A journey from librarian to information technologist, *Rilisar Bull* 8 (1) Jan-Mar 1993: 1-3.

Laments that nothing has been done by the library profession to enhance the career brightness, to attract bright young persons to the profession, except for asking for more salary and benefits. States that time has come to upgrade library and information science into information technology. Mentions that RILISAR has decided to introduce a competent post-graduate Diploma Course from 1993 for developing Information Technologist.

KADIRI, J A 64

Librarianship as a career in Nigeria, *Int Lib Move* 14 (1) Mar 1992: 19-25.

Defines career, library, and librarianship. Gives origin of library and librarianship, types of libraries, duties of a librarian, education and training, and qualifications. Discusses entry requirements, career structure, and prospects in Nigeria. Concludes that librarianship compares well with other professions in terms of training and remuneration.

KALYANE, V L and KALYANE, S V 65

Librarianship in 2000 A D, *Univ News* 30 (35) Aug 31, 1992: 73-74.

States that libraries and books will continue to exist even in 21st century though DTP will be there and libraries will be equipped with CD ROMs, more micros and fax machines, but browsing will continue. Mentions that library professionals have to accept the challenge in giving uptodate information, acquire managerial skills, and let others feel your importance in information handling.

KAPASI, HEERA 66

Indo-US relations: Understanding and friendship through libraries, *DL*, 247-252.

Discusses about Indo-US relations in the area of books and libraries. Traces the origin of the opening of the first USIS libraries in India and gives an account about their growth and development into automated library systems. Points out about the services these libraries have been rendering to their users who include Indians also. Mentions also about their interaction with Indian libraries.

KUPPUSWAMI SASTRI, S 67

Kosavan Acaryah, *LM*, 130-132.

Gives the meaning of 'Kosavan Acaryah' as to have a library is to be an educator. States that a true librarian finds a suitable reader for every book and a suitable book for every reader in the library so that the library resources could be put to maximum use.

LAHIRI, A 68

Poised for dramatic change, *NISSAT Newsletter* 12 (4) Oct-Dec 1993: 1.

Explains how information market scenario is in for a dramatic change in India from the libraries of universities laboratories etc. to the emergence of NIC and NISSAT to the ENVIS and BTIS in the eighties, to the information systems as NCSI, TIFAC, DELNET, CALIBNET, etc of the mid-eighties to the latest developments by the newspaper houses, INFOTEX '93, etc.

MALHOTRA, NIRMAL 69

An address to young librarians, *CLIS Observer* 10 (3-4) July- Oct 1993: 62-66.

Describes various methods as to how to increase efficiency and effectiveness of academic library usage under financial limitations. Based on personal experiences discusses rules of conduct for librarians, library rules, organising work, identifying needs of users, acquisition planning, library staffing enhanced services, personal relations, resource sharing with the help of which efficiency and effectiveness can be increased.

MISHRA, SANJAY and SINGH, YOUD VIR 70

Library in newspapers of 1992: A content analysis, *Jl Info Sci* 3(4) Apr-June 1993: 201-209.

Makes an attempt to review the newspaper articles relating to books and libraries published during various conferences organised in 1992 to mark the birth centenary of Dr S R Ranganathan, among others, to disseminate the latest developments.

NAGARAJAN, S 71

Introduction, *CTIT*, 1-3.

States that information science was totally a neglected subject till independence. Mentions efforts made to identify internal sources of information including the setting up of NISSAT and its national centres, the NICNET at governmental level, the efforts of the non-governmental agencies. Identifies malady of non-coordination, and effect the remedy of building our own detabases in many areas.

NANDI, SUBODH GOPAL, 72

Library profession and its code of ethics, *Int Lib Move* 15 (3) Sept 1993: 101-107.

Explains profession conceptually. Discusses that librarianship is a profession. Describes code of ethics, and code of ethics for library profession. States that library associations should keep pace for the advancement of the profession.

OJHA, D C, *Ed* 73

Advances in library and information science, Volume 4: Information communication, Jodhpur: Scientific Publishers, 1993, xv, 208 p.

Includes 14 articles by authors representing a variety of perspectives. Discusses about information communication technology and their impact on libraries, information communication management, user-oriented libraries and information centres, problems of acquisition in S & T libraries, INIS, etc. to cope with the ever increasing mass of information.

OHJA, D C and SHARMA, C D, *Eds* 74

Advances in library and information science,Volume 3: Information systems: Science and technology, Jodhpur: Scientific Publishers, 1992. xvi, 288 p

Contains 18 contributions by authors representing various libraries and information centres in the country about various information systems and centres for science and technology, the use of emerging technology, software packages, library and information networks. Presents plans and prospects for National Information System in the field of S & T.

RAJAGOPALAN, T 75

Rapid strides in library science, *In* Ravi, N (Ed), *The Hindu speaks on libraries,* Madras: Kasturi & Sons, 1992, pp 285-287.

Deals with the rapid strides made by the libraries as a result of recent developments in science and technology and the social sciences, the efforts of Raja Rammohun Roy Library Foundation, and the ILA report on national policy, and other developments as CD-ROM. Reports about the ILA conference held in Madras in 1991.

RATH, MOORTTIMATEE and RATH, PRAVAKAR 76

Sociology of librarianship, Delhi: Matibha Prakashan, 1992. 163 p.

Discusses about the role of library in the social context and how it can be an instrument in changing the reading habits of the people at large by providing its useful services to them directly as well as indirectly.

RAVI, N, *Ed* 77

The Hindu speaks on libraries, edited by N Ravi, Madras: Kasturi & Sons, 1992. xvi, 303 p.

Includes the selection of articles, news, views, editorials, reports, etc on libraries covering the period from 1918 to 1992 for the benefit of librarians and information scientists. Gives a general view of the developments in this field over the past seven decades and a half. Arranged in chronological order covering 150 items on the subject of libraries and books.

SAROJA, G 78

Professionalism in librarianship - some perceptions, *LID*, 81-86.

Defines profession. Aims at knowing the value of library profession in the eyes of professionals and public on the basis of data collected from library professionals, research scholars and staff of various Depts of S V University, through two sets of questionaire. Presents analysis of various library professionals and public. Gives discussion of results. Makes useful recommendations for raising the status.

SEWA SINGH 79

From librarianship to information science, *Univ News* 30 (35) Aug 31, 1992: 75-78.

Mentions that social changes have their impact on libraries and librarianship. Points out the recent changes in technology and their impact on university libraries and came in a shift in emphasis from collection development to providing information and access to information outside, a step towards computerized networks. Describes change in information storage, information transfer, computerized databases, online information networks, electronic publications, and all these call for new role for the professionals as recorded knowledge consultant. Calls for change in LIS education curricula in view of the above, new skills and ability through short term courses in IT.

SUBBA RAO, C V 80

Professional problems and their solutions, *Her Lib Sci* 31 (3-4) July-Oct 1992: 247-250.

Describes some problems faced by LIS professionals in India, such as Pay Commission's Review Committee recommendations, cadres for librarians, work standards, aptitute tests, etc. States that *Her Lib Sci* is opening a 'Professional Forum' to which the librarians can write about the problems and solutions.

SUBBA RAO, C V 81

Structural organisation for the library profession, *AGLIS Jl* 9, 1993 (Abstract only).

Advises care to orient computers to classification and inter linkages of electronic speed to research speed, and planning for time for social absorption and change of research habits in the library profession according to the needs of time.

TREHAN, G L 82

To young librarians, In *Souvenir* of Chandigarh Library Association, 1992.

Gives a piece of advice to the young generation of librarians, through this poem, to work hard for the cause of the library profession, and give service with dedication and devotion.

VYASMOORTHY, P 83

One liners for the librarian, *Luck Libn* 24 (2) July-Sept 1992: 97-103.

Introduces the concept of one liners. Explains what one liners have in common with epigrams, quotes, slogans, sayings, jokes, etc. Mentions important features and uses of one liners and role played by them in librarianship. Gives a list of more than 90 one liners in the Annexture. Discusses use of computer program.

020(1) Ranganathan and LIS

ANNAMALAI UNIVERSITY, DEPARTMENT OF LIBRARY AND INFORMATION SCIENCE, ANNAMALAINAGAR 84

Dynamics of librarianship; felicitation to luminaries in the profession - Birth Centenary publication of Dr S R Ranganathan, Annamalainagar: Department of Library and Information Science, Annamalai University, 1992. x, 327+14 (unnumbered) p.

Includes 32 articles divided into four Sections. Section A-Memorabilia (5papers); Section B-Papers on Ranganathan's contribution (Papers 6-12); Section C-Library and Information Science Education (Papers 13-22); Section D-Other areas (Papers 23-32). This publication is brought out as Birth Centenary Publication of Dr S R Ranganathan, and as a felicitation to luminaries in the profession such as V Durairajan and S R Ranganathan.

BARUA, P 85

Ranganathan's contribution to library science: A brief appraisal, *Coll. Lib* 8(1-2) 1992: 7-10.

Mentions that there are greatmen in every walk of life and Dr S R Ranganathan was one of them in Library Science. Gives his birth and education. Explains his role as a teacher and librarian at the University of Madras, Banaras Hindu University, and University of Delhi. Discusses the honours and fellowships Ranganathan received. Describes his contribution to the subjects of classification, cataloguing and indexing, library movement, etc.

BHATTACHARYYA, G 86

Ranganathan: An outstanding philosopher of science, *Lib Sci slant Docum & Inf Std* 29 (2) June 1992: 59-64.

Presents an analysis and approach to scientific method and the criteria for deeming a subject-field as a science. Analyses contributions to this modelling. Identifies Ranganathan's spiral of scientific method as a basic model to the field which is an elegant approach as that of Thomas Kuhn. Feels that this contribution of Ranganathan is a seminal one.

DEVARAI, RAJASHEKHAR S and DAMODARAM, T 87

Ranganathan and the professional development of librarians: Study in professiology, *Univ News* 30 (45) Nov 9, 1992: 11-13.

Discusses about S R Ranganathan's achievements, professional image and status. Describes librarianship as a profession. Explains Ranganathan's vision, approach and the professional model, while describing his voluminious contribution of 60 books and 2,000 articles. Highlights the legacy of Ranganathan called Rao Sahib which is far advanced and ahead of our times, especially as far as philosophy and theory of LIS are concerned. Concludes with the best tribute to him and Ranganathan's inspiring prayer.

GOPINATH, M A 88

Ranganathan's concept of "live library" and the role of the library profession, *DL,* 14-28.

Describes Ranganathan's achievements in library profession. Discusses his Five Laws of Library Science and his views on emerging library service, and the new emerging dimensions of the profession. Describes impact of information systems developments, information resource management. Narrates information science and its connection with other disciplines. Gives purposes of library as given by Dr Ranganathan and mentions about his integral approach.

GUPTA, A K 89

Ranganathan and the library science, *Coll Lib* 8 (1-2) 1992: 11-13.

Mentions about the birth and death of Ranganathan, and his reluctance to embrace librarianship. Discusses his contribution with reference to the totality of librarianship, as he himself was a complete man, dedicated to his profession. Observes that Ranganathan's activity level throughout his life time reflects a total, selfless commitment to library science.

PANDURANGAM, S 90

The man who enriched library science, *IPLA Souvenir*, 1992. 2 p.

Discusses about the achievements of Ranganathan and his contribution to the enrichment of library science by voluminous writings, developing and organising libraries, establishing library associations, opening library education schools, drafting library bill for enactment as library acts, etc.

RAMOLA, K C 91

A massiah for the library profession, In *Souvenir* of CLA, 1992.

Describes the birth, education and appointment of S R Ranganathan as librarian of the University of Madras. Discusses his activities and achievements as librarian. Discusses his contribution to the library profession in the form of writings such as his Five Laws of Library Science, Colon Classification, Prolegomena to Library Classification, and others. Explains his contribution to the profession of librarianship as a massiah.

RANGANATHAN on distinctive mission of Indian librarianship 92

for vitalising library service, *In* G L Trehan and Girja Kumar: *Ranganathan Birth Centenary Monograph*, Chandigarh: Chandigarh Library Study Circle, 1993, pp 14.a - 14.b.

Reproduces the distinctive mission of Indian librarianship as given by Dr S R Ranganathan after India's independence and advised the librarians to activate their inner spirit to vitalise the library service to users.

RANGANATHAN's call for changeover to new ideas for 93

dynamic library service: Changing environment, new concepts and new ideas, *In* G L Trehan and Girja Kumar: *Ranganathan Birth Centenary Monograph,* Chandigarh: Chandigarh Library Study Cirlce, 1993, pp 27-28.

States that in view of the changes in the profession, librarians must inculcate new ideas and change their outlook to serve their readers better for a better tomorrow.

RANGRA. V K 94

Ranganathan-apostle of librarianship, *DESIDOC Bull* 12 (5) Sept 1992: 7-12.

Focusses attention on the human aspect of the personality of Ranganathan. Describes his entry into the profession and problems he faced in it. Gives briefly his contributions and achievement.

Traces his leanings towards spiritualism and mysticism and their influence on his work. Comments on his style in writing and public speaking. Pleads that to pay a befitting homage to him in the Centenary Year, Ranganathan be posthumously honoured with the highest Republic Day Award.

SATIJA, M P 95

Ranganathan practitioner, *RILISAR Bull* 8 (1) Jan-Mar 1993: 4-25.

Describes in detail the manipulation of laws and certain special normative principles (derived from Five Laws of Library Science) to develop work in the various branches of library and information science. Discusses the methodology of classification, cataloguing, chain indexing, book selection, physical bibliography, and methodology of research in library administration.

SHARIFY, NASSER 96

An encounter with a genius: A sentimental reflection on Ranganathan, *Her Lib Sci* 32 (1-2) Jan-Apr 1993: 48-54.

Refers to the understanding of philosophy of S R Ranganathan. Describes first encounter with Ranganathan at the University of Pittsburgh, and the opportunity to act as his host. Narrates the first conversation with the genius of Ranganathan. Expresses gratitude for the personalised service to the great genius. Makes observation on his humility, his views on religion, his tackling of the entire field of library and information science. Refers to the honour of being awarded Kaula Gold Medal.

020(1) FIVE LAWS OF LIBRARY SCIENCE

ADELMAN, JEAN S 97

A memory of S R Ranganathan, *DL*, 1-2.

Remembers the author's contact with Ranganathan, with particular reference to his contribution of Five Laws of Library Science and their relevance. States how the author in few weeks contact with Ranganathan continues to inform some of the attitudes and actions as a librarian to this day.

BEDI, RAJINDER 98

The father of present libraries, In *Souvenir* of CLA, 1992.

Describes that Dr S R Ranganathan's Five Laws of Library Science are the basis of library science, and on the basis of his contribution of Five Laws only, he can be called as the father of present libraries.

COCHRANE, PAULINE A 99

Information technology in libraries and Ranganathan's Five Laws of Library Science, *Libri* 42 (3) July-Sept 1992: 235-241.

Defines information technology (IT). Discusses that Ranganathan's Five Laws can serve as useful guidelines and criteria for assessing IT's value in library and information services. Identifies advantages of IT if sensibly used in libraries. Concludes that IT should be used in libraries to provide reference, referral and other services, as well as automating library operations.

FAROOQUI, FARHANA 100

Induction of Five Laws of library science in the National Library, Calcutta, *RAT*, 50-53.

States that the Five Laws of library science are the basic philosophy behind the existence of the libraries, their services and characteristics. Describes the Five Laws and their induction in activities of the National Library (of India), Calcutta. Concludes that the National Library has been functioning in true confirmity with the Five Laws of Library Science.

GOPINATH, M A 101

Public relation in libraries, Five Laws and library civics, *DL*, 298-306.

Discusses the importance of public relations in libraries. Describes the suggestion of the Five Laws of Library Science to commend public relations as a service. Gives the public relations activity, functions, media and some public relations activity in libraries, such as knowing the readers, advertising library and information products, active interaction, etc. Puts forth also Ranganathan's views on the subject.

JAMAL, NAYYER 102

Computer: Saves the time of the readers: Its relevance to S R Ranganathan's Fourth Law, *RAT*, 54-57.

Discusses the various activities of a library such as acquisition, cataloguing, circulation, current awareness services, selective dissemination of information, indexing, etc which can be adopted to save the time of the readers as well as staff by using computer. States that similarly other activities such as reference service for which the use of computer can provide the services to the readers without wasting their time.

JAYARAJAN, P 103

The increasing relevance of the Five Laws of Ranganathan, *DESIDOC Bull* 12 (5) Sept 1992: 21-23.

Describes Five Laws of Library Science as the most seminal contribution of Dr S R Ranganathan to librarianship which have more relevance today. Mentions the message of Five Laws focussing on 'the user', which transformed the Indian libraries and the profession. Comments that Ranganathan had high expectations from younger generations of librarians.

KULDIP CHAND and GIAN SINGH 104

Impact of information technology on Ranganathan's Five Laws, *PP*, 21-26.

Lists the Five Laws of Library Science as given by Dr S R Ranganathan. Defines information technology (IT). Examines the impact of IT on all the Five Laws substituting 'Book' with 'Information'. Concludes that the new IT will create two classes - those who can pay, and those who can not pay for searching databases.

MUKHOPADHYAY, KABITA 105

Ranganathan's Five Laws of Library Science and its practical implementation, *Coll Lib* 8 (1-2) 1992: 17-21.

Describes the Five Laws of Library Science developed and published by Dr S R Ranganathan in 1931 which are the fundamental contribution giving principles and techniques for the proper functioning and management of libraries based on scientific principles. Explains the Five Laws, one by one, for this purpose. Concludes by inspiring the librarians to take an oath in the Birth Centenary Year of Ranganathan to make the library of the readers, for the readers, and by the readers.

NAGARAJAN, M 106

Five Laws of library science - foundation for quality service, *D L*, 238-246.

Traces the origin of Five Laws of Library Science of S R Ranganathan. Explains in detail the Five Laws one by one which helped to analyse the various activities and services in libraries, and make the libraries to meet the recreational, informative, educative, and inspirational needs of the modern society. Concludes that in the rapidly developing twentieth century the impact of Five Laws in libraries is unmeasurable.

SHARMA, RAVINDRA N 107

Books are for use: Ranganathan Centennial year, *Coll & Res News* 8, May 1992: 502.

Describes Ranganathan's Five Laws of Library Science as his work of seminal value. Discusses about the First Law of Library Science: "Books are for Use" in the present context of changes and developments taking place in technology in books and other formats of reading materials.

SURATI, DAKSHA VINOD 108

Ranganathan's Fourth Law of Library Science and communication revolution, *LIS*, 65-72.

Defines communication and discusses in relation to the Fourth Law of Ranganathan. Traces development of communication media in human history prior to 1948 and afterwards also as the new communication era in which emphasis is made on electronic communication, microelectronics in communication, telecommunications, etc. where library need to transform itself in an 'Information Agency'.

VISWANATHAN, T 109

Library as growing organism, *Lib Sci slant Docum & Inf Std* 29 (3) Sept 1992: 135-138.

Delivered as a Ranganathan Centenary Lecture at the Documentation Research and Training Centre, Bangalore on 9th August, 1992. Looks at the validity of the Fifth Law of Library Science in the context of advancements in modern technology and their impact on libraries. Explains the problems and prospects of CD-ROMs.

VISWANATHAN, T 110

A reflection on Dr Ranganathan's Fifth Law, *Ann Lib Sci & Docum* 39 (2) June 1992: iii-v.

Points out Ranganathan's contribution to library and information science. Mentions the Five Laws of Library Science created by him. Explains the Fifth Law 'Library is a Growing Organism': the two types of growth. Describes the impact of information technology (IT) on the ways libraries grow in the future. Discusses about electronic library with CD-ROMs. Mentions its inherent problems also. Mentions about the problems of use, classifying CD-ROMs, publisher's role, etc. Discusses about the telelibrary which may function much the same way as telephone exchanges linking it with other libraries, and making the entire world as one, which is like today's network.

VOHRA, RANJANA 111

Ranganathan: A trendsetter, In *Souvenir* of CLA, 1992.

Describes S R Ranganathan as one-man library movement. Explains his variegated contributions to the profession, particularly the Five Laws of Library Science through which he enunciated the philosophy of librarianship. Pays tribute to him in this Centenneial year.

WEERASOORIYA, W A 112

Five Laws of LIbrary Science: A philosophycal perspective, and their farreaching implications and extensions, *Lib Sci slant Docum & Inf Std* 29 (2) June 1992: 77-84.

Discusses the integral nature of S R Ranganathan's Five Laws of LIbrary Science. Develops the implications of the Five Laws to library networking and delineates a program of action for the network. Emphasises that Five Laws are of immense potential in many fields such as education, political science, besides in library and information science.

020 (1) LIS - National Policy

BARUA, B P 113

National policy on library and information systems and services for India: Perspectives and projections, Bombay: Popular Prakashan, 1992. 188 p.

Describes in this book the national policy India has evolved over the years with regard to the growth and development of information systems and services. Discusses the roles played by the Indian Library Association and the Raja Rammohun Roy Library Foundation of which the author has been Director. Outlines the perspectives and the projections of the national information policy as well as the future outlook.

DOSA, MARTA 114

Future perspective on information policy research needs, *INICAE* 11 (1) Mar 1992: 5-12.

Puts up a preliminary framework for an approach to research needs. States four dominant activities involving practice, education, research, policy formulation. Presents the role of research in addressing information planning and polity problems. States potential research topics on policy analyses. Suggests a modest and workable proposal.

GROLIER, ERIC de 115

Library and information policy perspectives and Ranganathan's heritage, In *Papers*, 58th IFLA General Conference, New Delhi, 30 August - 5 September 1992, pp 0.1 - 0.5.

Presented as the opening address in the Plenary Session of the 58th IFLA General Conference on 30th August 1992 at New Delhi. Discusses about Ranganathan's conceptual framework for national library and information policies, organization and design of national library systems, role of public, academic and special libraries in satisfying information needs, users and their needs, staff training and development, impact of national policies on scientific technological, cultural and social development, role of regional and international cooperation. Highlights the present value of Ranganathan's heritage.

KAULA, P N 116

Essential ingredients of National Policy on Library and Information System for India, *Her Lib Sci* 31 (3-4) July-Oct 1992: 200-208.

Describes implications of tremendous growth and diversification of knowledge. Explains a policy document and policy implications in various sectors. Discusses education system and NEP document. Refers to the plans of Ranganathan. Discusses policy documents of RRRLF, ILA, NAPLIS. Comments on the essentials of National Policy. Refers to the modernisation of library and information services and Public Library Policy. Emphasises on the national responsibility of UNESCO's medium term plan for library and information services.

NATIONAL policy on library and information system, 117
PLD, 156-173.

Explains the National Policy on Library and Information Systems developed as a result of a Committee appointed by the Government of India in October 1985. Gives its terms of reference. Reproduces the draft of the Policy prepared by the Committee which includes Introduction, objectives, Public library system and bibliographical services, manpower development and professional status, modernisation, general professional issues, implementing agencies and financial support.

NAVALANI, K 118

National information policy and the Third World countries, In *Papers*, 58th IFLA General Conference, New Delhi, 30 Aug - 5 Sep 1992, pp 0.5-0.8.

Gives need and history of national information policy. Discusses aims and salient features of the proposed National Policy of Library and Information Systems of India. Highlights gaps and disparities in information access in the Third World countries. Identifies main problems in policy implementation. Stresses that policy should give emphasis to the needs of the children and the new literates, rurals and have-nots of the information. Makes a few suggestions.

SIMON, ELISABETH 119

Information policy as cultural policy: Cultural, economic and societal aspects, *INICAE* 12 (2) Sept 1992: 242-245.

Reports about the International Conference on Information Policy as Cultural Policy held on Oct 17-23, 1992 in Thomasberg (Germany), attended by 75 high level participants from all over Europe and beyond. Points out goals of the meeting. Mentions the topics discussed. Explains conclusions from the presentations helpful for building of a new Europe.

020 (1) Library Literature. LIS - Literature

KANKACHARY, M 120

Library science literature in Telugu (1915-1991); a select annotated bibliography, *ILS* 5p.

Contains a list of library and information science literature published in Telugu language arranges alphabetically under subject heading such as Administration and Organization, Book Selection, Cataloguing, Classification, Documentation, Reference Service, etc. The entries are not numbered, however.

KUMAR, P S G 121

Library literature in Indian languages: Problems and probable solutions, *Timeless Fellowship* 15, 1993: 16-19.

Discusses problems of producing library literature in Indian languages such as lack of good authorship, lack of standard terminology, limited markets, and poor purchasing power of individuals. Suggests as solution that the government should organise competition among authors for writing books, workshops for writers, efforts be made at state and national level to standardise terminology, role of book exhibitions, need for quick revision of works. Opines that private agencies need encouragement in the production and distribution of books, etc.

SHUKLA, K H and SONI, N N 122

Growth of library and information science books in Gujrati: An appraisal, *ILA Bull* 28 (3-4) Oct-Mar 1993: 111-115.

Traces history of the LIS education in Gujrat. Analyses growth of LIS books in Gujrati language published in different subjects for the use of those who know and understand Gujrati well.

020 (1) LIS - Endowments

VANKATAPPAIAH, V 123

Prof Kaula Endowment for Library and Information Science: A brief report (1973-1993), *Her Lib Sci* 31 (3-4) July-Oct 1992: 230-237.

Explains the activities of the Kaula Endowment including Medlas and Prizes, Awards, publications of books, journals, Kaula Series, Centenary celebrations of Iyyanki, S R Ranganathan, other projects and programmes currently under preparation and gives future plans also.

020.14 Terminology

SATIJA, M P 124

Indian sources of library and information science terminology, *Jl Lib & Inf Sci* 16 (2) Dec 1991: 129-143.

Explains the importance of standardisation of terminology in LIS. Examines the contribution of S R Ranganathan, and also brings out the role of Indian Standards Institution. Describes some of the important sources on LIS terminology published in India.

TERMNET SECRETARIAT, VIENNA 125

Programme and activities of International Network for Terminology (TERMNET), *INICAE* 11 (1) Mar 1992 : 106-109.

Gives constituent organizations at international level, supernational organizations, national organizations, universities, software house, etc. Lists specified aims. Mentions its working programme including seven language thesaurus, and other activities.

020.16 LIS - Bibliographies

HANDBOOK of libraries, archives and information centres in India, Volume 12: Libraries, archives and information technology; an annotated bibliography, 1970-1990, pt 2, edited by B M Gupta, New Delhi: Aditya Prakashan, 1992. xxxviii, 474 p. 126

Includes 2935 entries, as a continuation of Pt 1, Volume 11, on the remaining subjects from LIS Education and training to Use Studies and surveys arranged in alphabetical order. Entries are further arranged alphabetically by author under each subject heading. Many entries do not have any annotations, while in others the size of annotation varies.

020.218 Standards and Standardization

BRINKHOFF, NORBERT 127

Towards standards in language engineering: EAGLES, *INICAE* 12 (1) Mar 1993: 85-88.

Aims at accelerating the provision of common functional specifications for the development of large scale language resources, called EAGLES (Expert Advisory Group on Language Engineering Standards). Gives its history and objectives. Discusses implementation of EAGLES. Mentions targets for 1993 and beyond.

DESHMUKH, P P 128

Standardization of library and information services; with special reference to scientific and agricultural libraries, New Delhi: ABC Publishing House, 1992.

States that if a library has to render effective and efficient service, it is necessary to formulate standards for each and every aspects of library service like planning and design of library building, norms for staffing, acquisition of serials, norms for stock taking, library automation, etc. Deals with the standards prescribed by ICAR for agricultural university libraries.

GURCHARAN SINGH 129

Dr S R Ranganathan - images and echoes: Work on documentation standards, *Her Lib Sci* 32 (1-2) Jan-Apr 1993: 3-7.

Refers to the contribution of Ranganathan. Mentions entry of Ranganathan into library profession with no looking back. Discusses the work of Ranganathan in standardisation, formulation of national standards on documentation. Describes some personal traits of Ranganathan, his unbounded energy for dedicated work, his working pattern at the Indian Standards Institution (now BIS), his knack for involving others into work and setting his standards.

GURCHARAN SINGH 130

With Dr S R Ranganathan on standards for documentation, *Ann Lib Sci & Docum* 39 (2) June 1992: 38-45.

Mentions that Ranganathan gave the pioneer lead to the activity of developing and applying standards in India in documentation, information retreieval, etc. Describes the infrastructure for standards. Discusses the role of Documentation Sectional Committee under Dr Ranganathan and thus came the 'Evolution of Documentation' and the fourth standard of ISI was on the practice for make up of periodicals. Mentions about other standards also. Discusses some of the work qualities of Ranganathan as experienced by author.

INTERNATIONAL ORGANIZATION FOR STANDARDIZATION, GENEVA 131

International standards on documentation and information, *INICAE* 11 (1) Mar1992: 95-104.

Explains that the scope of ISO covers standardization in all fields except electrical and electronic engineering. Provides a list of bibliographical data of international standards dealing with documentation and information obtainable from ISO member bodies.

SANKAR REDDY, M 132

Standardization in library organisation and methods, *CS*, 144-152.

Attempts to describe the standardisation efforts of Telugu University Library in the areas of book acquisitions, union catalogue preparation, ILL and circulation of documents. Stresses the role of Bureau of Indian Standards in formulating the standards in these areas.

020.25 LIS - Directories

PAST Students gazette, *Timeless Fellowship* 15, 1993: 84-86. 133

Gives a brief list of 35 successful candidates in B L I Sc during 1992-93, and a list of 10 M L I Sc students who passed in 1992-93. Also gives their present addresses and positions.

020.3 LIS - Dictionaries. LIS - Encyclopedias

COREA, ISHWARI, OJUANDO, GAD DAVID and FARUQI, KHALID KAMAL, *Eds* 134

Encyclopedia of information and library science, New Delhi: Akashdeep Publishing House, 1993. 10 volumes.

Attempts to include the terms from all the fields of library and information science discussing about new techniques, uses of equipments. Includes also such subjects as printing, publishing, binding, application of computers. It has terms from data processing, computer, microcomputer and desk publishing. Defines terms both in brief as well as in detail. Gives also illustrations.

RAMAIAH, L S and TAHER, MOHAMED 135

A dictionary of library and information science quotations, New Delhi: 1993.

Brings together 3415 quotations from the writings of ancient sages to the present practitioners on various facts of the subject, serves as a ready reference tool to comprehend the subject more particularly from Dewey to Ranganathan.

VIJAY KUMAR, P and SOOD, S P 136

Library and information science: A general knowledge encyclopedia, Jaipur: RBSA Publisher, 1991. 320 p.

Offers a new approach to the presentation of general knowledge about the different areas of LIS. Attempts to bring in a nutshell, to the knowledge of librarians and LIS students, all important aspects and events pertaining to the field of LIS. Divided into 25 convenient chapters each dealing with a specific branch of LIS containing in all over 2,500 entries in form of questions.

020.5 LIS - Journals

AFOLBI, MICHAEL 137

Productivity of journals which published Nigerian library literature, 1910-1985, *Ann Lib Sci & Docum* 39 (4) Dec 1992: 139-144.

Studies productivity of journals publishing articles on librarianship in Nigeria during 1910-85, to determine number of articles published by each journal, number of journals published in Nigeria, articles predominantly in English on the subject of librarianship.

ANAND, J K 138

Periodicals in library and information science in India: A review of their growth and development, *Univ News* 30 (5) 1992: 117-120.

Reviews the growth and development of LIS periodicals in India over the years in this century. States that most of them are published in English language, and are contributing to enrich the LIS literature.

JAGTAR SINGH and MEADOWS, JACK 139

Electronic serials for library and information specialists on Internet, *Aslib Proc* 45 (9) Sept 1993: 234-241.

States that amount of online information relevant to library and information activities has expanded rapidly, particularly due to Internet development. Presents results of a survey of coverage of Internet concerning the work of library and information specialists. Emphasises on the availability of relevant electronic journals.

NATIONAL SCIENCE LIBRARY, NEW DELHI 140

Secondary sources and primary periodicals in library and information science, *Her Lib Sci* 31 (1-2) Jan - Apr 1992: 92-95.

Analyses NUCSSI database to study the availability and distribution of LIS primary serials and the 400 most important secondary sources, namely *Library Literature*, and *LISA*. Compares the serials covered in *Library Literature* and *LISA*, 1987 with the serials intake of National Science Library, 35 university libraries and other libraries in different regions.

020.621 International Organizations

020.621 (1) ASTINFO

CONSULTATIVE Committee meeting, *NISSAT Newsletter* 12 (4) Oct-Dec 1993: 7-9. 141

Gives a brief overview of the PGI/ASTINFO activities. Mentions about the country reports focussing on the infrastructural facilities, online access etc. Outlines the UNESCO/PGI programme for 1994-95. Mentions about the ASTINFO evaluation report. Gives the recommendations emerged from the discussion.

020.621 (1) FID

KAULA, P N 142

The first joint FID/CR and ISKO seminar, *Her Lib Sci* 32 (3-4) July Oct-1993: 256-259.

Reports about the first joint FID/CA and ISKO Seminar in Madrid on 20 October 1992 attended by 11 members including the author. Mentions about the five papers presented at the seminar, the discussion held, comments made. Points out the suggestions made for future with reference to UDC.

KAULA, P N 143

46th FID Congress and Conference, *Her Lib Sci* 32 (3-4) July-Oct 1993: 237-238.

Reports about the joint FID/CR and ISKO Seminar field on 20 October 1992 with Prof. Nancy Williamson, Chair-person FID/CR, in chair. States that Prof Emilia Curras was the local Secretary of the Seminar which continued from 21 to 24 October and participated by over 80 participants. Mentions that 46th FID Congress was held in Madrid, 27-30 Oct 1992.

020.621 (1) IFIP

INTERNATIONAL FEDERATION FOR INFO PROCESSING 144

12th World Computer Congress, *INICAE* 12 (1) Mar 93: 95-97.

Reports about the 12th World Computer Congress (IFIP Congress '92) held in Madrid, Spain from 7 to 11 Sept 1992 on the theme "From Research to Practice". Mentions its programme, technical programme and other details.

002.621 (1) IFLA

DHEERENDRA, P T 145

IFLA: Harbinger of progress in library and information science, *IJILIS* 6(1-2) Jan-June 1993: 58-72.

Gives an outline of genesis, objectives and membership of IFLA. Examines its organisational structure. Indicates its long term policy and Medium-Term Programme. Gives a detailed account of the Five Core Programmes, viz, UBCIM, UAP, PAC, Universal Dataflow and Telecommunication (UDT), and ALP. Provides information about various grants, scholarships and fellowships offered by IFLA.

GROVER, VINOD KUMAR 146

IFLA - its genesis and activities, *Int Lib Move* 14 (2) June 1992: 53-56.

Describes the genesis of IFLA and its development since 1927, after the World War II, and the present status. Examines the main activities of IFLA, including in Third World countries.

IFLA and the Third World, *NISSAT Newsletter* 11 (4) Oct-Dec 1992: 15-19. 147

Discusses the relations of IFLA with the Third World countries, particularly through its programme ALP started in 1984. Presents some interviews of leading functionaries of IFLA to know their views on the subject.

MANGLA, P B 148

IFLA and PAC core programme, *ALR*, 121-131.

Discusses about the development and establishment of IFLA into a prestigious body. Explains its core programmes with special reference to PAC, i.e. Preservation and Conservation. Discusses some of the major activities under this Programme regarding publications, AV programmes, conferences and seminars, etc. Discusses activities of Regional centres ad points out bright future of IFLA/PAC.

MANGLA, P B 149

IFLA and PAC core programme, *LIS*, 173-182.

Discusses the establishment and development of IFLA programmes. Describes its core programmes with special reference to Preservation and Conservation (PAC), officially launched in April 1986. Gives objectives of PAC, and some of its activities including publications, audiovisuals, general awareness, surveys, training, preservation, databases, etc.

THE PRESIDENT speaks: Interview with IFLA President Robert Wedgeworth, *NISSAT Newsletter* 11(4) Oct-Dec 1992: 12-14. 150

Speaks about the programmes of IFLA, its relation to developing countries, whether Conference is the right kind of instrument, and the strength of library associations. Remarks that IFLA is not what it used to be. Outlines strategy for the future of IFLA activities says the President in an interview.

020.621 (1) 58th IFLA Conference

IFLA Conference on Ranganathan

CHATTERJEE, AMITABHA 151

World comes to India: A momentous meet of librarians, *Iaslic Bull* 37 (4) Dec 1992: 277-290.

Traces the background of holding of 58th General Conference of IFLA in New Delhi in 1992. Gives a summarised description of various events such as pre-Conference seminar, COMLA Workshop, Indo-US-SAARC Conference of LIS professionals, satellite meetings, inaugural session celebration of birth centenary of S R Ranganathan, various lectures, various bodies meetings, technical sessions, the exhibition, the IFLA Express, the special issues and publications, the visits, resolutions taken. Gives a short resume of interview with the President and Secretary-designate of IFLA.

GOPINATH, M A 152

58th IFLA General Conference (30th August -5th Sept 1992, New Delhi) on library and information policy perspectives, *Lib Sci slant Docun & Inf Std* 29 (4) Dec 1992: 213-216.

Reports in detail about the Inauguration of the 58th General IFLA Conference held in New Delhi on the occasion of Dr S R Ranganathan's Birth Centenary Year. Discusses about the Plenary Session with Dr Eric de Grolier as the speaker. Reports on sectional meetings on mobile libraries, Bibliographical control, Classification and indexing, Editors of library journals, Parliament libraries, Interlending and Document delivery, Acquisition and Exchange, Library theory and Research, National Libraries, etc.

IFLA: CONFERENCE theme and programme (30 Aug - 5 Sept, 1992), *NISSAT Newsletter* 11 (2) Apr-June 1992: 10-11. 153

Mentions the main theme of the 58th General Conference of IFLA to be held during 30 Aug - 5 Sept, 1992 at New Delhi. States that the Plenary Session will be addressed by Eric de Grolier with the focus on Dr S R Ranganathan.

IFLA 58TH General Conference, New Delhi: 154

An international festival for librarians in India, *NISSAT Newsletter* 11 (4) Oct-Dec 1992: 3-11.

Describes the event held in New Delhi during 30 Aug - 5 Sept 1992, attended by 1324 delegates and organised by the Indian Library Association. Discusses the Inauguration by Human Resource Development Minister Arjun Singh, and speeches by IFLA President, and others. States that the Plenary Session was addressed by Dr Eric de Grolier who spoke on relevance of Dr Ranganathan. Mentions about other special features of the IFLA Conference.

INTROSPECT and prospect: Conference participation, *NISSAT Newsletter* 11(4) Oct-Dec 1992: 20-24. 155

Explains about the participation of 1294 delegates from 80 countries, with 410 participants from India, at the 58th IFLA General Conference held at New Delhi to commemorate the Birth Centenary of Dr S R Ranganathan. Discusses about the technical content as IFLA - 92 was preceded by ten seminar/workshops and followed by one seminar.

KALIA, D R 156

IFLA General Conference 1992, New Delhi, *CLIS Observer* 9 (3-4) July-Dec 1992: 47-56.

Gives report about the 58th General Conference of IFLA held in New Delhi from 30 August to 5 September 1992. States that in all 832 participants came from abroad, and 358 from India. Mentions that in all 137 papers were submitted of which 80 were printed and circulated. Gives a country wise break of the participants in Appendix - I. Gives a list of papers presented at the Conference.

KAULA, P N 157

The opportunity of a century: Time for introspection, *Her Lib Sci* 31 (3-4) July-Oct 1992: 250-252.

Discusses the appeal made by the author in the Birth Centenary Year of Dr S R Ranganathan, when 58th IFLA Conference was held in New Delhi during 30 Aug - 5 Sept 1992 sponsored by the Indian Library association. Appeals that the income that ILA has made out of this international Conference should be properly used such as in setting up of an Endowment and Research Institution in commemoration of Ranganathan.

KRISHAN KUMAR 158

A momentous library conference, *The Hindu*, Delhi, Sunday, Aug 30, 1992. Special Feature, A.

Describes about the 58th General Conference of IFLA being held in New Delhi from Aug 30 to Sept 5, 1992 to coincide with the birth centenary celebrations of Dr S R Ranganathan in which about 1500 delegates are likely to participate. States that there will be exchange of information with librarians from all over the world, book exhibitions, literary project, etc. Calls it the biggest conference to be held in the history of Indian librarianship.

LAHIRI, A 159

The jamboree that was, *NISSAT Newsletter* 11 (4) Oct-Dec 1992: 1.

Discusses about the IFLA - 92 held in New Delhi, the biggest event of the century for the librarians and information scientists in India, which was organised here to mark the Birth Centenary Year of the great Indian librarian Dr S R Ranganathan.

LAHIRI, A 160

A lifetime opportuinity, *NISSAT Newsletter* 12 (2) Apr-June 1993:1.

Raises questions as to what to do with the money - lacks of Rupees - earned by a group of professionals while organising IFLA 1992 in New Delhi : Makes many useful suggestions such as the advancement of LIS in India through research and education for the welfare of LIS professionals, or a scheme of visiting professorship, research scholarships, on the job training could be instituted.

MANGLA, P B and SATIJA, M P 161

IFLA General Conference, New Delhi, 1992, *Int Lib Move* 15 (1) Mar 1993: I-V.

Reports about the 58th IFLA General Conference held in New Delhi in commemoration with Dr S R Ranganathan's birth centenary year, during 30 Aug - 5 Sept 1992. Reports about the inauguration, the key theme, important issues discussed and resolutions passed, etc.

NATIONAL policy on libraries in offing, *The Hindu*, 31st August 1992. 162

Reports about the inauguration of the 58th IFLA General Conference held in New Delhi on 30th August 1992 by the Human

Resource Development Minister, Arjun Singh who said that the policy of library and information system will be implemented in the next five years.

RANGANATHAN Birth Centenary: A watershed in librarianship (A centenary report), *Lib Sci slant Docum & Inf Std* 29 (3) Sept 1992: 163-164. 163

Presents a report about Ranganathan's Birth Centenary year which recorded a good response from several individuals and institutions from India and abroad such as IFLA Conference held in New Delhi at the invitation of the Indian Library Association. In the Plenary Session, Dr Eric de Grolier, a contemporary of Dr Ranganathan since Dorking Conference days, presented a review on Ranganathan. Gives account of other conferences also held in commemoration of Ranganathan's birth centenary year. These include Third International Conference on Informetics (Bangalore, 1991), DRTC Workshop, etc. Makes a mention of the special publications, special numbers of several periodicals dedicated to the memory of Ranganathan, lectures, postal stamp, etc.

RANGRA, V K 164

IFLA - 92 and the Third World, *Patriot*, Sept 28, 1992.

Describes the IFLA-92 Conference held in Delhi to mark the Birth Centenary of Dr S R Ranganathan, as a club of Western librarians to a large extent. Feels that the cause of the Third World librarians was neglected, though IFLA has a special section on Advancement of Librarianship in the Third World (ALP).

THE RESOLUTIONS, *NISSAT Newsletter* 11 (4) 165
Oct-Dec 1992: 29-32.

Gives resolutions adopted at the IFLA 58th General Conference, 1992 on the topics of disscussion such as Government support, socio-cultural impact, education and training, professional associations, standards and guidelines, user satisfaction, case studies, etc.

RESOLUTIONS passed at the IFLA Conference 166
held at New Delhi from August 30 to September 5, 1992, *CLIS Observer* 10 (1-2) Jan-June 1993: 37-40.

Lists various Resolutions topic by topic, passed at the 58th General Conference of IFLA held at New Delhi to celebrate the birth centenary of Dr S R Ranganathan.

020.621 (1) ISKO

KRISHAN KUMAR 167

International Society for Knowledge Organization marches forward, *Lib Her* 30 (1) Apr 1991: 35-37.

Describes the background to the formation of ISKO in 1989. Discusses the aimes, activities and future programmes. Points out that ISKO will establish itself as a major force at the ininternational level in the field of knowledge organization.

020.621 (1) ISKO - First Conference

RAJU, A A N 168

First international ISKO Conference: A report, *Her Lib Sci* 31 (1-2) Jan-Apr 1992: 61-62.

Reports about the First International Conference on Tools for knowledge Organization and Human Interface organised by the International Society for Knowledge Organization (ISKO) for 14-17 Aug 1990 at Darmstadt, West Germany in which some 200 delegates from 23 countries participated. After Inaugural session there were 12 Plenary sessions, 12 Workshops devoted to different aspects of the theme. Gives summary of the conference proceedings.

020. 621(1) ISKO - Second Conference

ASUNDI, A Y, SRIDHAR, APARNA and SREELATHA, G 169

Second International ISKO Conference on Cognitive Paradigms in Knowledge Organisation: A review, *Lib Sci slant Docum & Inf Std* 29 (4) Dec 1992: 217-222.

Reports in detail about the Second ISKO Conference held at Madras during 26-28 August 1992 organised as part of Ranganathan Birth Centenary celebrations. Reports about the inauguration and the eight Technical Sessions in which 29 papers were presented by authors from 15 countries.

020.621 (1) UNESCO

LAHIRI, A 170

UNESCO's information activities in India, *CLIS Observer* 10 (2) Jan-June 1993: 26-29.

Attempts to assess the impact and contribution of UNESCO - ASTINFO, UNESCO/PGI activities in the overall development of library and information services in India including introduction of modern technology in the post-1985 period. Appends a list of supported events, seminars, workshops/training courses.

020.62242 (1) IIS, London

INSTITUTE OF INFORMATION SCIENTISTS, LONDON 171

Text Retrieval Conference, *INICAE* 12 (1) Mar 1993: 102-104.

Explains the Conference programme held in London, 12-14 October 1992. Mentions other details about the Institute of Information Scientists, regarding its membership, special groups, conference fee, etc.

020.62254 (1) AGLIS

020.62254 (1) AGLIS Convention-1991

RANGRA, V K 172

AGLIS National Convention and Seminar '91, *Her Lib Sci* 31 (1-2) Jan-Apr 1992: 73-76.

Reports about the AGLIS Convention held on 24 October 1991 at INSA, New Delhi with 200 participants. Theme chosen was 'Marketing of Information Services and Products' on which Prof T Viswanathan, Director INSDOC, presided. Technical session was chaired by Prof P B Mangla with 11 papers presented followed by discussion. Mentions the recommendation made at this occasion.

020.62254 (1) AGLIS Convention-1993

CHADHA, R K 173

AGLIS Annual Convention, *Her Lib Sci* 32 (3-4) July-Oct 1993: 253-256.

Reports about the AGLIS Annual Convention for 1992-93 held at Jaipur during April 9-11, 1993 attended by about 200 participants. It was inaugurated by Prof P N Kaula. Describes the six technical sessions in which 20 papers were presented. In the Concluding session resolutions were presented and adopted.

SHARMA, PANDEY S K 174

Presidential address, *AGLIS Jl* 9, 1993: 1-8. 174

Delivered at the AGLIS Annual Convention, 1992-93 held at the University of Rajasthan, Jaipur during April 9-11, 1993 on the occasion of the Diamond Jubilee Year of AGLIS. Discussed about the conference theme: Computer and Libraries and Image of Library Profession. Also pays homage to Dr S R Ranganathan.

020.62254 (1) IASLIC

IASLIC, CALCUTTA 175

Annual report and audited statement of accounts, 1991, Calcutta: IASLIC, 1992, n.p.

Covers the various activities of IASLIC during 1991 and the report of the Executive and Finance committees from October 1991 to September 1992.

IASLIC, CALCUTTA 176

Annual report and audited statement of accounts, 1992, Calcutta: IASLIC, 1993, n.p.

Gives information about the IASLIC Council, 1992 and 1993, Annual General Meeting held on 27.12.92, JOCLAI meeting, 15th National Seminar held from 26-29 Dec 1992 at Annamalai University, membership, general and serial publications, medals , study circle meetings, lectures, Librarians Day, Education Division activities, Librarian of the year, Association Library, accounts and finance.

IASLIC, CALCUTTA 177

List of members as on 30 September, 1993, Calcutta: IASLIC, 1993. 50p.

Includes a list of all types of members of Iaslic, such as Honorary members (4), Donor members (2), Life members (678), members abroad (12), Ordinary members (217), and Institutional members (377+51).

IASLIC, CALCUTTA 178

Memorandum of Association; rules and regulations (as amended upto 1991), Calcutta: IASLIC, 1992. 8 p.

Includes the Memo of Association registered under the West Bengal Socities Registration Act XXI of 1961. Gives objectives of the Association. Covers rules and regulations and the amendments made.

KAPOOR, S K and SEN, SUBIR K 179

Instead of an Editorial, *Iaslic Bull* 38 (4) Dec 1993: 145-146.

Explains some of the changes to be incorporated in the *Iaslic Bulletin* from December 1993 onwards regarding the conference/

seminar proceedings, delay in publication, some oddities and their explanation is given.

MUKKHERJEE, NIRMALENDU 180

Dr Ranganathan and the Iaslic, *Iaslic Bull* 37 (3) Sept 1992: 155-161.

Gives an account of the views Dr S R Ranganathan had expressed about the IASLIC (Indian Association of Special Libraries and Information Centres), Calcutta. Analyses these views and shows how far these are justified and relevant in the present context. Also observes that many of these ideas of Dr Ranganathan were taken up by the IASLIC in later years.

020.62254 (1) IASLIC - 15th Seminar

FIFTEENTH National Seminar of IASLIC at Annamalainagar, 181

26-29 December, 1992: Summary of proceedings, *Iaslic Bull* 37 (4) Dec 1992: 245-246.

Reports about the 15th IASLIC National Seminar conjointly organised by the Dept of Library & Information Science and the Library of Annamalai University during 26-29 Dec 1992. Mentions the Inauguration made by the Lieutinent Governer of Pondicherry who stressed the need for adoption of futuristic approach with recent models and techniques of information retrieval. Dr (Mrs) M Surya, welcomed the delegates and guests, and the Vice Chancellor remarked that development in computers etc have led to multimedia approach to information retrieval. Ms Heera Kapasi gave the Presidential Address, and Dr M A Gopinath presented the Keynote address. The Minister of Education released the Felicitation Volume. Discussion on Thematic sessions was held on 27 Dec on the theme 'IR-Models and Techniques' based on 23 out of 36 papers. The Concluding session was held on 29 Dec presided over by Dr S Seetharama, Vice President, IASLIC. The Valedictory function was presided over by Dr M A Gopinath.

FIFTEENTH National Seminar of IASLIC, Technical Sessions: 182

Summary of proceedings, *Iaslic Bull* 37 (4) Dec 1992: 259-272.

Reports about the Technical Sessions and the Summary of proceedings on the theme of the National Seminar -Information Retireval: Model and Techniques. Director of Seminar Dr I K Ravichandra Rao, and Repporter General I R Nanganagouder

Gives details about four Thematic Sessions and their themes, the issues and the discussion held in each Theme. Provides the Recommendations made at the Seminar. Reports also about the SIG meetings for SIG: Computer Applications, chaired by I K Ravichandra Rao: SIG: Informetrics, chaired by C V Subba Rao.

IASLIC 15th National Conference, Annamalainagar, 183
26-29 Dec 1992, *Souvenir*, Annamalainagar: Annamalai University Library, and Dept of Library & Information Science, 1992, unnumbered pages.

Brought out as Birth Centenary celebrations of Dr S R Ranganathan, the luminary in the field of library and information science, on the occasion of the 15th National IASLIC Seminar hosted by Annamalia University Library and the Dept of Library & Information Science.

020.62254 (1) IASLIC - 34th General Meeting

IASLIC, CALCUTTA 184
34th Annual General Meeting of.IASLIC: Proceedings, *Iaslic Bull* 37 (4) Dec 1992: 273-275.

Reports about the 34th Annual General Meeting of IASLIC held on 27 Dec 1992 in the Sastri Hall of Annamalai University under the chairmanship of Dr SM Ganguly, Vice President of IASLIC which was attended by 79 members. Discusses about the five Agenda items.

020.62254 (1) Indian Library Association (ILA)

CHOPRA, H R 186
Indian Library Association: Origin, development, activities and achievements, *Int Lib Move* 14 (2) June 1992: 65-72.

Traces origin of the ILA. Describes its structure in terms of membership, income, headquarters, etc. Discusses various activities regarding conferences, seminars, publications, development of public libraries, library legislation, extension programmes, National Library Week, awards, advice for information, projects, etc. Lists achievements of ILA.

INDIAN LIBRARY ASSOCIATION 187
59th annual report on working of the Association and audited statement of accounts for the year 1991-92, Delhi: ILA, 1992. 52+8 p.

Gives information about the old and new ILA councils, meetings held, and the details about the presidential address given at the 37th All India Library Conference, the Seminar held in 1991 and its recommendations. Reports about the JOCLAI meeting, IFLA Conference and its programme in which people came from 81 countries. Includes information about its accounts also.

020.62254 (1) ILA -38th Conference

ALL INDIA LIBRARY Conference, 38th, Bhubaneswar, 21-24 Nov 1992, Quality life through libraries: Presidential address, by C P Vashishth, Delhi: ILA, 1992. 6 p. 188

Discusses the need for libraries in our country. Emphasises the need for Rural Library and Community Resource Centre (RLORC) in enhancing the development process. Explains the role of children libraries and school libraries in India. Delivered as the Presidential Address at the 38th All India Library Conference held at Utkal University, Bhubaneswar, Nov 21-24, 1992.

ALL INDIA LIBRARY Conference, 38th, Bhubaneswar, 21-24 Nov 1992, *Souvenir*, Bhubaneswar: Dept of Library & Information Science, 1992. 39+many unnumbered pages. 189

Brought out on the occasion of the 38th All India Library Conference of Indian LIbrary Association, held at Bhubaneswar (Nov 21-24, 1992) during the Ranganathan Birth Centenary celebrations. Includes some articles about library and LIS education in Orissa.

INDIAN LIBRARY ASSOCIATION, DELHI 190

Library and information technology: In pursuit of excellence: Seminar papers; XXXVIII All India Library Conference, Utkal University, Bhubaneswar, November 21-24, 1992, edited by C P Vashishth, O P Sharma, A P Gakhar and Dev Raj Singh, Delhi: ILA, 1992, xii, 318 p.

Includes 43 papers on the whole array of topics divided into 6 Sections on Library and Information Services; New and Innovative Measures; Automation and Computerisation; I R Systems; Development in Information Industry; and Human Resource Development.

020.62254 (1) Indian Public Library Association

INDIAN PUBLIC LIBRARY ASSOCIATION, HYDERABAD 191

Grandhalaya vikasmu: *Souvenir:* All India Public Libraries Conference, held at Sri Venkataeswara Vignana Mandir, Guntur, 25-28 February, 1992. Unnumbered pages, Hyderabad: Indian Public Library Association, 1992.

Includes 19 papers including the Keynote Address by Prof P N Kaula. Covers public library development in many states of the country in the Conference papers, edited by Samson Ramakrishnaiah and T.V. Ramanaiah.

020.62254 (1) National Convention of Library Associations

VASHISHTH, C P 192

National Convention of Library Associations, *Her Lib Sci* Jan-Apr 1992: 76-83.

Reports about the National Convention of Library Associations held on 6-7 Feb 1992 at New Delhi, hosted by JOCLAI presided over by P N Kaula in which 150 delegates from 49 institutions participated. Mentions Review Committee report recommendations. Lists various resolutions adopted on this committee report, on library legislation, networking of libraries, activating library associations, and on non-professionals heading the library system.

VASHISHTH, C P 193

National Convention of Library Associations, New Delhi, February 6-7, 1992: A report, *ILA Bull* 27 (4) Jan-Mar 1992: 194-201.

Reports about the National Convention organised by JOCLAI at Pragti Maidan, New Delhi, presided by P N Kaula, and participated by 150 delegates. It discussed Review Committee Report, library legislation, library networking, activating library associations, and so on.

020.62254 (1) Medical Library Association Conference

CONCLUDING SESSION, *ML*, 761-768. 194

Gives detail information about the Concluding session of the 6th International Congress on Medical Librarianship. Discusses about the resolution of adoption of Congress report and the points of discussion. Proposes vote of thanks on behalf of participants as also by the Secretary General, National organising committee.

CONCURRENT Session, 1A, *ML*, 594-599. 195

Gives a reporting of this session at the 6th International Congress on medical librarianship. The theme of this session was 'National Information System & Policies', and was chaired by Adrian Senadhira. Mentions about the presentation of papers and the discussion that followed.

CONCURRENT Session, 1B, *ML*, 600-602. 196

States the theme of this session as 'Resource Sharing & Coordination'. The chairperson of this Session was Ms Elizabeth Buntz. Discusses about the papers presented and discussion held.

CONCURRENT Session, IC, 10, *ML*, 603-605. 197

Mentions the theme of this Session as 'Sources for Health Information', which was chaired by Henry J Lemkan with Linda Parr as Reporteur. Describes the presentation of papers followed by discussion.

CONCURRENT Session 1D, *ML*, 606-607. 198

Reports about this session which was termed as late paper session, and chaired by C Dabral with Daniel Addo as Reporteur.

CONCURRENT Session 1E, *ML*, 608-612. 199

Gives details about this Late Paper session cahired by A G Patil with R P Kumar as Reporteur. Mentions about the presentation of papers and the discussion that followed.

CONCURRENT Session 2A, *ML*, 626-628. 200

Mentions its theme: 'National Information Systems and Policies II'. It was chaired by Frances Groen. After the introductory remarks gives details about the papers presented and discussion held.

CONCURRENT Session 2B, *ML*, 629-635. 201

States the theme: Search Training and Use of Bibliographical Sources'. It was chaired by Liisa Salmi. Reports about three papers and the lively discussion that followed each paper.

CONCURRENT Session 20, *ML*, 636-638. 202

Reports about the theme: 'Periodicals as a Source of Information'. It was chaired by Demetrio R Cichi. After giving introductory remarks, mentions about the papers presented and questions raised.

CONCURRENT Session 2D, *ML*, 639-641. 203

Gives the theme of this session as 'Information Need: Problems & Solutions' which was chaired by Toshinobu Suga with Lucilda Hunter and Jean Gurney as Reporteurs, Reports about the three papers presented in this session and the discussion held.

CONCURRENT Session 2E, *M*L, 642-645. 204

Mentions that the theme of discussion was 'Access to Information'. It was chaired by Derek Law with R P Kumar as Reporteur. Gives details about the papers presented and questions raised by the participants.

CUNCURRENT Session 2F, *ML*, 646-650. 205

Reports about this session and its theme 'Information Seeking & Information Programmes' and was chaired by Richard Hsieh with Ursula Hansan as Reporteur. Discusses about the papers presented on the various aspects of the theme and the discussion held after each presentation.

CONCURRENT Session 3A, *ML*, 672-674. 206

Mentions the theme of this session: 'Service - an overlooked aspect', chaired by Susan Crawford with Helga Patrikios as Reporteur. After introductory remarks gives the presentation of papers and discussion on them.

CONCURRENT Session 3B, *ML*, 675-677. 207

Reports the theme of this session as 'Medical Library Cooperation', chaired by Paul Weiss with Beryl Bailey as Reporteur. Gives details about the three papers presented in this session with points raised for discussion.

CONCURRENT Session 3C, *ML*, 678-680. 208

Reports the theme of this session as 'Medical Libraries & their Role', chaired by Ms Laxmi Mansingh with Ms Chhaya as Reporteur. Mentions about the three papers presented on the theme and the discussion held.

CONCURRENT Session 3D, *ML*, 681-686. 209

Gives detail about the papers presented on the theme of this Session: 'Medical Librarianship Today', chaired by Ms Liisa Salmi with June Rider Jones as Reporteur. Mentions about the papers and questions raised for discussion.

CONCURRENT Session 4A, *ML*, 687-690 210

States the theme: 'User Instruction and Users Needs' for discussion and presentation of papers. It is chaired by Ms Ursula Hansen with Mast T Hodges as Reporteur.

CONCURRENT Session 4B, *ML*, 691-695 211

Mentions the theme of this seession as 'Networks', chaired by Marc Walckiers. Mentions about the presentation of two papers on the theme and the comments of the participants.

CONCURRENT Session 4C, *ML*, 696-700. 212

Mentions the theme of this session as 'The Electronic Library', chaired by Khin Thet Htar, and Hilda Nasser, the Reporteur. Gives information about the papers presented here and the discussion held.

CONCURRENT SESSION 4D, *ML*, 701-705. 213

States the theme of this session as the 'Library Management & Organisation', chaired by Ms Elizabeth Buntz with Teodore Oker-Blom as Reporteur of the session. Mentions about the presentation of the three papers and discussion held.

CUNCURRENT Session 4E, *ML*, 706-712. 214

Reports about the theme of the session: 'Bibliographic Control and Information Methods', chaired by Ms Lucilla C Hunter with Ms Shane Godbold as Reporteur. Mentions about the three papers presented and discussion that took place.

INAUGURAL SESSION, *ML*, 555-563. 215

Reports about the inaugural session of the Sixth International Congress on Medical Librarianship held in Sept 1990 in New Delhi. States that welcome address was given by Goran Falkenberg (Chairman, International Organising Committee), Address by Derek Law, and Introduction to Congress by C Dabral (Chairman, National Organising Committee), Inaugural address by Prof M G K Menon.

PLENARY session, *ML*, 564-574 216

Describes the Plenary Session 1 of the Sixth International Congress on Medical Librarianship, 1990 theme of which was 'Key to Resources' and chaired by R Srinivasan. Keynote address was delivered by Dr U Ko Ko, Regional Director, WHO, and who emphasised on achieving the social goal of 'Health for All by the year 2000' for which a reorientation of medical libraries and cooperation networks are necessary.

PLENARY Session 2, *ML*, 575-590. 217

Discusses about the Keynote address delivered at this session by Dr B Loginov, USSR, State Central scientific Medical Library, Moscow. Discusses about the main ideas and facts about the construction of the Soviet medical information system, called Soyuzmedinfom. Gives details about the scheme of IT, and generation and use of Soviet biomedical database. Includes another Keynote address by Lois Ann Colainni of NLM, USA on the changing role of the medical librarian.

PLENARY Session 3, *ML*, 591-593. 218

Mentions its theme as 'Key to Resources' chaired by Vallutina Comba. Gives details about the papers presented in this Session on the different aspects of the theme.

PLENARY Session 4, *ML*, 613-621. 219

Describes about the review of proceedings of 25 Sept 1990 about the Plenary Session1. It was chaired by Goran Falkenberg with Fiona M Picken as Reporteur General. Explains about the reports earlier sessions.

PLENARY Session 5, *ML*, 622-625. 220

Discusses about the theme of this Session as 'Key to Health Professionals', chaired by Paul Weiss, with Tony McSean as Reporteur. Mentions about various presentations and the discussion on papers.

PLENARY Session 6, ML, 651-655. 221

Gives details about this open forum where consideration of draft resolution to form an International/World Association of Medical and Health Science Librarians was discussed under the chairmanship of Gorman Falksenberg. Gives the charter and draft of constitution of WHOSLA.

PLENARY SESSION 8, *ML*, 666-671. 222

Reports about this session on the theme: 'Keys to Information at Grass-root level' chaired by Ms Khin That Htar. Gives details about the presentations and the discussion on them.

PLENARY SESSION 9, *ML*, 713-750. 223

States that this Plenary session is the WHO Session which is chaired by Dr Hussain Gezaity with Dr U Myg Tu as moderator and Ms M Teodore oker-Blom as Reporteur. Presents the details of the Panel discussion.

PLENARY Session 10, *ML*, 751-760. 224

Gives details about the presentation of summary report in this Plenary session, chaired by Dr Doren Falkenberg, with Ms M Fiona Mackey Picken as the Reporteur General.

PRE-CONGRESS Session, *ML*, 523-554. 225

Describes in this one day Seminar on the occasion of the Sixth International Congress on Medical Librarianship held in Sept 1990 in New Delhi. It was chaired by Dr J P Jardel of WHO and co-chaired by Dr Harcharan Singh from India. Provides a brief about the presentation of papers of the discussion that took place.

020.62254 (1) Raja Rammohun Roy Library Foundation (RRRLF)

BARUA, B P 226

Raja Rammohun Roy LIbrary Foundation - programmes and activities, *ILS*, 4p.

Describes the main objectives of RRRLF, the function of State Library Committee, Assistance from Foundation for public library development. Gives its programmes and other activities for the development of libraries in the country so that reading habits and library movement could be developed.

BARUA, B P 227

Two decades of the Foundation, *TDF*, 1-14.

Traces the origin of the Raja Rammohun Roy Library Foundation. Explains its objectives. Mentions about its location and administrative development. Describes its early years, the perspective scheme ofwork, progress of work upto 1980, and during 1980s and upto 1990. Discusses about the research cell and special library, lectures and seminars organised, financial help to associations. Mentions about its various publications. States that it drafted NAPLIS and submitted to the Govt of India. Concludes with major bottlenecks and the total impact in 20 years.

RAJA RAMMOHUN ROY LIBRARY FOUNDATION, CALCUTTA 228

Two decades of the Foundation (1972-1992): Souvenir brought out on the occasion of the 20th Anniversary Celebrations, Calcutta: Raja Rammohun Roy Library Foundation, 1993. 87 p.

Includes seven articles on the various aspects of public library services and library legislation including one on RRRLF. Brought out on the occasion of the Foundation's 20th anniversary, includes many informative photographs and messages from all over the country.

020.62254 (1) Society for Information Science (SIS)

020.62254 (1) SIS - XI Conference

XI SIS Annual Convention : Current trends in information technology surveyed, NISSAT Newsletter 11 (1) Jan-Mar 1992: 9-12. 229

Describes the XI SIS Annual Conference held at NCL, Pune during 20-22 January 1992 on the theme of Current Trends in IT. Discusse about its inauguration, fellowships given, open session, and five technical sessions on various aspects of the theme. Includes recommendations made as a result of the discussion.

RECOMMENDATIONS, *CTIT*, 190-199. 230

Includes 12 recommendations adopted by the Society for Information Science at its XI National Convention and Conference held at NCL, Pune during 20-22 January 1992 on various aspects of information policy.

SEWA SINGH and KULDIP CHAND 231

Current trends in information technology and impact on information scene in India: A report, *SISCOM* 12 (3-4) Mar-Apr 1992: 1-5.

Reports about the XI Annual Convention and Conference of the SIS held at the NCL, Pune, 20-22 January 1992 on the abovegiven theme which was divided into 5 Technical Sessions. Recommendations were made in the last session of the Conference.

020.62254 (1) SIS - XII Conference

INFORMATION management for Rural Development: Its parameters-XII SIS Annual Convention, *NISSAT* Newsletter 12 (2) Apr-June 1993: 8-11. 232

Reports about the XII SIS Convention and Conference held during 28-30 January 1993 at IICT, Hyderabad on the theme of Information Management for Rural Development, in which 35 LIS professionals, scientists, technologists, administrators, experts, etc participated. Mentions about inauguration, Hon Fellowships, five technical sessions, and the Plenary session. Gives the recommendations made at the Conference.

020.622541 (1) Confederation of Librarians Association of Northern India (COLNI)

COLNI - Confederation of Librarians' Association of Northern India; a vibrant example of inter-state cooperation, In *Souvenir* of CLA, 1992. 233

Discusses the initiative taken by Chandigarh Librarians Association for the formation of COLNI about three years ago. Mentions aims and objectives of COLNI. Includes extracts from some of letters from professionals and others regarding the formation of the Confederation.

020.62354 (1) All Orissa Non-Government College Library Association

ALL ORISSA NON-GOVERNMENT COLLEGE LIBRARY ASSOCIATION 234

General conference, *IJILIS* 6 (1-2) Jan-June 1993: 155.

Reports about the state level conference of All Orissa Non-Government College Library Association held on 24 January 1993 at Cuttack, and presided over by Dr B B Shukla, attended by 155 delegates from different parts of the state of Orissa. Enumerates important resolution adopted at the Conference. Mentions the new office bearers of the Association.

020.62354 (1) Andhra Pradesh Library Association

ANDHRA PRADESH LIBRARY ASSOCIATION 235

Seminar on public library system at cross roads, Vijaywada: Andhra Pradesh Library Association, 1992, various pagings.

Covers papers in Telugu including 12 papers in English about the role of public libraries in the society. The papers were presented at the 36th Conference of the APLA which was held at Vijaywada during 11-12 January 1992.

SARADA, RAVI 236

Andhra Pradesh library Association, *ILS*, 4 p.

Traces historical development of Andhra Pradesh Library Association and its contribution to village libraries, library conferences, publications, library education, library pilgrimage, mobile libraries, spring festivals, adult education etc. States that the Associations through its activities promoted a massive library movement.

020.62354 (1) Madras Library Association (MALA)

MADRAS LIBRARY ASSOCIATION 237

Report of the Executive Committee, 1 April 1992-31 March 1993: Presented at the 50th meeting held in Madras on 19 June 1993, Madras: MALA, 1993, unnumbered pages.

Contains a detailed report of the various activities of MALA as well as others associated with the celebration of the Birth Centenary of Dr S R Ranganathan. Gives also information about the 2nd International ISKO Conference held in Madras in August 1992, and other events held world wide. Mentions some special publications brought out in this centenary year. Also includes Resolution on Ranganathan passed by the American Library Association.

020.623545 (1) CHANDIGARH LIBRARIANS ASSOCIATION

CENTENARY celebrations, 1992; a report, 238
In *Souvenir* of CLA, 1992.

Reports about the programmes and activities of Chandigarh Librarians Association which organised functions throughout the year of 1992 to celebrate the birth centenary of Dr S R Ranganathan. It organised such activities as Slogan writing contest, Cartoon making contest, Essay writing, Exhibition of charts, Ranganathan stamp release function, etc.

CHANDIGARH LIBRARIANS' ASSOCIATION: A name to reckon with, In *Souvenir* of CLA, 1992. 239

Traces the origin of Chandigarh Librarians' Association in 1977 when the Library Society was set up to look into the interests of the colleagues, changed to Chandigarh Librarians' Association in 1988 to broaden the area of its activities. Mention its other activities also.

CHANDIGARH LIBRARIANS' ASSOCIATION 240
Souvenir, Chandigarh: CLA, 1992.

Brought out to commemorate the Birth Centenary of Dr S R Ranganathan (1892-1992). Includes article about Ranganathan in addition to various messages, etc.

020.62354 82 (1) TamilNadu Library Conference

MUTHUSWAMI, M 241

Tamil Nadu Library Conference, *Her Lib Sci* 32 (3-4) July-Oct

1993: 239-240.

Reports about the First Tamil Nadu Library Conference held on 12 and 13 March 1993 in the University of Madras, and inaugurated by the Speaker of Tamil Nadu Legislative Assembly, and presided over by the Vice Chancellor of the University of Madras. Mentions about the awards and prizes, release of book on library movement.

020.688 Library Marketing

CHAKRABARTI, BHUBANESWAR 242

Marketing - the "in" work in library land - its potential for academic libraries, *Coll Lib* 7 (1-4) 1991: 7-17.

Discusses the concept of marketing and its application in non-profit organizations. Mentions the structure of marketing. Explains the application of marketing in academic libraries. Discusses market analysis, market segmentation, market mix, etc.

HARTONO, BAMBANG 243

Marketing library services, *ML*, 187-192.

Defines marketing. Explains the application of conceptual system of marketing to the marketing problems of libraries. Discusses the use of marketing principles in library. Hopes to provide the needed introduction to marketing to librarians as library managers.

KANKACHARY, M 244

Market segmentation for information services, *ALE*, 16-22.

Defines marketing and market segmentation. Describes aims of marketing as buyer-seller relationship, advertisement, profit motive, pricing, distribution. Applies the principles of market segmentation to library and information segmentation discussing the role of people, place and price. Suggests that in view of their application to LIS in India case may be taken to improve it in future. Concludes that a national level policy be framed to highlight the marketing concept.

LAHIRI, A 245

Time for service orientation, *NISSAT Newsletter* 11(2) Sept 1992: 1.

States that in a situation arisen out of budget crunch the librarians have to follow measures to reduce the cost of supply.

Stresses on a new service oriented approach whereby the consumers of library services should be satisfied. Recommends the adoption of marketing approach under the new situation.

020.7 LIBRARY AND INFORMATION SCIENCE EDUCATION LIS EDUCATION

AMUDHAVALLI, A and BAVAKUTTI, M 246

Towards better education for librarianship, *LISI*, 174-179.

Laments on the static situation of LIS education as started decades ago. Discusses for the betterment of LIS education resources -men, money, materials -in the context of its constraints. Identifies these constraints like course duration, curricula, teaching methods, evaluation system, teaching staff, students, and cooperation and coordination. Suggests few means and methods to improve the situation.

HARRISON, COLIN 247

Specialist education and training; FID/ET seminar, *INICAE* 11(2) Sept 1992: 266-268.

Reports about the FID/ET Seminar on Specialist education held in conjunction with the FID 45th Congress. Describes about the research techniques and training for research as well as general training of information professionals.

JENA, PUSHPANJALI 248

Reminiscences of education: An outline of psyco-educational analysis, *LIS*, 22-28.

Analyses the basic factors to improve library educational methods by studying the psycho-educational patterns. Focuses on three aspects of learning: creative ability, learning or acquisition ability, and development of abilities for problem-solving.

KAULA, P N 249

Rethinking on the pattern of education for information management, *INICAE* 12 (2) Sept 1993: 212-221.

Refers to the task of information professionals in putting knowledge to work. Discusses information sector and the accelerated technological change. States the impact of technology and closure of several existing LIS schools. Examines dimension of information industry. Discusses patterns of education needed caused by the impact of IT. States the trends in developing countries and the steps taken in India to meet the challenge. Puts forth the views on accreditation, cooperative relationship and development of personnel.

LAHIRI, *RAMANSU* 250

The serial publications in LIS education: A study, *Timeless Fellowship* 15, 1993: 57-68.

Discusses the scope of serial publications as learning material in the background of some basic factors directly involved in LIS education. Highlights graphic instruction, technique of information analysis, synthesis and consolidation so that the professionals can prove themselves useful, effective, efficient guides in information literate persons.

NEWTON, V and JEBAKUMAR, I AZARTAH 251

Need for professional training for health science libraries in India, *ITAH*, 249-257.

Explains the need for professional training for increasing the knowledge and skills of personnel in health science libraries. States that in China a five year course for medical library and information service is given. Discusses the trends in library science training in India, and the impact of IT on it. Describes the areas such as circulation, technical works, acquisition of documents, reprographic techniques, medical terminology where training is required. Proposes a curriculum for health science library and information services.

RAJYALAKSHMI, D 252

Challenges of post-industrial society on library and information science education, *LISI*, 111-119.

Mentions about the challenge to the profession from the emergence of information society resulting in interjection of information science into library science and overlooking LIS curricula. Discusses role of information or high technology revolution and the competencies needed under new pressures. Mentionsthat LIS graduates are not as prepared as they should be and libraries are losing usefulness. States however that non-traditional job market is large and highly dynamic.

RANGANATHAN, S R 253

Training of special librarians and imported confusion number two, *Iaslic Bull* 37 (3) Sept 1992: 119-127.

Reprinted pro Iaslic Bull 2 (1-2) Dec 1957: 32-38, in view of its relevance under the heading 'Thus wrote Ranganathan'. Points out the gap in the West between the public librarians and special librarians. States that UK is attempting to integrate the course of training for both the public and special librarians. Discusses the position in India which is just the opposite. The training for the two is already integrated with the necessary differentiatiion at appropriate points. Suggests a plan for strengthening this integrated course and avoiding dissipation.

SATYANARAYANA, R 254

Education for information resource management, *CS*, 132-143.

Discusses the concept of Information Management (IM) and its need. Interprets concept on Information Resource Management (IRM). Discusses in this context information sources, services and systems. Refers to the establishment of a programme in this new field of study and the new professional skills associated with IRM. Concludes by advocating that IRM education programme be started in India for meeting the information needs of the society.

020.7 (1) LIS Education- National Policy

KRISHAN KUMAR 255

A proposal for national policy for library and information science education, *LISI*, 135-141.

Gives a brief history of LIS education in India. Describes need for national policy. Defines national policy. Mentions its basis and scope. Explains the need for a National Commission on LIS Education as well as an Indian Council of LIS as autonomous body. Discusses also the need for setting up a National Institute for LIS. Mentions its functions and records to be maintained. Gives the role of Government in formulation and implementation of the national policy.

LAXMAN RAO, N and KARISIDDAPPA, C R 256

Library and information science education policy in India, *DL*, 175-185.

Defines policy. Gives historical background of policy and LIS education policy. Explains Ranganathan's contribution to LIS education. Presents the present scene of LIS education, policy presentation and implementation. Discusses relevance of policy documents developed by various bodies/agencies. States the need for a new policy document for which gives guidlines and standards.

020.7 (1) LIS Education Through Distance Education

HARISH CHANDRA, LOHIA, J S and Hans Raj 257

Library and information science teaching through distance education, *Univ News* Sept 13, 1993:

Gives importance of distance education. Mentions its objectives in respect to LIS teaching. Discusses the problems in teaching LIS through distance education. Points out to re-orient and revamp the efforts for teaching LIS through distance education. Point out to re-orient and revamp the efforts for teaching LIS through distance education. Provides a table of universities offering distance education programmes.

INAMDAR, N B and CHANDRASEKHARA RAO, V 258

Library and information science education through distance learning: A case study of M L I Sc programme of A P Open University, *LISI*, 86-96.

Gives historical background of distance education. Mentions programmes of studies at A P Open University. Describes the M L I Sc programme, its admission requirements, profile of students, course contents, methods of instruction, preparation of course material, use of audio visuals, study centres, assignment and evaluation and examinations. Concludes that the course should be continued but improved further.

MANORAMA SRINATH, SENTHIL KUMARAN, and STEPHAN, LAWYED 259

Supply and demand of manpower in library profession in Tamil Nadu, *RDAL*, 91-94.

States that in view of the technological changes and their impact on education and training of library and information professionals, distance education programmes serve no useful purpose. Gives data of the output through regular and distance education courses in Tamil Nadu, number of candidates registered for employment in Madras from 1980 to 1990. Emphasises the urgent need to decrease the supply of professional output; and demand should rather be increased.

RAMESH BABU, B 260

Distance education in library and information science, *LID*, 227-243.

gives an overview of LIS education in India. Mentions about

development of distance education in India. Describes distance education in LIS at various levels such as Certificate, Diploma, Bachelor's and Master's programmes. Mentions the universities offering these programmes through distance education. Explains in detail the case of Madras University with reference to enrollment, sourse material,method of instruction, personal contact programme, feedback, and problems. Offers useful suggestions.

RAMESH BABU, B and GANGADHAR RAO, P 261

Master's degree in library and information science through open learning: Case study of the University of Madras, *Lib Rev* 40 (4) 1992: 21-26.

Traces the genesis of open learning in LIS at the University of Madras. Discusses about the introduction of MLIS through open learning, giving details about admission requirements, course contents, preparation of study materials, method of instruction, and feedback. Concludes that there is scope for improvement.

RAMESH BABU, B 262

Measures to strengthen correspondence courses in library and information science, *ALR*, 267-277.

Give a background of correspondence courses in LIS in India. Identifies pitfalls if offering LIS courses through correspondence system. Suggests suitable remedies so as to achieve professional standards in LIS education. Concludes that this system of education has come to stay as a viable system in all the universities. Appends a list of universities offering LIS courses through distance education system.

SATYANARAYANA, P, YADGIRI, R and YADGIRI REDDY, M 263

Library resources and services to distance learners, *ILS*, 3 p.

States the need for distance education in India, and its application to LIS education also. Mentions functions of the university, college, and public libraries in India in relation to distance education for the development of library resources and services.

020.7 (1) LIS Education - Institutes

INAMDAR, N B 264

Institute of Library Science, Hyderabad, *ILS*, 6 p.

Narrates the story of establishement of the Institute of

Library Science which had blessings of Dr S R Ranganathan, and reproduces his letter of 7th Dec 1953 to K M Ujlambkar. Recounts the Board of Studies, syllabus, and other details of the course, Board of examiners, faculty, finances, etc.

RAMESH, P 265

Bird's eyeview of Central Institute of *LIbrary* Science, Hyderabad, *IPLA Souvenir*, 2 p.

Discusses the establishment of the Central Institute of Library Science, Hyderabad meant to train librarians through Certificate Course. Mentions that it also conducts user education programmes in library science - also conducts course on school on school librarianship for working teachers as incharge of libraries.

RISWADKAR, M R 266

Six years with Institute of Library Science (ILS), *ILS*. 4p.

Recounts the years spent in the Institute as teacher and learnt programme management, among many other things. Remembers the work done here as a social cause, dedication of teachers and others, its library, etc.

SUBBA RAO, B V 267

State Institute of Library Education Research and Training (SILERT): An overview, *ILS*, 2 p.

Set up in 1986 as part of the Directorate of Public Libraries, it aims to oversee the conducting of pre-service training course by the recognised institutes, in-service training for librarians, etc. Mentions that it will undertake publication work also.

YOUNIS SULTAN 268

Professional colleges in rural areas: A profile of Mariar College of Library Science, Khammam - AP, *ILS*, 2 p.

Describes about the establishment of the college of Library Science at degree level in 1991. Proposes to introduce Computer Application to Library Operations from 1992-93 academic year.

020.7095 LIS Education - Asia

DICKSON, IAN E 269

Research into training and education of information professionals in Asia and Oceania, *INICAE* 11(2) Sept 1992: 164-177.

Reviews research carried out in Education and Training of information professionals in Asia and Oceanic region. Describes a case study of implementation of a course that develops IT in conjunction with Management Studies for mature-age students in full time employment. Involves off-campus self paced materials, computer managed learning, 24-hour access to course materials, etc.

020.70954 LIS Education - India

KONNUR, M B 270

Information technology and the future training for librarianship: Some implications for developing countries, *LID*, 177-179.

Brings forth the importance of IT and its application in L & I work. Describes role of LIS educators in new library situations created by IT applications, reflecting changes in the LIS curricula for future training. Mentions about the reflecting changes in the LIS curricula for future training. Mentions about the IT contents introduced in BLISc course of Poona University. Concludes that there is need to adopt IT contents introduced in BLISc course of Poona University. Concludes that there is need to adopt new techniques and new ideas.

AGRAWAL, S P and MANOHAR LAL 271

Library and information science education in India: Achievements and perspectives, *LISI*, 29-49.

Describes the present position of LIS education in India including Ranganathan's contribution, various courses, accreditation, overview. Discusses about change in nomenclature, duration of courses, course contents, course trends, etc. Points out the trend towards change in courses. Mentions research activities, teaching methods, teaching standards, manpower planning particularly in new areas. Makes some suggestions to improve the quality of LIS education. Gives course contents of selective universities/institutes in Appendix.

ASUNDI, A Y 272

Library science education in India: An evaluative profile, *DL*, 144-156.

Gives introduction of LIS education in India. Discusses stock of courses in universities and courses, admissions in these courses. Describes the status of librarians. Explains state of libraries and services, evaluation of courses, education and employment, research activities.

020.7095 (1) LIS Education - Developing Countries

CHATTERJEE, AMITABHA 273

Library and information science education in India: Achievements, problems and prospects, *LISI*, 50-59.

Traces briefly history of LIS education in India. Mentions about leading role of Delhi University and the significant achievement. Discusses some problems of proliferating numbers, degradation of degrees, lack of infrastructure, lowering of standards, differences in course contents, relevancy and orientation, lacuna in training, etc. Discusses other issues as accreditation, need for national policy to give clear direction to LIS education. Mentions necessary measures to improve and maintain quality of LIS education.

CHOPRA, H R 274

Information technology in the library and information science education in India, *Jl Inf Sci* 3 (2) Oct-Dec 1992: 93-98.

Defines IT. Hightlights the changing concept of librarianship in view of literature explosion, societal awareness, role of technological development, etc. States that there is need to revamping the curriculum to provide specialised training to budding librarians. States that to cope with changed needs and trends,certain new courses, useful for future librarians and information scientists, covering automation, should be introduced and equipments required be provided.

DESHPANDE, K S 275

Education for librarianship: Stray thoughts of an old-timer, *LISI*, 60-70.

Mentions the traits of a librarian who is teacher-cum-practitioner. States library and the Dept as twins. Describes the academic nature of a librarian's work in book selection, classification and cataloguing, bibliography, library management, etc. States that topics for M L I Sc dissertations should help in research and scholarship to the candidates. Discusses some structural matters as three year M L I Sc, internship, two separate courses, LIS at the undergraduate level, college of library science possibility may be explored. Discusses image of the profession, guidelines from users of our products. Gives a thinking about future. Mentions the Indian scene.

DHANASEGARAN, G 276

Library and information science education in India, *DL*, 157-164.

Discusses about LIS Education in India from 1929, Indian library schools, Library association schools, higher studies in library science. Discusses about Sarada Ranganathan Chair, teaching of library science, and role of Ranganathan and the University Grants Commission, and impact of the contribution of Ranganathan.

INAMDAR, N B 277

National workshop on library science education, *Her Lib Sci* 31 (3-4) July-Oct 1992: 256-261.

Reports about the National workshop on 'Library Science Education at Certificate Level and Library Service in Rural Areas' organised by the Institute of Library Science, Hyderabad from Dec 15-17, 1991 in collaboration with Raja Rammohun Roy Library Foundation.

INSTITUTE OF LIBRARY SCIENCE, HYDERABAD 278

Souvenir, edited by S Sudarshan Rao: Published on the occasion of the inauguration of the Institute's own premises and National Workshop on Library Science Education at Certificate Level & Library Service in Rural Area, 15-17 December, 1991, Hyderabad, Hyderabad: Institute of Library Science, 1991, n. p.

Dedicated to Dr S R Ranganathan in his Centenary Year, includes articles on libraries, library science education, library associations in Andhra Pradesh by various authors.

KAULA, P N 279

Hundred years of library and information science education: Evaluation and trend, *LISI*, 3-13.

Delivered as Keynote address in Nagpur Seminar in Oct 1987, discusses about state control on education, impact of Dewey's contribution, pattern of education in India including impact of Ranganathan's contribution. Discusses about evaluation of LIS education and achievements of hundred years in US, UK, etc. Gives observations on vital issues including professional content in teaching, uncontrolled growth of schools, inadequate library facilities. Describes impact of information revolution for new image, new tasks,etc accreditation, etc. Calls for taking the country towards 21st century.

KHAN, H A 280

Library and information science education in India, *LISI*, 142-153.

Aims to provide the trends or changing scene of LIS education in India such as from library science to library and information science. Evaluates their impact on education and training. Suggests certain measures which would be helpful in the formulation of a positive action oriented LIS education policy for India in the decades to come.

KUMAR, P S G 281

Education for librarianship in India: Perspectives, performance and projections *LISI*, 17-28.

Traces history of LIS education in India since Baroda school, and the various courses started at a later stage. Discusses role of IASLIC, IATLIS,INSDOC, UGC, etc. Mentions about the growth in LIS schools, their status, course contents, faculty and its growth. Brings forth the contribution of teachers based on a bibliography of Indian library literature compiled by Dr Sewa Singh and I V Malhan. Mentions the physical facilities and teaching aids. Describes some points of projectionthat need our attention.

KUMAR, P S G and VASHISHTH, C P 282

Library and information science in India, New Delhi: Sterling, 1992. xii, 220 p.

Includes 20 selected papers, including the Keynote address of Prof P N Kaula presented at the ILA-IASLIC-IATLIS-AGLIS Seminar on hundred years of library education held at Dept of Library & Information Science, Nagpur University, in Oct 1987 in which 73 delegates from all over India participated. The papers cover a wide variety of subjects like performance, problems and prospects of library schools; strategies for future as restructuring, new technology, continuing education, etc; planning LIS programmes, and so on.

LAXMAN RAO, N and KARISIDDAPPA, C R 283

Library and information science education policy in India, *Luck Libn* 25 (1-2) Mar-Jun 1993: 32-39.

States that National Policy provides guidance for library and information science education progremmes. Ranganathan's contribution to the development of library and information science education is phenomenal. Mentions the attempts made to prepare a

National Policy on LIS. Says that the UGC should take initiative to prepare a National Policy for LIS education on the basis of earlier recommendations and the present needs. Points out that the UGC should supervise its implementation and update it from time to time.

NARASIMHA RAJU, G V S L and KAMAIAH, P 284

Library and informatikon science education in India: A new approach, *LISI*, 180-186.

Attempts to present LIS as a full-fledged discipline like engineering, medicine and law. Describes that training needs demand a new look at the gamut of course requirements and duration of training, keeping in mind the overwhelming changes in information needs of contemporary society. Pleads for the introduction of LIS courses right from post-secondary level of education.

NAVALANI, K 285

Library and information science education in India, *DL*, 128-143.

Traces historical development of LIS education in India to the present. Discusses various ailments LIS education is suffering from. Gives a critical look at the contents of courses in most of the universities.

SEWA SINGH 286

Library and information science education, *DL*, 107-127.

Traces beginning of LIS education in India, and its development in post-independence periods. Mentions about the open university courses. Discusses level of LIS education. Explains present manpower turnout. Discusses access to information, impact of IT. Points out the gap in the curriculum. Mentions the need for research and other academic activities, continuing education programmes. Offers some useful suggestions.

UNIVERSITY GRANTS COMMISSION (INDIA), COMMITTEE ON CURRICULUM DEVELOPMENT ON LIBRARY & INFORMATION SCIENCE 287

Report, New Delhi: University Grants Commission, 1992. 157 p.

Explains the need for new and changing curriculum for LIS schools in India. Discusses the report prepared by the Curriculum Development Committee of the UGC under the chairmanship of PN Kaula.

020.7095413 LIS Education - Orissa

MAHAPATRA, G 288

History and development of library and information science education in Orissa: A synopsis, In *Souvenir, 38th All India Library Conference,* 21-24 Nov 1992, Bhubaneswar, pp 21-25.

Gives in brief objectives and origin of LIS education in India. Mentions origin in Orissa about a decade or so old. Discusses levels of library education and the types of organisation involved in it. Mentions intake capacity and teaching facilities. Outlines the admission criteria. Gives an overview of syllabus, and research and publications.

020.7095414 LIS Education - West Bengal

BARUA, B P 289

Library & information science education: An overview, *LID*, 213-226.

Traces history of LIS education in India since 1911. Gives development of LIS education in West Bengal, enumerating different levels of LIS courses including Certificate level, Degree level, PG level, and Ph D level. Mentions the universities where these courses are taught. Describes the faculty strenght and teacher-student ratio. Mentions about library literature being produced in West Bengal. Gives observations and necessary steps to be taken to improve and maintain the quality.

020.709543 LIS Education - Madhya Pradesh

PRASHER, R G 290

Library and information science education in Madhya Pradesh, *Univ News* 31 (16) Apr 19, 1993: 10-19.

Explains in detail about the ten teaching departments of LIS in Madhya Pradesh about the courses run, Heads and their qualifications with status, staff strength, annual budget, building, computer, library, admission procedure, fees, schemes of papers at different levels, students work at M L I Sc level, quality of products, professional activities of teachers, constraints in development. Lists steps for the improvement of the LIS Depts. Suggests for rationalisation of M L I Sc topics, raisnig standard of LIS education, particularly in professional activities, etc.

020.7095483 LIS Education - Kerala

DEVARAJAN, G 291

Library science education in Kerala: A survey and assessment, *DL*, 165-174.

Provides a brief account of LIS education and libraries in Kerala. Tells about the new courses on the anvil. Also gives the manpower position in Kerala. Gives some observations useful for further improvement of LIS education in the state.

020.7095484 LIS Education - Andhra Pradesh

CHANDRAN, D, RAMESH BABU, B AND RAMESH, G 292

Library and information science education in Andhra University: Problems and prospects, *LID*, 203-212.

Provides an overview of LIS education in India. Gives genesis of LIS education in Andhra Pradesh where library movement and library education were seen growing in parallel way. Discusses about the institution offering LIS education in A p, admission requirements, medium of instruction, changes in the levels of library education, research activity, availability of staff. Identifies some problems in training of librarians. Gives some useful suggestions.

RAJU, A A N 293

A bird's eyeview of library and information science education in Andhra Pradesh, *ILS*, 4p.

Deals with the LIS education in Andhra Pradesh at semi professional level. Describes also the various university courses such as Bachelor's course, B L I Sc through distance education, Master's degree, research courses, NISIET training progreammes, continuing education progremmes, etc.

020.71 LIS Schools

HAVARD-WILLIAMS, PETER 294

The changing roles of library schools: Into strategic planning, *Lib Prog (Int)* 13 (1-2) Jan-Dec 1993: 1-7.

States that when LIS schools are being closed in America, the Dept of Library and Information Science at the University of Botswana is branching out into new areas. Describes information as a tool for planning as a paper in this University. Makes reports about other papers, Workshop on Strategic Planning, etc. Points out new concepts, processes and procedures to be followed.

PADHI, P and RATH, M 295

Department of library and information science: A decade's achievements, In *Souvenir, 38th All India Library Conference*, Bhubaneswar, Nov 21-24, 1992, pp 7-10.

Traces the history and development of the Department of Library and Information Science which was set up in 1981 at the Utkal University with B L I Sc course, and started M L I Sc degree course in 1983-84, and later Ph D also. Mentions the achievements, areas of research, etc. Reports the other distinctions of the Dept which has to shoulder many responsibilities in the future.

020.71 (1) LIS Schools -Accreditation

PICHAPPAN, P 296

Department of Library and Information Science; a profile, In *Souvenir*, XV National IASLIC Conference, 26-29 Dec 1992, hosted by Annamalai University Library and Dept of Library & Information Science, Annamalai University, 1992, pp 77-79.

Provides the picture of the setting up and development of the Dept of LIS at the Annamalai University which is running different courses at the point.

SHUKLA, R K 297

Library and information science schools in India: Need for accreditation, *LISI*, 157-164.

States the need and purpose of standardisation. Defines accreditation. Traces history of accreditation. Discusses accrediation of LIS education in USA and UK. Describes the situation in India identifying problems in LIS education. Points out the urgent need of standards in certain areas in Indian situation such as finance, curriculum faculty, admission procedure, library facilities, building. Identifies agencies for accrediting schools like ILA, UGC, IATLIS, Indian Library Science Council.

020.71 (1) LIS Associations

BRIEF REPORT of the Karnataka University Library and Information Science Association, 1992-93, *Timeless Fellowship* 15, 1993: 87-88. 298

Gives the names of the new office bearers of KULISA - Karnataka University Library and Information Science Association. Mentions about inauguration of the KAULISA. Describes its other activities, special lectures, one-day seminar. etc held during the year.

020.711 LIS Education -Courses and Curriculum]

ALVI, W A 299

Library and information science education in India: Need for remodelling the programmes, *LISI*, 165-173.

Discusses the course contents of the syllabi for Bachelor's programme in India with respect to their objectives. Explains the need for reframing, deemphasise on Colon Classification and Classified Catalogue Code and less emphasis on canons in classification and cataloguing. Discusses the duration of B L I Sc programme, inadequacies in course content. Makes some suggestions regarding modifying in syllabi, increase in duration, post-education training, consolidation of LIS schools, etc.

CHANDRAN, D 300

Introduction of computer-based curses in library & information science education: Problems and prospects, *LID* 192-201.

Stresses the importance of LIS education in the present information society with salient features of developing countries. Presents an overview of the past and present syllabus in LIS education in India. Compares how the present syllabus is not suitable to meet the future challenges of the society. Stresses need to add computer-base information courses in the curriculum. Provides insight into the capabilities, benefits, problems and limitations of new courses. Gives a few suggestions.

IT APPLICATIONS to LIS: NCSI training course Bangalore, *NISSAT Newsletter* 11(1) Jan-Mar 1992: 13-14.301

Mentions the objectives of the one-year training course started by the National Centre for Science Information set up at the IISc, Bangalore, and is funded by the UGC. Gives the minimum qualifications for admission to the course. Mentions the teaching methods followed. Gives a summary of the course content.

KAMAIAN, P and CHETTY, P RAJARATHNAM 302

Need for job-based curriculum in library and information science education, *LID*, 187-191.

Defines curriculum. Describes core curriculum and ancilliary curriculum. Mentions various types of courses offered in Indian LIS schools. Points out available jobs in LIS centres. Compares manpower production with job opportunities in library and information centres. Concludes that curriculum has to be continuously revised in the changing socio-economic conditions.

KARISIDDAPPA, C R and LAXMAN RAO, N 303

Course on computer application in LIS curriculum at Master's degree level in India, *Luck Libn* 24 (4) Oct-Dec 1992: 138-143.

Examines the relevance and nature of computer training of LIS professionals/trainees. Emphasises that there is no need to convert LIS professional as hardware/software experts. Suggests a draft curriculum for the inclusion of a course on computer application in the Master's programme in LIS in Indian universities.

KARISIDDAPPA, C R and LAXMAN RAO, N 304

Course on computer application in LIS curriculum at Master's degree level in India, *DL*, 88-96.

Discusses the relevance of computers and the need to use them in libraries in present times. Makes a plea that the course on computers be introduced in the LIS education progremmes at least at the Mater's level so as to produce well trained professionals.

KONNUR, M B 305

Computer applications in libraries: An elective papers at B L I Sc level, *LISI*, 126-132.

Describes the need to introduce computer applications in libraries at B L I Sc and M L I Sc levels. Mentions institutions having this paper at M L I Sc level. Describes various aspects of the course such as objectives, course contents, faculty, assessment of students and examinations etc as being given at the University of Poona.

LAHKAR, NARENDRA 306

Courses in librarianship and university library service in the sheffield University: An informative study, *LIN*, 49-26.

Explains the courses of study, course contents, methods of instruction, library services, computerised library systems, BLCMP library service, record retrieval, users' interface. Discusses about the search options as title search, author search, etc. Discusses author's experience gained during his study for one year in the University of sheffield, UK.

LAXMAN RAO, N and RATNA RAO, N 307

Teaching management in library science courses, *DL*, 318-327.

Discusses about the relevance of management course for librarianship and the status of management courses in Indian university library schools. Explains how to teach management course.

MANORAMA SRINATH 308

Library education and librarianship - a conflict between theory and pragmatism, *DL*, 189-194.

States the need for restructuring of library schools curricula in view of the change of the concept of librarianship. Evaluates the management techniques in curricula and textbooks and their relevance. Lays emphasis on research in library schools, apprenticeship training. Makes some suggestions.

MISHRA, SANJAYA 309

Education for preservation and conservation of library materials in Indian library schools: A proposal, *Lib Her* 31 (1-2) Apr-Sep 1992: 33-41.

Defines the terms preservation and conservation. Discusses the need of preservation and conservation education in India. Outlines the present position of PAC education. Presents a proposal for PAC education in Indian library schools with its objectives, course contents, teaching facilities, research needs, etc.

NAVALANI, K 310

Library and information science education at Master's level in India: A survey, *LISI*, 73-85.

Makes a distinction between Library Science and Information Science. Discusses what constitutes information science. Conducts a survey of the existing courses from about 30 universities out of which 15 syllabi were received. Makes a paperwise analysis of MLISc courses of these universities. Finds out about the weightage to information science. Discusses the analysis in view of the aimms and objectives of LIS education concludes that professional education needs redefinition.

RAJU, A A N 311

LIS courses in India: Levels, admission requirements and placement. *DL*, 97-106.

Gives introduction of LIS education in India. Discusses about the levels of courses offered in India, admission requirements of various courses, as also holding of Entrance test. Mentions also about the placement of trained manpower in different sectors.

SATIJA, M P 312

A case for a diploma in Indian Librarianship, *Luck Libn* 25 (1-2) Mar-Jun 1993: 6-24.

Makes a case for a Diploma in Indian Librarianship as there is need to offer short-term but intensive and full time courses in the various specialisations including the one under consideration.

SEN, B K, ARORA, R and KARANJAI, A 313

The changes context and the LIS education in India, *DL*, 195-212.

Brings home the point that in LIS education the course contents should be amended from time to time to keep step with changes in the context. Discusses change in the context in LIS. Discusses LIS course content and that new areas have emerged for which detailed course contents are given. Outlines a model of the course.

SIVA REDDY, K and SOMASEKHARA RAO, K 314

Library and information science education in India - a case for need based curriculum development, *LID*, 180-186.

Provides a brief about development of LIS education in India to the present. Describes about the struggle for independent status of LIS education in India to the present. Describes about the struggle for independent status of LIS courses with the encouragement from the UGC. Mentions papers taught at BLISc and MLISc levels. Reviews the existing curriculum designed long ago. States that with the information explosion, new developments, development of IT, new training courses are needed where modern technology is used.

SURYA RAO, G and ABBULU, G E P 315

Desired changes in library and information science education in the wake of new information technologies, *LIT*, 302-306.

Scans though the sayllabi for different Departments of LIS at the university level or run independently in Andhra Pradesh and in some other states at B L I Sc, MLI Sc or M Phil levels, and also on the basis of literature available in different documents.

VAISHNAV, A A and DEO, V N 316

Current job market and LIS curricula; a pragatic study, *Her Lib Sci* 31 (3-4) July-Oct 1992: 191-200

Identifies trends in current job market for library and information centres in India. Analyses advertisements appeared in *University News* and *Employment News* from January 1988 to August 1989 in various cadres. Describes positions by organisations, designation, qualification, age, experience to prepare a profile of manpower needs. Compares the job market, and present curricula. Suggests changes in the present curricula. Points out anamolies in advertisements.

020.715 LIS Education - Continuing Education.

In-Service Training

YADAGIRI REDDY, J 317

Norms and standards in LIS education in Andhra Pradesh with special reference to course curriculae, *ALR*, 279-286.

Gives background of LIS education in India. Mentions present situation of LIS education in AP. Discusses course curricula at Certificate and BLISc levels in formal and non-formal system. Makes a mention of MLISc, M Phil and PhD programmes also. Suggests that universities should concentrate on higher level courses leaving Certificate programmes to professional bodies.

020.715 Lis Educaation - Continuing Education
In Service Training

JANARDHANA RAO, S S 318

ILA/NISSAT training programme, *Her Lib Sci* 31 (3-4) July-Oct 1992: 262.

Reports about the 15th ILA/NISSAT Workshop on Computer Application in Library and Information Activities sponsored by the DSIR and organised by ILA in collaboration with Sir C R Reddy Autonomous College Library, Eluru, A P in which 20 librarians participated.

NAWE, J 319

Need and priority areas for continuing education for sub and professional information, library and archives personnel in Tanzania, *Int Lib Move* 14 (3) Sept 1992: 152-160.

Explains the need for continuing education in Tanazania,

highlights areas for continuing education. Describes mode of provision of continuing education such as seminars, workshops, conference, etc. Lists demand for librarians, documentalists, and archivists in Tanzania. Adds appendix for lower and higher government standard library examination content.

PALEKAR, B R 320

Summer school for librarians at Pondicherry, *Rilisar Bull* 8 (2) Apr-June 1993: 22-24.

Reports about a training course on 'Management of Library and Information Service in Engineering Colleges' for librarians of engineering colleges, organised at Pondicherry to exchange ideas and experiences for efficiency and effectiveness to library services in which about 35 delegates participated. Inaugurated by Dr T Viswanathan, Director, INSDOC, and directed by K Nityanandan.

PICHAPPAN, P 321

Continuing education for librarians through distance education, *LISI*, 212-218.

States that in view of the technological trend and their implications for libraries, librarians are unable to become masters in IT. Calls for further education of librarians to develop more sophisticated management techniques and expertise in information resource management, information system, communication technology, etc.

RAJU, A A N 322

Continuing education programmes for teachers in library and information science and academic library professionals in South India, In *Papers*, 58th IFLA General Conference, New Delhi, 30 Aug - 5 Sept 1992: 7.3-7.4.

States that NPE has recognised the need for improving the quality of education in India. Refers to the UGC's scheme for orientation/Refresher courses and the establishment of Academic Staff Colleges. Estimates the number of academic library professionals working in the catchment area of Academic Staff College of Osmania University and the number of courses in LIS to be conducted to cover them all. Hightlights five refresher courses conducted by Academic Staff College of Osmania University and their unsfulness and impact on the professionals of South India.

SETHI, A R 323

Continuing education programmes for academic libraries, *ALE*, 23-30.

Explains the need for continuing education (CE) for all library personnel. Identifies areas of CE progremmes for the academic library staff such areas as academic updating, library techniques, library management, user studies, IT, R&D, and public relations. Looks at the changed scenario in academic libraries. Describes some agencies which should cooperate to execute the CE progremme include libraries, and library professionals. Makes a case for CE centre to frame guidelines.

TAHER, MOHAMMED 324

Curriculum for inservice training of health science librarians, *ALD*, 81-83.

Outlines the need for training progremme of health science librarians. Discusses the objectives of in-service training. Describes the syllabus of course for this type of training. Concludes that continuing education should be a regular progremme to establish contacts through seminars, refresher courses, workshops, etc.

020.716 LIS EDUCATION-TEACHING METHODS

PATEL, JASHU 325

A comparative study of methods of evaluating library science students in UK and USA: A research proposal, *Jl Lib & Inf Sci* 18 (2) Dec 1993: 67-81.

Describes need and justification of the study based on literature. Enumerates objectives and limitations of the study. Lists underlying assumptions. Gives tentative hypotheses and definitions of terms. Describes plan of the study covering research methodology, significance of project and probable results. Gives also outlines of research chapters.

ROUT, R K 326

Planning workshop -cum-information processing laboratories for library schools, *LISI*, 187-196.

Assesses the methods of teaching of LIS in India for offering practical education, to fulfil the need of a professional course. Offers suggestions for setting up workshop-cum-information processing laboratory with different units, in every school to achieve the above goal.

020.717 LID Education -Teachers

MAHAJAN, S G 327

Development of library and information science teachers, *LISI*, 199-211.

Presents the LIS teaching scene in India particularly after 1985. Discusses problems in recruiting teachers regarding qualifications, research experience, specialisation, publications of high quality, production of teaching materials, innovations in teaching methods. Suggests for training of teachers.

020.72 LIS Research

CHAKRABARTI, BHUBANESWAR 328

Research in librarianship: A bird's eye view, *Coll Lib* 9 (1-4) 1993: 1-13.

States the purpose of library as innovative and experiment. Traces the development of innovations and experiments. Defines research and gives its importance. Ientifies purpose of research. Discusses nature of research in LIS. Hightlights some trends of research in LIS. Describes the research methodology followed in LIS. Concludes that team research in equally important for the productive use of the theories and techniques from other fields in research to library service.

CUBILO, JULIE 329

Positioning research activities: Problems and quest for solution, *INICAE* 12 (1) Mar 1993: 42-62.

Discusses research as an important activity because it helps to learn from past mistakes, provides better understanding of information systems, anticipates changes. Explores some of the issues for stimulation of research. Highlights that quest for answers to unexplored questions will come from open discussion and research. Points out challenges to be faced from policy makers, funding agencies, officials, information system users in the search for viable research solutions.

DOUGLAS, DEPHANE 330

Research in Caribbean library and information education and training, *INICAE* 12(1) Mar 1993: 17-24.

Discusses the factors that influence the information system and in the formulation of information policy and planning. Explains information environment and its impact on education and training of information studies, core formal research methodology courses and programmes conducted in Dept of Library Studies, University of West Indies. Describes research and research activity for practicing information specialists. States also the areas of research needed to support the policy and planning activities.

IBRAHIM, ABBAS 331

Ranganathan Institute of Library & Information Science for Applied Research (RILISAR): Developments in MIS for record management/library automation & information technology, *Rilisar Bull* 8 (1) Jan-Mar 1993: 26-28.

Describes the need of MIS for automation of record management/library and information handling for which are needed specialists in IT in this new information age. Mentions about good career progression in this area for which a course is being initiated by RILISAR from April 1993.

IFFIDON, SAM E 332

Research degree progremmes in librarianship: Critical areas and the Nigerian job marker, *ALE*, 31-43.

Defines research degree programme. Discusses the pattern of library education in Nigeria. Identifies areas of importance which include user studies, book stock, library architecture, library technology, library society, librarians, management, cataloguing and classification, library education, etc. Describes the employment opportrtunities available to research degree holders. Gives various suggestions to improve the situation of research in Nigeria.

IJARI, S R 333

Research in library and information science: A case study, *Timeless Felloship* 15, 1993: 9-15.

Provides a bird's eyeview of doctoral research activities in LIS in the five universities of Karnataka. Mentions that so far 44 Ph D degrees have been awarded by these universities except Bangalore and Mangalore. Gives detailed information of research faacilities in tables and appendices. Makes suggestions to avoid duplication and promote a high standard research in LIS.

KANNAPPANAVAR, B U, ARABAGONDA, N N and BHAT, CHANDRAKANT 334

Planning a thesis: Some observations, *IJILIS* 5 (3-4) July-Dec 1992: 282-289.

Deals with the theoretical aspects of the thesis writing. Discusses in detail the selection of title, reviewing of literature, methodology, analysis of date, use of statistical analysis, use of diagram, charts, summary and findings, etc.

KOMALA RAO, R and SAMPATHA CHARY, K 335

Recent advances in library research methods in medical sciences: A study, *ITAH*, 243-247.

Describes research process, and library research methodology. Discusses as to how the modern medical research is confronted with the literature explosion, varies information research methods and to get research findings published in the best journals in the least time. Mentions two styles of giving references.

KRISHAN KUMAR 336

Research methods in library and information science, New Delhi: Har-Anand Publications in association with Vikas Publishing House, 1992. 317 p.

Divided into 20 chapters, discusses in detail about the research methods as survey, historical, experimental, scientific method. Discusses about other data gathering techniques as observations, questioning, interview, etc. Makes also a comparative study of research approaches and methods. Describes the application of statistical methods including bibliometrics as applicable to LIS.

OHDEDAR, A K 337

Research methodology, Calcutta: Bengal Library Association, 1993. x, 142-6 p.

Deals with such topics on the subject as meaning and characteristics of research; kinds of research and research methods; steps of research design; organisation, analysis and interpretation of data; writing the reports; modern trends in research; development of research in India.

OHDEDAR, A K 338

Study and research on Ranganathan, *IASLIC Bull* 37 (3) Sept 1992: 145-153.

Suggests the possible means of research and study on

Ranganathan in three broad directions: (i) Ranganathan's works; (ii) his career activities and achievements; (iii) his life and personality. Suggests the use of published and unpublished sources including sources of oral history. Suggests creation of "Ranganathan Research Library" where all relevant sources be collected for the purpose. Enumerates possible categories of sources and lists already available sources. Hints at a few specific research problems.

RAJU, A A N 339

Library and information science research in India, *ALR*, 13-23.

Defines research. Points out need for research in LIS. Lists advantages. Mentions impediments to research. Traces genesis of LIS research in India. Gives output of LIS research in India in recent years, particularly research output in academic librarianship. Lists some topics for prospective LIS research. Appends a useful list on 'Research Output in Academic Li brarianship'

SATIJA, M P 340

Garnering the fruits of research, *LISI*, 99-107.

Gives importance of research and Ph D degree. Mentions research in LIS and introduction of Ph D in LIS. Describes research in LIS in India starting with Delhi University at Ph D level, M Phil and M L I Sc levels. Discusses the situation of bibliographical control of Indian LIS dissertations. Mentions various such sources compiled for different purposes. States the need to keep track about research in progress.

ATIJA, M P 341

Ranganathan and team research, *Her Lib Sci* 32 (1-2) Jan-Apr 1993: 11-17.

States the advantage of collective thinking and research. Gives examples of collaboration work initiated by Ranganathan. Discusses Ranganathan's work through research circles like Classification Research Group (London), Library Research Circle, Delhi, in association with students and associates. Refers to his writing work, research work, etc and faith in learning through discussion.

ASTIJA, M P 342

Ranganathan and team research, *D L*, 59-68.

Describes the team work in librarianship and Ranganathan's contribution to it by involving more professionals in various activities, starting of study circles as Library Research Circle, Delhi, consultation with colleagues, etc to promote team research.

SATIJA, M P 343

Research in librarianship before and after Ranganathan: An overview, *PP* 27-45.

Traces history of libraries through the ages. Discusses story of research in librarianship in other countries as well as in India. Explains the period of research in library and information science after Ranganathan emerged on the scene, particularly its establishment at the University of Delhi.

SEETHARAMA, S 344

Ranganathan, the methodologist, par excellence, *DL*, 69-80.

Looks at Ranganathan and his contributions from a different angle or perspective, and discusses him as a methodologist par excellence. Discusses his methodologies as spiral of scientific method, planes of work, postulational approach, depth classification design, reference service, cataloguing, planning, job analysis, etc.

SEETHARAMA, S and KARISIDDAPPA, C R, *Eds* 345

Current research in library and information science; Festschrift to Professor M R Kumbhar, Jaipur: R B S A Publishers, 1993. xii, 219 p.

Includes 15 articles on different aspects of LIS, particularly on terminology, classification, indexing, user information services, IT, etc in honour of Prof M R Kumbhar. Reports about the current research being done at various places in LIS in India. Includes a Foreword by S Parthasarathy.

SHARMA, DEV RAJ and SHARMA, D K 346

Doctoral theses in library and information science accepted by Indian universities (1990-1992), *CLIS Observer* 9 (1-2) Jan-June 1992: 39-45.

Lists receipients of Ph D degree in LIS from various Indian universities during 1990-1992, arranged in alphabetical order with more information on the year of award, title of thesis, university, name of guide, and present address of awardee.

020.79 LIS - Awards

AWARDS & honours, In *Souvenir* of CLA, 1992. 347

Mentions some of the awards and honours Dr S R Ranganathan received both at home and abroad as a result of his massive contributions.

VENKATAPPAIAH, V 348

Dr Bjorn Tell is the recipient of the Kaula International Award for 1991, *Her Lib Sci* 32 (1-2) Jan-Apr 1993: 105.

Gives information about the receiving of Prof Kaula International Award for 1991 by Dr Bjorn Tell, a distinguished professional and till recently Director of University Libraries, Lund University, Sweden. He has served UNDP / UNESCO, FID, IFLA, European Economic Commission, among others.

VENKATAPPAIAH, V 349

International Kaula Award presented to Professor Meyriat: Presentation function in Paris, *Her Lib Sci* 32 (1-2) Jan-Apr 1993: 101-104.

Reports about the International Kaula Gold Medal and Citation received by Professor Jean Meyriat in Paris on 18 March 1992 in recognition of his significant contributions to international social science documentation, in association with UNESCO and other international bodies.

VENKATAPPAIAH, V 350

Kaula Aware for 1990 to Prof Curras, *Her Lib Sci* 31 (1-2) Jan-Apr 1992:157.

Reports that Prof (Dr) Emilia Curras, noted library and information scientist has been selected for Kaula Award for 1990. She is the Director of Department of Scientific Documentation in Madrid, Spain, and has authored several treatises and research projects, and also 56 articles, and so on.

VENKATAPPAIAH, V 351

Recipient of Ranganathan -Kaula Award for 1992, *Her Lib Sci* 32 (1-2) Jan-Apr 1993: 106-107..

Reports that N B Inamdar got the Ranganathan-Kauala Award for 1992 for his contribution to the profession for librarianship particularly as Librarian of Osmania University, Hyderabad.

020.8 LIS - Anthologies

KARISIDDAPPA, C R, SANGAM, S L and MAHESWARAPPA, B S, *Eds* 352

Current studies in library and information science (Felicitation volume of Dr S R Gunjal), Delhi: Manak Publications, 1993. xii, 354 p.

Contains 28 articles contributed in honour of Prof (Dr) S R Gunjal of Gulbarga University, by experienced and senior members of the profession. Covers on a variety of current topics valuable to know new developments in LIS.

TEJOMURTY, A and KUMAR, S, *Eds* 353

Library and information science: Trends and challenges: Essays in honour of Professor S S Agrawal, New Delhi: Indus Publishing Company, 1993. 192 p.

Includes 21 essays by a cross-section of LIS authors of India on a variety of subjects such as library library management, academic and research libraries, associations, and institutions, and on Prof S S Agrawal in honour of whom this volume is published.

020.9 COMPARATIVE LIBRARIANSHIP

SEWA SINGH 354

Comparative librarianship and Ranganathan's writings, *Her Lib Sci* 32 (1-2) Jan-Apr 1993: 29-35.

States the emergence of comparative librarianship as a new development in the study of library and information science outside India. Refers to the work of Ranganathan and teaching methodology involving comparative analysis and study. Discusses his work in comparative classification, comparative cataloguing, comparative library services, comparative library legislation, comparative library development progremmes and plans. Mentions his work for development of library system for India to achieve "free book service for all".

020.9 (1) INTERNATIONAL/WORLD LIBRARIANSHIP

COBLANS, H 355

Ranganathan in the international scene, *SRR*, 22-25.

Comments on the international impact of Dr S R Ranganathan and his contribution right from the days of his honorary membership of the FID in 1957. Discusses about his being invited by UNESCO, his association with the Classification Research Group (London), International Organisation of Standards, IFLA meetings, the honours and awards he received including the D Litt degree from the University of Pittsburgh. Concludes by saying that he became a "conscience" for the West - a corrective for their assumptions on name forms, cataloguing rules, classification prejudices, etc.

KABIR, A F M FAZLE 356

Ranganathan: The educator and his influence on the Western world, *RAW*, 61-70.

Relates the contribution Dr S R Ranganathan made to the library education in India through discussion-based teaching, and was equally well known for his teaching excellence in the West. Also discusses his influence on library practice, classification, service philosophies. Concludes that Ranganathan was a 'Renaissance Man', and it certainly seems the "Age of Ranganathan" which will continue to be with the library world for years to come and continue to provide a base for the realisation of the concept of total library service.

KAULA, P N 357

Impact of Ranganathan's concepts and techniques on international librarianship, *Her Lib Sci* 32 (1-2) Jan-Apr 1993: 36-43.

Refers to the two phases in the world librarianship: Pre-Ranganathan era and Ranganathan - era. Describes the beginning of Ranganathan era with the publication of Five Laws of Library Science. Mentions international contacts and advisory role of Ranganathan with such agencies as the United Nations, FID, UNESCO, ISO, IFLA. Evaluates the work of Ranganathan at international level, the honours and wards given to him. Mentions high tributes paid by distinguished personalities and associations including the Library Association (UK), and American Library Association.

SHARMA, RAVINDRA N 358

Ranganathan and the West, *RAW*, 158-169.

Discusses the contribution made by Ranganathan to librarianship. Describes his impact on the West and the Honours he received from various institutions. Gives the importance of his Five Laws of Library Science for which the West has been grateful to him. Narrates his travels from East to West because of his involvement in the Western and international librarianship. Discusses Colon Classification and the Classified Catalogue Code, and their impact on Western librarians. Mentions about his lectures trips to the West. Explains his contribution to terminology for introducing many new words to the field of library and information science. Mentions about the tributes paid to him after his death. Concludes that Ranganathan was the leader of the profession, and the unquestioned giant of 20th century library science.

SHARMA, RAVINDRA N 359

Ranganathan's impact on international librarianship through information technology, *Libri* 42 (3) July-Sept 1992: 258-267.

Describes briefly, with extensive literature review, the impact of Ranganathan's contributions on international librarianship, especially in Europe and the USA. States that application of information technology (IT) in library and information science has not diminished the value of his contributions; and rather more areas of their usefulness are being identified. Also that IT is enabling the realisation of Ranganathan's vision of a user centred, user-friendly information service implied in his Five Laws of Library Science.

020.92 BIOGRAPHY OF LIBRARIANS, LIS TEACHERS, ETC

020.92 A Agrawal, SS

SURATI, DAKSHA VINOD 360

Professor S S Agrawal : A noble teacher, *LIS*, 20-21.

Describes Professor S S Agrawal as a teacher of library cataloguing where he would follow the discussion method, quiz method, interrogative examination, and the like.

TEJOMURTY, A 361

Professor Agrawal as I knew him, *LIS*, 17-19.

Narrates about the birth, education, professional education. Describes the professional positions he held from 1956 at Delhi and then at Vikram University where he retired in 1993. Narrates his qualities as a sincere teacher, researcher, and as a writer as he has published 20 articles and 4 books out of which three books about librarianship are in Hindi.

020.92 C Comaromi, John P

SATIJA, M P 362

In memoriam: John Phillip Comaromi, 1937-1991, *Luck Lib*n 24 (1) Jan-Mar 1992: 42-44.

Describes about the birth, education - academic and professional - career, and contribution to Library and information science as teacher; and to classification, particular to DDC as its Editor. Highlights his contribution, his vision to take the DDC to the 21st century.

SATIJA, M P 363

John Phillip Comaromi, 1937-1991; in memorium, *Int Lib Move* 14 (3) Dept 1992: 106-109.

Discusses the birth of Dr J P Comaromi, his education, and his achievements with reference to his work as Editor of Dewey Decimal Classification 20th Edition. Mentions his other major works, and gives a brief account of his personality.

020.92 D DESHMUKH, PP

STANLEY, M K 364

Prof PP Deshmukh: A profile, *IJALIS* 20, 1992: 32.

Provides a brief biographical account of Prof P P Deshmukh who retired as Librarian of Punjabrao Krishi Vidyapeeth Library, Akola, in Jan 1993. Mentions about the various professional postions he held. Outlines his contribution to LIS literature by writing articles and books.

020.92 DI Dickinson, A D

SATIJA, M P and AGRAWAL, S P 365

Contribution of Asa Don Dickinson, *CLIS Observer* 10 (3-4) July-Dec 1993: 48-53.

Describes about the arrival of Dickinson in Punjab in 1915 on the invitation of the Punjab University, Lahore. Discusses about this contribution in starting a short term training course. Mentions about his book the *Punjab Library Primer*. Gives details about his contribution to standardization in furniture and stacks, open access, book selection, processing of books, labeling and pasting, accession in register, cataloguing, classification with Dewey Decimal Classification.

020.92 DU Durairajan, V

AMBU, D 366

Professor V Durairajan; a multi facet personality, *DL*, 10-13.

Records appreciation of the valuable services rendered by Prof V Durairajan, to the development of Annamalai University and the services he rendered, list of publications, membership of professional bodies, teaching experience, temprament, etc.

GOVINDARAJALU, T 367

Prof Durairajan; a multi-faceted gentleman, *DL*, 5-6.

Describes Durairajan's contribution in the growth and development of Annamalai University Library, particularly the Reprographic Secion which he well equipped for his users. Describes him as a multifaceted gentleman.

GURUSWAMY NAIDU, N 368

Professor Durairajan, as I know him, *DL*, 7-9.

Discusses about Durairajan, as librarian, his qualities as a professional and as a man who had the power of inspiring his subordinates who had love for their work.

PRASAD, N N 369

Prof Durairajan, my good friend, *DL*, 3-4.

Pays tribute to Prof V Durairajan and his contributions to the growth and development of Annamalai University, Library and the Department of Library and Information Science.

RAGHAVAN, S 370

Prof V Durairajan I Know, *DL*, ix-x.

Discusses about the contribution of Prof V Durairajan in building the services, collection, etc of the Annamalai University Library. Mentions about Durairajan's qualities.

RANGACHARI, A V 371

Prof V Durairajan - an appreciation, *DL*, i-vii.

Discusses about joining of Prof V Durairajan a Librarian and Head, Dept of Library and Information Science, and his contribution to the development of Annamalai University Library. Discusses about the services he started such as routing of journals, compilitation of bibliographies, CAS, interlibrary loan, teaching of LIS courses, etc.

020.92 G Gunjal, S R

BIRADAR, SOMNATH S 372

Dr S R Gunjal as an ideal teacher, *CS*, 352-354.

Describes about the impressions the author and about Professor S R Gunjal as a teacher at Gulbarga University. Mention about the good qualities he was endowed with, and the love and care he gave to his students in his life.

KARISIDDAPPA, C R 373

Dr S R Gunjal: A profile, *CS*, 1-4.

Describes about the birth, education and contribution of Dr Gunjal to library profession as a teacher, writer, researcher, manager of library. Discusses about him as a person also.

020.92 I Inamdar, N B

PROF N B Inamdar - a short biography, *ALR*, xix, xx. 374

Describes briefly about Prof Ianamdar's early education, his birth, higher education from USA and then coming to Osmania University Library in 1980 as its Librarian till his retirement in 1990. Highlights his work and contribution as University Librarian in improving upon the exsiting library services. Mentions about the various postitions he held in the professional organisations. Mentions about his writings in book and article form.

020.92 K Kaula, P N

CURRAS, EMILIA 375

In honour of Professor Kaula: Impact of his work in Spain, *Her Lib Sci* 32 (3-4) July-Oct 1993: 213-217.

Gives a brief account of Prof Kaula's visit, work and activities in Spain. Mentions the invitation from the Ministry of Education and Science, Govt of Spain to work on a research project for three months. Describes the arrival, stay and working of Kaula, his visits and lectures in various universities and institutions in Madrid, Barcelona, etc. States the honours and awards he received and the indelible impact of his contribution.

MALHAN, I V and SATIJA, M P 376

Among the immortanls, *Her Lib Sci* 31 (1-2) Jan-Apr 1992: 88-90.

Discusses about the multifaceted personality of P N Kaula as lantern bearer, internationalist, who is honoured with two

Festschrits Volumes in 1979 and 1991. Reviews the second *Festschrift* - a collection of 52 essays grouped under 20 themes with varied range from 14 countries.

RAWAT, P P 377

International Kaula Felicitation Committee, *Her Lib Sci* 32 (1-2) Jan-Apr 1993: 107-110.

Describes life and contribution of Kaula. Describes him as the most inspiring educator, his varied and longest innings in journalism. Refers Kaula as the most prolific writer. Mentions his world wide impact of contribution, awards instituted, thesis on Kaula, etc. Refers him as an embodiment of humility and other virtues.

SHUKLA, B B 378

Professor P N Kaula: His works, contribution and impact on international library and information field, Cuttack: Bharati Publications, 1993. xvi, 328 p. illus.

Includes ten chapters on the contribution of Prof P N Kaula for the development of libraries, developement of professional organizations, as a library scientist and as educationist, development of thought and practice, development of professional journalism, impact of Indian library scene, dimensions of Kaula's works and contribution, etc. It is the result of author's D Litt degree in library and information science considered as world's first D Litt thesis

VANKATAPPAIAH, V, GUPTA, S R and RAWAT, P P 379

International felicitation and honours to Prof P N Kaula in Oct 1993, *IJILIS* 6(1-2) Jan-June 1993: 149-153.

Describes that Prof PN Kaula will be felicitated internationally by the International Felicitation Committee at New Delhi, and also to Dr B B Shukla for his outstanding academic attainments of D Litt, original theories in abstracting, library movement and creation of library consciousness among the people of Orissa.

020.92 KU Kumbhar, M R

OUR felicitation to Professor M R Kumbhar, *CRL*, vi. 380

Describes highly the leadership qualities of Prof M R Kumbhar who retired as Head, Dept of LIS, Karnataka University on the completion of his 60th year in April 1985. Describes his professional approach in teaching and research guiding which has been helpful, systematic and precise. States that he had a profound vision, leadership qualities and single minded dovotion.

PARTHASARATHY, S 381

Foreword, *CRL*, vii-ix.

Describes in brief the life, work, contribution of Prof M R Kumbhar who used to walk long distances to listen to Dr S R Ranganathan. States that he took keen interest in establishing Dept of LIS, Karnataka University in 1962 and efficiently build the Dept to research level. He provided solid support to DRTC progremmes of research. Sympathetic to others problems he never wanted any award for himself.

PROF M R KUMBHAR: Obituary, *IJILIS* 6 (3-4) July-Dec 1993: 168. 382

Reports that Prof M R Kumbhar formerly Prof and Head, Dept of LIS, Karnataka University, Dharwad died on June 23, 1993. Mentions that he was a member of many Journals and bodies and initiated Ph D programme at his University. He also served at Maniput University Library after retirement i 1985.

020.92 L Lazar, Peter

OBITUARY: Dr Peter Lazar, *NISSAT Newsletter* 12 (1) Jan-Mar 1992: 16 383

Records with profound sorrow the death of Dr Peter Lazar in Budapest in June 1992. He was a most distinguished internationally renowned information scientist held the post of Director General of the Technical Library and Information Centre for several years in Budapest. Mentions about his outstanding contributions, and pays humble tribute to the multifaceted and versatile personality of the great man.

020.92 R Ranganathan, S R

AGARWAL, S C 384

He ushered a new era...., In *Souvenir* of *CLA*, 1992.

Relates Ranganathan's contribution, achievements, honors and awards he got in India and abroad including the title of Padam Shri, and honour of National Professor of Library Science in India. Pays rich tributes to this glittering personality in his Birth Centenary Year.

AHLUWALIA, J K 385

Legacy of Dr Ranganathan, *Ann Lib Sc & Docum* 39 (2) June 1992: i.

Writes in this Editorial of the Special Number of this old journal, as a homage, about the contribution of Dr Ranganathan to the field of library and information science. States that as a prolific writer, as a teacher he had few peers, and is called 'Messiah of Library World'. Mentions about his association with Indian National Scientific Documentation Centre (INSDOC) during its formative years, and also as the founder Editor of the *Annals of Library Science,* as it was then called.

ARORA MADHURI 386

Father of library science: Dr Ranganathan, *Aryan Heritage* 11(97) Dec 1992: 22-23.

Deals with Ranganathan's birth, brief lifeaccount, awards, degrees, honours etc which he received during his life time. Describes his contribution to librarianship. States that he laid the foundation of library and information science education in India and that we are following the same pattern even now.

BALACHANDRAN PILLAI, S 387

Dr S R Ranganathan: The father of library movement in India, *PLD*, 1-5.

Discusses about the life and work of Ranganathan, his education, his career at different places, his library tour, contribution in setting up INSDOC and DRTC. Describes his role in developing public library system in India, the books and articles he write, formulation of Five Laws and the prizes, awards and acknowledgments he received for his contribution to LIS. States that Sayers called his period as 'The Age of Ranganathan'.

BALRAM KAUR 388

Guiding light to the librarians, In *Souvenir* of *CLA*, 1992.

Remembers Ranganathan's contribution, his dedication, devotion, humility, austerity,and philanthropy. Particularly in creating a Professorship in Library Science at the University of Madras and also the Sarada Rangenthan Endowment for Library Science (Bangalore). Which is continuing with his good work. Pays rich tributes to him in the Birth Centenary year.

BANKAPUR, M B 389

Dr S R Ranganathan - a live specimen of librarianship, *IJILIS* 5 (3-4) jULY-DEC 1992: 253-257.

Describes Ranganathan as an intellectual elite who rose from humble origin. Gives account of his life and works which led to the 'Age of Ranganathan'. Describes his qualities as a man. Makes an assessment of his work in the field of librarianship. Describes Ranganathan as the perfect representative of the 20th century who accomplished something that no else did at the time.

BERA, CHITTARANJAN 390

Dr S R Ranganathan: A great teacher and roganiser of library science. *Coll Lib* 8 (1-2) 1992: 26-27.

Pays tribute to Ranganathan as a great teacher and organiser of library science. Concludes that we the Indian workers in library and information field should practise Ranganathan's ideas of library service which will raise and strengthen the status and importance of library service in modern society.

BHARGAVA, G D 391

Dr S R Ranganathan - My teacher and mentor, *PP*, 109-115

Describes Ranganathan as a great man who opined that library professionals should not live on profession but for it. Recaptulates author's initiation in the library profession as Ranganathan's student, his association and meetings with Ranganathan and first hand study of Ranganathan as a teacher who was a hard task master, and a professional seer par excellence.

BHATIA, JASPAL KAUR 392

Our godfather, In *Souvenir* of *CLA*, 1992.

States that due to his unique contribution to the field of librarianship Ranganathan will be remembered in the days to some as a benefactor and our godfather. Pays rich tributes to him for initiating the library movement in India as well as for establishing a large number of libraries and making people realise the importance and usefulness of these temples of knowledge.

BHATIA, KK and GUPTA, S P 393

In the footsteps of the great master: Some innovative information service at CRRI, *AGLIS JI* 9,1993 (Abstract only).

Describes the various information services being given at the Central Road Research Institute, New Delhi such as 'Emerging technologies', 'Global Developments', 'Pragmatic Development', Emerging Terminology', and so on in the footsteps of the great master, Ranganathan. Concludes that these innovations have helped the user of the library.

BOSE, ANINDYA 394

Ranganathan: An impressionistic view, *RAW*, 170-173.

Discusses about the asuthor's small meetings with Ranganathan. Relates the interesting character traits which impressed the author. Lauds the monumental contribution of Ranganathan to the field of librarianship. Concludes that his work and contribution impressed the author more than Ranganathan as a person. Mentions further that we need a Ranganathan at the moment to integrate the relevant segments of information science into library science so that the discipline can move forward and remain viable.

CHOPRA, H R 395

Dr S R Ranganathan: Father of library movement in India, In *Souvenir* of *CLA*, 1992.

Discusses about Ranganathan's Five Laws, Colon Classification, Classified Catalogue Code, and other contributions as a librarian and library and information science teacher. Mentions his association with professional bodies at national and international level such as ILA, FID, IFLA, UNESCO, etc. Mentions about the awards he received in India and abroad. States that by holding the 58th Conference of IFLA at New Delhi from 30th August to 5th September, 1992, the world of librarianship has paid rich tributes to him in his Birth Centenary year.

CHOPRA, RAJINDER 396

Still remains an ideal for me, In *Souvenir* of *CLA*, 1992.

Pays tributes to Ranganathan who loved his students, and was ideal for many including the author, Recaptulates some of the fine memories as a student of Ranganathan who was a disciplinarian but also took personal interest in his students. States that he had complete devotion and dedication to librarianship. Mentions about his other qualities of simplicity wearing dhoti and kurta but deeply plunged in the study of his subject.

CHOCHRAINE (ATHERTON), PAULINE 397

The influence of Ranganathan upon library and information science, library education, and me, *RAW*, 50-60.

Describes the significance and depth of the Five Laws of Library Science propounded by Dr S R Ranganathan as they offer guidance and rationale we (the Americans) need. Discusses the influence of Law 2 on need for use studies, improving catalogue use, focus on the reader, principle of least action, and cooperation. Discusses influence of Law 3 on catalogue and readers requirements, with regard to the structure of catalogue. Discusses influence of Law 5 on the human side, professional education, the challenge of change in library education, change of attitude, relating library education to library problems. Acknowledges Ranganathan's influence on her philosophy of library science. Outlines a chronology of Ranganathan- (Atherton) Cochrane relationship.

COMAROMI, JOHN P 398

Ranganathan's influence on American librarianship, *PP*, 123-129.

Explains how Dr S R Ranganathan's ideas entered the United States of American via United Kingdom where they did not stir much initially, and had no immediate effect on library classification. States that Ranganathan provided a rationale and a vocabulary for classification construction such as facet analysis. Describes about the influence of Ranganathan on Dewey Decimal Classification, the latest edition.

COMAROMI, JOHN P 399

Ranganathan's influence on American librarianship, *RAW*, 10-16.

Traces the beginning of Ranganathan's relationship with America to his dialogue with Henry E Bliss, and subsequent comparison of Colon Classification and the Bibliographic Classification. Discusses the influence of Ranganathan's Five Laws of Library Science upon the practice of American librarianship. States that Ranganathan provided a rationale and a vocabulary for classification construction, facet analysis. Discusses the roots of PRECIS in Ranganathan's classificatory ideas, his substantial influence on Dewey Decimal Classification and its revisions. Concludes that but for Ranganathan's ideas the Americans may not had at their disposal the analytical tools that Melvil Dewey did not have them.

DAHLBERG, I 400

Editorial: Ethics and knowledge organization in memory of Dr S R Ranganathan in his centenary year, *Int Classif* 19 (1) 1992: 1-2.

Pays tribute to Ranganathan by bringing out this Special Number of *International Classification*, Includes four articles on and about Ranganathan's contribution. Gives a brief account about his life and the hard work he used to do for the profession. Outlines some of his qualities in relation to ethics.

DASGUPTA, KALPANA 401

Introduction, *RAT*, v-vi.

States that this compilation, *S R Ranganathan" A Tribute*, has been prepared with the sole idea of paying tribute to the doyen of library and information science from the general staff members of the National Library (of India), Calcutta. Gives the resume of the ten articles included in the compilation on Ranganathan's different contributions to the field of library and information science.

DESHPANDE, V W 402

Dr S R Ranganathan, librarian extraordinary, *Bhavan's Ji* 39 (20) May 31, 1993: 26-27.

Recounts some of the most interesting, but full of advice, anecdotes from the life of Ranganathan as librarian, and the service he rendered to his users, big and small, rich and poor alike. Pays tribute to him on the occasion of his Birth Centenary year celebrated in 1992 all over the world of librarianship.

DR S R RANGANATHAN - a sketch, *Bhavan's Jl* 403

39 (20) May 31, 1993: 18-19.

Provides a brief and sketchy picture of Rangnathan's birth, achievements and contributions to the field of libraries and librarianship. Describes that his sole aim was to bring alive the First Law of Library Science, ie, "Books are for Use". Pays tribute to the great master.

DR S R RANGANATHAN: A tribute (on the occasion of his Centenary celebrations), Calcutta: The National Library, 1993. vii, 57 p. 404

Brought out as a tribute to the great master, S R Ranganathan on the occasion of his Centenary celebrations by the staff members of the National Library. Includes ten articles contributed by the staff of the National Library of India on different aspects of library and information science and tries to highlight Ranganathan's contribution, image of his life and work in the field of libraries and librarianship.

DUDLEY, EDWARD, *Ed* 405

S R Ranganathan, 1892 - 1972, New Delhi: Ess Ess Publications, 1992. 39 p. (First Indian Reprint; originally published by the Library Association, London, 1973).

This Indian reprint brought out on the occasion of the Birth Centenary celebrations of Ranganathan includes six valuable papers contributed by his admirers and friends in England who applied Ranganathan's ideas in classification, documentation and indexing, laws of library science, etc to the British librarianship successfully.

FINKS, LEE W and HAUG, JAMES D 406

Ranganathan's contribution to American librarianship, RAW, 71-97.

Pays personal tributes (by the first author) to DR S R Ranganathan. Attempts to measure Ranganathan's influence in a quantitative manner by using the method of a combination of citation and content analysis to the entire population of articles in American and Canadian publications which refer to or review Ranganathan's articles and books cited in *Social Science Citation Index*, and *Library Literature*. Concludes that Ranganathan's publications had influence upon American and Canadian authors particularly in the subject of classification, and they also recommended his works favourably.

FLYING LIBRARIAN; first and the only 407

In Souvenir of *CLA*, 1992.

Mentions some of the firsts achievements of S R Ranganathan both at the national and international level such as establishment of MALA, first Public Library Act, UGC Committee on Library affairs, first full time University Librarian of the Madras University, first Librarian to be awarded Padamshri, and so on at the national level. At the international level first librarian to tour Europe and USA, first to attend IFLA, chairman of the FID Committee, Vice President of FID, and so on.

FOSKETT, D J 408

Ranganathan's professionalism, *S R R,* 19-21.

Remembers Dr S R Ranganathan as a 'Whole man' who, in his writings, interpreted his approach to the profession of librarianship. Describes his guiding principles by which one should act, and these embody in his Five Laws of Library Science. States that Ranganathan was an internationalist by his approach, and he always acknowledged his debts to Dewey.

FRIIS-HANSEN, JENS B and ENGEL, SVEND 409

Impact of the contribution of Ranganathan in Denmark, *Her Lib Sci* 32 (1-2) Jan-Apr 1993: 44-47

Mentions the study of work of S R Ranganathan by Danish librarians. Describes the influence of Ranganathan on various writings in Denmark, particularly of Kirkegaard, Jenson, Hansen, etc. Reproduces excerpts from the Kaula Endowment Lecture delivered by Kirkegaard, tribute paid to Ranganathan and the homage paid by Hansen on passing away of Ranganathan. States that theories propounded by Ranganathan are studied at Danish Royal School of Librarianship. Mentions about his visit to Copenhagen to deliver lectures. Illustrates the influence of Dr Ranganathan on Danish librarianship.

GANAPATHY, V 410

Father of library science in India, *In* Ravi, N (Ed), *The Hindu speaks on libraries*, Madras: Kasturi & Sons, 1992, pp 278-279.

Deals with the birth, early education, professional training, appointments, work and contributions of Dr S R Ranganathan whose Birth Centenary celebrations are being celebrated at Thanjavur District Library. Describes his achievements and recognition he received in India and abroad. Discusses about the special meetings organised by Thanjavur District Library to lauch the centenary celebrations of the doyen of library science.

GARFIELD, EUGENE 411

A tribute to Ranganathan, the father of Indian library science, *RA W*, 121-128.

Discusses life and works of Ranganathan. Mentions his objection to the prevailing classification systems and as a result gave the new classification system called Colon Classification. Describes his contribution to cataloguing and other fields also, such as library science education, public libraries. Mentions that his contributions were acknowledged many times over, both in India and abroad. Pays tribute to the great man on the occasion of his Birth Centenary celebrations.

GAURI, KUL B 412

Language as ritual in the library discourse of Ranganathan, *RA W*, 112-120.

Examines the nature of Ranganathan's style and discourse which is derived and based on a specific category of Hindu scriptures and literature. States that his style reflects the use of the language as ritual derived from his cultural moorings. Mentions some of the unique features of Ranganathan's discourse such as the creation and use of metaphors, expanding the use of words to express and shape his thinking and writing.

GIAN SINGH 413

He was an institution in himself, In *Souvenir* of CLA, 1992.

States that through his works and deeds, Ranganathan carved out for himself a permanent niche in the library movement. Mentions that he dealt with all aspects of the library, and his writings will act as the guidelines for the generations to come. Pays tributes to him as a genius, held in high esteem.

GIRJA KUMAR 414

Creativity in the thought of Dr S R Ranganathan, *Ann Lib Sc & Docum* 39 (2) June 1992: 46-51.

Points out Ranganathan's religious and cultural background. Describes him as a pragmatist, and the other side of his personality as a believer in occult philosophy. Discusses impact of mysticism on him and his work, impact of Indian religious scriptures on his writings. Gives the spirit of the library as envisaged by Ranganathan. Draws analogies and three planes of work. Mentions about his intellectual essence, Ekavakyata principle, holistic principle. Describes his intellection, creativity, intuition, etc.

GIRJA KUMAR 415

Creativity in the thought of Dr S R Ranganathan, *CLIS Observer* 9 (1-2) Jan-June 1992: 25-32.

Discusses impact of religion, occult, mysticism, and Indian scriptures on Ranganathan. Mentions the spirit of the library which he enjoyed and practised. Discusses his freedom of intellect and

Ekvakyata principle of unity of ideas, holistic principle, intellection, and creativity in detail.

GIRJA KUMAR 416

Indian roots of Dr S R Ranganathan's thought, *Jl Lib & Inf Sc* 17 (1) June 1992: 1-16.

Argues that the mainsprings of Ranganathan's thought are derived from his oriental origins. Points out that some people say that his many ideas had emerged from his spiritual background. Mentions that he had great moral sense due to his Brahmanic background. Describes the place of intuition, creativity, imagination and mysticism in the development of his thought.

GIRJA KUMAR 417

The library scientist: Remembering S R Ranganathan, *Frontline* 9 (17) Aug 15-28, 1992: 58-60.

Describes Ranganathan as quintessential intellectual at par with such scientists as Sir C V Raman and Charles Darwin. Explains his seminal contribution to the field of library and information science such as *Colon Classification*, Five Laws of Library Science, theory of classification, and *Prolegomena, Classified Catalogue Code*, establishment of Documentation Research and Training Centre, Bangalore. Narrates his tormentoes at the University of Madras.

GIRJA KUMAR 418

Prince amongst librarians, *The Times of India*, Aug 9,1992.

Portrays brief sketch of life and contributions of Dr S R Ranganathan who is considered as the prince amongst the librarians. Reflects Ranganathan's devotion to librarianship with intellectual stimuli and hard work compiled with creativity, mysticism, and intuition.

GIRJA KUMAR 419

S R Ranganathan: An intellectual biography, New Delhi: Har-Anand Publications 1992. 327 p.

Divided into two parts, Part I deals with Ranganathan as 'The Man' giving account of his life in his social milieu, his activities and achievements. In Part II the author makes an assessment of Ranganathan's work and personality as 'The Intellect'. Evaluates Ranganathan's fundamental laws and canons, application of scientific method, faceted classification, postulational approach and mnemonics, etc. Presents his psyco-analytico study and social environment in which he worked. Deals with Ranganathan's value system, the holistic approach, and his creativity.

GIRJA KUMAR 420

S R Ranganathan; an intellectual par excellence, *In* G L Trehan and Girja Kumar: *Ranganathan Birth Centenary Monograph*, Chandigarh: Chandigarh Library Study Circle, 1993, pp 29-35.

Discusses Ranganathan's birth, his contribution which went on to transform beyond recognition what has today emerged as the discipline of library and information science. Describes him as an intellectual par excellence who had no hesitation in comparing him with such stalwarts as Charles Darwin and Sir C V Raman. Mentions that in this field all his contributions flowed from one single idea - Five Laws of Library Science.

GOPINATH, M A 421

Ranganathan's perspectives and achievements: Guest Editorial, *Lib Sci slant Docum & Inf Std* 29 (3) Sept 1992: i-iv.

States that Ranganathan lived through a period of renaissance where libraries had a primary objective of preservation which he enlarged. Emphasises that Ranganathan's perspectives are to be analysed in this context. States that he had an analytical mind and he put his ideas in a logical and systematic approach which put everything in a holistic context. Gives at the end American Library Association Resolution adopted by it on Jan 29, 1992.

GOPINATH, M A 422

Summary of the work and achievements of Dr S R Ranganathan, *Lib Sci slant Docum & Inf Std* 29(2) June 1992: 47-57.

Presents in this Summary the work and achievements of Dr S R Ranganathan in a chronological fashion. Arranges the contents under such headings as Summary of chief events, Endowments, Honours/Awards, Family, Education, Employment, Honorary work, Library Development Plan, Library Bills, Committee works in India and outside, Conferences in India and outside, Associations works, Library tours, Periodicals editing, Books published, Indian standards, Library catalogues, and Articles contributed.

GUPTA, K BALASUNDARA 423

Father of Library Science, *In* Ravi, N (Ed), *The Hindu speaks on libraries*, Madras: Kasturi & Sons, 1992, pp 280-281.

Describes the work and contribution of Dr S R Ranganathan who invented Colon Classification which earned him international fame. Deals with his other contributions as PMEST, CCC, Five Laws, and many more. Mentions about the places he worked and the awards and honours he received from abroad.

GUY, RANDOR 424

The high priest of library science, *The Hindu*, New Delhi, Sunday, Aug 30, 1992, Special features, B.

Narrates the biography of Dr S R Ranganathan who was born in a Brahmin family of Tamil Nadu. Describes him as a popular teacher after his scholastic career in Madras, and taking up the job of Madras University Librarian. Discusses his sojourn to England, his contribution to the cause of libraries. Recounts his memoirs, his innings at Madras, Banaras Hindu University, Delhi University. Mentions his simple living and simple habits, his sense of humour.

HARJIT SINGH 425

S R Ranganathan - an exemplary teacher and guide, *DESIDOC Bull* 12 (5) Sept 1992: 13-15.

Narrates author's experiences with Ranganathan and the profession of documentation while at Documentation Research and Training Centre, Bangalore as a student. Discovers qualities in Ranganathan as he made DRTC a gurukul. States that he was an interesting speaker with stories fron Puranas, and equally prolific writer who believed in work only.

HARRISON, K C 426

Ranganathan and British librarianship, *RAW*, 17-31.

Mentions briefly S R Ranganathan's early years. Describes the first visit of Ranganathan to England in 1924 to study librarianship, and his interest in classification led to the publication of Colon Classification in 1933. Brings out relationship between Ranganathan and B I Palmer, and Five Laws, Colon Classification and chain indexing began to be studied in England. Discusses impact of Ranganathan on British National Bibliography through his classificatory principles; and his influence in forming Classification Research Group when his faceted ideas were discussed. Brings out relationship of Ranganathan with Maurice Gwyer in Delhi; Ranganathan's library tour of England in 1948, meeting British librarians, his contribution to *The Library World*, a British monthly journal. Mentions about the British tribute paid to him at his death in 1972.

JAYARAJAN, P 427

Ranganathan's contributions - Fundamental and seminal, *The Hindu* Sept 2, 1992.

Describes S R Ranganathan's works as seminal. States that Ranganathan's contributions to library science are as significant, if not more, as those of Sir C V Raman to Physics and Rabindranath Tagore to literature.

JAYASWAL, P K 428

Ranganathan: A professional par excellence, *AGLIS Jl* 9,1993 (Abstract only).

Traces the formulation of Five Laws based on Vedic philosophy, and correlated the sociological needs of the nation and their fulfilment through library service. Describes Ranganathan as a professional par excellence who had user and service at the forefront.

KATARIA, J K 429

Remembering Ranganathan, In *Souvenir* of CLA, 1992.

Praises Ranganathan while highlighting his qualities in the form of a poem. Describes him as ocean of knowledge, enforced laws of library science, gave us the reference service like Vivekanand's knowledge of God, his PMEST, etc. helped in synthesis.

KAULA, P N 430

International Ranganathan Centenary Committee: Programme of activities, *Her Lib Sci* 31 (1-2) Jan0Apr 1992: 157-159.

States that the Committee is set up to celebrate the Birth Centenary of Dr S R Ranganathan for which 70 papers from 26 countries have been collected to bring out a volume of papers. Explains about starting the Ranganathan Research Bulletin, collection of letters, postal stamp release, and showing a film on him, and special Centenary Numbers of library journals are being brought out in India and abroad as a mark of respect to the Master.

KAULA, P N 431

Ranganathan remembered: Birth Centenary celebrations, *Her Lib Sci* 32 (3-4) July-Oct 1993: 218-236.

Describes in brief the various events and celebrations of Ranganathan's Centenary beginning with Ranganathan International Centenary Committee constituted primarily by the author. Discusses international celebrations as IFLA 58th General Conference in New Delhi, ISKO Second Conference at Madras. Explains celebrations in India including seminars, lectures, book exhibitions, etc. Appends the ALA Resolutions on Ranaganathan.

KAULA, P N 432

Remembering Ranganathan: His work in Delhi, *Her Lib Sci* 32 (1-2) Jan-Apr 1993: 54-69.

Mentions the invitation to Ranganathan for joining the University of Delhi, his appointment as Honorary Professor of Library Science in 1947, and his work in that capacity till 1955. Describes his work as the President of the Indian Library Association (1944-53), work on projects and invitations from FID, UNESCO, IFLA, ISO, British Council. States Ranganathan's work in establishing Delhi Public Library, Indian National Scientific Documentation Centre, Union Catalogue, Library Research Circle, professional journals, UGC Library Committee, UGC Review Committee. Refers to the Farewell Address on his departure from Delhi.

KAULA, P N 433

Remembering Ranganathan : His work in Delhi, *Jl Lib & Inf Sci* 17 (1) June 1992: 17-32.

Describes the work carried out by S R Ranganathan from 1947 to 1955 during his stay as a Professor of Library Science at Delhi University. Discusses his activities as President of the Indian Library Association. Mentions about his tour of 1948 and participation in international activities. Enumerates his contribution to the development of libraries in India and research on library and information science. Concludes by referring to Ranganathan as 'master educator'

KAULA, P N 434

S R Ranganathan as library scientist and benefactor, *In* G L Trehan and Girja Kumar: *Ranganathan Birth Centenary Monograph*, Chandigarh: Chandigarh Library Study Circle, 1993, p 36-d.

Describes Ranganathan as a library scientist par excellence, and the greatest benefactor. States that his contribution encompasses the entire domain of library and information science. Extracts taken from *Library Today* (Hyderabad) for January 1992.

KAULA, P N 435

Some episodes from Ranganathan's life, *Her Lib Sci* 32 (1-2) Jan-Apr 1993: 69-84.

Mentions the opportunity of the author to work closely with Ranganathan and plethora of correspondence between the two. Relates a number of episodes from the life and work of Ranganathan. States the episodes relating to his work: uncertainty in facet sequence, designing of classification, reference service, etc; relating to life: singly meal a day, no newspaper reading, no calling on highups, etc. and work as value of character, white bedsheet, faith in destiny, etc.

KAULA, P N 436

Works by and on Ranganathan published during the Centenary year: State of the art review, *Her Lib Sci* 32 (1-2) Jan-Apr 1993: 94-100.

Evaluates works published during the Birth Centenary year of Ranganathan which according to the author, includes 13 books, and 11 Special Numbers of journals published material on Ranganathan. Gives a review of all what is published during 1992.

KAULA, P N and VENKATAPPAIAH, V 437

Ranganathan International Centenary Volume Committee: An appeal, *IJILIS* 5 (1-2) Jan-June 1992: 153-156.

Makes an appeal about contributions for Ranganathan's Centenary Volume as he has been the master-architect in the domain of library science, library scientist par excellence, the great benefactor, world wide impact of his contribution, etc.

KHERA, RAJ 438

We owe our today to him, In *Sourvenir* of CLA, 1992.

Regards Ranganathan as the father of library science in India who brought overall development in the profession, and we owe everything to this great man who will always be worshipped by all seekers of informations. States that he by dint of hard work, attachment to a cause, worked for the welfare of the library staff in India.

KONNUR, M B 439

Dr S R Ranganathan: American view, *PP*, 131-137.

Explains about Dr S R Ranganathan's ideas propounded through his writings on classification and cataloguing in particular, on American thinking in these fields. Discusses also Ranganathan's concept of pre-natal classification and cataloguing, his Five Laws of Library Science. Mentions about Ranganathan and the American honours bestowed upon him in recognition of the importance of his works.

KRISHAN KUMAR 440

Editorial, *Jl of Lib & Inf Sci* 17 (1) June 1992: 2 pages.

States in the Editorial of this Special Number of the *Journal of Library and Information Science*, Volume 17, Number 1, June 1992 that it is brought out as a tribute to Dr S R Ranganathan in the year of his Birth Centenary. Includes ten articles on and about the various aspects of the contribution of S R Ranganathan written by various scholars in the field including Prof P N Kaula, Girja Kumar, and others.

KRISHNA RAO, D B 441

Some facets of Ranganathan's personality, *In* G L Trehan and Girja Kumar: *Ranganathan Birth Centenary Monograph*, Chandigarh: Chandigarh Library Study Circle, 1993, pp 36.a - 36.c.

Reprinted from the *Herald of Library Science*, Vol 12, April - June 1973, describes Ranganathan as a store of Himalayan energy, had intense love for library science, was a symbol of work - chastity, and as a teacher used effective teaching methodology. Concludes that he was a great force in the library world for nearly fifty years who was respected in all countries of the world where library consciousness had developed.

KUMAR, P S G 442

Kaula and Ranganathan: A perspective, *In* V Venkatappaiah (Ed), *Dimensions in library and information science*, New Delhi: Concept Publishing Company, 1991, pp 523 - 533.

Presents an analysis of the work of P N Kaula and that of S R

Ranganathan pointing out latter's impact on Kaula as librarian, teacher, Editor, project designer. Refers to the work that Kaula did for S R Ranganathan in popularising his ideas. Also records views of S R Ranganathan on P N Kaula.

KUMAR, P S G 443

Ranganathan; a multi-faceted personality, New Delhi: D K Publishers, 1992. xii, 240 p.

Tries to analyse the real librarian in Ranganathan, a master educator and a great humanist. Starts with a biographical note on him. Highlights Dr S R Ranganathan's outstanding contribution in various branches of librarianship in a systematic way and in a simple language. Studies the personality and philosophy of the man - Ranganathan and mysticism, a fitting tribute to Ranganathan in his Birth Centenary year as it gives a comprehensive view of Ranganathan and his work.

LANGRIDGE, D W 444

Ranganathan and mysticism, *SRR*, 26-27.

Explains the concept of 'Mysticism' the way Ranganathan used it, though he himself was not a mystic anyway. States that in his writings, the religious beliefs are implicit; through his continuous and wholeness approach to his works, he was termed as Karmayogi.

LANGRIDGE, D W 445

Unified vision of library science (Development of Library Science, 2), *Lib Sci slant Docum & Inf Std* 29 (2) June 1992: 91-97.

Review of *Library Science Today* (1965), edited by P N Kaula, reprinted from *Lib Sci slant Docum* 3 (2) June 1966: 101-113. Points out that wholeness in the life and work of S R Ranganathan, stemming from the spiritual foundations of scholarship and learning presented in Indian tradition. Describes his art, discovery, and humour, his application of scientific method to librarianship, his pioneering research in library science, his method of teaching, integration of theory and practice, unification of library science by Five Laws, his approach to classification, etc. Emphasises that essays under review highlight the holistic approach of Indian librarianship.

LETTERS OF Ranganathan - I, *Iaslic Bull* 37 (3) Sept 1992: 187-202. 446

Includes six letters from Bernard Plamer / Ranganathan correspondence collection covering the period from 1949 to Ranganathan's death. Gives an insight into Ranganathan's personality and developments of his thoughts on classification. These letters are published in this Special Number of *Iaslic Bulletin* coutsey of Mr Russel Bowden of Library Association (U K), and Mr S C Biswas, New Delhi. The collection is presently used in the Information and Library Studies Library at the University College of Wales, Aberystwyth.

LETTERS OF Ranganathan - II, *Iaslic Bull* 37 (3) Sept 1992: 203-217. 447

Presents the text of 13 letters between Ranganathan and Mahalanobis, with an introduction by M A Gopinath (of D R T C). Indicates not only warmth and friendship but also abiding interest they had in the development of the Documentation Research and Training Centre, as a centre for research, development, education in library, and documentation and information science.

LETTERS OF Ranganathan - III, *Iaslic Bull* 37 (3) Sept 1992: 219-229. 448

Includes 13 letters written to different persons on different occasions at different times, and on different subjects. The letters reveal Ranganathan's deep concern and involvement with the issues and problems of the profession as well as the careers of the students and young librarians. The letters were addressed to B Guha, B K Ghosh, Amitabha Chatterjee, among others.

MANINDER YASH PAL SINGH 449
We owe our bread and butter to him, In *Souvenir* of CLA, 1992.

States that by enumerating Five Laws of Library Science, Ranganathan brought a revolution in libraries as books were made the living things. Explains his manifold contributions to the field of library science. Describes him as the founder of the Indian Library Association and many other associations in different states. Mentions about his foreign tours, and his success in bringing librarians on par with teaching faculty. Pays gratitude and reverence to this great soul.

MARTIN, L M 450

Ranganathan for 90s: A conversation with Hemlatha Iyer (of Schools of Information Science and Policy, SUNY Albany), *Technalities* 11, 1991: 12-14.

Reports about the conversation the author had with one of the Indian library science teachers settled in an American University. Describes about the relevance of Ranganathan's writings and contributions towards librarianship in the modern times when some changes are being effected as a result of the technological developments.

McILWAINE, I C 451

Ranganathan and University College, London, *RAW*, 32-41.

Describes in detail the association of Ranganathan since 1924 with the University College, London where he studied librarianship. Mentions about the papers he offered, record for which is still available in the College. Describes his expericne, his remarks as the College student in London and that he is not forgotton there till today.

THE MIRACLE man, S R Ranganathan, *Lib Today* 14 (9) Sept 1992. 452

Deals with the voluminous contribution of Dr S R Ranganathan to the field of library and information science in general, and chain indexing, classification, cataloguing, library education in particular. Mentions about the awards and honours he was bestowed upon during his life time, both in India and from abroad.

MITTRA, D K and KOTNALA, V 453

Dr S R Ranganathan: The path finder, *RAT*, 1-5.

Describes Ranganathan as a path finder to the library and information science as he engaged himself in finding 'path' for the betterment of the library profession. Gives in short early years of his life, his entry to the library field, his perception about the profession and his achievements in the field. Deals also with scene in India soon after Ranganathan's death. Gives his idea about 'library service'.

MOHANRAJAN, P A 454

Library science: Dr S R Ranganathan's contribution, 1924-44, an analysis, Madras: Mohanvalli Publications, 1992. 112 p.

Brings together Ranganathan's earlier contribution as the First Librarian of the University of Madras. Discusses Ranganathan's experiments in organisation, administration, reference service, library classification, library cataloguing, and teaching of library science as a subject of study. Provides an insight into Ranganathan's working methodology. Includes a select list of his publications.

MOHANRAJAN, P A 455

The miracle man, *The Hindu*, Aug 9, 1992.

Gives a biographical sketch of Dr S R Ranganathan. Discusses his contribution to the field of librarianship, reflecting all aspects of this miracle man in the world of LIS who touched the heights of it in and outside country.

MOHANRAJAN, P A 456

S R Ranganathan, the miracle man, *In* G L Trehan and Girja Kumar: *Ranganathan Birth Centenary Monograph*, Chandigarh: Chandigarh Library Study Circle, 1993, pp 37-38.

Describes Ranganathan's achievements and contribution to the field of libraries and library science. Describes him as a miracle man who organised the Madras University Library so ably. Talks about his unfulfilled desire of a national enactment of public library law. Recounts the honours he got, the departments of library science he organised, the donations he gave to the University of Madras.

MOOKERJEE, SUBODH KUMAR 457

Sri Shiyali Ramamrita Ranganathan - a remeniscence, *Coll Lib* 8 (1-2) 1992: 4-6.

Recollects meetings of the author with Dr S R Ranganathan from time to time. Discusses Ranganathan's unique contributions to the field of library and information science at the world level. Relates many interesting anecdotes and experiences of the meetings of the author with Dr Ranganathan.

MURTHY, S S 458

Editorial, *DESIDOC Bull* 12 (5) Sept 1992: 2.

Speaks about the Special Issue of this Bulletin published by the Defence Scientific Documentation Centre, devoted to the memory of Dr S R Ranganathan, father of library movement in India, on the occasion of his Birth Centenary which falls on 12 August, 1992. Includes five articles on the life and work of Ranganathan in this Special Number.

NAGPAL, NEELAM 459

Had a will made of the hardest of steel, In *Souvenir* of CLA, 1992.

States that though born with poor health but his will was made of the hardest steel because of which he dominated the scene of Indian librarianship till his last day. Points out that he gave new dimensions to the library science by way of his contributions which were varied and many. States that he immortalised himself through his works and will continue to inspire generations to come.

NANAK, M P S G 460

Remembering Ranganathan today, *Information Management Report*, August 1992: 12-14.

Outlines the career of Dr S R Ranganathan and his influence on library and information science theory. Describes briefly the influence of his Five Laws of Library Science and Colon Classification scheme.

NAVALANI, K and SATIJA, M P 461

Introduction, *PP*, ix-xiii.

Narrates the story of Ranganathan's life, education, entry in librarianship, training in United Kingdom, reorganisation of Madras University Library, writing of books on library and information science, coining new terminology, working at the Banaras Hindu University Library, Delhi University, Vikram University, Ujjain, establishing library associations, associations with other bodies such as FID, etc, honours he received.

NAVALANI, K and SATIJA, M P ,*Eds* 462

Petits petals: A tribute to S R Ranganathan, New Delhi: ABC Publishing House, 1993. xiv (unnumbered), 150 p.

Includes 16 articles written by Indian and foreign contributors on life, works, personal experiences, and the effects of Ranganathan's ideas as felt in other countries. Describes more about Ranganathan's influence on classification, and on library practices in other countries, his efforts to institutionalise research in library science. etc. Pays tribute to Dr S R Ranganathan in his Centenary celebrations.

NEELAMEGHAN, A 463

Introduction, *Libri* 42 (3) July - Sept 1992: 171-175.

Writes about Ranganathan and his Danish connections in this Special Number of *Libri* (from Copenhagen), Volume 42, Number 3, 1992 brought out as dedication to his work, and edited by the author. Includes eight papers on assesment of Ranganathan's contribution to classification, information retrieval, Five Laws of library science, his impact on international librarianship, etc and gives their resueme.

OJHA, D C 464

A giant remembered: Dr S R Ranganathan (1892-1972), *IJALIS* 20, 1992: 20-23,

Describes early period of Ranganathan, his entry in the library profession, his contribution to LIS in India. Discusses about the library literature he produced, formation of library associations and organisations he helped in setting up and development. Mentions about the honours and recognitions he received.

PALMER, B I 465

Ranganathan as a person, *SRR*, 14-18.

Describes the life, education, and contribution of Ranganathan to the field of librarianship. Traces his contact with Ranganathan and narrates some of the characteristic features of his personality.

PALMER, B I 466

Ranganathan, the man and his works: View through a bibliography (Biography Series 1), *Lib Sci slant Docum & Inf Std* 29 (2) June 1992: 99-108.

Reprinted from *Library Science slant to Documentation*, vol 6 (3) September 1969: 273-288. Presents a review of the book *Essays in personal bibliography* (1967) compiled by A K Dasgupta on S R Ranganathan. Draws attention to the usefulness of the librametric study in bringing out the pattern of distribution of the works by and on Ranganathan by subjects, by quantity, by language, by period etc. Mentions briefly each of the major works of Ranganathan and its impact, commenting in particular the Five Laws, Colon Classification, Classified Catalogue Code, theory of library cataloguing, library development plans, and library legislation. Gives a glimpse of some aspects of Ranganathan's personality. Concludes with an appeal for updating the bibliography.

PANDURANGAM, S 467

Dr S R Ranganathan, 1892-1972, *ILS*, 3 p.

Recollects Ranganathan's association with the Institute of Library Science, Hyderabad, and he is remembered by many of its members. Describes his contribution to the field of library and information science and the importance he gave to small professional matters.

PARTHASARATHY, S 468

Shiyali Ramamritam Ranganathan: Guest editorial, *Lib Sci slant Docum & Inf Std* 29 (2) June 1992: 43-45.

Highlights breifly in this Guest Editorial of this Special Number of the quarterly journal *Library Science with a slant to Documentation and Information Studies*, dedicated to the memory of Ranganathan, his work, contribution and achievements in the profession of librarianship who built libraries in Madras; Banaras Hindu University; Delhi; and also started teaching departments. Narrates his sojourn to Zurich, and then work at DRTC, Bangalore; his associatiion with FID, IFLA, Classification Research Group (London), and other international bodies. Mentions that he had close association with spirtual persons.

PARTHASARATHY, S 469

S R Ranganathan: Made librarianship a profession, *The Hindu*, Aug 21, 1992.

Discusses about the life and contribution of Dr S R Ranganathan whose Birth Centenary year is being celebrated in 1992 by, among others, holding an International IFLA Conference in New Delhi. Describes Ranganathan as a man who made librarianship a profession in India as well as elsewhere.

RAHA, SOMNATH 470

Dr S R Ranganathan: A profile, Calcutta: West Bengal College Libraries Association, 1992. 12 p.

Provides a profile of Ranganathan pointing out the mission of his life to create and develop library movement in the country. Includes two papers - one in English and the other in Bengali presented at Dr S R Ranganathan Birth Centenary celebrations held on 9th August 1992 at Presidency College, Calcutta. Pays tribute to Ranganathan and discusses his life and mission.

RAJALAKSHMI, V and PAL, R 471

Ranganathan and the Annals, *Ann Lib Sci & Docum* 39 (2) June 1992: 62-68.

Mentions that Ranganathan was the founder-editor of the *Annals* (1954-63). Analyses Ranganathan's contributions published in *Annals* (total 87, which is 50% of the total published in volumes 1-10). Makes a subject wise analysis revealing that 50% were on classification only. Reveals further that it was followed by cataloguing, documentation, teaching/training in library science, library and information science in general, standards, serials, and bibliographies. Gives a complete list of Ranganathan's papers published in the *Annals*.

RAJAN, T N 472

The relevance of Dr Ranganathan's ideas in the information age, *Ann Lib Sci & Docum* 39 (2) June 1992: 31-33.

Examines briefly the relevance of Ranganathan's ideas and contributions in the present context of information age. Cites implications of his Five Laws and interprets their value in the present day information handling problems. Lists a few areas for the application of his methodology of subject structuring. Mentions groundwork for library routines as analogous to algorithms for computer programming and analysis for PERT/CPM. Suggests that his ideas are valid even today for serious study.

RAMAN NAIR, R 473

Dr S R Ranganathan: The father of library movement in India, *Jl Info Sci* 4(2) Oct-Dec 1993: 69-76.

Describes the early life of S R Ranganathan, his entry into library profession and achievements in LIS thereby becoming unquestioned giant of the 20th century LIS with his vision, innovations, and planning with roots in Indian culture and tradition. His leadership raised to new heights the library movement, library science, and library services.

RANGANATHAN, S R 474

A librarian looks back: An autobiography of Dr S R Ranganathan, appended with an evaluation of his life and work, by P N Kaula, New Delhi: A B C Publishing House, 1992. (Kaula Series in Library Science, 11). xiv, 485 p, 34 photographs.

This autobiography of the great Indian library scientist, Dr S

R Ranganathan has been divided into two parts. Part A gives Ranganathan's professional career and his days of struggle, learning, work, experiments at the Library of the University of Madras. This Part starts with the background of his application to the post of the University Librarian in July 1923 and ends describing the last days of his association with the University. Part B describes Ranganathan's activities with different professional associations and conferences with special reference to the Madras Library Association and the Indian Library Association. This part goes upto the year 1963. Evaluates Ranganathan's contribution in the last part prepared by Kaula (Part C). The autobiography was serialised by Ranganathan under the heading 'A Librarian Looks Back' in the quarterly journal *Herald of Library Science* (1962-1972).

RANGANATHAN and the West: A chronology, 475
RAW, 174-177.

Outlines the events, arranged in chronological order, in the life and career of Dr S R Ranganathan beginning from his birth on 12 August, 1892 to his death on 27 September, 1972. Mentions only those dates which concern his visits to the Western countries. It is reprinted from *S R Ranganathan 1892-1972*, edited by Edward Dudley, London: The Library Association, 1974, pp33-40, and also from *Library Science Today: Ranganathan Festschrift*, Volume 1, edited by P N Kaula, Bombay: Asia Publishing House, 1965, pp 779-782.

RANGANATHAN as a creative genius, library thinker 476
and humanist, *In* G L Trehan and Girja Kumar: *Ranganathan Birth Centenary Monograph*, Chandigarh: Chandigarh Library Study Circle, 1991, pp 14.c - 14.d.

Describes Ranganathan as a creative genius, thinker and humanist who gave his philosophy of librarianship in his Five Laws, and considered duty to do good to others. Describes Ranganathan as an intellectual giant, a scholar, a pattern maker, a protagonist of free book service for all.

RANGANATHAN as a creative writer, *In* G L Trehan 477
and Girja Kumar: *Ranganathan Birth Centenary Monograph*, Chandigarh: Chandigarh Library Study Circle, 1993, pp 15 - 18.

Describes Ranganathan as a creative writer who produced a

corpus of library literature of about 60 books and a bumper crop of articles, research papers, speeches, addresses, messages, reviews, etc during the 50 years of his professional career. Discusses about his book *Five Laws of Library Science*. Explains impact of Ranganathan's writing as contained in Classified Catalogue Code and chain procedure. Describes the last phase of his life in which also despite failing health and blindness, he continued doing creative work. Mentions about his last wish also.

RANGANATHAN Birth Centenary : A watershed in librarianship (A Centenary report), *Lib Sci slant Docum & Inf Std* 29 (3) Sept 1992: 163-164. 478

Reports about the good response the Ranganathan's Birth Centenary year recorded from several individuals and institutions in India and abroad including the 58th General IFLA Conference held at Delhi where Dr Grolier presented a review on Ranganathan; at Madras was held Second ISKO Conference; several books were published and special issues of several journals were also brought out in India and abroad. Mentions about the lectures delivered, stamp released, film produced, and so on.

RANGANATHAN in action at DRTC and writing work at home *In* GL Trehan and Girja Kumar: *Ranganathan Birth Centenary Monograph*, Chandigarh: Chandigarh Library Study Circle, 1993, pp 19-23. 479

States that Ranganathan was a Karmayogi who used to work all the time at DRTC, Bangalore and at home also. Discusses about the ILA Conference at Bangalore in 1978, organised lectures under Sarada Ranganathan Endowment for Library Science, discussion of academic and professional problems, no coffee or tea to visitors, note book for communicating academic and professional matters, and his writing work at home on a charpoi, and thus contrinued doing research work.

REMEMBERING Ranganathan at Chandigarh, *In* G L Trehan 489 and Girja Kumar: *Ranganathan Birth Centenary Monograph*, Chandigarh: Chandigarh Library Study Circle, 1993, pp 43-44.

Discusses about the function organised by the Chandigarh Librarians Association and the T S Central State Library on November 26, 1992 to celebrate the Birth Centenary of Dr S R Ranganathan. Describes about the glowing tributes paid to

Ranganathan in regard to his massive contributions to library profession, and who worked his entire life for the upliftment of the profession as for him it was only service to the society.

ROY, P B 481

Ranganathan: Paying Gurudakshina, *Isalic Bull* 37 (3) Sept 1992: 137-143.

States that Ranganathan was not only a teacher but a Guru par excellence in library and information science. Analyses some of his major contributions which help in solving current as well as future problems. Explains that the most appropriate *gurudakshina* would be to take steps in propagating and utilising Colon Classification and Classified Catalogue Code in all libraries and perpetuating them by producing manuals and workbooks in Indian languages, organising camp training courses, doing research, etc.

S R RANGANATHAN: A tribute, Calcutta: The National Library, 1993. 57 p. 482

Published as a tribute to Ranganathan in his Birth Centenary year by the staff members of the National Library (of India), Calcutta, it includes 11 papers, all by the library personnel of the National Library only, on the great Master's life, work and contributions. By publishing this monograph the National Library has acknowledged its debt to Ranganathan.

S R RANGANATHAN: A world librarian, 483

Library Times International 9 (1) July 1992: 14.

Written as Editorual, describes briefly the contribution of Ranganathan to libraries and librarianship in India, the books and articles he wrote, his library tours abroad, the awards he received, the honours he got, and the international seminars/ conferences/ meetings held in the Birth Centenary year of the great man Ranganathan.

S R RANGANATHAN's reminiscences of some 484

eminent personalities in the Punjab library world, *In* G L Trehan and Girja Kumar: *Ranganathan Birth Centenary Monograph*, Chandigarh: Chandigarh Library Study Circle, 1993, pp 39-42.

Describes S R Ranganathan's meetings with such library personalities of the state of Punjab as A C Woolner whom he met at the First Indian Library Conference in October 1933 in Calcutta, who had faith in the social value of libraries; Lala Labhu Ram, librarian Punjab University, Lahore met Ranganathan at the same Conference; Rattan Chand Manchanda met him at Banaras in 1930 and at Madras in 1934; and Sant Ram Bhatia, Editor of the *Modern Librarian* and *Indian Librarian*. Ranganathan also met K M Asadullah from Punjab on various occasions, when he occupied the seat of dignity in the Imperial Library, Caluctta.

SARKAR, TAPAN 485

S R Ranganathan: A socialist leader of the century, *RAT*, 6-9.

Attempts to focus the socialist impact on Dr S R Ranganathan in reference to the socialist movement in the world. Turns to the definition and history of socialism. Presents Ranganathan in reference to the socialist movement of the 20th century who continued the legacy of the socialists, reassembeled the Fabian Socialists and devoted to the development of library and information science.

SATIJA, M P 486

Birth Centenary literature on Ranganathan: A review, *Third World Libs* 4 (1) Fall 1993: 17-25.

Reviews the literature in the form of books and journals published on Dr S R Ranganathan during his Birth Centenary year. Concludes that most of the literature is on classification, five laws, and their relevance in the information technology environment.

SATIJA, M P 487

Information sources on the life and work of Ranganathan, *Her Lib Sci* 32 (1-2) Jan-Apr 1993: 84-94.

Mentions the earliest bibliographies on Dr S R Ranganathan. Refers to the Ranganathan Festschrift, Volume 1and 2. Mentions the British contribution, the doctoral work done on Ranganathan, special issues of journals brought out as memorial numbers on Ranganathan, his autobiography, and a number of works brought out in the Centenary Year.

SATIJA, M P 488

Life and mind of Ranganathan, *IJILIS* 5 (3-4) July-Dec 1992: 245-252.

Mentions about birth and education of S R Ranganathan. Explains the role of Ranganathan in librarianship in producing standard literature on librarianship. Discusses impact of Hindu Scriptures and some people on Dr S R Ranganathan.

SATIJA, M P 489

On his birth centenary, *DESIDOC Bull* 12 (5) Sept 1992: 3-6

Brings out a life sketch of S R Ranganathan as a legend. Gives account of the achievements and milestones he set during his life span and how the current status of libraries and profession differs from that of his dreams. Highlights the national and international recognition of his work, and the awards and laurels conferred to him.

SATIJA, M P 490

Padamshree S R Ranganathan - a legendary figure, a dreamer and a visionary, *In* G L Trehan and Girja Kumar: *Ranganathan Birth Centenary Monograph*, Chandigarh: Chandigarh Library Study Circle, 1993, p 36.

Outlines the most importanct events and achievements in Ranganathan's life. Showers praises on him for his immense contribution. Mentions about some of the awards and honours he received. States that he is being addressed as the "Librarian to the World" by the American Library Association, and his time is also calleld as "Ranganathan Age".

SATIJA, M P 491

S R Ranganathan and method of science, New Delhi: Aditya Prakashan, 1992. ix, 181 p.

Divided into 13 chapters revealing Ranganathan's insights, synthetic capacity, intution, etc. Discusses him as scientist who wanted to create research in library and information science. Describes the objective and systematic methods he followed in his writings. Developed from the author's Ph D work, it includes an appendix of Ranganathan's works.

SATIJA, M P 492

S R Rangnanthan: A tribute, *Univ News* 30 (35) Aug 31, 1992: 151-153.

Describes birth, education, and librarianship of Ranganathan. Describes him as a prolific writer and author. Discusses his contribution to facet analysis. Describes him as a crusador for Indian librarianship, yet he had international obligations and the world was a big family for Ranganathan who worked for international librarianship.

SATIJA, M P 493

S R Ranganathan: A tribute to the scientist, *LIS*, 168-172.

Describes life, works, and everlasting contributions to Indian librarianship by Dr S R Ranganathan. Discusses his role at international level and with such international agencies as Unesco, ISO, FID, etc.

SATYANARAYAN, R 494

Dr Ranganathan and library profession: A centenary tribute, *Iaslic Bull* 37 (3) Sept 1992: 129-135.

States that the significance of Ranganathan's contribution to library and information service has yet not been assessed fully. Discusses in a general way his contribution of dynamic theory of classification, Colon Classification, symbiotic relationship between classification and subject indexing, formulation of POPSI; etc. Touches upon his association with FID, Unesco, his influence on PRECIS and AACR - 2, his role as a teacher and a crusader of library development and library legislation in India.

SEN, SUBIR K 495

Introduction, *Iaslic Bull* 37 (3) Sept 1992: 97-100

Discusses about the material published in this Special Number of the quarterly journal from Calcutta, *IASLIC Bulletin*, Volume 37 (3) September, 1992, brought out commemorating the Birth Centenary of Dr S R Ranganathan. Describes the potential area of research and study needed in respect of Ranganathan's personality and contributions. This sperial issue includes 11 articles by various Indian authors including three by Ranganathan himself. Also includes letters of Ranganathan with introduction by Gopinath. Mentions Ranganathan's links with *IASLIC* of which he was an honorary life member.

SETHI, A R 496

Aesthetics in Ranganathan, *Jl Lib & Inf Sci* 17 (1) June 1992: 89-101.

Points out that aesthetics and librarianship were quite close about 100 years ago but now they are not. Discusses concept of aesthetics. Examines aestheics in Ranganathan's works, style and personality. Points out that Ranganathan termed his own intensive aesthetic experiences as intuition and did not use the term "aesthetics" in his writings. Suggests that librarianship should come closer to aesthetics.

SHARIFY, NASSER 497

An encounter with a genius: A sentimental reflection on Ranganathan, *Her Lib Sci* 32 (1-2) Jan-Apr 1993: 48-53.

Refers to the understanding of philosophy of S R Ranganathan. Describes first encounter with Ranganathan at the University of Pittsburgh, and the opportunity to act as his host. Narrates the first conversation with the genius of Ranganathan. Expresses gratitude for the personalised service to the great man. Makes observations on his humility, his views on religion, his tackling of the problems of the entire field of LIS. Refers to the honour of being awarded Kaula Gold Medal to the author.

SHARIFY, NASSER 498

Remembering Ranganathan: A sentimental reflection, *RA W*, 149-157.

Describes author's interest in Ranganathan's works and contribution. Relates meeting with him at the Pittsburgh University, and their living together at author's residence, when Ranganathan narrated his life story. Discusses about the conversation that took place between the two professional personalities about the works and contribution of Ranganathan, about religion, integrity of knowledge, his mission to raise the status of Indian libraries and librarians, etc.

SHARMA, N K 499

A tribute to Dr S R Ranganathan, *AGLIS Jl* 9, 1993 (Abstract only).

Throws light on the different phases of S R Ranganathan's professional career and its impact on library and information science profession in India. Highlights his first contributions made to the field of librarianship which earned acclaim for him.

SHARMA, RAVINDRA N 500

Ranganathan and the United States, *PP*, 139-146.

States that Ranganathan was the only librarian to have contributed to all branches of library and information science which made him famous. Writes about his contributions to American librarianship particulary through Five Laws of Library Science which were appreciated by many. Discusses also his contribution to classification, cataloguing, the honours he was given, the terminology he introduced, tributes and views displaying the American influence.

SHARMA, R N, *Ed* 501

S R Ranganathan and the West, New Delhi: Sterling Publishers, 1992. xii, 179 p (Foreword by Partricia Glass Schuman, President ALA).

Published to celebrate the birth centenary of Dr S R Ranganathan, who introduced much needed reforms in Indian librarianship and made a deep impact on international librarianship. Includes 16 articles on the life and work of Ranganathan contributed by well known authors from Canada, USA and England. Brings out deep impact of Ranganathan on the West and therefore deserves to be recognised. Also includes a chronology of Ranganathan and the West. Gives also the two resolutions passed by the American Library Association during its mid-winter meeting held in January 1992 to celebrate Ranganathan's birth centenary.

SIDHU, A S 502

President speaks, In *Souveni*r of CLA, 1992. 2 p.

Tells that Dr S R Ranganathan was tireless and dedicated scholar who emhasised the role of libraries in the society in continuing education, removal of illiteracy, agency for progress and development of a nation. States that the fittest tribute to Dr Ranganathan today would be to make every citizen of India library minded, as desired by him, and also to open the doors of our libraries to all those who long for these.

SRIVASTAVA, A P 503

Lasting impact of Ranganathan, *Ann Lib Sci & Docum* 39 (2) June 1992: 34-37.

Observes that Ranganathan strongly believed that knowledge represented real power. Discusses Ranganathan as a pattern maker in librarianship. Mentions how he welded ideas and practice of his age into coherent and convincing form of lasting value. Mentions about Ranganathan's Newtonian and Aristotelian approach of succint analytical thinking. Describes him as one who had belief in God like Einstein and other great pattern makers. Explains the concept of pattern recognition which is needed to examine his work from a new angle. Mentions about modes of formation of knowledge. States that he was pioneer for computer scientists.

STILES, WILLIAM G 504

That's the way it is, *RAW*, 139-148

Pays tribute to Ranganathan and states that he was a man

ahead of his times. Mentions his contribution as a classificationist with a proper study of order. Relates experiences meeting Ranganathan and learning many things from him, such as facet analysis and its use in reference work, his advice as to pass the examinations easily. Talks about Ranganathan and cognition, Personality perceived through what is left, and other fundamental categories, etc. Marks it a tribute from one librarian to another for his past efforts.

STRANGE but true, In *Souvenir* of CLA, 1992. 505

Puts forth some examples from the life of Ranganathan full of ups and downs, successes and defeats, bore the brunt and scars of many but left too much for us to emulate and follow his ideals. Mentions about his several strange likings, tastes which one would never believe, but are surely true.

SUBBA RAO, C V 506

Controversies on Dr S R Ranganathan, *PP*, 13-20.

Narrates the stories about some of the controversies surrounding Ranganathan. Lists seven of such episodes from his professional life beginning from the University of Madras, and on other professional issues such as stock taking, salary scales, Colon Classification, etc.

SUKIASYAN, E R 507

Ranganathan and the Soviet Union, *Lib Sci slant Docum & Inf Std* 29 (2) June 1992: 65-76.

Identifies the various features that have led to a culture-bond between India and Soviet Union. Presents the various events that have led to the admiration of Dr S R Ranganathan commends in the Soviet Union. Analyses the contribution of Ranganathan and recommends greater attention towards the seminal contributions to library science and service.

SUTINDER SINGH 508

A moment of reflection: Editorial, *Univ News* 30 (35) Aug 31, 1992: 2.

Brought out as a Special Issue dedicated to the memory of Prof S R Ranganathan who is veritably described as the Father of Library Science in India. Deals with Ranganathan's life, career, achievements, contribution, honours and awards. Mentions about the holding of IFLA 58th General Conference in New Delhi in 1992 to honour Dr Ranganathan who had given his all to the cause of libraries and librarians.

TALWAR, B L 509

A consummate genius, In *Souvenir* of CLA, 1992.

Mentions Ranganathan as a consummate genius in the field of library and information science in India who raised the status of the profession, fought for the service conditions of library personnel, and wanted the librarians to be dedicated and devoted to the cause of the profession. Salutes this great saint who sacrificed his life for the profession.

THAKUR, G S 510

A great genius, In *Souvenir* of CLA, 1992.

Showers praise on the great genius of library and information science, Dr S R Ranganathan on the occasion of the bringing out an informative Souvenir on him during his Birth Centenary Year, 1992.

THUS SPAKE Ranganathan, In *Souvenir* of CLA, 1992. 511

Quotes from the great master his views on the profession, libraries, appeal to new generations of India, departmental libraries, research and university libraries, school and college libraries, library training, library facilities for research in LIS, development of library system according to a plan, avoid subscription library system, and value of library service and library legislation.

TREHAN, G L 512

A library prophet and a humanist, In *Souvenir* of CLA, 1992.

Lists briefly the major events of his life and major contribution of this library prophet, Ranganathan, to the library profession. Points out his Five Laws of Library Science revolutionised world's library thought.

TREHAN, G L 513

Looking back at my contact with Ranganathan: Lingering fragrance, *In* G L Trehan and Girja Kumar: *Ranganathan Birth Centenary Monograph*, Chandigarh: Chandigarh Library Study Circle, 1993, pp 7-14.

Discusses author's contact with Dr S R Ranganathan. Deals with the study of Ranganathan's works, correspondence with the author, and Ranganathan's reminisceneces of Punjab library world, etc.

TREHAN, G L and GIRJA KUMAR, *et al* 514

Ranganathan Birth Centenary monograph: Padamshree S R Ranganathan - a creative genius and an intellectual par excellence, Chandigarh: Chandigarh Library Study Circle, 1993. 44p.

Includes articles by such eminent Indian writers in librarianship as Girja Kumar, D B Krishna Rao, P N Kaula, P A Mohanrajan, G L Trehan, and others on the various facets of life and works of S R Ranganathan by the Chandigarh Library Study Circle which celebrated the occasion on 26 November, 1992. It has a Foreword by K M Ujlambkar.

TREHAN, G L 515

Ranganathan Jayanti: S R Ranganathan a creative genius, *In* G L Trehan and Girja Kumar: *Ranganathan Birth Centenary Monograph*, Chandigarh: Chandigarh Library Study Circle, 1993, pp 1-5.

In this long poem, the author discusses about Ranganathan's life, birth, education, training abroad, career, professional contribution in the various fields. Makes special mention of his Five Laws of Library Science, facet analysis, Colon Classification, Prolegomena to library classification, fundamental categories, etc.

TREHAN, G L 516

A tribute to Padamshree S R Ranganathan at his Birth Centenary 1992, *In* G L Trehan and Girja Kumar: *Ranganathan Birth Centenary Monograph*, Chandigarh: Chandigarh Library Study Circle, 1993, p 6.

Pays tribute to S R Ranganathan and his voluminous but scientific contribution to the field of library and information science, on the occasion of his Birth Centenary celebrations.

A TRENDSETTER, In *Souvenir* of CLA, 1992. 517

Explains the qualities of S R Ranganathan who worked for 18 hours a day and opened the library for maximum number of hours, and did unique work not for the sake of money but for serving his readers, and by dint of his hard work set many trends.

VERMA, I B 518

And we march on, In *Souvenir* of CLA, 1992.

Discusses about the personality of S R Ranganathan, his contribution to the field of librarianship and library and information science education during the half a century he remained on the library scene. Mentions about the qualities of Ranganathan. Pays tribute to him on behalf of the Chandigarh Library Association.

WELLS, A J 519

Ranganathan's influence on bibliographic services, *SRR*, 11-13.

Describes briefly about Ranganathan's influence on bibliographical services, particularly in relation to indirect influence on Indian National Bibliography, British National Bibliography, and others which used chain indexing of Ranganathan.

WOOD, KATE 520

S R Ranganathan; a chronology, *SRR*, 28-35.

This chronology appended to the book produced by the Library Association, London (1973), is based on the earlier sources such as Ranganathan Festschrift Volume 1, Essays in Personal Bibliography, Festachrift Volume 2, and other sources, and hence is not uptodate.

YAHYA HAROON K 521

An epic portrayed, *Her Lib Sci* 31 (1-2) Jan-Apr 1992: 83-87.

Reviews the autobiographical work of S R Ranganathan, *A librarian looks back* which is divided into three parts. Part A includes chapters on professional career of Ranganathan. Part B is devoted to his professional contribution through associations, library legislation, etc. Part C deals with Ranganathan's personal glimses at various phases of his life and work, contribution, honours and awards, chronology of life and list of major publications by and on him.

SPECIAL NUMBERS OF INDIAN JOURNALS ON RANGANATHAN

ANNALS OF LIBRARY SCIENCE AND DOCUMENTATION, Volume 39, No 2, June 1992. 522

This quarterly journal etited by J K Ahluwalia published a Special Number on Dr S R Ranganathan, who, incidently, was the founder of this Journal, way back in 1954. This Special Issue has ben brought out in commemoration with the Birth Centenary celebrations of the stalwart of Indian librarianship, as well as a respected librarian and writer at the international level. Includes eight papers, besides an Editorial, by such friends and associates as Girja Kumar, A P Srivastava, T N Rajan, Gurcharan Singh, M A Gopinath, etc.

BHAVAN'S JOURNAL, Volume 39, No 20, May 31, 1993. 523

This non-professional journal has published a Special Number, Volume 39, No 20, May 31, 1993, dedicated to the memory of Dr S R Ranganathan. Published by Bhartiya Vidya Bhavan, Bombay, this Special Issue carried a coloured photograph of Dr S R Ranganathan on the cover of the *Journal*, and includes three articles on the life and works of Dr Ranganathan.

CLIS OBSERVER, Volume 9, Nos 1-2, January-June 1992. 524

This Issue of this quaterly journal edited by D R Kalia includes only two articles ahout Ranganathan's contribution to the field of library and information science. Pays tributes to the great master on the occasion of his Birth Centenary Year being celebrated world wide.

COLLEGE LIBRARIES, Volume 8, Nos 1-2, 1992. 525

This Special Number has been brought out as Dr S R Ranganathan Commemoration Volume, by the West Bengal College Libraries Association, Calcutta. It contains eight messages, an Editorial, and a few words from the Convener. Besides, it has included seven articles on the life and works of Dr S R Ranganathan. Pays homage to this great teacher and organiser of Library Science. However, all the authors of this Special Issue are from the state of West Bengal only.

DESIDOC BULLETIN OF INFORMATION TECHNOLOGY, Volume 12, No 5, September 1992. 526

This Special Number of this Bulletin of Defence Scientific Information and Documentation Centre, Delhi, has been brought out as Dr S R Ranganathan Birth Centenary Issue. Includes five articles on Ranganathan's life, career and contribution by the authors from within the country as tribute to this exemplary teacher and apostle of librarianship. Includes also a brief but well written Editorial about Ranganathan's contribution.

FRONTLINE, Vol 9, No 17, August 15-28, 1992. 527

This fortnightly magazine published by Kasturi & Sons, Madras, published four articles including one of S R Ranganathan, the library scientist and father of the Colon Classification, marking his Birth Centenary celebrations. The other three articles and write-ups are on different aspects of libraries and library science.

HERALD OF LIBRARY SCIENCE, Volume 32, Nos 1-2, January - April, 1993. 528

This Issue edited by P N Kaula has been published as a Special Ranganathan Centenary Number as a tribute to him in his Birth Centenary year celebration. Dr S R Ranganathan has been a regular contributor to this quarterly journal being published since 1962 first from Banaras and now from Lucknow. It includes three photographs of Dr S R Ranganathan, and covers 13 articles written by library and information professionals from all over the country including two from abroad (Denmark and USA). The articles touch some episodes from his life, career, and professinal contributions. The Editor has contributed three articles on different aspects of Ranganathan including Centenary literature.

IASLIC BULLETIN, Volume 37, No 3, September 1992: 529
97-243, Edited by S K Kapoor and Subir K Sen.

Brings out a Special Number as "S R Ranganathan Birth Centenary Commemorative Issue". This is the only Special Number which includes three articles by Ranganathan himself published earlier in the same journal. Besides this, includes eight more articles by the various authors from across the country. Another special feature of this Special Issue is that it includes three sets of letters of Ranganathan written and received by him. It also covers book reviews of some of the books published on Ranganathan in 1992. Includes a well written 'Introduction' by Subir K Sen about the Speical Number.

IJILIS NEWSLETTER., 1992, Cuttack. 530

Brought out as a Special Issue of this *Newsletter* marking salutations to the Father of Library Science in India on his 101st birthday. Reports about the various celebrations organised in the country on the occassion of Ranganathan Birth Centenary. Publishes a photograph of Padamshree S R Ranganathan on the title page.

INDIAN JOURNAL OF INFORMATION LIBRARY & SOCIETY, Volume 5, Nos 3-4, July-December 1992, Edited by B B Shukla. 531

Brought out as a Special Number on Ranganathan Centenary and Orissa Library Movement, with a photograph of Ranganathan, giving its salutations to him. Edited by B B Shukla, this Issue includes three articles on the life, and contribution of Ranganathan by four Indian authors. Pays tribute to the Father of Library Movement in India in the year of his Birth Centenary celebrations.

INDIAN BOOK CHRONICLE, 1992. 532

It has brought out a Special Issue on Dr S R Ranganathan to commemorate his Birth Centenary Year (1992) by publishing book reviews of such books as were written on him to mark the occasion.

INDIAN BOOK INDUSTRY, Volume 45, No 2, 1992. 533

Published as a Special Issue on Dr S R Ranganathan, Father of Library Movement in India, to commemorate his Birth Centenary Year by publishing book reviews of such books as were published on him during 1992 to mark the occasion.

JOURNAL OF LIBRARY AND INFORMATION SCIENCE, Volume 17, No 2, December 1992, Edited by Krishan Kumar. 534

This six monthly journal of the Department of Library and Information Science, University of Delhi, has published this as a Special Issue to mark the Birth Centenary celebrations of Dr S R Ranganathan who established this Department way back in 1947-48. Includes articles on the life and work of S R Ranganathan by his close friends, his students and associates, thereby paying tributes to the great luminary in the field of library and information science, when international conferences are being held all over to mark the occasion.

LIBRARY HISTORY REVIEW, Volume 3, No 4, 1992. 535

This quarterly journal from a private Publisher based at Calcutta, carries only one article in its volume 3, No 4, December 1992 on Dr S R Ranganathan as a token of tribute to this great Indian library scientist and Father of Library Movement, on the occasion of his Birth Centenary Year.

LIBRARY SCIENCE WITH A SLANT TO DOCUMENTATION AND INFORMATION STUDIES, Voulme 29, No 2, June 1992. 536

Devoted to documentation and information studies, this quarterly journal founded by Dr S R Ranganathan himself in 1964, is now published by the Sarada Ranganathan Endowment for Library Science, Bangalore. It brought out a Special Number Volume 29, No 2 June 1992, dedicated to Dr S R Ranganathan on his birth centenary. It carries a Guest Editorial on Ranganathan by S Parthasarathy (of the Institute of Information Studies, Madras); a summary of the work and achievements of Ranganathan by M A

Gopinath; and seven more articles by Indian and foreign authors. This journal has also published its Volume 29, No 3, September 1992 as Special Number on Dr S R Ranganathan as it carries a Guest Editorial on Ranganathan by M A Gopinath, one article by Ranganathan himself, a couple of more related articles, and a Ranganathan Birth Centenary report. The No 4 for December 1992 of the same Volume also carries one article on Ranganathan as well as Reports of the 58th IFLA General Conference and Second International ISKO Conference, held to commemorate the Birth Centenary of Dr Ranganathan.

LIBRARY TODAY, Volume 14, No 9, September 1992. 537

This monthly library periodical is published by the Andhra Pradesh Public Library Association, Hyderabad, contains two articles on the lilfe and works of Dr S R Ranganathan in commemoration with his Birth Centenary Year falling in 1992, and celebrated world wide.

LUCKNOW LIBRARIAN, Volume 24, Nos 1-4, 1992. 538

This quarterly journal published by the U P Library Association, Lucknow published on all the four Numbers of Volume 24 for 1992, a photograph of Dr S R Ranganathan as a mark of respect and tribute to him during the Birth Centenary celebrations.

NISSAT NEWSLETTER, Volume 11, Nos 1-4, 1992. 539

This quarterly Newsletter of the National Information System in Science and Technology, Department of Scientific and Industrial Research, Government of India, New Delhi, carried on all its four Numbers a coloured photograph of Dr S R Ranganathan, the Father of Library Movement in India. Also it reported from time to time about the Birth Centenary celebrated in various institutions in the country and elsewhere.

TIMELESS FELLOWSHIP: Annual Journal of Library and Information Science, Volume 15, 1993. 540

It is published as an Annual from the Library and Information Science/School of Studies, Karnataka University, Dharwad. In its Volume 15, 1993, it carries one article on Ranganathan and his contribution to the development of reference service, a library service so dear to him.

UNIVERSITY NEWS, Volume 30, No 35, August 31, 1992.
Editor: Sutinder Singh. 541

Although this has been brought out as a Special Issue on University Libraries in order to present a state of the art report on the university libraries in India, yet it carries a photograph of Padamshri S R Ranganathan on the title cover, and two articles on Ranganathan's autobiography, as a tribute on his Birth Centenary. It was released on the occasion of the 58th IFLA General Conference held during 30 August - 5 September 1992 in New Delhi. Includes an Editorial 'A moment for reflection' about Ranganathan's life, career, achievements, and contributions.

NEWSPAPERS

THE HINDU, August 30, Sunday, 1992. 542

This famous; more than a century old daily newspaper published from Madras, brought out a Special Supplement on Libraries and Dr S R Ranganathan, and distributed free to the participants on the opening day of the 58th IFLA General Conference, held in New Delhi during 30 Aug - 5 Sept 1992 to mark the Birth Centenary celebrations of Dr S R Ranganathan.

020.92 S Sastry, R S

SATYANARAYANA, K B 543

The influence of R S S on ILS, *ILS*, 1 p.

States the influence of Mr R S Sastry, a teacher at the Institute of Library Science, Hyderabad, during the period 1960-1985, Hightlights his qualities as a teacher who would take interest in his subject.

020.92 SE Sengupta, I N

RAY, DIPAK KUMAR, CHOUDHURI, ABHA and CHOUDHURI, ARUN 544

Dr Indra Narayana Sengupta: An information scientist of international reputation, *IJILIS* 5 (1-2) Jan-June 1992: 149-152.

Describes Dr I N Sengupta as a man, his education and positions he held. Discusses about the awards, honours he got, and the discovery of his law in Bibliometrics which made him known all over the globe.

SHUKLA, B B 545

Indra Narayana Sengupta: His publications and other achievements, *IJILIS* 5 (1-2) Jan-June 1992: 126-148.

Pays a tribute to Dr I N Sengupta on his superannuation, and the Special Number of IJILIS brought out in his honour. Provides appendices listing his publications, bibliographies, professinal experience, honours and awards conferred on him, membership of professional committees, projects completed, research achievements, etc.

SHUKLA, B B 546

The work and impact of a pioneer scientometrist of the world: A study of the contribution of Dr I N Sengupta, *IJILIS* 5 (1-2) Jan-June 1992: 23-40.

Discusses comprehensively and with wide spectrum the contribution of Dr I N Sengupta that made him the foremost scientometrist/information scientist of the world. Makes a mention of the awards, honours, etc given to him and the Festschrift volume given to him.

020.92SH Sharma, J S

PROF J S Sharma: Obituary, *IJILIS* 6 (3-4) July-Dec 1993: 167. 547

Reports that Dr J S Sharma, former University Librarian, BHU, Librarian-cum-Prof and Head, Dept fo LIS, Panjab University, Chandigarh, and University Librarian-cum-Professor and Head, Dept of LIS, Jammu University, died on 2 January 1993 at his residence in Delhi. Mentions that he started his career in 1954 at New Delhi. He was Vice President of IASLIC and ILA, and President Punjab Library Association. He was a prolific writer, and a Festschrift Volume was presented to him in 1988.

020.92 V Viswanathan, C G

OBITUARY: Prof C G Viswanathan, *Luck Libn* 24 (4) Oct-Dec 1992: 169-170. 548

Reports about the demise of Prof C G Viswanathan on 9th Dec 1992 in Lucknow. States that he was born on 2 January 1907 in Tamil Nadu. Mentions about his contribution to LIS in the field of cataloguing and public libraries in which he wrote books also.

PROF C G Viswanathan: Obituary, *IJILIS* 6(3-4) July-Dec 1993: 167 549

Reports that Prof C G Viswanathan former University Librarian, BHU, and G B Pant University of Agriculture and Technology, Pantnagar, and later Head, Dept of LIS, Lucknow University died in Lucknow on 8 Dec 1992. Mentions that he started his career in 1931 at Andhra University, and has been a prolific writer. States that he was presented a Festschrift volume also.

020.9 LIBRARY MOVEMENT

LIS - HISTORY

CHANDETH, M A 550

The battle of ignorance, *LM*, 172-173.

Explains that in order to dispel ingnorance, make men better citizens, library movement as initiated by Madras Library Association is essential.

CHANDRASEKHARAN, N 551

The library movement, *LM*, 54-56.

Describes the idea of library movement to have a small, useful and working library in every village in this vast country so that it could spread free education to all. States that the Government agencies in the villages can start public libraries on a small scale and gradually extend the network. Highlights the role of students.

DUGGAL, K S 552

Needed a library movement, *The Pioneer*, New Delhi, Aug 25, 1992.

Stresses upon the organization of a neetwork of libraries and Nehru also wished libraries to be established in the country which should purchase good books in different Indian languages. Says that in India we spend very less on library services in comparison to other countries. Concludes that in India also a library movement is needed to give salvation to authors.

KRISHNASWAMY AYYAR, K V 553

The library movement and mass eduction, *LM*, 39-42.

Mentions the main purpose of library movement is to educate the illiterate. Highlights the role of local organisations and associations, public bodies, individials, students, etc can work in this movement, and all this be supported by a library in each village.

KRISHNASWAMY AYYAR, K V 554

The library movement for the educated classes, *LM*, 151-155.

Points out that the educated people donot generally continue intellectual pursuits except those in law, medicine, teaching, etc. For all these educated classes there are some good libraries in Madras and more libraries in Indian languages can also be set up. States that for further development of reading libraries may organise lectures, talks, etc.

KRISHNASWAMY AYYAR, K V 555

The library movement for the quasi educated, *LM*, 82-85.

Explains that important aspect of the work of library movement is educating those who have just learnt to read and write and preventing them from lapsing into illiteracy. Highlights the role of library service in this regard as provided by Municipalities in urban areas and they should also provide for travelling libraries. Mentions the nature of books to be stocked in libraries.

KRISHNASWAMY AYYAR, K V 556

The scope of the library movement, *LM*, 8-9.

Explains the term 'Library Movement'. Defines it as understood in the Western countries, that is the extension side, viz., the eduction of the illitrate, and links diffusion of knowledge with books and Madras Library Asociation. Stands for this library movement which comprises three different heads of work.

MADRAS LIBRARY ASSOCIATION, MADRAS 557

The library movement: A collection of essays by diverse hands, Madras: Madras Library Association, 1929, Reprinted by Government Press, 1992. Various pagings.

Includes essays on library movement divided in five sections: English (52), Tamil (9 articles), Telugu (8), Canarese (6), and Malayalam (9 essays). Includes also various messages containing the one from His Excellency the Right Honourable Viscount Goschem of Hawkhurst, and a Foreword by The Rt. Hon V S Srinivasa Sastry. The Reprint includes a Preface by Dr Suseela Kumar, the present President of MALA.

POPLEY, H A 558

Libraries for the million, *LM*, 21-23.

Describes about the beginning of the library movement in India and in Punjab and Baroda. Tells the joy one gets from the public library. States that library movement faces the difficulty of suitable literature in vernaculars. Suggests that Cooperative Socieites should establish at least one library each.

RAKHAKRISHNAN, S 559

The library movement, *LM*, 158-160.

Hightlights need for libraries now in India though in the past the teachers were librarians themselves. Mentions that to raise the general level of librarians they will have to respect their position. Discusses the need of weeding, careful selections of books, particularly on India.

RAGHUNATHAN, B 560

A plea for a people's library, *LM*, 69-72.

Discusses that the success of library movement depends on the production and popularisation of books in vernacular particularly the old classics, biographies, adventures, religion, philosophy, literature, etc. Mentions that books in vernacular should be well brought out and should be handy and be kept in libraries for people.

RAMASWAMI AYYAR, C P 561

The library movement, *LM*, 156-157.

Explains the value of books. States that libray movement in India is still in its infancy though we had great centres of learning in the past. Points out the need for a library movement on Baroda lines.

RAMASWAMI AYYAR, S 562

The library movement in relation to rural reconstruction, *LM*, 111-113.

Lays emphasis on the need of rural reconstruction, removal of ignorance and illiteracy. States that for this purpose library movement appears useful and indeed essential.

RANGACHARIAN, T 563

The place of the cinamatograph in the library movement, *LM*, 35-38.

Discusses the need of adult education in India in view of its vast illiteracy, and use of films for spread of knowledge. Highlights place of cinema in education, and library movement can start and maintain film libraries all over the land.

RANGASWAMY IYENGAR, A 564

Journalism and the library movement, *LM*, 167-168.

Shows the important part journalism can play in popularising the libray movement. Suggests to create reading habits through newspaper and then set up libraries and reading rooms for the public at large.

RUTHNASWAMY, M 565

The library movement and political education, *LM*, 10-11.

Describes that library movement is essential for political progress and political education. States that library movement is also important for rural reconstruction.

SARANATHA AYYANGAR, V 566

The problem of popular culture in India, *LM*, 27-30.

Describes about the state of learning and respect for scholarship. Discusses the problem of culture bound up with the rise of teachers of men. States that we need library movement for the cultivation of thought, these can fill up the gaps in our lives, and educate the educated.

SATYAMURTI, S 567

The library movement and Swaraj, *LM*, 26.

States that to combat illiteracy and ignorance, library movement is essential. Points out that elementary education and adult education should be supported by library facilities.

SESHA AYYANGAR, K V 568

Library movement and night schools, *LM*, 161-162.

Makes a case for night school libraries to cater to the educational needs of the adults, and impart knowledge about cultural heritage of the country.

SIVASWAMY AYYAR, P S 569

The library movement: Some lines of work, *LM*, 5-7.

Describes the primary object of library movement, its scope and how it should be helpful in removing illiteracy and diffusion of knowledge, and create reading habits in the literate class. Also discusses the functions of the Library Association in establishing libraries in every Municipality and Taluk centre.

SRINIVASA AYYAR, N S 570

The library movement, *LM*, 94-95.

Highlights that library movement is essential for mass education. States that there should be network of organizations which will link the cities with villages.

SRINIVAS IYYANGAR, P T 571

The need for the library movement, *LM*, 86-89.

Discusses about the books which are now produced in larger number, as real knowledge can be acquired by reading books. Emphasises that library movement is must for democracy.

SUBRAHMANYAM, N 572

Some thoughts on the library movement, *LM*, 90-93.

Describes about the subjects on which books should be acquired in the library for the people.

VENKATARAMA SASTRI, T R 573

The library movement and national uplift, *LM*, 59-62.

Describes library movement. Gives its scope and the tasks can be achieved through it, including spread of knowledge, educating masses to attain universal literacy through public libraries.

VENKATARAMANI, K S 574

The library movement, *LM*, 57-58.

Highlights the role of library movement in the spread of democracy, and amelioration of man and social justice, and mass education. Talks of library cess and pass a law for it.

020.95 Librarianship - Developing Countries

GURUSWAMY NAIDU, N, *Ed* 575

Librarianship in devloping countries, New Delhi: Ess Ess Publications, 1992. xii, 266p.

Divided into six seetions, it contains 27 articles in all on such aspects as planning of library services in developing countries, acquisition of reading materials, professional development, public libraries and user studies, LIS education, distance education and libraries. The papers are those presented at a National Seminar on 'Librarianship in Developing Countries' held at S V University, Tirupati in 1991.

020.954 Library History - India

LIS - India

BISWAS, S C 576

Wanted an action plan for library modernisation, *The Hindu*, Madras, June 4, 1991.

Divides modern librarianship in India into Ranganathan era, era of stagnation (1970s), and the movement towards modernity (1980s). Traces the developments that took place in the 1950s and 1960s in librarianship as well as in its training. Identifies major constrints in development such as economic recession, no new staff, less funds, deterioration of quality service, and library use is decreasing. Points out that the National Library is not doing its functions effectively and so is INSDOC. Highlights the alarming situation prevailing in Indian librarianship where modrnisation will not be easy, but an action plan may be prepared for this purpose as soon as possible.

DEVIS, DONALD G (Jr) and TAHER, MOHAMED 577

Library history in india: Historiographical assessment and current trends, In *Papers*, 58th IFLA General Conference, New Delhi, 30 Aug - 5 Sept 1992: 7.10-7.11.

Mentions that the status and role of library history in Indian librarianship has a proud past. Deals with the historiography of libraries and librarianship in India, present day considerations and some modest projections.

SEWA SINGH 578

Growth of library and information science in India: Some thoughts, *CTIT*, 150-166.

Discusses the growth of LIS education in India, with an overview of the present scene. Lists the infrastructure of library and information development. Evaluates LIS education course contents. Discusses role of faculty, their research and publication activity, student intake, employment avenues, and need for accreditation. Looks at the trends and issues, perspectives, performance and strategies for change in the new social, economic and technological environments.

020.954 Library Movement - India

BARUA, B P 579

Library movement in India: Problems and prospects, *Granthana* 4 (1-2) Jan-July 1993: 9-18.

Defines library movement as it is composite and continuous movement. Emphasises the need for adoption of National Libray & Information Policy, establishement of an efficient administrative structure and provision of adequate resources for library services. Discusses role fo library associations, voluntary organisations, local governmetns, people's participation. Explains some new concepts and ideas for public library development.

BOSE, SREEKANTA and ROY, RADHAKANTA 580

Library thought of Pandit Ishwarachandra Vidyasagar, *Coll Lib* 7 (1-4) 1991: 21-22.

Describes the contribution of Iswarachandra Vidyasagar towards library consciousness. Mentions his love for books and need to preserve them. States that he was library-minded person.

GHANI, MD USMAN 581

Dr S R Ranganathan'contribution to library movement in India, *RAT*, 10-15.

Describes about the Indian library scene at the time of Ranganathan's entry into profession and the background in which he worked from Madras, the initial library workshop. Discusses his contribution to education and research, Five Laws, library classification, cataloguing, AACR, his work at Delhi, Insdoc, BHU, Bangalore, activities at government level, his contribution to the National Library.

GROVER, VINOD 582

Librarianship in India: Its genesis, growth & current trends, *IJILIS* 6 (1-2)Jan-June 1993: 73-83.

Deals with the role of libraries in differenct segments of education, occupation, trade and business with emphasis on the genesis, growth and development in librarianship and role of library associations. Discusses also librarianship as an academic discipline, current trends in librarianship especially computer technology in libraries, new communication techniques, networking of information. Concludes that though librarianship in India has developed fast since Independence, yet it needs more funds for further development.

KUMAR, SUSEELA 583

Libraries and library science in India, *IFLA Jl* 18 (2) 1992: 94-107.

Traces the growth of libraries - public, academic, research, special, S&T, medicine, agriculture, social sciences, humanities and arts, government libraries, national libraries in India explaining their services and role in the growth of their areas of work. Discusses about LIS education in India since Ranganathan's time to the present showing growth in schools and courses. Explains the role of professional associations. Highlights recommendations of NAPLIS. Discusses the process of modernisation of information centres and systems with the availability of new IT leading to networking.

MAITY, PRATIK and MAITY, GOUTAM 584

A scientific approach to the problems before library movement in India, *Coll Libs* 9 (1-4) Jan-Dec 1993: 28-34.

Discusses the role of library in a class divided society like that of India. States that library is a capitalist enterprise in a capitalistic society as in India. Mentions and discusses that libraries open to all are actually not for all the people as it is dominated by one class fo people and may not be good always for working people. Explains that the dream of secular, scientific, democratic library system is still to be accomplished. Mentions that the root cause must be searched. Makes suggestions to make it a people's university.

REFURBISHING the sagging image of our libraries, 585

The Hindustan Times, Sept 3, 1992; also in *Fortnight* 5 (9) 15 Oct 1992: 1.

Points out that the library movement can succeed only if it becomes people's movement. States that it is a welcome idea that the Ministry of Human Resource Development is contempolating a national policy on libraries which should refurbish the sagging image of our libraries.

VASHISHTH, C P 586

Advancement of librarianship in India, *Jl Lib & Inf Sci* 17 (1) June 1992: 102-114.

Mentions early public libraries, establishement of National libraries in India. Enumerates national documentation centres. Discusses library/information infrastructure. Mentions about information services provided at the national level. Discusses public library system. Describes roles of professional associations at the national level. Describes briefly library and information science education. Mentions about school library including their standards.

020.95413 Library Movement - Orissa

RATH, P K 587

Library movement in Orissa, In *Souvenir*, 38th All India Library Conference, Bhubaneswar, 21-24 Nov 1992, pp 30-36.

Describes the library movement in the state initiated after 1936 when Orissa was separated from Bihar. Discusses the growth of public libraries, academic libraries, LIS education, library literature and research. Gives the contributiion of library associations/academic institutions and individuals. Mentions role of government in library development. Concludes that movenment lacks planning and support.

020.95414 Library Movement - West Bengal

SHARMA, AJAY KUMAR 588

History of library movement in British Bengal during twentieth century, *Int Lib Move* 15 (4) Dec 1993: 161-168.

Makes a historical survey of the British Bengal in 20th century. Gives history since Babur, discusses the achievements of Humayun, Akbar, Jehangir, Aurangzeb in the development of libraries. Describes the destruction of the Library Aurangzeb set up and the loss of vauable books and other records.

020.954162 Library Movement - Assam

PHUKAN, GAJEN 589

Looking back at the library movement in Assam, *LIN*, 11-16.

Writes the reminiscences of author's close link with All Assam Library Association particularly in regard to organising the Eighth Open Conference of the Association in 1964. Recounts that Assam library movement dates back to 1938. Makes suggestions to mobilise and strengthen the public libraries mostly in rural areas through the Assam Library Association.

020.95417 Library Movement - Manipur

SINGH, KHOMDON (Th) 590

Why library movement is necessary in Manipur, *IJILIS* 5 (3-4) July-Dec 1992: 266-272.

Mentions implication of library movement. Defines a public

library giving its objectives and functioning. Narrates the historical development of public libraries in Manipur in brief. Suggests the ways and means for the success of library movement in the state. Concludes that the Manipur Public Libraries Bill of 1988 be converted into an Act for the success of public library set up in the state.

020.95455 Library Movement - Punjab

SUKHDEV SINGH 591

Library movement in Punjab from nineteen thirties to sixties, *Int Lib Move* 14 (1) Mar 1992: 26-38.

Describes the beginnings and development of library movement in Punjab during the period 1930-60. Gives some useful appendices.

020.95482 Library Movement - Tamil Nadu

SRINIVASACHARI, C S 592

Earliest evidence of the library movement in Madras, *LM*, 133-135.

Traces the history of earliest establishment of library in Madras since 17th century which served as the official library of the Company and housed in Fort St George. States that a catalogue of the books was prepared.

020.95483 Library Movement - Kerala

RAMAN NAIR, R 593

Origins of people's library movement in Kerala, *Granthana* 4 (1-2) Jan-July 1993: 29-36.

Traces history of a hightly specialised and efficient service with recorded information organised and managed by people, that existed in ancient Kerala. Explains how the influence of this tradition and the requirements of the educational, social and political reform movements of later half of 19th century caused the establishment of small libraries in villages that gave birth to a unique people's library movement in Kerala.

020.95484 Library Movement - Andhra Pradesh

VENKATAPPAIAH, V 594

Pioneers of Andhra Pradesh library movement, *ILS*, 5 p.

Makes an attempt to briefly sketch the profiles of such

pioneers of library movement in Andhra Pradesh as I V Ramanayya, S V Narasimham, M Hanumantha Rao, Nagabhushnam, Gopal Rao Ekbote, Kodati Narayana Rao, and so on.

021.2 LIBRARY AND SOCIETY

LIBRARY AND COMMUNITY

GANDHI, J S 595

Library as a social system, *Univ News* 30 (35) Aug 31, 1992: 37-39.

Explains social system theory and its application to the library system in that it is too a working social system. Gives characteristics of library as a social lsystem. Mentions some studies of library system and library profession in India. Visualises it in the cultural context, the organisational context.

JOSHI, S C and ROUT, R K 596

Role of library in the development of society, *PLD*, 93-98.

Gives importanc of public library as social institution. Discusses knowledge and society for which education of masses is essential where public libraries can function more effectively. Describes their role in cultural progress also and the role of information for development of society and increasing literacy, utilization of leisure time. Concludes that public libray plays a significant role in the development of society.

SETHI, A R 597

Libraries and social transformation: A development communication approach, *Jl Lib & Info Sci* 18 (2) Dec 1993: 142-153.

Describes concept of social transformation. Discusses social role of information. Examines role of libraries in social transformation. Discusses dilemma of developing countries whether or not to accept the eastern style of development model and the role of IT in it. Mentions Indian society as no longer traditional, but powerless to become modern. Concludes that development communication offers a new approact to achieve the goal of sustainable librarianship.

021.1 (1) Library and Economic Development

IFFIDON, SAM E 598

Role of libraries in the economic and industrial development, *PLD*, 82-92.

Mentions importance of libraries in nation's economic and

industrial development. Discusses the situation of libraries in developed countries and their role in educational, scientific and industrial development in USA, Canada, GDR, role of trade and commerce libraries in Britain. Describes also the role of libraries in the economic and industrial development of Nigeria. Explains the role of academic, public and special libraries. States that it is, however, difficult to determine the contribution of libraries in this regard and the unsatisfactory situation. Makes suggestions for improvement.

021.24 Library and Educational Role

CHOPRA, H R 599

Role of libraries in life long education, *Lib Prog (Int)* 11 (1-2) Jan-Dec 1991: 1-4.

States that library is an essential organisation in life.long education of society. Mentions that public libraries are good agencies towards literacy drive. Discusses the activities of different kinds of libraries. Concludes that libraries play significant role towards imparting education at every stage in the life of a person.

SASTRY, R S 600

Libraries, learning and the child, *ILS*, 5 p.

Deals with the role of education and libraries in children personality development. Quoted extensively in support of the children's books.

021.24 (1) Library and Adult Education/Literacy

DILLI, K T 601

Libraries pivotal role in promoting literacy, *The Hindu*, Madras, 3 Nov 1992.

Deals with the important role the library can play as a social agency, in promoting the cause of literacy and therby benefitting different groups in the society through its services.

DIMATTIA, ERNEST A (Jr) 602

Libraries and literacy: A global to local perspective, *CLIS Observer* 9 (1-2) Jan-June 1992: 3-15.

Presented at Literacy/Library Symposium co-sponsored by National Book Trusts and USIS, New Delhhi held on 3 Sept 1992 in which the author speaks of the great importance of literacy in India and the need for its linkage with libraries. Discusses some of the things that are happening in various parts of the world, and brings both global and local pictue of the literacy mosaic.

GOSWAMEE, RAM 603

Adult education and libraries, *LIN*, 1-4.

Mentions about the concept and need for adult education. Gives statistical information about illiteracy in world and India. Discussesa about the Adult Education programmes initiated by the Government of India to increase literacy. Points out the need for a network of public libraries in both urban and rural areas for the success of Adult Education programmes. Describes the follow up programme of a library for Adult Education.

NARASIMHAN, S 604

The library movement and mass education, *LM*, 96-101.

Explains the need of mass education in India with high rate of illiteracy. Stresses on the development of reading habits with the help of libraries.

VARALAKSHMI, R S R 605

Post-literacy programmes - the role of libraries, *SPLS*, 1.1-1.5.

Traces out the existing literacy and post-literacy programmes including Naitonal Literacy Mission and Jana Siksha Nalayama. Emphasises the role ought to be played by the libraries in these programmes. Makes suggestions on the models and methods that can be adopted in implementing programmes.

021.24 (1) Libraries and NEP

MITRA, N L 606

Towards a New Education Policy and response of UGC, *Univ News* Jan 18, 1993: 12-13.

Deals with the New Education Policy developed by Govt of India in 1986, and the response of the UGC in fulfilling its needs by setting up more libraries for higher education support.

021.24 (1) Libraries and Distance Education

ABRAHAM, ALEXANDER 607

Libraries and distance education, *Int Lib Move* 14 (2) June 1992: 82-91.

Explains the term distance. Identifies formal and non-formal education. States the situation of distance education in India and national policy on education and distance education. Mentions media in distance education, role of library in education and various services to be rendered by the library and the role of librarian in distance education system.

KARISIDDAPPA, C R and RAMADEVI, V 608

Library services for promoting distance education in India, *LID*, 254-261.

Highlights importance of distance education. Gives its objectives. Explains role of library in distance education system. Discusses distance education at international level, and national level. Gives a case of the Ambedkar Open University, Hyderabad regarding the services, material, package, etc. Concludes in favour of open learning system where library is placed at the centre of the learning process.

021.64 Library Cooperation

ALBERANI, VILMA 609

Cooperation for a better exploitation of resources in health services: The Italian information system, *ML*, 7-13.

Mentions that information may be used efficiently only through cooperation and resource sharing. Presents a cooperative programme for a national information system in health science in order to meet information needs of people working in this field. Gives an outline of situation of biomedical libraries survey regarding the role that the Italian National Institute of Health with its information structure is assuming.

AMANO, YOSHIO 610

A consideration of the cooperative activities between the National Centre for Science Information System (NACSIS) and the Japan Medical Library Association (JMLA), *ML*, 15-19.

Outlines the activities of the NACSIS in Japan, especially its cataloguing database for books and periodicals which are held in the whole university libraries. Discusses the present situation and the future feasibility of cooperative activities with medical libraries most of which are affiliated with the JMLA.

YOON, BONG-JA, KIM, HO-BAE, LEE, SUNG-HA and SUGA, TOSHINOBU 611

Medical library cooperation in case of Korea and Japan, *ML*, 491-494.

Discusses importance of cooperation among libraries.

Describes the establishment of Korea Medical Library Association and Japan Medical Library Association. Discusses their activities, officers, education, publication, ILL. Gives the analysis of the present state and the two associations course for future advance.

021.642 Union Catalogues

SANTIAGO, SUZANNE 612

ISDS and union catalogues, *Jl Lib & Inf Sci* 16 (2) Dec 1991: 160-166.

Presents the organizational structure and working procedure of ISDS that account for the content of ISDS database. Attempts to define the good usage of ISDS by union catalogues with computer systems. Explains the practical issues regarding creating a union catalogue satabase, and its maintenance.

021.65 LIBRARY NETWORKS/INFORMATION NETWORKS/COMPUTERISED LIBRARY NETWORKS

AHUJA, J P S 613

CD-ROM networks: Building information workstations in organizations, *LIT*, 276-282.

Describes that CD-ROMs are commercially available for searching databases primarily bibliographic in nature. Compares CD ROM vs online searching. Explains the CD ROM networking, LAN for effective information dissemination. Describes the CD ROM LAN. Touches on the problems associated with CD ROM LANs.

ALVI, WAJIH A 614

National library & information services networking: Prerequisites, problems and suggestions, *CTIT*, 177-186.

Describes the need for networking in view of the information explosion. Discusses the concept of resource sharing. Explains IT and its application to networking. Describes the prerequisites for networking. Discusses the Indian scene of LIS networking and the problems. Offers various suggestions.

ARORA, JAGDISH 615

Computer networks for the libraries in India: Current scenario, *AGLIS Jl* 9, 1993 (Abstract only).

Discusses the need and significance of computer and communication networks for the present day librarianship. Gives historical perspective of library networks in India like NICNET, INDONET, I-NET, CALIBNET, BONET, DELNET, ERNET, INFLIBNET, BTISNET.

ASHOK BABU, T and SASTRY, P S 616

Public libraries and networking, *IPLA Souvenir*, No. 15, 4 p.

Gives importance of public libraries. Defines network. Presents the facilities available for establishing public library networks, and how a network like Andhra Pradesh Libray Network (APLIBNET) can be successfully implemented. Includes also a birds' eyeview of some of the national and international networks for the information of public librarians.

BARUA, P and SAIBABA, B 617

A plan for cooperation and networking among engineering and technological libraries in India, *Ann Lib Sci & Docum* 39 (3) Sept 1992: 101-105.

Mentions some problems librarians are facing. Describes the concept of cooperation. Explains the need for cooperation among Indian engineering and technological libraries on the basis of a survey through questionnaire sent to 162 such libraries.

CHADHA, RAVINDRA KUMAR 618

Right to information: Network of government libraries in India, *AGLIS Jl* 9, 1993.

Makes a case for need to have a proper publication policy, increased accessibility to extract information by Parliament, enactment of an adequate freedom of information act establishment of a National Referral Centre of government publications, and a strong network of government libraries to provide freedom of information.

CHAKRABARTY, BIPUL KUMAR 619

Need for a Zoological Information Analysis Centre in the national network, *ALD*, 60-74.

Explains the role of the Zoological Survey of India in the network of information analysis. Discusses the need for the national network on zoological information. Gives objectives of National Network of Zoological Sciences. Describes the need for a computerized database on this Network. Emphasises the role of information analysis for quick access and retrieval of information.

Mentions skills needed for the Bioscience network of information within the databases. Makes a case for a national network of information systems in view of the Bioscience research in India. Suggests some solutions to the problem.

CHARYULU, UVN 620

Information network for rural development, *NIRD Newsletter* (69) Aug 1993: 6.

Makes a case for an information network to be established for rural development by providing the people easy access to sources of information. Outlines the benefits that can be accrued from such a netwrok.

CLACSO 621

Information and communication network: Social science, *INICAE* 11 (2) Sept 1992: 264-266.

Deals with the goals of CLACSO information and communication network, services provided, access to scientific work. Mentions about International Network of Information for Development (IDIN).

CSIR LIBRARIANS discuss networking and library management, *NISSAT Neewsletter* 12(4) Oct-Dec 1993: 14-17. 622

Reports about the two-day meeting of Heads of CSIR libraries to discuss several important issues of vital concern to the scientific community of CSIR in regard to library and information services. States that there were seven technical sessions chaired by Prof T Viswanathan, Director INSDOC. Strsses the need for making the services of the library and information centres more dynamic.

DUBEY, YOGENDRA 623

Modeling and simulation in the development of desision support system for library resource sharing networks, *COP*, 160-172.

Defines a decision support system (DSS). Discusses DSS support to phases in decision making process. Explains modeling components in DSS though no well developed design tools for model formulation exists. Describes design model and cognitive factors for DSS, with the help of system analysis. Gives application of modeling and simulations and their use in library resource sharing networks. Discusses the methodology. Gives architecture of resource sharing simulation system with the validity and reliability of models.

GAKHAR, A P 624

Networking and sharing of information in art and culture among the countries of South Asian region, *ILA Bull* 28 (1-2) Apr-Sept 1992: 43-47.

Traces the history of exchange of information among the countries of South and South East Asia. Desccribes certain pre requisites for creation of network and dwells upon various programmes initiated in Kala Nidhi Division of Indra Gandhi National Centre for Arts.

GUPTA, S P 625

Telematics in library and information management system, *AGLIS JI* 9, 1993 (Abstract only).

Discusses need for resource sharing and networking of libraries. Gives importance of components of telematics and its applications in library and information services at CRRI including online access to information and resource sharing through E-mail.

HAZARIKA, BIJOYA 626

Network of public libraries in Assam, *IPLA Souvenir*, No. 14, 4p.

Outlines development of public libraries in Assam and creation of district libraries and their buildings and the Dept of Libraries was upgraded to Directorate. Discusses about the various services offered by the different libraries. Explains the expansion and development of this library network upto the rural areas and support the public library movement.

INDO - BRITISH meet: Focus on library networking, *NISSAT Newsletter* 11 (4) Jan-Mar 1992: 3-6. 627

Describes the library networking drive in India which owes its inception to the sustained efforts in recent years of NISSAT of DSIR, Government of India. Discusses the fresh impetus it received with the Indo-British meet jointly organised at the India International Centre by DELNET, the British Council and NISSAT during 14-15 Jan 1992.

INFORMATION access: Networks continue to widen, *The Hindu*, Madras, 27 Jan, 1993. 628

Discusses about the 40 General Information Service Terminals: National Informatics Centre (GISTNIC) booths set up around the country - the largest public access database in Asia - covering tourist and travel, education, medical directories, rural technology, a massive datastore on Indian and world economy brought in as MEDLARS from th US, INDDOC's own SIRNET, ERNET, all these taken together open floodgates of international information.

JASMER SINGH 629

Punjab public library and information network: A proposal, *LIT*, 208-217.

Explains the condition of public libraries in Punjab and the present administrative set up. Makes a proposal for public library and information network. Gives network objectives. Mentions the need for finances and their sources. Explains need for library legislation. Gives some suggestions for planned development of public library and information network in Punjab.

JOSHI, P G 630

Library and informationnetworks, *ALIS,* V 3, 215-228.

Defines the need of networking concept in the light of knowledge explosion, printing and communication, revolution. Describes the type of networking systems and their functions and services. Highlights important library network and some information systems, viz, NCSI, INSDOC, NICFOS, AGRIS, INIS, and HELLIS.

KAUL, H K 631

Library networks; an Indian experience, New Delhi: Virgo Publications, 1992. 264 p.

Presents a systematic stydy of library networks. Analyses the efforts made in India by NISSAT and UGC. Deals in eleven chapters, with a global view of library networks, automation of Indian libraries, promotion of Indian libray networks, etc. Describes the essential features of a functional network.

KAUL, H K 632

Library networks in India, *DL*, 272-297.

Studies the growth of library networks in India giving their objectives, services, etc. States that it is through networks that the libraries not only share resources but provide excellent and fast services to their users.

LAHIRI, A 633

Time for coordinating mechanism, *NISSAT Newsletter* 11 (3) July-Sept 1992: 1.

Discusses that with the change in information scenario, a large number of library resource sharing networks such as CALIBNET, DELNET, BONET, etc and SIRNET, ERNET, INFLIBNET, etc are under various stages of computerisation. Suggests that a flexible collection coordination mechanism is required to be set up.

LAXMAN RAO, N 634

Networking and communication of information, *Timeless Fellowship* 15, 1993: 28-56.

Explains that information is the sixth basic need of human being and quality of information increases its value. States that the latest technological developments provide opportunity to improve communication which have resulted in networks. Describes networks LAN, MAN, WAN, etc. Gives idea about ISDN and OSI. Describes in detail the networks development in India. Discusses their impact on library and information services.

MAHAJAN, S G 635

Resource sharing and networking of university libraries in India, *Univ News* 30 (35) Aug 31, 1992: 79-85.

Makes a mention of information society, information explosion and access to information which has grown tremendously but information resources are decreasing because of devaluation and cuts. Points out resource sharing as the way out. Discusses advantages of networking and networks in India such as NICNET, ERNET, I-NET, SIRNET,etc. Discusses INFLIBNET in detail with implementation mechanism etc. Identifies the task ahead.

MITRA, ASHOK 636

Some reflections on networking and libraries, *TDF*, 67-69.

Explains capabilities of computer. Discusses about these capabilities leading to the various developments in the library contest, particularly in preparing MARC and library networking for resource sharing, use of CD ROM, electronic book and electronic publishing.

OPEN, MERLITA M 637

Medical and health libraries link to the total health program - the HERDIN development framework (Phillippines), *M L*, 319-326.

States that HERDIN initially worked on the concept of a library network transcended to a bigger picture where all major players in the health information community were identified and linkages were established. Describes network as evolving, dynamic and takes into context all related developments, complementation defines its reasonable success.

PAREKH, HARSHA 638

Library networks: Moving from informal to formal, *Univ News* 31 (14) Apr 5, 1993: 4-7.

Discusses about the advantages of library networks for the purpose of resource sharing. Makes a survey of some of the college and university librarians to ascertain their faith in the library and information networking including INFLIBNET.

PRASAD, Y V SILVA 639

Network of public libraries & information centre in India, *IPLA Souvenir*, 6 p.

Defines networking. Spells out the need for library networking. Gives prerequisites for library networking. Discusses network functions. Explains network models, and the technology for network implementation. Describes the Indian scenario regarding networking where progress is slow.

SHARMA, NARINDER KUMAR 640

A plea for academic library system in India, *CLIS Observer* 9 (1-2) Jan-June 1992: 23-24.

Makes a plea for an Indian National Academic Library and Information System (INALIS) to pool the resources of academic libraries to meet with the changing educational requirements. Concludes that the INALIS should be integrated with the National Library and Information System.

SINGH, SURYA NATH 641

A bibliographic online information network for biomedical libraries/TICs in India, *ML*, 443-451.

Discusses the need for sharing of information resources in biomedical R&D in India through an online network. Highlights main features, advantages, drawbacks of various systems used for resource sharing. Discusses briefly problems and issues involved in organising a bibliographic information network for Ministry of Health. Highlights salient features of proposed centralised information network for health. Suggests a proposal for national biomedical R & D online information network model. Enumerates main problems and advantages, and so on.

STONE, MARTHA B 642

The future of world agricultural information networks, *LT*, 236-251.

Reviews present day information networks and how they have evolved as a result of new IT. Discusses needs of the end user and how they influence the design of information networks, evolving role of information systems on transfer process at various levels. Discusses role of AGRIS in this connection.

TEJOMURTY, A and BOSE, KAUSHIK 643

Computer networks in India, *DL*, 220-237.

Describes the development of computer networks in India. Discusses the various general data/information networks, such as NICNET, INDONET, specialised information networks including INFLIBNET, DELNET, CALIBNET. Explains some other specialised networks such as ONGCNET, etc.

ZHENG XIN - QUING 644

The network development and resource sharing of medical libraries in China, *ML*, 487-490.

Discusses inter library cooperation and network of China's medical libraries during the early developing period, 1950-65; almost standstill period 1966-76; new developing period 1977-84; and formal setting up of the network. Analyses existing problems in setting up a more scientific and rational system of medical literatues. Tries to put forward the solutions. Indicates how to make the collection development policy full of effect.

021.65 (1) APINESS

APINESS Regional Advisory Group- New Delhi Meeting, 645

NISSAT Newsletter 12 (1) Jan-Mar 1993: 8-10.

Describes the Third Meeting of the Regional Advisory Group of the Asia Pacific Info Network in Social Sciences hosted by

ICSSR on behalf of UNESCO at New Delhi during 25-27 Aug 1992 in which 13 representatives participated in addition to the observers from many other Associations. Mentions the objectives of the meeting. Gives the issues and solutions that emerged.

HARINDER KAUR 646

Asia Pacific Information Network in Social Science (APINESS), *AGLIS JI* 9, 1993 (Abstract only).

Traces the history of APINESS. Discusses its framework, constituents of the system, its action programme and various activities. Describes the role of NASSDOC as national contact point in furthering APINESS activity.

TYAGI, K G 647

Regional Advisory Group of Asia Pacific Information Network in Social Sciences, *INICAE* 12 (2) Sept 1993: 239-241.

Describes about the Third Meeting of the Regional Advisory Group of the Asia Pacific Information Network in Social Sciences (APINESS/RAG-III), hosted by ICSSR at New Delhi during 25-27 Aug, 1992, and attended by 13 representatives of the APINESS. Describes about the Opening Session, and Business sessions. Points out the major issues and solutions that emerged at the Meeting.

021.65 (1) ASTINFO

9th ASTINFO: New Delhi hosts Regional Seminar on Library 648 Networks and Ninth Consultative Committee Meeting, *NISSAT Newsletter* 12 (4) Oct-Dec 1993: 3-6.

Reports about the Regional Seminar on Library Networks followed by the Ninth ASTINFO Consultative Committee Meeting organised by NISSAT on behalf of Government of India and UNESCO during 25 Sept to 1 Oct 1993 at Surajkund, was attended by 17 ASTINFO members. Discusses about the Technical Sessions on various topics. Describes the recommendations adopted.

021.65 (1) BONET

BOMBAY Library Network commissioned, *NISSAT Newsletter* 12 (1) Jan-Mar 1993: 3-4. 649

Reports that BONET was inaugurated on 6 Nov 1992 by DOE, Govt of India. Mentions its aims to build a low cost library information stystem between libraries in Bombay with focus of ILL rather than on computerising individual libraries. Describes ILL activities of BONET and the annual subscription payable by members.

GANPULE, S R 650

Bombay Library Network, *Her Lib Sci* 32 (3-4) July-Oct 1993: 251-253.

Reports about the BONET inaugurated by the Secretary, DEO, Govt of India at the National Centre for Science and Technology on 6 Nov 1992. Describes the aims of BONET as to build a low cost library information system, and promoting cooperation between libraries in Bombay. Mentions the inter library activities of interest to BONET. Mentions also the annual subscription fee payable by BONET members.

021.65 (1) Commonwealth Network

COMMONWEALTH SECRETARIAT, LONDON 651

Commonwealth network on information technology, *INICAE 11* (1) Mar 1992: 104-106.

Proposes to set up a Commonwealth - wide network of IT to provide a vital link between member countries for sharing of information technology and innovations. It will be called COMNET-IT.

021.65 (1) DELNET

KAUL, H K 652

DELNET: An overview, *Iaslic Bull* 38 (3) Sept 1993: 113-122.

Traces roots of DELNET and the efforts that led to its establishement. Attempts to show the database created and the softwares and format being used in Delhi libraries. Describes progress made in the rationalisation of periodical acquisitions. Makes an assessment to find out the most economical approach for creating bibliographic databases. Describes the operation of E-mail and need for standards. Mentions that work on the compilation of union catalogue has begun. Concludes that DELNET will develop in the coming years.

KAUL, H K 653

Delhi Library Network (DELNET), *INICAE* 11 (2) Sept 1992: 209-231.

Discusses the cooperative effort in networking and genesis

of DELNET. Explains areas of standardization and promotion of database in DELNET libraries. Refers to the participating libraries. Presents achievements of DELNET, starting extension of its activites and its future progremme. Mentions net‥orking and its operations among libraries. Gives hardware configuration for DELNET libraries.

021.65 (1) INFLIBNET

INFLIBNET: Current programme, *NISSAT Newsletter* 12 (3) July-Sept 1993: 19. 654

Reports about the current programme of INFLIBNET launched in May 1991. Mentions its aims, services such as catalogue based, database, document supply service, collection development, communication based services. Describes its First Phase commenced in April 1993 identifying 11 university libraries for automation.

PAREKH, HARSHA 655

Library networks: Moving from informal to formal, *Univ News* 31 (14) 5 Apr 1993: 4-7.

Explains the concept networks and its use in sharing information. Discusses about UGC's INFLIBNET and its awareness among librarians. Describes about frequency of help sought from other libraries for various reasons. Works out scope for different types of libraries. Discusses dependence among different types of libraries. Describes the hopes for the future about INFLIBNET.

VAISHNAV, A A 656

INFLIBNET problems and prospects, *Int Lib Move* 15 (1) Mar 1993: 11-16.

Describes the prospects and problems of INFLIBNET based on the report of the Inter Agency Working Group of UGC. Offers various suggestions to remove the problems.

021.65 (1) INTERNET

ASANO, SHOICHIRO 657

Operation of the INTERNET Backbone, *INICAE* 12 (1) Mar 1993: 92-95.

Describes that LAN is proceeding repidly in universities, hence their network is essential. Explains the present network configuration. Mentions the concept of subscribing to SINET. Gives the future developments of this network.

021.65 (1) KRISHINET

SHARMA, RAMESH DUTTA 658

KRISHINET: The agricultural information network for India, *CTIT*, 187-197.

Explains the need for information and databank in agricultural informaion services as there exist some gaps in lab and land. Discusses the proposals of ICAR for the 8th Five Year Plan including KRISHINET. Also duscusses about international agro network. Points out the urgent need of Indian agro-network.

021.65 (1) NERULIBNET

KUNDU, A K and PANDA, N M 659

NERULIBNET for resource sharing among university libraries in North Eastern region: A blueprint, *Univ News* 31 (26) June 28, 1993: 11-15.

Points out the present economic crisis acting on Indian librarianship. Highlights the inevitability of a computer based communcation network programme termed as NERULIBNET (North Eastern Regional University Library Network) to promote resource sharing among university libraries in the NE. Proposes a blueprint for it and suggests a few guidelines for its effective implementation.

021.65 (1) PUNENET

And now it's PUNENET, *NISSAT Newsletter* 11 (3) 660 July-Sept 1992 : 3-6.

Reports about the launching of PUNENET feasibility study for which was already ready. It is to be implemented in four phases and would provide such network services as union catalogue, CAS, SDI, authority data, library automation, ILL, document transfer/copy, access to national/international databases.

021.65 (1) LAN

AHUJA, J P S 661

Building a microcomputer base Local Area Network for libraries: From concept to percept *Luck Libn* 24 (1) Jan-Mar 1992: 1-10.

Defines IT. Describes the need for netwroking a library with various constituent units of its parent organisation. Puts forth a case for building a micreocomputer based LAN to achieve this goal. Compares also the characteristics of a mini-computer based system with those of a microcomputer based system.

DESIKAN, P A and MUTHUSAMY, R 662

Local area networks: A system for TIC, *STIM*, 132-143.

Gives the advantages of library computerisation. Describes in detail the requirements of hardware and software for the Combat Vehicles Research and Development Establishment (CYRDE), Ministry of Defence, Madras. Defines LAN and gives its characteristics. Discusses role of Fileserver in LAN. Describes the hardware system and its components for such a local area network.

RAMCHANDER RAO, K 663

Resource sharing at local level: HYNET - a proposal, *ALR*, 247-256.

Gives the need for resource sharing. Describes the past efforts made in resources sharing and cooperation at regional and local level. Presents the library scenario at Hyderabad with rich resources in different subjects. Reports about the survey of 35 libraries in the twin cities of Hyderabad and Secundrabad and proposes a network HYNET at local level. Gives its advantages and salient features.

TEJOMURTY, A and BOSE, KAUSHIK 664

Local area network: How it can work in a university information system, *LIT*, 218-223.

Mentions importance of LAN. Gives definition of LAN and is found practicable as well as attractive for libraries. Discusses how LAN can work in a university information system, and gives its applications. Lists advantages and disadvantages of LAN. Proposes setting up of LAN at Vikram University, Ujjain.

021.65 (1) RESOURCE SHARING

ABRAHAM, ALEXANDER, 665

Resource sharing in university libraries: A myth or reality, *RDAL*, 77-85.

Defines ressource shairng. Mentions objectives, and need for resource sharing. Discusses factors for successful resource sharing. Explains problems in resource shairing in India libraries, identifies areas of resource sharing. Describe ILL system. Gives various recommendations on resource sharing in Indian libraries. Offers suggestions

CHANDRA KUMARAN NAIR, M 666

Resource sharing in medical libraries and its significance in new information technology, *RDAL*, 35-43.

Mentions factors influencing resource sharing activities. Explains medical information, sources and information needs, biomedical informatics, medical library situation in Kerala. Makes a proposal for resource sharing in the medical libraries in Trivandrum. Mentions NISSAT progremme for the rationalisation of periodical acquisitions. Discusses significances of IT in resource sharing through computer network, LAN, MEDLINE on CD-ROM, interfacing, etc.

DUCHOW, SANDRA R 667

Resource sharing in hospital libraries: New technologies, new directions, *ML*, 131-138.

Explains that keys to enhanced information environment in hospital library are to be found in recent technology development specifically in automation, microcomputers, telecommunication. Reviews briefly history of these developments. Discusses application of these technologies in hospital libraries and implications for resource sharing through the use of online searching facilities, E-mail, Fax capabilities. etc. Gives an overview of the extent to which some Canadian hospital libraries are using the new IT for resource sharing.

KONNUR, M B 668

Resource sharing in university libraries: The international scene, *Univ News* 30 (35) Aug 31, 1992: 93-97.

Traces the origin of resource sharing in library field. Describes objectives, activities and levels of resource sharing. Discusses resource sharing in UK, USA, and other countries as FRG, Portugal, Latin America, Pakistan, etc. Discusses resource sharing in India in detail upto the INFLIBNET. Concludes that in view of the inadequate finances, resource sharing is needed more.

KORALE, S R 669

An overview of medical literature resources in Sri Lanka, *ML*, 211-229.

Outlines development and growth of medical institutions and

facilities. Identifies user categories and user demand. Introduces HELLIS Sri Lanka, a network set up under WHO, concerned with shairing of resources. Provides absence of any core list of midical journals, hence need to develop such a list for guidance. Focuses on te need for close cooperation and coordination between medical libraries.

PANDAY, S P 670

Resources sharing amongst medical libraries in Bihar and their networking, *ITAH*, 235-241.

Makes a survey of 11 medical libraries in Bihar. Explains the concept and scope of resource sharing. States that need for resource sharing comes from the rapid growth of informaiton centres and literature, the capacity of storage, financial constraints, and rise in the cost of publication. Discusses the importance of resource sharing and need for developing a network of medical libraries in Bihar.

RAKHAKRISHNA MURTHY, S 671

Sharing of information resources through inter-library loan and other facilities, *ML*, 285-293.

Explains that resource sharing through ILL and photocopying facilities among health science libraries will solve some problems of the requirements of scientists. Discusses need for and advantages of resource sharing. Suggests few guidelines for better resource sharing programme. Also suggests ILL facilities, policies and proposals for photocopying. Describes few international resource sharing networks in India and the world.

RAINA, ROSHAN 672

Resource sharing and cooperation, *Her Lib Sci* 32 (3-4) July-Oct 1993: 248-251.

Reports about the meeting of the librarians of all the four IIMs to discuss various issues related to 'Resource sharing and cooperation', among them, on 26-27 June 1993. Mentions about the Business Session, discussion and the various recommendations made in this regard.

RESOURCE sharing in petroleum sector libraries: 673

IOC National convention, *NISSAT Newsletter* 11(2) Apr-June 1992: 3-4.

Reports about the two day convention of the libraries in the petroleum sector in India organised by the Indian Oil Corporation in New Delhi during Apr 9-10, 1992. Mentions its aims, inauguration and participation. Discusses that six technical sessions were organised and papers suggested different methods for resource sharing. Mentions the recommendations emerged out of the two day Convention.

RAJAN, A C 674

Resource sharing among college libraries in Kerala, *RDAL*, 44-52.

Explains need and purpose of resource sharing. Discusses important components of resource sharing, facilities available, pre-conditions, problems, development stages etc. Proposes resource sharing in arts and science colleges in Kerala, with proposed areas of operation. Discusses role of UGC and INFLIBNET.

SATPATHI, J N 675

Resource sharing of periodicals among the medical and bio-medical libraries in Calcutta, *Isalic Bull* 37 (1) Mar 1992: 15-21.

Points out that there are more than 40 medical libraries in Calcutta which procure multiple copies of costly foreign journasls but still can't satisfy all the users needs. Makes a case for resource sharing by forming a network of libraries which enable to avoid duplication and also acquire other important journals without extra expenditure. Discusses essential features of network.

021.7 PUBLIC RELATIONS

BAKIGHIR, DOMINIC A G 676

Public relations in university libraries in Nigeria, *Int Lib Move* 14 (1) Mar 1992: 12-18.

Defines public relations (PR). Discusses PR in university libraries in Nigeria where the audience is the public at campus, the general public, and the university libraries' PR with other libraries. Stresses on the need for good PR for quality service.

ISAAC, DOROTHY 677

Public relations in academic libraries, *ALR*, 153-160.

Discusses about higher education and role of academic libraries. Discusses the role of public relations (PR) in academic libraries for their full potential and improvement of services. Mentions need for PR. Discusses techniques for promotion and PR. States that PR efforts can strengthen the image of the library and staff morale.

JAGGA RAO, N V and PRAFULLA CHANDRA, T V 678

Role of public relations in university libraries, *ALR*, 183-195.

Explains PR. Mentions need for PR. Discusses planning of PR with a six point model. Describes the organisation of PR department in university library, and the activities to be taken up by it. Calls for launching 'Friends of the Library' movement enlisting private support for various programmes.

SANGAM, S L and KONNUR, P V 679

Public relations activities in Karnataka State public libraries, *Ialsic Bull* 38 (4) Dec 1993: 169-173.

Discusses the importance of PR activities in furthering the effectiveness of the services rendered by public libraries. Proposes a scheme of PR activities for Karnataka public library system including advertising and publicity, multimedia, extension and educational activites. Stresses the need for proper training of public library staff regarding PR activities to make them capable of communicationg the essence of the library to their clientele.

022.3 LIBRARY BUIDDINGS

PLANNING AND DESIGN

DORAN, BEATRICE M 680

Key to access: The flexible library building, *ML*, 125-129.

Mentions that to the traditional three essential components-personnel, colleciton, and reading facilities - of library building, a fourth component, technology, has been added. Defines a flexible library building. Discusses the new medical library building, shape and size, flexible space management, floor loading, designing facilities for high technology future with computer, CD-ROM, E-mail, flexible environment for future.

SANKARAIAH, K 681

Physical conditions in academic libraries, *RDAL*, 1-7.

Sets out the important general principles of planning which aim at ensuring physical conditions in libraries conducive to growth consisted with their aims and academic objectives, their efficient functioning, and the good services.

SIEVANEN-ALLEN, RITVA 682

Library space as a key to aceess, *ML*, 435-438.

Identifies main factors causing changes in the housing of books through the ages. Relates the functions of a library. Discusses the open access plan in library buildings with reference to planning the medical library. Discusses the future of the library in view of the paperless society.

022.3172 University Library Buildings

DESHMUKH, P P 683

Planning and design of university library building, *IJALIS* 21, 1993: 16-25.

Gives guidelines for planning a library building. Emphasises that a healthy collaboration of librarian and architect will result in a beautiful and functional building. Gives norms for site selection. Provides guidelines for planning and interior, ventilation, air conditioning, lighting. Discusses locations of various sections. Gives a sketch plan of Punjabrao Krishi Vidyapeeth, Akola.

HEMASUNDER NAIDU, G and GUNJAL, S R 684

Agricultural library buildings and their structure in India, *Her Lib Sci* 32 (3-4) July-Oct 1993: 190-198.

Emphasizes role of library building in rendering effective service. Reveals that about 40% of the agricultural libraries possessed independent library buildings. Works out the areas utilised for various functions. Suggests that libraries housed in non-functionsal buildings should plan for new library buildings.

022.9 Library Equipment, Furniture, etc.

SUBBARAO, C V 685

Library furniture case study, *Lib Her* 31 (1-2) Apr-Sep 1992: 42-44.

Narrates as to how librarian faced a situation of new racks with fixed shelves against professional demands of adjustable shelves. Points out nuts and bolts catalogue card cabinet was rejected as it could not accommodate 5"x3" cards. Points out unhelpful attitude and non-cooperation of the administrative powers resulting in the better qualified librarian to move to another institution.

023 HUMAN RESOURCE DEVELOPMENT. LIBRARY PERSONNEL. MANPOWER DEVELOPMENT. STAFFING PERSONNEL MANAGEMENT

CHAKRABARTY, BIPUL KUMAR 686

Information manpower-strategic issues for development, *Ialsic Bull* 38 (2) June 1993: 67-72.

Analyses the demand for library and information workers during 1988 as advertised in five national dailies. Stresses the need for training the suitable manpower by laying greater emphasis on IT and information management to meet the present day needs.

CHATTERJEE, AMITABHA 687

Human source development for library automation in India, *LIT*, 307-311.

Emphasises upon the need for developing suitable human resources for library automation in view of the computer and networks making their way into library and information centres. Outlines course contents for suitable training.

COMBA, VALENTINA 688

Managing library staff in an Italian medical library, *ML*, 93-96.

Aims to discuss the human resources, salaries of staff in the university medical library and in the national health service. Offers various suggestions about the staffing in the Italian medical libraries. Concludes that in spite of lack of motivation and low salaries, creative solutions are possible.

DEO, V N and VAISHNAV, A A 689

Central job market and L & I S curricula: A pragmatic study, *LIS*, 55-64.

Attempts to profile various facets of manpower demands in libraries and information centres which can show market demand or current job market. Indicates the complimentary role the educational institutions should play in implementing new courses.

DESIDOC, DELHI 690

Manpower development activities, *DESIDOC Bull Inf Tech* 11 (2) Mar 1991: 3-6.

Presents the activities, programmes and achievements of DESIDOC in the area of manpower development for which it has arranged training programmes, seminars and conferences, professional lectures, technical advice and consultancy.

DEVARAJAN, G 691

Manpower resorces in university libraries in Kerala: A survey, *RDAL*, 103-110.

Discusses universities and university libraries in higher education. Describes the relevance of manpower in university libraries and role of INFLIBNET. Discusses higher education and university libraries in Kerala. Analyses data collected from published and unpublished sources regarding qualifications, manpower positions. Estimates prospective requirements of manpower

GOEL, PREETI 692

Academic librarians in India: An overview, *Univ News* 30 (35) Aug 31, 1992: 57-61.

Outlines the academic institutions in India which have libraries and are considered as heart of the university's work. Gives their organisational structure. Discusses the status, pay scales and qualifications of academic librarians in India. Describes the librarian's position in an academic library. States that to solve multidimensional problems of libraries, librarians have to acquire managerial ability and professional skills.

MAHAPATRA, KEDARNATH 693

Qualitative development of human resources in librarianship, *LIT*, 283-288.

States that workforce management is essential for achieving productivity and efficiency. Advocates for quality culture in library, communication system is essential factor of human resource development. Discusses human relations leadership style, human resource training, and motivation which contribute to employee satisfaction.

MAHESWARAPPA, B S and SALMANI, G K 694

The demand for library and information workers in India: A content analysis of job advertisements during 1990, *Iaslic Bull* 38 (2) June 1993: 73-83.

Studies the demand for library and information workers and the employers' expectations based on the content analysis of 477 vacancies in five major newspapers. Concludes that the findings have implications for LIS education and training in India especially in bringing the mismatch between the type of products coming out of library schools, and the employment trends and the employers'expectations.

MURALIKRISHNA, C 695

Manpower planning in university libraries, New Delhi: Ess Ess Publications, 1993. iv, 142 p.

Includes five chapters on the important subject of manpower planning which include introductory chapter about the significance of the manpower in university libraries. Discusses about the methodology used to collect data, manpower planning in university libraries, workload of manpower is analysed, and conclusions derived. Offers some useful suggestions.

PENLAND, PATRICK R and MATHAI, ALEYAMMA 696

Academic librarian development, *ALD*, 22-30.

Explains the need for staff development in academic libraries for expanded informational and educational service and products. Defines staff burnout, its components and causes, and it must be reduced to minimum. Describes growth of knowledge and IT and their merger leading to changes in information environment. Concludes by offering suggestions so as to increase staff effectiveness.

PULLA REDDY, V 697

Importance ranking of incentives by professionals working in colleges and university libraries: A survey, *Iaslic Bull* 37 (2) June 1992: 55-65.

Analyses data collected using a questionnaire from a random sample of professional staff working in college and university libraries of Delhi. Reveals four top incentive factors: Recognition of work done, Good opportunity for promotion, Treating the work of professional staff at par with academic staff, and Adequate earning. Reveals that there is statistically significant agreement in the rank order of incentive items among various sub groups of librarians.

PULLA REDDY, V 698

Professional developmental activities of librarians working in university and special libraries of Andhra Pradesh, *LID*, 87-105.

Outlines objectives of study as reading of professional journals by librarian participation in seminars/conferences, etc, contribution to professional knowledge in articles and books, and to find out the differences between librarians working in university and special libraries in Andhra Pradesh. Analyses data collected from 195 librarians. Gives summary of conclusions. Offers suggestions for future research.

RAMAN NAIR, R 699

Human resource planning and development for automated library and information systems, *LIT*, 289-301.

Mentions about computer and automated library and informationl system in which human element is important. Gives functions and composition of ALIS in relation to manpower. Explains need for manpower development for which syllabus may be redesigned. Mentions the existing study facilities. Touches upon manpower relation, status and position.

RATH, PRAVAKAR 700

Staffing pattern for a State Central Library under the public library system, *IPLA Souvenir*, 6 p.

Deals with the need for planning a library system, public library system and its structure. Discusses role of State Central Library, organisational set up of a SCL, staffing pattern for each division/unit and its formula. Gives conclusions.

REWADIKAR, SHALINI 701

Staff development in university libraries in India; plans and prospects, *Univ News* 30 (35) Aug 31,1992: 125-128.

Stresses the need for staff and its education. Describes the changing demands on librarianship, while there are still conflicting views on librarianship. Discusses the information environment for which there is need to update the knowledge, skills and competence of staff. Outlines the staff development plan and the programmes on computer application and netwroks for the new challenges. Also mentions the future directions.

SATARKAR, S P 702

Staffing pattern in academic college libraries in Maharashtra: Review and recommendations, *Luck Libn* 24 (3) July-Sept 1992: 108-113.

Traces history of college libraries in Maharashtra. States that college libraries are growing fast in respect of collection and number of readers. Mentions that adequate staff often are not available to deal with the increasing load of work. Reviews all staff formulas, makes comments and suggests a new formula for consideration.

SEWA SINGH 703

Library and information manpower problems and prospects: A literature survey, *Jl Lib & Inf Sci* 16 (2) Dec 1991: 169-180.

Analyses the library and information science literature on LIS manpower on the basis of a survey which includes journals, bibliographic databases, monographs, dissertations and theses, and seminar/conference papers. Concludes that proliferation of literature on the subject is about a decade old. Brings out the role of professional associations and other organisations in this regard.

SHARMA, LOKESH 704

Psychological perspectives of library professionals, Delhi: Sahitya Kendra Prakashan, 1992.

Deals with the psychological problems, attitude and approach of the library and information professionals towards their jobs, and job opportunities. Gives interesting studies and findings which should be taken care of in the libraries of different sizes so as to increase the efficiency of staff.

SINGH, DEV RAJ 705

Career pattern of university library professionals in India, *Jl Lib & Info Sci* 18 (2)Dec 1993: 154-176.

Identifies different library positions held by professionals so far. Analyses career mobility of professionals in terms of their inter-organisational, interstate, intra-state, mobility and factors influencing mobility. Examines extent of upward mobility attained by the professionals in their career.

SINGH, DEV RAJ 706

A comparative study of career advancement of library professionals in university libraries in Punjab, Haryana, Madhya Pradesh and Uttar Pradesh, *Lib Her* 31 (1-2) Apr-Sep 1992: 65-71.

Presents the summary of Ph D thesis of the author submitted to the University of Delhi. Studies the professionals in the university libraries in four states in their socio-economic context to exam such issues as motivation behind their occupational choice, their commitment to the profession, channels of entry to university library set up, job mobility pattern, etc.

SINGH, DEV RAJ 707

Librarianship as a career, *Jl Lib & Info Sci* 18 (1) Jun 1993: 43-65.

Analyses different sources and factors which have motivated university library professionals to choose librarianship as a career. Concludes that inter personal sources were instrumental in the decision of a university libray professional to join librarianship, however, with secondary occupational choice, but does not like his offsprings, kith and kin to follow in his footsteps.

SINGH, DEV RAJ 708

University library professionals: Some sociological aspects, *Jl Lib & Inf Sci* 17 (2) Dec 1992: 158-181.

Analyses socio-economic and demographic data collected through questionnaire from 261 professionals employed in university libraries of Punjab, Haryana, UP and MP. Examines intergenerational mobility. Concludes that a university libray professional is a male of 47, and is married, entered profession at the age of 25, born in uppercaste Hindu community to an undergraduate father, and is in better occupation than his father.

SINGH, N GIRIDHARI 709

Development of manpower of the university and post graduate centre libraries in the North Eastern region of India, *LIN*, 67-74.

Explains the manpower planning and development in 7 university and 2 PG centre libraries in the NE region. Describes some human factors effecting manpower development on the basis of interviews and observations, including policy making, training facilities, brain storming, human relation, job description, etc. Concludes that Library Advisory Committees at state and regional level formed to advice library authorites to raise image of library services.

SUBBA RAO, C V 710

Chattopadhyaya Review Committee recommendations, *Her Lib Sci* 31 (1-2) Jan-Apr 1992: 91.

Reports about the recasting of the points and the items of work about the anamolies in the 'Recommendations and the Categorisation Table' of the Review Committee. The Discussion Group found the analysis on right lines.

SUBRAMONI, T K 711

Induction: An often neglected aspect of library personnel management, *Luck Libn* 24 (4) Oct-Dec 1992: 144-148.

States that present day senior librarians are senior managers also, so they are also concerned with management of staff. States that successful personnel managment in a library results in user satisfaction, achieving the objectives of the organisation and job satisfaction for the staff.

VARALAKSHMI, R S R 712

Emerging trends in academic libraries and changing role of manpower, *RDAL*, 95-102.

Attempts to examine some of the dominant influences on academic library environments of education, IT and netwroking. Discusses the manpower requirements to suit the changing trends of information society.

VENKATARAMANA, V 713

Manpower pattern and inadequacies of Indian university libraries, *IJILIS* 6 (1-2) Jan-June 1993: 49-57.

Describes the development of libraries with the establishment of higher education institutions and universities, and for manpower in libraries various standards have been established, but libraries are planned neither according to the staff formulae of the UGC nor staff standards are worked on scientific lines. States that adhocism and haphazard recruitment are seriously affecting service-oriented information dissemination in university libraries. Analyses existing manpower pattern, and suggests meaningful planning for the growing information needs of the changing world.

023 (1) Academic Status. Professional Status

AWOGBAMI, POPOOLA A 714

Full academic status for Nigerial librarians: An agenda for the 21st century, *Int Lib Move* 15 (1) Mar 1993: 33-40.

Determines the reactions of all types of Nigerial academic librarians towards academic status based on a questionnaire. Concludes that librarians were supportive of faculty status, though some still dissented.

KEERAN, K M 715

Status of health science librarians in Tamil Nadu, *ITAH*, 153-159.

Points out that the present position of health librarians and library service is most critical. Gives present proposed qualifications for librarians. Calls for change of designation from 'librarian' to 'Medical Library & Information Officer'. Deals with the low status of librarian who is not a member of any committee. With his low salary there are no promotional appointments, and this leads to low status of library. Makes suggestions to solve the problems that are being faced by medical librarians fo Tamil Nadu.

SINGH, DEV RAJ 716

Academic status for university and college librarians, *Lib Her* 30 (1) Apr 1991: 20-29.

Makes out a case for academic status. Discusses the recommendations of Ranganathan Committee. Describes the position during Fourth Five Year Plan. Mentions the beginning of disparity with Third Pay Commission and its restoration. Discusses Merit Promotion scheme and recommendation of Mehrotra Committee. Suggests that librarians should work towards social acceptance.

023 (1) STAFF FORMULA

KAMAIAH, P 717

Staff formulas and standards in assessing the staff strengths and categorization in the university - a critical study, *CS*, 118-131.

Presents the staff formula of Ranganathan and the UGC. Includes guidelines for appointing professional staff. Considers the standards for professional staff in UK and Canada. Examines staff pattern of UGC. Analyses critically the problems of implementing staff formulas and classification of professional positions in the university libraries in India.

LAHIRI, RAMANSU 718

The human side of the library: In search of a model; a brief study on North East, *Her Lib Sci* 32 (3-4) July-Oct 1993: 199-203.

States the limitations of manpower in providing qualitative service. Observs that exsiting staff pattern has always been neither appropriate nor realistic in the context of the complex nature of service required today. Presents a model for conducting studies in differenct backgrounds and regions in that a standard staff formula can be framed according to the needs of the time.

MALHAN, I V and ALI, G 719

Desired professional competence and psychological traits of professional librarians as perceived by teachers and postgraduate students of Jammu University, *Luck Libn* 25 (1-2) Mar-Jun 1993: 45-51.

Presents opinion of 100 teachers and students of Jammu University regarding the qualities, qualifications and role of a librarian. Analyses statistically weightage given to various parametrs of professional competence and psychological traits. Interprets major findings of the analysis.

PULLA REDDY, V 720

An enquiry into the incentives for professional staff working in college and university libraries, *LID*, 106-123.

Mentions some studies done already on incentives for employees. Makes effort to know the relative importance of incentive items as perceived by the professional staff working in college and university libraries in Delhi. Gives analysis of data collected through questionnaire. Discusses each item of incentive such as recognition of work done, opportunity for promotion, work at par with academic staff, adequate earning, job security, training facilities, and so on.

023.8 Inservice Training

KANKACHARY, M and MORE, S 721

Computerisation of public libraries in India: Manpower development through in service training, *Luck Libn* 24 (4) Oct- Dec 1992: 133-137.

Explains the main components of computerisation of library and information system. Stresses the need and necessiety of manpower. Emphasizes the in-service training. Suggests a methodology for conducting training programmes for computer applications in public library system.

023.9 Job Analysis and Job Classification

BAKIGHIR, DOMINIC A G 722

Regular performance assessment of librarians in developing countries, *Int Lib Move* 15 (2) June 1993: 46-52.

Defines performance assessment. Mentions need and

importance of performance assessment of library in developing countries by ascertaining whether the staff have been assigned to the right jobs, and which units each staff is most suited.

BARMAN, RAJNI KANTA 723

Job analysis and job classification in university library personnel administration, *LIN*, 23-38.

Defines job, job analysis, job description, job specification. Discusses purporposes of job classification, its advantages and areas in university library. Gives UGC categories of library personnel. Mentions the jobs to be performed suggested by staff Inspection Unit of Ministry of Finance. Examines various types of designations found in the university libraries of North East region. Concludes that a precise classification is vital for proper and smooth running of university library.

023.9 (1) Library Ethics

Professional Ethics. Code of Conduct/Ethics

GURUSWAMY NAIDU, N 724

Professional ethics: An end or erosion, *ALR*, 161-169.

Explains 'ethics' and code of ethics. States that in the professional circle it is a forgotton area. Mentions that equation with other professions sometimes is fatal to the profession, but says that librarians are not saints. States that though Ranganathan did not use the term 'ethics' in his writings, but his whole life was full of it and he practised it, but now the models are changing. Enumerates the Code of Ethics accepted by the American Library Association in 1938.

023.9 (1) Job Performance

PULLA REDY, V 725

Job preferences in university and special libraries, *Lib Sci slant Docum & Inf Std* 30 (1) Mar 1993: 6-10.

Analyses data collected from a random sample consisting of 183 professional staff working in university and special libraries, reveals their first preference to referecne work. Reveals that there is considerable agreement statistically in the order of preference of jobs among various sub-groups of professional staff.

STANLEY, M K 726

Hurdles in performance appraisal, *IJALIS* 20, 1992: 37-44.

Explains purpose of performance appraisal to facilitate changes in individual behaviour to stimulate achievement in goals. Criteria for effective and ineffective performance are frequently difficult to define. These hurdles are unavoidable. Discusses appraisal techniques. Gives evaluation of performance appraisal techniques.

023.9 (1) Staff Qualifications

SINGH, DEV RAJ 727

Library professinals' response towards need for enhancing qualifications: An analysis, *ILA Bull* 28 (3-4) Oct- Mar 1993: 61-73.

Analyses responses collected through questionnaire from 261 professionals working in university libraries of Punjab, Haryana, UP and MP. Examines their qualifications at entry point and improvement in it thereafter and their views to enhance it in furture. Concludes that in university libraries they have improved their qualifications during service.

023.9 (1) Recruitment

GURUSWAMY NAIDU, N 728

Composition of the staff: A forgotton factor, *CS*, 110-117.

States that supporting staff in univertsity libraries is dominating compared to professionals, and the imbalance is an immediate threat to the organisation culture of the library automation notwithstanding. Identifies factors responsible for the imbalance. Emphasizes to have a staff recruitment policy.

025 DOCUMENTATION. INFORMATION

ASUNDI, A Y 729

System of information organisation for national development with reference to India, *CS*, 95-109.

Explains importance of information organisation for national development in India. Highlights different dimensions of global changes. Gives broad categories, forms of presentation of information, major organisations providing information and data for planning and the structure of statsitical system of India.

BADIANE, EL HADJ MALICK 730

Decentralizing public health literature: The case of the Senegaleese experience, *ML*, 29-30.

Gives importance of the role of information and documentation in improving health staff competencies. Gives justification of the decentralisation of information. Discusses the process of decentralization in three stages, viz., the analysis of the situation; the setting up; the evaluation and the follow up of the program.

BANERJEE, S B 731

Information communication management in industries: Strategic issues, *ALIS*, V 4, 83-102.

States that industries are the instruments for structural change and economic developement. Tries to draw attention of administrators, planners, and decision makers for considering information as a key element in decision making. Attempts to bring into help a conflicting situation that persists with regard to its availabiliry, accessibility and use.

CURRAS, EMILIA 732

Information science - information as a dialectic interactive sytem, *COP*, 419-431.

Statess that now a days we refer to the information era and the information society, hence need to study the theoretical basis of information. Provides a brief summary of the theory of information from the 80s . Defines information as a phenomena and as a process. Mentions how, from personal ideas, information is derived and becomes information science. Discusses the systematic approach of information. Establishes dialectic inter-relations of both system to know clearly the concepts and behaviour.

DUTT, K L 733

Documentation of Indian literature: The pioneering role of Sahitya Academi, *DAB*, 278-284.

Mentions objectives of Sahitya Academi and the projects in hand. Discusses about the National Bibliography of Indian Literature and its compilation, scope, objectives, etc. Also discusses about other documentation activities such as cumulative index to Indian Literature, mimeographed series of catalogues, Indian literary index. Mentions about the on-going projects.

HABLE, M K 734

Right to information: A sine qua non for democracy, *The Hindu*, 13 Oct 1992: 17.

Explains the importance of information, and the right to

information stems from the right to know. States that right to information provides opportunity to have information from the public authority. Describes the right to information as sine qua non for democracy.

HOLZL, J 735

Cognitive modelling of technology information, *COP*, 139-145.

Mentions information is one of the three elementary factors of technology and thus essential. Discusses the role information plays for communication in technical land economic areas. States that Information Management is must for handling today's flood of information. Discusses application of technology and product databanks. Displays the fast growing importance of online and CD-ROM databases. Introduces INPADOC in Vienna as an exchange of technical and product research. Mentions difficulties also.

JOSHI, S C 736

Role of information in the twentyfirst century, *Ann Lib Sci & Docum* 39 (3)Sept 1992: 94-100.

Explains the phenomena of information explosion taking place currently. Defines information and gives its characteristics. States that it is an indispensable resoruce. Discusses impact of technology on information and the emergence of information technology and micrographics. Forecasts that in the 21st centruy there may be paperless society and 'wire city'.

KUMAR, P S G 737

Ranganathan's contribution to documentation, *DL*, 29-35.

Describes Ranganathan's contribution to the field of documentation in the demarcation of documentation activity, facets of documentation, preparation of various kinds of documentation lists. Discusses documentation activities throught such organisations as FID, BIS, INSDOC, DRTC.

PARTHASARATHY, S 738

Ranganathan and documentation in India, *Jl Lib & Inf Sci* 17 (1) June 1992: 33-38.

Mentions SR Ranganathan as a builder of institutions. Describes his work/role in the formulation of standards for documentation. Gives background leading to the establishment of INSDOC, and DRTC. Concludes that the impact of Ranganathan on the development of documentation activities in India has been considerable.

RAMAIAH, L S 739

Humanism and the need for documentation, *DAB*, 38-42.

Traces the tradition of humanities. Gives the scope of humanities. Provides definition of humanities with the subjects of study. States that humanistic studies are based on libraries and books. Points out the need for Documentation Centre in arts and humanities. Concludes that as the National Library of India is not adequate, a national centre for arts and humanities should be set up

RAMAIAH, L S and KANKACHARY, M *Eds* 740

Documentation and bibliographic control of the humanities in India, New Delhi: Aditya Prakashan, 1992. xv, 349 p.

Discusses the present position of the humanities, their importance, and the state of their bibliographical control. Includes 33 papers divided into 8 sections relating to the importance of the humanities, classification schedule for humanities, problems and prospects, institutional profiles and documentation and bibliographical centres proposals. Gives three appendices. It is dedicated to Padamshri S R Ranganathan in his contenary year.

RAY, DIPAK KUMAR and CHAUDHURI, ARUNA 741

The multiple role of logical approach in the information, *IJILIS* 5 (1-2) Jan-June 1992: 72-77.

Deals with the role of logic in informaion, information representation. Describes that logic helps in library network technology, search service network, logical information base, language and concepts, and so on.

SEETHARAMA, S 742

Towards an information centred society in developing countries, *LID*, 3-15.

Highlights information environs in developing countries where information flow is not smoth and compatible to users needs. States that in order to achieve 'Inormation for All by 2000' integrated effort of different groups of users as Government, information users, information professionals, is needed. Explains the role of information professionals in putting knowledge into action by way of LIS education and research; design of appropriate information services and products; marketing of information; application of IT; resource sharing; professional ethics.

SENADHIRA, ADRIAN 743

WHO generated information: Production, distribution, bibliographic control and retrieval, *ML*, 503-508.

Deals with the WHO generated information made available through a range of publications and unpublished material produced at WHO headquarters and regional office. Discusses also the CIP, the basic guides and tools for retrieving WHO publications and documents.

SURYANARAYANA, Y V and RAMAN, M 744

Library and documentation services at Central Tobacco Research Institute, Rajamundry, *IJALIS* 20, 1992: 24-31.

Discusses in detail objectives and activities of library and documentation services at CTRI, Rajamundry. Gives briefly achievements of the library in providing library and documentation services during 1987-91. Discusses various information services, computerisation activities, resource sharing, reprographic services, Institute's research publications and distribution, CTRI Research stations libraries development, staff position, etc.

TYAGI, K G 745

The challenges in the access to information in South Asia, *ALR*, 239-245.

Explains need for free flow of information in South Asia in view of its meagre resources. States the data in social sciences is more complex therefore there is need for databases in social science literature. Makes a case for need for regional cooperation and networking in these countries and need for manpower training programmes which will help in enhancing information access.

VAISHNAV, A A and BAPAT, N G 746

Software for local documentation list in MUL, *LIT*, 157-170.

Points out that to meet the information needs of users, a modern library has to think of such information services as CAS, Reference service, location service, etc. Describes the local documentation list of Marathawada University Library. States the need for computerisation of local documentation lists and the software developed for it.

VIJAYAKUMAR, K P 747

Library publications and their production, *Her Lib Sci* 31 (3-4) July-Oct 1992: 174-179.

Discusses the need for bringing out library publications. Examines various types of publications brought out by libraries, their characteristic features, and method of arrangement of items. Gives useful hints on the typographical layout and production. Mentions also BIS standards for preparation and layout of publications.

VISWANATHAN, T and JOSEPH, A 748

Cost containment of information products and services, *ML*, PC 21-34.

States the importance of information as essential ingredient for development of nations but the cost of information is rising. Mentions that time has come to find means to contain costs of information products and services. Discusses such ways and meansof cost containment of such information services as abstracting and indexing services, print products, online databases, optical media products. Catalogue services, and document copy supply. Presents library coopeation, information sharing networks, E-mail systems, and electronic publishing as major cost saving measures.

025 (1) Information/Paperless Society

BANKAPUR, M B and KUMBAR, MILINATH 749

The concept of paperless society, *IJALIS* 21, 1993: 46-48.

Mentions the growing importance of information. States that with development in communication and printing technology books and journals are available in machine readable form and also online. There is a growing concern that paper will cease to be medium of storage and transfer of information making present day libraries redundant. The present day 'Information Society' is paving way for a 'Paperless Society', but optimists argue that inspite of technological breakthrough paper will continue to be the preferred medium for storage and communication of information.

025 (1) Information Policy

FOLDI, TAMAS 750

Information policy and transition to the market economy, *INICAE* 12 (1) Mar 1992: 5-17.

States that government has in the planned economy direct control over the information system and large scale producer of information. Points out that a transition from planned economy to market economy is narrowing the role of government in information field. The compositon of information suppliers undergoes many changes. Stresses the need for a broad based information environ under post-communism. Describes the main tasks of informatiion policy in the transformation process including devlopment of technology infrastructure, E & T of information specialists, etc.

025 (1) Information Explosion

BALASUBRAMANIAN, ALLADI SARADA 751

On information explosion, *DESIDOC Bull Inf Tech* 11 (5) Sept 1991: 3-8.

Mentions that the rat-race among scientists has led to indiscriminate publishing of scientific literature resulting in an incontrollable explosion of scientific literature. States that scientists in the world are devising ways and means of arresting this flood of publications. Examines a few suggestions in details, chief among which is the vital role played by the editors of archival journals in sifting the more important from the less significant publications.

025 (1) Documentation and Information Centres

PAREKH, HARSHA 752

UGC's information centres, *Univ News* 30 (35) Aug 31, 1992: 87-91.

Discusses about the services of the UGC's information centres, particularly the two centres, at Bangalore the National Science Information Centre (IISc), and at Bombay the National Information Centre (SNDT Women's University). Describes their current awareness, document delivery, retrospective search, referral, training, etc. Mentions about the future plans also.

SRINIVASLU, P 753

Andhra Pradesh Information centres - tools and communications, *IPLA Scouvenir*, No 17, 2 p.

Deals with the crucial role the Information Centres play in the communication of information in the state at various levels. Describes the set up of Information Centres in AP and their District Information Centres. Explains their activities of maintaining a reading room and meeting the needs of adult education programmes.

025 (1) ACML

KALANDER, SULAIMAN 754

The role of "Arab Centre for Medical Literature" (ACML) in the promotion of medical information systems and services in the Arab world, *ML*, 201-206.

Gives historical background of Arab Centre for Medical Literature setup in May 1981. Mentions its objectives. Discusses the use of Arabic language in the medical fields and translation of world literature in Arabic. Discusses the medical information activities and services. Mentions ACML's printing, publishing and distribution activities. Makes a case for the setting up of "Arab Medical Information Network" to cover all these activities.

025 (1) Centre on Rural Documentation

RAJU, K A 755

Centre on Rural Documentation - a profile, *ILS*, 3 p.

Traces genesis of Centre on Rural Documentation (CORD). Elucidates its objectives and functions. Deals with the resource base of CORD, its documentation activities, publications, computerisation with the help of NIC. Discusses perspective of CORD.

025 (1) IARIC

BORAIYAN R 756

International Agricultural Research Information Centres - an outlook, *Lib Prog* (*Int*) 12 (1-2) Jan-Dec 1992: 17-25.

Elucidates the major objectives of International Agricultural Research institutes. Gives outline of day to day activities of information centres affiliated to the research institutes of agriculture, forstry, cassava and field beans, dryland agriculture, maize and wheat, rich, semiarid tropical crops, etc. Discusses their library and information services. Concludes that an integrated information on agriculture effort is needed. Concludes that an integrated information on agriculture effort is needed to expand the quality and quantity of information on agricultural research.

025 (1) Indian Council of Humanities Research

SOMARAJU, P 757

Indian Council of Humanities Research (ICHR): A national plan, *DAB*, 297-303.

Describes importance of information in human endeavour in modern world so that information source documents be developed. Defines humanities with its subject coverage. Discusses problems of bibliographic control in humanities in India. Makes a case for the setting up of an ICHR which will serve as a national apex body. Mentions its aims and functions. Gives cetain conclusions.

025 (1) ICSSR - Southern Regional Centre

KHAN, MASOOD ALI 758

ICSSR - Southern Regional Centre and its documentation services in regional languages, *ILS*, 2 p.

Describes the documentation services in social sciences offered by the ICSSR - Southern Regional Centre. Provides bibliographies in regional languages, indexes of articles from Telugu and Urdu periodicals and newspapers, indexes of articles on women from Telugu and Urdu sources.

025 (1) INIS

BALAKRISHNAN, M R 759

INIS: A computer based international nuclear information system *ALIS*, V 4, 31-64.

Mentions need for a computerised based information system. Explains the beginning and functioning of INIS. Identifies scientific and technical literature published within the country and output activities. Deals with the conventional and non-conventional data in which IAEA is interested. Gives also information about its liasion with other international databases through online and magnetic tapes.

025 (1) Institute of Ethiopian Studies - Documentation Centre

GUPTA, SUSHMA 760

Institute of Ethiopian Documentaion Centre for Research on Ethiopian Studies, *Int Lib Move* 15 (4) Dec 1993: 198-208.

Traces brief history of the Institute. Provides aims and objectives of the Institute. Describes various activities of the Institute which comprise of publication and organising conferences and seminars. Makes suggestions for further improvement by performing its functions more effictively and by compiling various bibliographies, indexes, etc.

025 (1) INSDOC

INDIAN National Scientific Documentation Centre, New Delhi, S&T activities: 1991-92, *CSIR News* 43 (6) Jan30, 1993: 78-80. 761

Describes about the growth and development of Indian National Scientific Documentation Centre, New Delhi. Discusses about its various services offered to its users. Mentions about the information products prepared by it. Points out its automation programmes and future plans.

INSDOC is forty, *NISSAT Newletter* 11 (2) Apr- June 1992: 7. 762

Describes that on 20 March 1992 INSDOC celebrated 40 years of its formation. Discusses the activities arranged to celebrate the occasion. Prof M S Swaminathan deliveered the Foundation day lectue on 'Information Technology and National Nutrition Security'. Mr N Vittal, Secretary, DOE, delivered the Keynote address. Dr S K Joshi, Directory General, CSIR, presided over the function.

025 (1) NACSIS

INOSE, HIROSHI 763

Activities of National Centre for Science Information Systems, *INICAE 11* (1) Mar 1992: 81-95.

States the objectives of NACSIS established in April 1986. Describes its organization, library network connections, information retrieval services containing 36 kinds of databases, E-mail service, electronic bulletin board system and electronic developmental activities.

INOSE, HIROSHI 764

The National Centre for Science Information Systems: Services and activities, *INICAE 11* (2) Sept 1992: 252-255.

Gives the genesis of NACSIS and its establishement for promoting its status to inter-university research institute and renamed as NACSIS in 1986. Describes its initial activities, operation of network, database service, activities base on research, its education programmes, information retrieval service, etc.

OHNO, KIMIO 765

Future possibilities of NACSIS services abroad, *INICAE* 11 (2) Sept 1992: 258-261.

Discusses about the international circulation of academic information throught NACSIS in the area of cataloguing information services, information retrieval services, E-mail service, secience information network, etc. Concludes that NACSIS intends to explore the future possibilities of services abroad.

025 (1) NASSDOC

KAUL, INDIRA 766

Use of information technology in social science documentation services with special reference to NASSDOC, *CTIT*, 167-176.

States the need of communication of social science information. Describes the role of NASSDOC (of ICSSR) in information communication and designing of its services, products, etc. Describes the development of local databases on locially available materials and databases acquired in NASSDOC. Points out impediments and gives suggestions.

025 (1) NHDC

RAY, ROMA 767

National Humanities Documentation Centre: An alternate model, *DAB*, 315-319.

Explains humanities. Describes the Indian scenario of humanities development, and the need for the establishement of a NHDC. Points out the growth of archives for preserving the records produced by government. States this to be important task of NHDC. Proposes the alternate model of NHDC.

YADGIRI REDDY, J and RAMAIAH, L S 768

Source and services in the humanities: A proposal for NHDC, *Jl Lib & Inf Sci* 17 (2) Dec 1992: 182-190.

Defines humanities. States that documentation and bibliographic activities in humanities are less despite information explosion in this area. Pleads for the establishement of a National Humanities Documentation Centre (NHDC) in order to remedy the situation of bibliographic control. Discusses objectives and functions of the model for the proposed centre.

025 (1) NICIPA

RANA, M S 769

Nationa Information Centre for Indian Protected Areas (NICIPA), *WII Newsletter* 6 (3-4) July-Dec 1993: 46-48.

Discusses in detail need for setting up a NICIPA, its objectives, functions and services. States that the facilities available at the WII Library and Documentation Centre with modern equipments, specialised collections, trained staff, are ideal for establishment of a NICIPA in India.

025 (1) NISC - CBRI

SINHA, S C 770

Planning National Information Centre for Building Technology - a proposal for CHRI, Roorkee as NISC in housing sector, *Int Lib Move* 15 (2) Sept 1993: 120-132.

Describes the CBRI as the SIC for Building Technology. Explains the model plan of Information System for Building technology with its proposal features, functions, organization, subject field, capital cost, manpower, recurring expenditure, source of revenue. Gives suggestions.

025 (1) NISSAT

OJHA, D C 771

NISSAT: An overview, *ALIS*, V 3, 167-178.

Provides information about NISSAT's objectives, and organisational set up. Describes the Sectoral, Regional and Local information centres. Discusses also the NISSAT's activities and its contribution to the R & D scientists. Reviews overall NISSAT programme sponsored by the DST.

UPGRADE NISSAT infrastructure to reinforme efforts - 772

Evaluation committee report, *NISSAT Newsletter* 12 (3) July-Sept 1993: 22-23.

Gives the brief report of the five-members Committee headed by Maj General A Balasubramanian constituted in Aug 1991 to evaluate the activities of NISSAT and how to improve its performance. Says that the financial resources of NISSAT are not commemorative with the expectations from the system. Gives the main findings and suggestions of the Committee. Mentions also the recommendations.

025 (1) TIC/PERA

KHAN, K M 773

Technical Information Centre of Production Engineering Research Association, *Int Lib Move* 14 (4) Dec 1992: 170-181.

Describes about the activities and services of TIC of PERA set up in 1946 in Leicestershire, England. Discusses its loan services, reference services, translation services, technical publication service, and discussion for industries and members.

025.02 Technical Processes

Technical Operations

JASMER SINGH 774

Technical processing and its role in optimising use of college libraries: A survey report, *Luck Libn* 24 (1) Jan-Mar 1992: 16-31.

Explains technical processing. Reviews technical processing in college libraries. Uses questionnaire and interview methods to gather required information on the subject. Applies Chi-square Test and Normal Deviate Test to study level of significance or homogeniety of proportions among various categouries of users. Gives suggestions to improve technical processing to optimise use of college libraries.

MISRA, V N and PHADKE, D N 775

Study on unit costing of technical processing in an academic library, *ALIS*, V 4, 151-165.

Discusses the theory of 'unit cost' and its application to the libraries for cost analysis purpose. States certain attempts made in India at Govt and non Govt levels to pay down certain norms and standards for job performance.Concludes with a case study to work out unit cost of technical processing in the Central Library of IIT, Bombay.

025.0285 Computerisation of Library Operations

Library Automation. Library Computerisation

ABRAHAM, DEBORAH V H 776

Maximising computer power for public service, *Iaslic Bull* 38 (4) Dec 1993: 147-153.

Describes that computers have made possible substantial gains for libraries in three areas: improved delivery of routine services, reference work, and recource sharing.Surveys the experience of US libraries with implications for Indian libraries. Discusses that in libraries throughout the world, computers are most importantly used to improve service to the user.

AMJAD ALI 777

Computerisation of media libraries, *Jl Inf Sci* 3(3) Jan-Mar 1993: 119-127.

Discusses the organization of new forms of documents as

photographs, microfilms, sound spools, tapes, discs, etc under the system of information. States that the application of computer in a media library provides economy in terms of cost of time. Makes special reference to the computerisation of the media libraries attached to the film and TV production organizations.

ASHOK BABU, T and SASTRY, P S 778

The personal computer & the public library, *IPLA Souvenir*, No 18, 2 p.

Describes the need for and advanteges of computers in libraries in housekeeping operations. Mentions that software packages are also available for libraries, and communication facilities have advanced enough to join the public libraries to the networks.

BHARGAVA, J K, SRIVASTAVA, R K and MURTHY, S S 779

Sanjay - an Indian library automation package based on CDS/ISIS, *Program* 27 (1) 1993: 566.

Explains the development of Sanjay - an Indian library automation package.Describes its special features in context with its users as an automation package based on CDS/ISIS for the various library operations. Mentions about its applications.

BURAGOHAIN, ALKA 780

Problems and prospects of library automation in greater Guwahati, *The North East Times*, Guwahati, 11 (125) Feb 7, 1992: 5.

Deals with the problems and prospects of application of computer etc to the various libraries and their operations in greater Guwahati so as to increase the effectiveness of library and information services.

CICHI, DEMETRIO R 781

Library automation: The Italian style, *ML*, 85-88.

Describes about the national library network (SBN) of Italy with the aims of reorganisation of library services, creation of a union catalogue, transmission of information in real time, a letter to documents through a national service. Discusses decentralized network, the SBN architecture, SBN's future. Explains the inside view of the system.

DASGUPTA, KALPANA 782

Planning, modernization and preservation programme in South Asian libraries; a seminar, Calcutta: National Library, 1992. 295 p.

Contains 25 papers contributed by eminent scholars in the field and presented at the International Seminar held in Calcutta on 31st December, 1990, covering the entire range of activities for modernization of library services, their proper planning and preservation programme specifically aimed at the South Asian libraries.

DILLI, K T 783

Computers in modern libraries, *IPLA Souvenir* 4 p.

Points out the stage has come when traditional library has to change into new information centres with computers in libraries, meeting the challenge of knowledge explosion. Mentions that India is doing progress in the area of science libraries and other networking as INDONET.

DILLI, K T 784

Computers in modern libraries, *In* N Ravi (Ed), *The Hindu speaks on libraries*, Madras: Kasturin & Sons, 1992, pp 282-284.

Explains the sea change the world of library and information centres are witnessing due to the information explosion in the post World War II period leading to the computers development and applications in libraries. Discusses the benefits of computer in a library, and how computer networks are being developed including INDONET, NICNET, and even S R Ranganathan was in favour of computer. Concludes that computer technology should be applied in view of the nature of users needs as users are the final link in information transfer.

DUTTA, NAMITA 785

The use of PCs in library automation, *ITAH*, 59-66.

Deals with the specific situation in introducing the PC culture in small and medium-sized medical libraries in India especially in Calcutta. Describes the critieria for selecting computers in different types of libraries. Includes development of programms on CDS/ISIS, in dBASE or and other software package exclusively for trhe specific needs of a library. Discusses advantages of LAN for medium-sized libraries. Reports about the problems medical libraies in Calcutta are facing, and tries to find out some remedial measures to overcome threse problems.

DWIVEDI, P N 786

Problems of automation and computerisation of library information system, *LIT*, 76-79.

Mentions problems of LAN, problems of suppliers, problems originating with library staff, problems of poor planning, poor design, and poor implementation. States that library automation can be healthy if these problems are discusses and solved.

ESSENTIALS FOR safe computing: Taking the pain out of PC use, *Jl Inf Sci* 3(1) July-Sept 1992: 53-55. 787

Emphasises the use of proper and suitable office equipments, furniture, setting up of computer installations, little common sense, adjustment of work habits, etc for the safe use of computers.

GANPULE, S R and WAYDANDE, H S 788

Computerisation in IIT Bombay Central Library: Cost benefit approach, *CTIT*, 39-46.

Points out need to evaluate library services with some tools and measure some of its aspects and computer costs and benefits. States that it is easy to measure the cost of computerisation. Discusses this attempt made to estimate the cost of computerisation of IIT Library, Bombay.

GARDNER, TRUDY A 789

Creative use of a library resource to provide better access to information within a limited budget, *ML*, 157-162.

Gives the goal of a health science library. Emphasises use of highly sophisticated computer technology to achieve its goals. Describes several steps any health science library can take to become an information management system without resort to computerisation; by using catalogue to act as an information management system.

GARG, B S 790

Computer vis-a-vis university libraries in India: Promise and reality, *Lib Her* 31 (1-2) Apr-Sep 1992: 24-32.

Points out in the information era past pattern of treating information no longer fit in present reality. Gives brief development of computer and its presence on Indian scene. Observes use of computers in Indian university libraries in its infancy. Presents a two-phased plan for introduction. Gives future prospects.

GOLAM AMBIA 791

Application of computer in different areas of university libraries, *LIT*, 73-75.

Makes a case for computerisation in university libraries in India, as automation will solve many problems. Identifies areas which can be computerised in acquisition, cataloguing, circulation, serial control, maintenance, information retrieval, stock verification.

GUPTA, S P 792

Management of computer-based library and information systems, *AGLIS Jl* 9.1993 (Abstract only).

Discusses the various library operations that have been computerised or are on the way hence these all for a sound management syustem as planning, design and implementation, selection of hardware/software, evaluation, staff motivation, etc.

HARAVU, L J 793

Library automation and networking in India - an overview of recent developments, *Ann Lib Sci & Docum* 40 (1) Mar 1993: 32-40.

Presents an overview of recent developments in library automation and networking in India. Raises issues believed to be of basic nature as a contribution to the on going debate and discussion on the subject in the country.

IBRAHIM, ABBAS 794

Automation era, *Rilisar Bull* 8 (2) Apr-June 1993: 2 p.

Written as an Editorial, states that computer age began in India in 1984 because of the policies of Govt of India to handle rapid growth of information. Points out the need for Management Information System (MIS) handled by a MIS personnel who should be trained accordingly. Mentions that RILISAR has developed a package CALIBRAN MIS helpful to automate managerial activities.

KATNA, A K 795

Library automation at IIT, Kharagpur, *AGLIS Jl* 9, 1993 (Abstract only).

Describes adoption of computer system for library use for day to day in house operations at IIT Library, Kharagpur. Describes the development of a database for over one lakh books for users via CYBER network. Discusses also the problems.

KUMBAR, T S 796

Electronic mail and its application for library and information services, *CS*, 329-338.

Defines E-mail. Presents beiefly its general use in India and information services where it can be used. Presents in brief the use of E-mail in libraries in USA, UK, Canada, and India. Gives hardware and software required for setting up an E-mail service. Mentions a few advantages and disadvantages of the system.

MISHRA, B N 797

Computer application in library and information science activities, *Lib Prog* (*Int*) 12 (1-2) Jan-Dec 1992: 31-37.

Presents the necessity of the computer application in library activities in the country. Gives the different fields, such as acquisition, circulation, maintenance, search nd query, periodicals, information exchange,which require the computerization. Narrates the WILIMAX and WILITRAX popularly known for the different house keeping operations.

MOHANDAS, M K and SHET, K C 798

Software for Indian libraries, *LIT*, 151-156.

Hightlights the library automation software packages and the problems associated with their use. Proposes new software package features for the Indian libraries to take a quantum jump into the 21st century. Discusses problems in available library softwares and desirable features for library software.

PAREKH, HARSHA 799

Need for library automation and modernisation, *Univ News* 30 (1) 6 Jan 1992: 2-4.

Hightlights need for automation libraries as a step towards modernisation and in order to improve the library and information services so that library users could be satisfied. Discusses other details needed for library computerisation.

PARIDA, BAMAN 800

Computer culture and communication network of libraries in India, *LIT*, 63-72.

States that computerisation has relieved the pressure of workload in libraries. Outlines genesis of computers and computer networks. Mentions development of computer-based library systems. Gives importance of telecommunications and data networks, online database access and networks, India's participation in international databases, online access to remote data centres in India, and databases on magnetic media and CD-ROM.

PASSI, B K, *et al* 801

Computers and libraries (computer based library management), New Delhi: 1992.

Discusses in its chapters about the computer based library management in the various house keeping operations to effect efficiency and improve library services for the end users.

PREM SINGH 802

Managing technological change in libraries, *The Administrator* 36, 1991: 67-84.

Deals with the growth and development of new technologies and their applications in libraries for the improvement of services as well as organisation and management brought out by the technological change.

RAMAREDDY, E 803

Components of library automation, *ALR*, 217-222.

Describes various components of library automation such as aim; processing; computer system and its location; computer software; data communication; system documentation; human resources; other resources such as equipments, furniture, terminals, printers; and environment including physical space, lighting, temprature, humidity, noise control, cleanliness, etc.

RAMA REDDY, E 804

Planning library automation, *IJILIS* 5 (1-2) Jan-June 1992: 41-47.

Describes the planning required in automating library services and related activities. Deals with the components of automation such as aim, processing, computer system, location of computer,computer software, data communication, system documentation, human resources, other resources, and environment.

RAMAN NAIR, R 805

Computer application to library and information services, New Delhi: Ess Ess Publications, 1993. xi, 278 p.

Includes 18 chapters on different aspects of computer applications, including computer systems, input/output, data storage, software, Hightlevel language, MS DOS, and so on. Discusses also about the computer terms used frequently by the users of the system.

RATHORE, JAGMOHAN S 806

Development of a computer based library storage and retrieval system, *Int Lib Move* 14 (4) Dec 1992: 182-189.

Provides a complete set of user instructions and implementation descriptions for suits of programs which support an online library database. Describes the system of a class of personalised information storage and retrieval systems to cope with the information explosion.

RAVICHANDRA RAO, I K 807

Library automation, 2nd ed, New Delhi: Wiley Eastern Ltd, 1992. 213 p.

Deals with four selective chapters adding two more of 'Introduction' and 'Conclusion' in this edition. Gives brief overview of introduction of automation in LIS field, definition of computer, flowcharting and algorithm; basic featrures of computers to give necessary conception in this field. Discusses about computerisation of library housekeeping operations. Describes MARC, LC MARC, UNIMARC, CCF, etc. Deals also with IR systems, selections of hardware, software, etc.

SEWA SINGH 808

Computer applications in Indian libraries: A study, *LIS*, 153-167

Gives importance of information and Information Age. Defines computer. Discusses development and use of computers in India. Explains computers in libraries, and the areas of their application. Mentions advantages of computerisation. Describes the Indian scene with an overview of computer applications with library and information functions.States the uses of libray networks already installed. Points out need for manpower training for this purpose.

SHARMA, PANDEY S K 809

Library computerisation: Theory and practice, New Delhi: Ess Ess Publications. 1993. 182 p.

Discusses in five chapters, A to H, about the library computerisation including hardware, software, operating system, applications of computers to library and information services, and so on.

SHARMA, PANDEY S K 810

Library computerization:Why? *AGLIS Jl* 9, 1993 (Abstract only).

Traces history of use of computers. Explains the need for

computers in libraries and information centers. Explains the need for computers in libraries and information centres. Highlights limitations of non-computerised library. Concludes that time saved by computerization could be used more fruitfully and effectively in providing useful servicves.

SHINGANKULI, S V and SINGH, R S 811

Computerisation of library activities at NCL: A case study, *CTIT*, 123-132.

Reviews the WILISYS system, the library and information system being used at NCL Library, Pune. Discusses its infrastructure, the database, modules of the software 'WILISYS' such as ordering, requesting, payment and billing, search and query, periodicals, registration, circulation, binding, holdings, etc.

SINGH, LAKHAN 812

Development of computer application in nuclear medicine information system: Review, *ML*, 439-441.

Outlines advantages of computer applications in information retrieval, CD-ROM storage and retrieval services and communication/networking services. States that these will enable both information specialist and user to utilise a vast wealth of resources unavailable in a non-computerized environment. Reviews the progress, update in modern IT. Describes new trends in information services and existing nuclear medicine databases international.

SINGH, SANJAY KUMAR 813

Computer application in libraries, *LIN*, 80-86.

Discusses importance of computer application in information handling and data processing as computers have moved in. Describes computer hardware and software. Explains the impact of new IT in transforming library and informing library and information services such as cataloguing, circulation, serial control, stock verification, maintenance of accounts. Discusses need for and advantages of computerisation. Points out problems in computerised information processing.

SINGH, VIRENDRA PRAKASH 814

Computer application in agricultural libraries with a special emphasis to the adoption of CD-ROM technology, *LIT*, 238-243.

Explains as to why use computers in agriculture libraries. Describes the computer applications in circulation control, stock verification, information and bibliographical retrieval, catalogues, bibliography. Forecasts that by 2000 every scientist will use a computer in office and home to retrieve information and CD-ROM will also be used.

TANAKA, AKIO 815

Library computerization in Aichi Medical University, Japan: A case report, *ML*, 467-472.

Discusses about computerisation of libraries in Japan by developing integrated automated library system where each subsystem supports the house keeping under satisfied conditon. Discusses in detail the book management as an example of computerization. Describes the future prospects that our library confronts with computerization.

VERMA, JITENDRA and KAPOOR, NEENA 816

Computerization of bibliographic records: A JNU experiment, *LIT*, 136-141.

Describes the computerisation of JNU Library, installation of computer and software package, adopted AACR and for computer applications and input sheet is based on CCF pattern for books, theses and serials. Gives the outputs such as Granthisuchi, Suchika, India and World Affairs, List of subscribed serials in Delhi libraries, etc. Mentions future plans also.

025.04 Automated/Computerised Information

Storage and Retrieval

ALLY SORNAM, S and SWAROOP RANI, B S 817

Impact of telecommunication technololgy on information access, storage and retrieval, *IR*, 100.

Discusses role of telecommunication technology, need for telecommunication in information industry, present development in telecommunication technology and their application in information access, storage and retrieval.

CHOWDHURY, S and CHOWDHURY, G G 819

Text retrieval systems: An overview, *IR*, 35-41.

Defines text retrieval systems. Mentions its characteristics. Presents the general guidelines for evaluating text retrieval systems.

Discusses major features of six microcomputer based text retrieval packages: BASIC, BRS/Search, CAIRS, CDS/ISIS, idea List and STATUS. Concludes in favour of CDS/ISIS on the basis of price factor.

KOUSHIK, MURLIDHAR 820

Dynamic hashing with distributed overflow space: A file organisation with good insertion performatnce, *Info Sys* 18 (5) 1993: 299-317.

Proposes a dynamic hashing scheme which uses a generalised exponential hash functions and a directory-based overlfow handling scheme. States it is designed to accommodate a variety of file growth rates and ensures that retrieval insertion and file expansion performance is non-cyclic.

MOHANDAS, M K and SHET, K C 821

Computerised information retrieval: An experiment at KREC, *IR*, 92.

Explains the difficulties even in computerised information retrieval situation with a case study of KREC Library. Discusses how 15 files have been created for each of the 7 classifications containg 5000 books. Describes the facilities provided by the retrieval system and saving time of users.

PANIGRAHI, PIJUSHKANTI and KANKACHARY, M 822

Automated information retrieval system in a university library, *LIT*, 178-187.

Explores the ways and means of retrieval functions. To perform these functions, there should be a database; it is difficult to retrieve the required information unless suitable retrieval techniques are applied. Gives reason of information retrieval system automation and the concepts of IRS. Discusses search formulation and also online searching.

SEETHARAMA, S 823

Evaluation measures in information retrieval systems, *IR*, 79-87.

States importance of information and computers application to it. Gives definitions of some terms. Provides a framework for Information Centre Evaluation. Enumerates the various evaluation measures. Discusses their applicability to IR systems. Explains the economic concepts of evaluation. Concludes that evaluation is a form of enquiry where the end product is information; while information is power, evaluation is powerful.

SUBBA RAO, S 824

Automated retrieval system: Leather science database, *IR*, 98.

Highlights computerisation of Leather Science Abstracts being published by NICLAI, CLRI, Madras since 1964 by using CDS/ISIS software. Presents database design in detail. Mentions about the expected products out of the database as generaation of various indices. Gives future plans to make available the database on communication networks.

VISHWA MOHAN, V and YADAGIRI REDDY, J 825

Machine retrieval: Problems and prospects, *IR*, 75-76.

States that the introduction of computers in information storage and retrieval has provided many avenues for wonderful storage and retrieval. The search strategies have improved the search capabilities, nevertheless not free of noise. Cites some examples to show the irrelevant retrieval which occurs in the machine retrieval.

025.04 (1) Artificial Intelligence (AI)

DATTA, SUBRATA, DUTTA, NAMITA and MAKHIJA, HEM LATA 826

Application of AI/ES in library and information science: A statistical analysis of papers abstracted in LISA (1980-1990), *IR*, 43-53.

Explains AI and ES giving their characteristics. Analyses statistically 370 articles from LISA form its coverage of AI application on LIS from 1980 to 1990. Presents information yearwise, continent-wise, and country-wise, indicating future trends of AI applications to LIS. States that though US and UK dominate the field, contributions from Germany, Russia, Japan, China, India are not insignificant.

RAMANO, GIOVANNI 827

An intelligent documentation system, *COP*, 442-451.

Mentions that even after improvements in the user interface, people have difficulties in accomplishing their tasks on a computer. The user's difficulties can be reduced by the construction of advice systems that assist her/him in solving problem. Outlines the literature on empirical studies about human advisors. Describes the architecture of an Intelligent Help System that is able to dynamically tailor the information provided according to the characteristics and needs of the particular user.

SUBRAMANIAN, M S 828

Artificial intelligence technology for information handling for 2001 A D: An overview, *Jl Inf Sci* 3 (3) Jan-Apr 1993: 111-117.

Highlights the concept of AI in terms of mental processes, decision making and learning. Emphasises working of AI system as per sets of rules and descriptors and specification. Projects the ongoing research interest in AI in US, Britain, and Japan and the development of ES. Describes recent developments in AI computer software products - INTELLECT, MAIL, PUFF, CONCUDEUS, PALLADIO. Concludes by cautioning the employed people the dangers of it, and suggests remedies.

025.04 (1) Expert Systems (ES)

GAUR, R C and GUPTA, S P 829

The application of Expert Systems and Artifical Intelligence technologies in Indian libraries and information centres, *ITAH*, 119-132.

Explains AI and ES introduced recently concerned with knowledge-based computer programs. Highlights applicationn of ES and AI in libraries and information centres in classification and cataloguing. IR, information services such as indexing and abstracting, online search and reference assistance. Gives an overview of present status of computerization in Indian libraries and information centres and possibilities of making use of ES and AI technologies. Discusses problems faced by Indian L & I professionals in using computers and application of ES and AI in L & I work.

GOPALAKRISHNANA, S 830

Expert system and its utilities in information retrieval, *Jl Inf Sci* 3(4) Apr-June 1993: 181-186.

Explains ES. Mentions objectives of ES. Gives key characteristics that an information retrieval system (IRS) related ES should possess. Menions limitations. Clarifies on the utility of the ES in the IRS by explaining objectives and comparing the different kinds of IR Expert Systems.

MAITY, CHANDANA 831

Expert systems in information retrieval, *IR*, 55-60.

States that information retrieval is one of the most challenging aspect due to information explosion. Information intermediaries are becoming more and more important for handling this vast amount of information. Mentions characteristics of ES. Points out problems in IR. Discusses ES functions as intermediatries in IR. Concludes with opportunities for research and limitations.

025.04 (1) Databases. Bibliographic Databases

AMJAD ALI 832

Information system for educational video: The case of an indigenous database, *AGLIS JI* 9, 1993 (Abstract only).

Discusses about the development of an indigenous database for the educational purposes. Describes its components, creation, and use.

ARORA, A M, KOCHHAR, V B and ELHANCE, D 833

Bibliographic database on materials resrarch in India: Design and development using dBase IV, *CTIT*, 141-149.

Mentions importance of R & D activities in materials science. Discusses about materials science, and database created for it by INSDOC. Describes why DBMS package dBase IV was used. Gives DBMS software development. Also mentions about cost aspect of the database and the programs for providing statistical analysis of information contained in the database.

ASHOK KUMAR and RAM KUMAR 834

Standardization of formats for creation, maintenance and use of computerised databases, *CTIT*, 26-38.

Mentions importance of standardization, and their need in bibliographic databases. Discusses about standardizing bodies and their standards for exchange of bibliographic data. Discusses the role of UNESCO in this area including CCF. Also discusses the Indian scenario and role of NISSAT.

BAOKAR, ANJALI, SUNDARESHWAR, P R and JOSHI, M R 835

Value-added global database search throught wide area network, *Desidoc Bull Inf Tech* 13 (3) May 1993: 3-9.

Discusses the access and search of global databases, value

addition through organisation of the received data and sharing of the organised data in the local area network. The original organised database when accessed and downloaded becomes an ACSII file. If the selected database is to be reconstructed at the reveiving end, it is a laborious task of maual data entry. Describes a program developed for automated conversion of the ACSII file into a standard database format.

BORAIYAN, R 836

Computerised databases in agriculture: An outlook, *IJILIS* 6(3-4) July-Dec 1993: 300-311.

Defines database and its types in detail. Outlines the products of databases. Describes major databases avaialable for agriculture such as AGRICOLA, AGRIS, BIOSIS, CAB ABSTRACTS, TROPAG, and RURAL.

CHHABRA, PAVAN, AGARWAL, NEERA and GUPTA, S P 837

Development of transportation and highway engineering database at CRRI, New Delhi, *AGLIS JI* 9, 1993 (Abstract only).

Discusses the experience gained in developing the Transportation and Highway Engineering (THE) database using UNESCO's mini-micro CDS/ISIS Version 2.3 for this purpose.

CHUDAMANI, K S 838

Knowledge-based system for data sources(KSDS) at IISc Library, *IR*, 61-63.

Attempts to develop a knowledge-based system for data sources (KSDS) at IISc Library. Follows a hierarchical organisation of knowledge at the first level. Uses the VP-Expert program developed for reference support as the basic model for developing a program in dBase III.

GHOSH, S B 839

Need for a national database of Indian medical literature as a feeder service to international databases, *ML*, 171-175.

Traces the tradition of medical science in India. Explains its growth in pre-independence period. Mentions available services for dissemination of medical information. Reveals the non-availability of a comprehensive database and information system in medical sciences. Makes a case for creation of national database for medical sciences in India in view of the inadequate coverage of Indian medical literature in international databases.

HUGAR, N C 840

Database activities in science and technology in India: A critical study, *LIT*, 114-125.

Gives importance of information and information generation and bibliographic control. Discusses data base activities in India listed in the Directory of S & T Information Systems brought out by DST. Collects salient features of the selected database with a checklist. Gives observations made and reports areas where databases can be created.

JOSE, J M and VISWANATHAN, T 841

Object-oriented database management systems-a new tool for information centres, *Ann Lib Sci & Docum* 39 (3) Sept 1992: 74-80.

States that object-oriented database management systems (OODBMS) are a recent development in the field of database systems, and their use will increase the efficiency cf an information centre. Highlights inadequacies of the present data models for new applications. Presents features of OODBMA and illutrated its usefulness by modelling typical application in any information centre.

JOSE, MERCY 842

Bibliographic databases in information storage and retrieval, *Luck Libn* 24 (2) Apr-June 1992: 82-93.

Attempts to redefine and reclassify databases on a broader perspective. Describes types of databases with special emphasis on online bibliographic databases in IR, databases in various subject fields, databases producing agencies and vendors. Emphasises contemporary role of databases in ISR in general, and library and information centres in India in particular.

KASHYAP, M M 843

Database technology: Basic concepts and terminology, *Lib Her* 30 (1) Apr 1991: 1-19.

Gives the definition and description of some of the key concepts and the terminology used in the domain of database technology. Describes the various shades of meaning associated with a term and the different terms used to represent a particular concept.

KASHYAP, M M 844

Integrated database design for a library system employing library techniques developed by Ranganathan and CDS/ISIS database management system, *Jl Lib & Inf Sci* 18 (2) Dec 1993: 82-141.

Discusses computerized library information systems. Examines rules stipulated by S R Ranaganathan in CCC, Ed 5 for construction of catalogues and preparation of documentation lists or bibliographies from the point of view of their relevance and suitability for creating bibliographical databases. Compares rules of CCC and AACR II regarding compatibility. Concludes that in devloping online catalogues/bibliographies it is not essential to follow the rules strictly of CCC or AACR - II.

KAWALE, A V, MISHRA, J K and DE, B K 845

DRILLREP: Research report database of Institute of Drilling Technology, *IR*, 94.

Explains about the creation of a PC-based, menu-driven database 'DRILLREP' using dBase III+software package for retrieving information from reports. States that the IR facility has been extended to all ONGC regions and institutes. Points out the non-availability of thesaurus on oil-well drilling, hence need to develop one.

KOCHHAR, V B, SUBBA RAO, A, ARORA, A M and ELHANCE, D 846

Materials research in India: A quantitative analysis of publications output in scientific journals, *Jl Lib & Inf Sci* 17 (2) Dec 1992: 198-207.

Highlights certain observations resulting from the study of a statistical sample from two secondary sources, viz, Indian Science Abatracts (ISA), SCI (CD ROM), while creating a database of Indian literature output in materials science research in India for a period of ten years from periodicals.

KULDIP CHAND and SHARMA, DARSHAN 847

Herbal database and information services for health, *ITAH*, 213-218.

Describes various herbal databases and information services available in India useful for mitigating diseases. Discusses such databases and information service as CCRAS Documentation Bulletin, Database on Indian Medical Plants, Economic Botany

Information Service (EBIS), Integrated Information Service, Medicinal & Aromatic Plants Infomation Services (MAPIS), National Products Database and Plant Information Database. Mentions also general science databases-Indian Science Abstracts. Concludes that regional language information services should also be brought out.

NAG, D K and CHATTERJEE, DEB SIKHA 848

Creating database on geology using CDS/ISIS, *LIT*, 107-113.

Makes a case for developing a database, a computerised bibliographic database, named GSIPUB. Discusses system configuration, database structure, defining database, creating database, printing database.

NARENDRA KUMAR and SEN, B K 849

Indian Science Citation Database : A bibliometric tool, *CTIT*, 12-17

Traces history of database creation. Discusses about the features of SCI database and facilities to search SCI database at INSDOC. Points out the need for the National Centre on Bibliometrics, and the need for Indian Science Citation Database (ISCD) Discusses about the packages developed for ISCD.

NEW SOFTWARE and databases available with NISSAT, 850

NISSAT Newsletter 11 (2) Apr-June 1992: 8-9.

Discusses about the new software and databases available with NISSAT for distribution. These include IDAMS (International Developed Data Analysis and Management Software), IDIS (Bi-directional Interface between micro-ISIS and IDAMS -PC), Serials Database and SDI Software. Mentions their features and charactristics, the hardware requirements, etc.

PIEGAS, MARIA HELENA ARATANGY and CEPEDA, LUIZA MARIA RODRIGUES 851

LILACS (Latin American Literature in Health Sciences) : An approach to its methodology, *ML*, 349-353.

Describes about the creation of LILACS database to control bibliographic health sciences literature. Discusses about its methodology and the guidance for preparing indexing manual and abstracts, etc.

RAM KUMAR and ASHOK KUMAR 852

Sharing of inhouse databases in India : Need for standardization, *ILA Bull* 28 (3-4) Oct-Mar 1993: 105-110.

Discusses briefly features and importance of inhouse databases being developed by various institutions in India. Emphasises need for standardization in record format and 'structure' in order to merge/exchange records effectively. Discusses various exchanging formats developed and accepted by international community.

RATTANANI, LEKHA 853

Electronic databases : Knowledge on tap, *India Today* 18 (21) Nov 1-15, 1993:129.

Deals with the development of databases under the influence of technology. Describes the benefits the society can reap from these electronic databases now available around the globe in all fields of human activity.

SAHNI, DEEPAK and SAHNI, NEERA 854

Modelling techniques for database design of information system, *Jl Inf Sci* 3 (1) July-Sept 1992: 37-47.

States the importance of database and DBMS. Describes that software development for computerised infomation system is crucial and difficult. Gives special emphasis to database design for library and information system.

SUNIL KUMAR 855

Facilities to access international database in Delhi libraries : A survey, *LIT*, 100-106.

Reports the survey to assess the facilities available to access international databases in libraries of Delhi. Visits made personally or enquired through phone and 1 1 libraries responded positively which were approached later personally with a questionnaire. Concludes that training courses on search strategy in online be given.

UPADHYAY, J L 856

Database generation using CDS/ISIS, *Luck Libn* 24 (2) Apr-June 1992: 66-81.

Mentions the hardware needed for CDS/ISIS software package. Gives a preliminary account of the experience of the author in database generation using Version 2.3 of CDS/ISIS. Explains in detail the different steps involved in the creation of a database giving examples from the Jute and Allied Fibres database.

WAHAL, DEEPAK and SRIVASTAVA, A K 857

Creation of CRIPS -a bibliographic database using mini-micro CDS/ISIS : An experiment at NBRI, *CTIT*, 18-25.

Describes the creation of CRIPS-Current Reserch in Plant Science-as a monthlky computerised CAS at NBRI Lucknow, on mini-micro CDS/ISIS Version 2.3. Discusses about creating a database, dataentry, sorting and printing of main text and list of journals consulted, and searching. Points out limitations of CDS/ ISIS.

WEIHS, ERICH 858

On the cliet-server concept of text related data, *COP*, 452-459.

States that database storage has been a specialised field in the past, but is now gaining general significance because of office automation, etc. An essential pre-requisite is the client-server archietecture which allows a meaningful segmentation of data processing. Discusses text-related data storage, and significance of databases in text retrieval, describes the components of text-related databases. Discusses the possibilities of distributed processing of text related data.

WHITTALL, STEVA 859

Renewable energy resources, *INICAE* 12 (1) Mar 1993: 90-92.

Describes renewable energy database including INSPEC Database which will help to preserve precious energy resources.

YAMADA, HISAO 860

Feasibility study on international exchange of East Asian databases, *INICAE* 11(1) Mar 1992 : 113-115.

Reports the feasibility study on international exchange of databases being carried out by NACSIS since 1989 and now in the final stage. Mentions various discussions and deliberations held in this connections.

025.04 (1) SOFTWARES. PACKAGES
SOFTWARE PACKAGES

CHAKRABORTY, BIPUL KUMAR 861

Software package for management of databases - an evaluation of CDS/ISIS, *ALIS*, V 3, 105-119.

Highlights trend of an integrated software package using CDS/

ISIS for information storage and retrieval purposes. Evaluates the different guidelines of DBMS for efficient and effective IR activities and the role of CDS/ISIS for proper utilisation and management of DBMS. Concludes that the integrated sets of CDS/ ISIS and IDAMS software packages are compatible within the databases.

JOSE, J M and VISWANATHAN, T 862

Software documentation on standards, *Ann Lib Sci & Docum* 39 (4) Dec 1992: 123-133.

Deals with software documentation and standards which occupy an important place in software engineering process. Discusses the need of software librarian as a part of sotware engineering team. Deals with evolving standardization process for the organisation using international standard guidelines. Presents some quality indicators for software documentation.

LAXMAN RAO, N and FORD, NIGEL 863

Software selection for Indian libraries, *CS*, 304-315.

Gives need and planning for automation in libraries. Discusses in detail factors to be considered in selection of software availability. Concludes that UGC should establish a Library Software Development Centre in cooperation with other organisations for developing software for Indian libraries.

LAXMAN RAO, N and FORD, NIGEL 864

Software selection for Indian libraries, *Lib Sci slant Docum & Inf Std* 30 (4) Dec 1993 : 146-151.

Examines the role of automation in libraries. The primary consideration for choosing software for automating library operations are explained. Discusses the availability of the required softwares and the factors to be considered for selection of softwares in the Indian context.

PANDA, SHREEMAYEE 865

Libr A : A computer software for LIS applications, *STIM*, 107-112.

States that Libr A is an integrated library software package for Mackintosh family of computers. Describes the six modules of Libr A including acquisition, catalogung, circulation, services, serials, online retrieval module. Concludes that though it has many attractive features, its limitations in Indian context is the problem of acquiring a Macintosh.

RANGRA, V K 866

Software packages for LIS operations and services, *AGLIS J1* 9, 1993 (Abstract only).

Discusses the system software and application software required for library operations such as acquisition, cataloguing, circulation, serials control, and information services including CAS, SDI, bibliographies, thesaurus construction, and maintenance, etc.

SAXENA, S C and MEHTA, S N 867

Software package for libraries, *ALIS*, V 3, 143-156.

Mentions application software developed in India for computerising various library and information activities. Discusses in brief some important sofware packages tested at international level. Suggests software package suitable for Indian libraries, particuarly DESIDOC.

SINHA, P K 868

Software for libraries, *ALIS*, V3, 121-142.

Explains and evaluates various types of software useful for library operations. Examines criteria for evaluation and selection of software package. Analyses areas of library work wherein computer can be used. Discusses various softwares developed by different libraries for each of library activities. Provides also sources of software for library packages.

VYASMOORTHY, P 869

Software packages in India for library and information work, *ALIS*, V 3, 157-165.

Presents information on indigenously produced software packages available in public domain for the Indian libraries. Gives details of hardware needed, library functions for which the package offers solution, based on the information gathered from manufactures' pamphlets and demonstrations.

VYASMOORTHY, P 870

Software packages in India for library and information work : A brief survey, *CS*, 316-328.

Gives a brief survey of indigenously produced commercially available priced softwasre packages useful for library and information work in India. Gives also a list of software firms in India for library applications.

025.04 (1) CDS/ISIS

CARINO, PATRICIA B 871

Status of CDS/ISIS training and use in Asia and the Pracific : A regional report, *NISSAT Newsletter* 12 (3) July-Sept 1993: 8-12.

Continues form Vol 12, No. 2, 1993, about training on specific library operations, training for network participants, CDS/ISIS training institutions, methodology and training materials, training problem, course duration, trainee-related problems. Concludes that the demand for and use of CDS/ISIS will continue to grow in spite of the problems.

CDS/ISIS : Fourth National Meet, Pune, *NISSAT* 872

Newsletter 12 (2) Apr-June 1993 : 3-7.

Reports abouth the Fourth National Meet of CDS/ISIS and NICHEM at the NCL, Pune during Jan 6-8, 1993. Mentions its aims and objectives. Discusses about the six technical sessions on reviewing the progress in promotion and application of CDS/ISIS packages. Mentions about introduction of 'SANJAY' package. Reports that sessions III to VI were devoted to presentation of user applications. Each sessioin was followed by an open house discussion. Gives the recomendations made.

CERN, GENEVA 873

Mini-micro CDS/ISIS application for high energy physics preprints, *INICAE* 12 (1) Mar 1993 : 89-90.

Points out that in order to facilitate participantion from less developed countries a stand-alone application, Micro PROP, based on the new vesion of UNESCO's Mini-Micro CDS/ISIS has been developed which will make several years' bibliographic records on preprints.

CHOWDHURY, S and CHOWDHURY, G G 874

Development of library management system using micro-CDS/ISIS, *Ann Lib Sci & Docum* 39 (3) Sept 1992 : 113-122.

Describes about CDS/ISIS developed by UNESCO. Gives a review of literature and distinct features of CDS/ISIS. Reports about a prototype circulation control system developed using CDS/

ISIS (Ver 2.3), giving features of these programms written in Pascal. Concludes that the prototype system will work satisfactory on a LAN.

DURAI, R and MARIASUSAINATHAN, S 875

Back volumes : Storage and retrieval of infomation through CDS/ISIS, *Int Lib Move* 14 (4) Dec 1992 : 175-178.

Describes the storage and retrieval of backvolumes information of a libary with the help of CDS/ISIS software package through the media of computer. Discusses features of CDS/ISIS through which we may create number of databases. It is available free of cost for non-profitable organizations from Unesco.

HARINARAYANA, N S and NAVALGUND, C U 876

Suitability of CCF for CDS/ISIS based IR system : Experience at the National Law School of India University (NLSIU) Library, *IR*, 96.

Discusses on the basis of experience of NLSIU Library staff that CDS/ISIS software has a number of inherent features which support CCF thus minimising the efforts needed by designer of database to adopt CCF.

ISIS-PASCAL utilities developed at NCSI, 877

NISSAT Newsletter 12 (2) Apr-June 1993 : 19-20.

Describes about the three general utility programs developed in ISIS-Pascal at the National Centre for Science Infomation by the one-year training course students as part of their course work. States about LODCOM.PAS, CLABMOD. PAS and SELFMT. PAS. Mentions that NCSI is willing to share the source listings of these programs with the CSD/ISIS user community.

JAIN, S L 878

dBASE and CDS/ISIS for bibliographic databases : A comparative study, *IR*, 97.

Evaluates the characteristics and operational features of dBASE III + and CDS/ISIS, the most commonly used database management software in library and information work. Concludes that dBASE offeres excellent choice in terms of simplicity, expertise available and conditional searching.

JOSHI, MANOJ K 879

Use of CDS/ISIS in the libraries of Delhi : An analysis, *ILA Bull*

28 (3-4) Oct-Mar 1993 : 95-104.

Identifies reasons for acquisition of CDS/ISIS by a large number of libraries in Delhi. Examines its use for various library transactions-processing-management systems, extent of database activities for bibliographic/non-bibliographic information storage and retrieval, and various services as provided by using the datbase/ maintained on CDS/ISIS. Gives also user evaluation.

MUKANGARA, F E 880

Understanding Micro CDS/ISIS-Version 2.3 and possible areas for improvement, *Int Lib Move* 15 (3) Sept 1993 : 108-112.

Explains the Version 2.3 CDS/ISIS in generalised information storage and retrieval system. Discusses its database designing and maintenance, database creation and maintenance, searching and retrieving, sorting and printing services, and limitation. Gives some recommendations also.

SREELATHA, G and APARNA SIMHA, T A 881

A user-inerface for information retrieval in CDS-ISIS datbases, *Lib Sci slant Docum & Inf Std* 29 (3) Sept 1992 : 127-134.

Discusses about the application of CDS-ISIS software package for effective information retrieval. States that it can all be developed on user-interface module and helpful enviornment be created for this purpose.

STATUS OF CDS/ISIS training and use in Asia and the 882

Pacific : Regional report, *NISSAT Newsletter* 12 (2) Apr-June 1993 : 12-16.

Based on country reports submitted by participants to the Asian Regional Training of trainees and meeting of distributors of UNESCO's CDS/ISIS software package. Reports about the survey conducted on the status of CDS/ISIS use in 14 countries. Mention also about the status of CDS/ISIS training at different levels.

USE OF IDAMS-PC in conjunction with Micro CDS/ISIS 883

through IDIS interface, *NISSAT Newsletter* 12 (4) Oct-Dec 1993 : 18.

Describes the IDAMS distributed by UNESCO first in its Main frame Version for microcomputers for professionals working in scientific environments. Mentions how the change from IDAMS to ISIS which is written in CDS/ISIS Pascal.

WALIA, R K 884

Computer assisted publication of bibliography using CDS/ISIS, *Jl Inf Sci* 3 (3) Jan-Mar 1993 : 151-160.

Describes problems in manualy compiling a bibliography. Stresses the need of a computer assisted system, which involves creation of the database using CDS/ISIS and various indices and has numerous advantages over the manual system. Concludes that it provides an efficient and effective way for searching and retrieving records.

025.04 CD-ROM Technology

AGARWAL, U K 885

CD-ROM technology : A powerful media for LIS activities, *ITAH*, 23-27.

Mentions that CD-ROM technology has developed at a fast pace and entered in LIS. Describes its storage capacity, accuracy, reliability, advantages, work station and state of fundamentals of applications and its operation. Records also the survey results produced within four years after its marketing began in 1985. States that the first hand experience on CD-ROM applications to LIS is fairly good.

CHOPRA, H R and GOEL, PREETI 886

Use of CD-ROM technology in less developd countries, *Jl Info Sci* 4 (2) Oct-Dec 1993: 49-57.

Provides information on CD-ROM technology begin used extensively in the information centres these days. States that this technology has very significant positive impact on access of information not only from taking end but also from giving end.

FIRST consortium meeting for CD-ROM of Asian 887 information on health and environment, *CSIR News* (21) Nov 15, 1993: 311-312.

Reports about the First Consortium Meeting held for CD ROM users on the subjects of health as well as environment.

MISHRA, SANJAY 888

A survey of CD-ROM in Delhi libraries, *LIT*, 244-253.

Mentions capabilities of CD-ROM as optical storage medium. Explains the potential value of CD-ROM. Reportss the findings of a survey of some Delhi libraries to find out if they have CD ROM drives, databases in CD ROM, and any problems in it. Mentions libraries having CD ROM.

MUJOO-MUNSHI, USHA 889

ROMs & WORMs : Optimal solution for archival storage, *Jl Lib & Inf Sci* 17 (2) Dec 1992 : 191-197.

Mentions that no library can have adequate collection in real terms to cater to user needs. Discusses five media choices for the data storage/recording, such as paper, magnetic media, CD-ROM, Erasable optical disks, and WORM. Mentions equipment cost and problems relating to technology. Examines application of optical storage for mass storage purpose.

PANDA, KRUSHNA C 890

CD-ROM : The modern papyrus, *LIT*, 256-266.

Traces the origin and abode of CD-ROM. Discusses the CD-ROM know how and its storage capacity. Gives the constituents of CD ROM and the taxonomy of products. Explains the pre installation ruminations and the cost factor. Discusses advantages and limitations of CD ROM. Concludes that it will continue to be used in libraries.

PANIGRAHI, PIJUSHKANTI 891

Information searching from CD-ROM databases, *IR*, 71-74.

Mentions some procedures of IR from CD-ROM databases and its helpfulness in satisfying user needs. Emphasises the search mechanism of interface software package of Silver Platter Info Ret Services (SPIRS). Presents some sample queries alongwith retrieved information. Mentions information about PYGMALLION which can exchange data from CD-ROM, DIALOG, to CDS/ISIS databases.

RAJYALAKSHMI, D and PADMAJA RANI 892

CD -ROM search strategies, *LIT*, 267-275.

Explains the search techniques for CD-ROM, in different databases, such as text searching text signatures, inverted signature trees, etc. Analyses the time required. Mentions how to read the data from a CD ROM. Compares the CD ROM v/s online searching.

RELAN, SONIA and KAKAR, VIJAY LAKSHMI 893

CD-ROM facilities at DESIDOC, *Desidoc Bull Inf Tech* 13 (1-2) Jan-Mar 1993 : 3-8.

Describes in detail CD-ROM systems, databases and CD NET networking system available at DESIDOC. Compares advantages and disadvantages of online and CD databases. Discusses problems faced in acquisition, installation of various databases, and also retrieval software problems of major CD database producers. Mentions future programmes also.

SAMAL, P K and GUPTA, SANGITA 894

CD-ROM for the library, *ITAH*, 9-22.

Provides a technological overview of the CD-ROM and relates into its distinctive information dissemination attributes. Describes the CD-ROM applications available for cataloguing aids, bibliographic searching, full-text searching, and networking. Mentions its limitations. Points out why CD-ROM is popular in India.

SEN, B K 895

Compact disc : New medium for information storage, *Univ News* 31 (3) 1993: 24-26.

Defines compact disc. Explains its possibilities and prospects as a new medium of information storage which is gaining popularity even in India. States that it will continue to be used in the times to come as a useful new storage and retrieval medium.

SHAH, G A, MANIKYA RAO, M, DESAT, A T and GAIKWAD, D T 896

CD-ROM in information storage and retreival : A case study of CWPRS, *IR*, 77-78.

States that to cater to the needs of the Central Water and Power Research Station, Pune, it has set up a CD-ROM unit and procured four CD-ROM databases. Narrates CWPRS library's experience in rendering services through CD-ROM dtabases to its users. Concludes that users are satisfied with it.

SUBRAMANIAN, M S 897

CD-ROM a new electronic media for document storage and retrieval, *Jl Info Sci* 4 (2) Oct-Dec 1993 : 77.

Describes CD-ROM as electronic media for document storage and retrieval. Explains structure, storage capacity and process involved in making CD-ROM disc. Highlights its features in terms of versatility, storage density, durability, cost, etc. States CD-ROM products in LIS field and the project on document delivery through CD-ROM by Commision of the European Communities.

SUBRAMANIAN, P V S and SRINIVASAN, R 898

CD-ROM : Emerging technology for database searching; impact, potentialities and problems, *ALIS*, V 3, 57-89.

Explains what is CD ROM. Discusses emergence of CD ROM technology, its advantages and disadvantages over the existing media, its impact on library and information application, products available in the market, problems of standardisation, and its furture. Gives a useful Appendix on available CD-ROM databases.

025.04 (1) Multimedia

RAMAIAH, C K 899

Multimedia : A new instructional tool, *INICAE* 11 (2) Sept 1992 : 177-186.

States the revolution caused by computer technology in the production, storage and retrieval of information. Mentions multimedia computing has influenced significantly the present process of teaching and learning. Explains need for multimedia, the requirements for basic media station, and authoring tools for designing the multimedia programmes. Discusses multimedia in E & T stating their cost effectiveness. Mentions some important multimedia applications.

025.04 (1) Online Searching/Retrieval

AGRAWAL, I K 900

Infrastructure and facilities for the development of online information industry in India : A proposal, *Lib Sci slant Docum & Inf Std* 29 (1) Mar 1992 : 15-25.

Presents a state-of-the-art infrastructural facility in telecommuication network in India. Presents a contemporary scenario on Pocket Switched Data Network and project the future of online information industry in India.

AMBRISH KUMAR and TYAGI, A K 901

Online searching of databases : An automatic approach, *Desidoc Bull Inf Tech* 11 (6) Nov 1991 : 3-9.

Describes a technique for automatic logon to Dialog host computer at Palo Alto, Califormia, USA. Discusses the software (in Procommunication Script) helps in connecting to the Gateway Packet Switching Service PAD at New Delhi provided by the VSNL. After connecting to the PAD, the software sends NUI, User Number, Password and loads up the search strategy. States that the software can be learnt by the librarians.

CHAUDHURY, ARUP RAY and SHARMA, P N 902

Online bibliographic information pricing, *STIM*, 118-127.

Deals with the charging of the online bibliographic services by the library and information centres. Discusses the pattern of pricing with components of search independent cost and per-search cost. Gives most prominent strategies followed by online vendors for pricing. Mentions charges for the retrieved information, and also for telecommunication facility.

CHOUDHURY, RINA 903

Online retrieval from physics database : operating philosophy, *IR*, 95.

Sketches breifly scope, facility and utility of online access to physics literature. Suggests a structure design for an interactive database of micro documents being published in India which will be compatible to the existing databases and also be suitable for the available online services in the respective fields.

DEODHAR, V G and SINGH, R S 904

Online information retrieval, *CTIT*, 109-122.

Gives importance of information and its problems and use of electronic gadgets for its storage and retrieval. Discusses computerised databases of two types. Explains telesearching and modes of telecommunication. Describes Indian scene in using new technologies including online searching of databases, role of some national centres, cost effectiveness of computerised databases. Gives suggestions to economise search cost.

GUPTA, SUDHIR and WALIA, R K 905

Role of Current Contents on Diskette (CCOD) in library information system, *LIT*, 92-99.

Studies the CCOD system requirements. Discusses features of CCOD such as browsing, browsing by discipline, browsing by source title/journal, searching, viewing, articles. Mention limitations, but CCOD is the need of the hour.

KASI RAO, V, RAMESH BABU, B and RANGASAMY, K V 906

Online information technology in the field of library and information science management environment (LISME): An overview, *Rilisar Bull* 8 (1) Jan-Mar 1993: 30-41.

Describes various concepts of online information technology and its vital role in LIS Management Environment. Suggests online system as essential for efficient and effective dissemination of information from several international databases to satisfy the user community in the minimum possible time.

KASI RAO, V, RAMESH BABU, B and RANGASAMY, K V 907

Online information technology in Library and Information Science Management Environment (LISME), *IR*, 91.

States importance of online information system. Mentions four stages of a search in an online IRS. Explains that online system can also be used for SDI as SDI-LINE of NLM, USA. Discusses that Indian can build a knowledge gateway node to help develop our own online host facility within the country.

MAHAJAN, NALINI 908

On-line information retrieval and patient care, *ML*, 247-251.

States that online IR provides effective and rapid delivery system. Discusses eight case studies showing that the physicians are increasingly using online searching as an important decision-making tool in patient care. Describes that the librarians searched MEDLINE, and other databases available through DIALOG and BRS. Identifies items of information needed for the specific patient problem.

RADHIKA RAMNATH 909

TIFACLINE : An online networked technology information system, *STIM*, 144-148.

Discusses about TIFACLINE aimed to be a nationally networked technical information system for online ascess. Describes the TIFACLINE concept, its information content, pilot project, special features, implentation details, etc. Concludes that it is the first system of its kind in the country.

RAGHU RAM, M and PALANIYANDI, M V 910

MEDLINE using NICENT : An information retrieval case study, *IR*, 65-70.

Deals with online retrieval of records from MEDLINE databases which is stored at Indian MEDLARS Centre, New Delhi. The access is being carried out through NICNFT. Discusses other technical processes involved in retreiving records like BRS/ Searchmate software, Crosstalk, alongwith NICNET features. Mentions about the users and user approach.

RAINA, ROSHAN and MISHRA, RAJESH K 911

Online search strategy : An experience, *Luck Libn* 24 (2) Apr-Jun 1992 : 63-67.

Explains Online Information Retrieval System (OIRS) facilitate interaction between researcher and databases through computers. Discusses with example, merits of a good search strategy to arrive at a best precision level. Results can be cent-percent target oriented if the searcher commands analytical ability, communication skill, and assumes the role of a partner with the user in the search process.

ROY, SATYABRATA 912

Establishment of an online information facility, *STIM*, 128-131.

Mentions that to access information, NISSAT has set up five online information centres in India. Gives objectives of the Centre. Discusses the characteristics and identification of the problem under organizational problems, technical problems, physical, economic, manpower problems, and so on. Concludes that Indians are just getting accustomed to paying for information.

SHARMA, JAIDEEP, RAM KUMAR and ASHOK KUMAR 913

Online information retrieval : A case for indigenous databses, *LIT*, 196- 202.

Mentions that online information is the talk of the day Defines database and gives categories. Discusses search of database and results can be obtained online or offline. Describes online services in India and are gaining popularity. Concludes that NISSAT sectoral centres have future plans to develop local databases and providing them online.

THAIVANAYAGAM, A 914

Modern technology and health science libraries online or CD-ROM databases ? *ITAH*, 49-57.

Deals with the characteristics of online provision, history of online system. Draws parallels between online and offline database provisions. Describes the characteristics of offline system. Explains the merits and demerits of online system. Summarises the features that best characterise online and offline products. Emphasises also the need of co-existence of the two types of databases without one threatening the future of the other.

VAISHNAV, A A 915

Online information technology : Implications on LIS education, *LISI*, 120-125.

States that online informaton science are recent in origin. Describes the technology of online information retrieval. Mentions kinds of searches possible, and type of databases. Discusses use of online services in India. Explains its implications on LIS education. States that a new curricula is necessary.

025.04 (1) OCR (Optical Character Recognition)

PRASAD, A R D 916

Optical Character Recognition (OCR) and its relevance to library and information work, *CRL*, 157-163.

Traces the development of OCR. Discusses types of OCR readers with latest technology. Describes the available OCR software. Proposes the setting up of a PC-based OCR workstation. Discusses also the OCR application in library and information services.

025.04 (1) E-Mail

KUMBAR, T S 917

Electronic mail and its application for library and information services, *CS*, 329-338.

Defines E-Mail. Presents briefly its general use in India and information services where it can be used. Presents in brief the use of E-Mail in libraries in USA, UK, Canada and India. Gives hardware and software required for setting up an E-mail service. Mentions a few advantages and disadvantages of the system.

PILLAI, M RAMASAMY 918

Application of E-Mail information, *ITAH,* 79-81.

Discusses hardware, software, and other interface requirement for E-Mail installation. Presents different types of E-Mail based information services. Highlights the application of E-Mail in enhancing end user and information system interaction under network environments. Presents overall scenario of network based services at national level promoted by ERNET, SIRNET, and GEMS (Gateway Electronic Mail Service), etc.

025.04 (1) Information Technology (IT)

BAJWA, DEEPINDER S, et al 919

Conceptualising the link between strategy, structures and information technology : Implications for computer based system configuration, *Vikalpa* 18 (4) Oct-Dec 1993 : 29-36.

Deals with the conceptualisation of the strategy, structure and IT, with its implications for the computer based systems being developed for various functions.

BARADOL, A K 920

The use of information technology in the libraries of medical, dental and engineering colleges of Mangalore University, *LIT*, 80-85.

Gives meaning of IT. Discusses need for IT to render more effective and efficient information services. Studies the use of IT in 12 medical, dental and engineering college libraries of Mangalore University. Makes some useful suggestions for improvement.

BEDI, D S 921

Information professional and the new technology, *Desidoc Bull Inf Tech* 11 (3) May 1991 : 3-8.

Highlights the impact of automation on staff and on administration of library operations in view of the recent technological developments. Emphasizes that the library administrators and managers must develop mecahnisms for dealing effectively with the changes caused by the introduction of new technology in a library. Discusses the guidelines recommended for introducing staff to the changes caused by the new technology. Concludes that any library set-up could benefit from implementing these guidelines.

CHAKRABORTY, ARUN KUMAR 922

Impact of new information technologies on libraries, *ALE*, 1-15.

States the importance of special library as leader in technological innovation and experimentation and these have helped in information transfer, information utilization, technological transfer, information access, etc. Describes the time for newer roles for information system for which information staff training is needed. Discusses in this information age the information technology and librarians and elucidates the effects of technological impact.

CHHOTEY LAL and BHATIA, S 923

Adoption of information technology by agricultural libaries in India, *Ann Lib Sci & Docum* 40 (1) Mar 1993 : 6-11.

Discusses the need of agricultural research and transfer of technology to attain the optimum level of productivity. Provides a state-of-the-art of agricultural libraries in India. Discusses their information services in relation to ICAR. Describes about the databases in Indian agricultural libraries. Points out constraints in application of IT. States that target achievement depends on motivation of librarians and support of scientists.

DAS, KAILASH CHANDRA 924

Information technology and libraries : A future for distant learners, *LIT*, 38-43.

Studies the effects of IT on distance education at two levels, first in the way the library delivers information, and secondly, in methods and modes of student study. Discusses IT and libraries, the ISR through videodiscs, CD-I, CD-ROM, optical disc, etc. giving future directions in information retrieval. Identifies the issues and problems.

ESPERANZA, M (Sister) 925

Workshop on Information Technology and Library Development, *Her Lib Sci* 32 (3-4) July-Oct 1993 : 245-248.

Reports about the Workshop on 'Information Technology and Library Development' organised at Patna Women's College Library on 23 April 1993 participated by librarians, library science students and library users. Mentions about the discourses on distance education and library, on IT, etc.

GAUTAM, J N 926

Modern information technology and libraries, *IJILIS* 5 (1-2) Jan-June 1992 : 95-116.

Describes concept of information and its growth. Discusses exponential growth of literature and need for bibliographical control of information. Narrates role of modern information technology, particularly computer technology and other sophisticated modern equipments in the context of storing, retrieving and disseminating information.

GOETZE, HEINZ 927

Development and application of technology, production, distribution, storage and retrieval of health science information - global perspective, *ML*, PC 39-43.

Mentions that medical literature is increasing at a fast speed. States that we are at the turning point where the introduction of electronic media will support the dissemination of diagnostic and therapeutic information. Describes that new problems create new soulutions in electronic publishing and new media which will improve rapid access to information and special data including publishing on demand.

KULDIP CHAND, *Ed* 928

Current trends in information technology: Its impact on information scene in India, New Delhi : Batra Book Service, 1993. viii, 199p.

Contains 19 contributed papers for the XI Annual Convention & Conference of the Society for Information Science held at the NCL, Pune during 20-22 Jan 1992. The theme "Current Trends in IT : Its impact on Information Scence in India" was discussed under 5 technical sessions : (1) Databases Creation; (2) User requirement, services offered, impact of DTP, etc; (3) Data online or offline; (4) Networking of the National Services; and (5) Marketing Strategies.

KULDIP CHAND 929

Impact of information technology on science information scene in India, *CTIT*, 4-11.

Defines IT. Describes the information scene in India such as IT in library operations and networks, database creation, database searching, online services, and DTP. Discusses also about education and training of the professionals in view of the changing requirements of society. Mentions also about costs of IT.

LAHIRI, A 930

IT : What the decade portends, *NISSAT Newsletter* 11 (1) Jan-Mar 1992: 1.

Predicts that IT revolution would continue through this decade also as thousands of microprocessors with above 100mn transistors will help reach a speed beyond comprehension of lod generation computer users. Discusses about the position of India in such a situation as it is way behind at the component level.

MISHRA, S , JOSHI, M K and MISRA, M K 931

Relevance of Ranganathan's contribution in the age of information technology, *Ann Lib Sci & Docum* 39 (2) June 1992 : 69-71.

Studies Ranganathan's ideas and philosophy revealing some amazing concepts which have the potential to solve the complexities of the present system. Discusses the relevance of the Five Laws, information organization, and retrieval, bibliographic record formats in the context of computer and communiction technology. Concludes that Ranganathan's ideas are seminal in nature and need careful attention from the professionals, academicians and researchers.

NAGI REDDY, Y 932

Impact of information technology on libraries, *Univ News* Sept 28, 1992.

Discusses about information explosion and need for application, CD ROM technology, databases, telecommunications, and information networks. Concludes that a modern day library has to become a gateway to the broadest world of scholarly information.

NAVALANI, K 933

Information technology and libraries : The Indian scenario, *LIS*, 114-123.

Gives the information infrastructure for science and technology in India with integral plan of NISSAT and its databases, other organisations and their databases, academic libraries, public libraries, and the databases they can follow, telecommunication networks and use of IT in Indian libraries. Discusses some of the problems as they donot follow a standard exchange format.

PARTHASARATHY, S 934

Fiche and chips : The library of the future, *Frontline* 9 (17) Aug 15—28, 1992 : 60-62.

Describes the impact of IT on the information storage system and the formats such as microfilm, microfiche. States that computer technology has made rapid progress due to microchip revolution. Discusses various generation of computer and rapid strides in telecommunication in transfer of digital information. Describes the impact of IT on Indian information systems including INSDOC, NISSAT, and networks as SIRNET, DELNET, CALIBNET, INFLIBNET, NICNET, INDONET, etc. Mentions that libraries will continue to be essential even in the year 2000

PAWAR, S S 935

Impact of new information technology in development of library services, *LIT*, 27-31.

Provides an overview of IT with its main features. Describes the impact of computer technology, storage technology and telecommunication technology. Discusses about computerised networks as INFLIBNET, CALIBNET, SIRNET, and development of video tex and E-mail. Gives an overall impact of IT. Mentions the need of new breed of library professionals for development of library services.

PUROHIT, KARUNA H 936

Information communication technology : Its meaning and application, *ALIS*, V 4, 75-81.

Defines information and IT. Provides guidelines for developing information system in the country. Describes role of computer, CD-ROM, facsimile and their application in rendering effective library services. States that new technology will play an important role in the management of libraries and information centres. Provides the concept of paperless libraries by the next century.

RAJASEKHARAN, K 937

New information technology for increasing access to agricultural information, *LIT*, 32-37.

Emphsises that the advent of computer in library and information activities, role of CD ROM, LAN, video cassettes, full text, laser discs, etc have revolutionised the methods and increased effectivness of dissemination of information. Discusses the future scenario as a result of IT and it is likely to pay the dividends.

RAJU, J SRIHARI 938

Information handling as a profession : Current trends and emerging opportunities, *INICAE* 12 (2) Sept 1993 : 221-226.

Refers to all pervading information environment. Discusses IT and its advantages. States evolution of online era and the development of online information system. Points out the growth of new information providers in business information. Discusses growth of new information providers in business information. Discusses growth of information networking, decision support system, CD-ROM phenomena causing challenge to the traditional information services.

RAVI, N, *Ed* 939

The Hindu speaks on information technology, compiled by the Editor, Madras : Kasturi & Sons, 1993. 403 p.

Follows the first volume on libraries in this series. Brought out on the occasion of the First International Conference on Database Production and Discribution -INFOTEX 93. Groups items under five IT categories : Impact Implementation and Maintenance; Development in Technology; Communication Facilities; Applications Databases; Information Sources and Services.

ROWE, RICHARD P 940

The impact of new technologies on medical library services in developing countries, *ML*, PC 7-13.

Mentions about the various global problems of population and health, poverty, illiteracy. States about the changing role of librarians. Explains the role and impact of IT in the library and information work including the development of CD-ROM, satellite communications. Identifies the potential application of satellite services to document delivery, conferencing, training, research, etc.

SAHOO, K C 941

Information technology vis-a-vis technical processing, *LIT*, 21-26.

Traces the origin of IT and its application in library operations such as technical processing, automated cataloguing, indexing/abstracting. Discusses general impact of new technology as advent of the microprocessors have introduced library automation at affordable price.

SETH, MAHENDRA KUMAR 942

Trends in information technology industry, *LIT*, 233-237.

Defines IT. Discusses trends in communication media, trends in storage technology, trends in publishing. Concludes that new technology offers the possibility of rapid collection, processing and distribution.

SEWA SINGH 943

Information technology and academic libraries in India, *Jl Inf Sci* 3(1) July-Sept 1992 : 11-24.

Defines IT. Points out that application of computers in information retrieval is catching up these days. Gives detailed account of new IT and libray computerisation. Attempts to identify the problems associated with computerisation and the challenges that the libraries have to face especially in academic libraries.

SEWA SINGH and KULDIP CHAND 944

Current trends in information technology and impact on information scene in India, *Her Lib Sci* 31 (3-4) July-Oct 1992 : 241-245.

Reports about the XI Annual Convention and Conference of the Society for Information Science held at NCL, Pune during 20-22 January 1992. Describes the inaugural function, the award presentation, Technical Sessions on Databases creation, Data online or offline, Networking, Marketing strategies. Gives also the recommendations adopted aat the Convention.

SHISHOO, J J 945

Library and information services: Impact of information technology, *LIT*, 1-9.

Mentions about the long journey from primitive system of communication to the present system of telecommunication and electronics as a result of technological revolution. Describes the use of electronic media such as electronic databases, gateway services. Describes the future scenario of libraries with electronic journals and paperless books. Discusses the impact of technology in relation to space, storage, reading room, access to information, and manpower requirement.

SINGH, S N 946

Impact of information communication technologies on libraries: Indian scenario, *ALIS,* V4, 1-20.

Explains the need of information communication technology for providing pinpointed, expeditious and exhaustive information services. Explains the role of IT in handling S & T information. Emphasises use of computer technology, communication technology, satellite communication and CD-ROM technology in rendering effective information services. Provides state of affairs of IT in India. Suggests for manpower training through UGC and DST, course revision. Advocates promoting awareness and utilization of existing information communication technology resources.

SINHA, A K 947

Information management in 21st century-new trends and technology, *Ann Lib Sci & Docum* 39 (3) Sept 1992: 106-1121.

Explains the terms 'information society', 'information explosion'. Describes information technology (IT), giving its components and users in library and information activities. Discusses about INFLIBNET, CALIBNET, information systems, ES, videotex, and teletext, micrographics, E-mail, information management, etc.

SUJATHA KUMARI, K 948

Library : A source for development of information technology, *SPLS*, 23-25.

Deals with the application of computer and information technology (IT) in library and the functions information systems must perform. Discusses information transfer, information storage and retrieval system, indexing systems.

SWAROOP RANI, B S 949

Digitizing libraries with today's information technology, *LIT*, 48-54.

Identifies the element brought in by IT. Describes advances in IT as electronic notebook, data discman, multimedia, E-mail, videotex, videoconferencing, audiotex. Discusses recent developments. States that we are passing through a transition and a period of adjustment is necessary.

TARIQ ASHRAF and SANJEEV KUMAR 950

Library and information services: Impact of new technology, *LIT*, 10-20.

Explains the genesis of IT and developments in new storage media, optical laser discs, communication media, document delivery services. Describes in detail the impact of IT on modern libraries.

TEJOMURTY, A and BOSE, KAUSHIK 951

Information technology in India comes of age, *LIS*, 124-134.

Defines information technology (IT). Mentions present status of IT in India. Discusses development of computer technology including hardware, software, applications in public or private sectors. Discusses development of communication technology. Points out need of national information policy as India is adopting new high-tech products.

TEJOMURTY, A and BOSE, KAUSHIK 952

Information technology in India : Where we are ?, *LIT*, 224-232.

Explains the current status of IT in India. Traces the development of IT in two main areas, ie, in the areas of computer and communication technology. Describes status of computer adoption in India. Mentions about manpower requirements.

VARALAKSHMI, R S R 953

Emerging trends in information technology and its impact on library environment, *INICAE*, 11 (2) Sept 1992: 232-243.

Defines IT. Emphasises the need for adopting IT in librarires and information centres. Provides a comprehensive introduction to the emerging trends of IT. Discusses impact of IT on information society. Highlights application of IT in the introduction of new activities and services such as online search, CD ROM search, E-mail, teletext/videotext, FAX, DTP, etc. Concludes that all types of libraries have to switch over to automation to offer effective library service.

VASHISHTH, C P, *Ed* 954

Library and information technology: In pursuit of excellence: Seminar papers of 38th All India Library Conference of ILA, Delhi: India Library Association, 1992. 318 p.

Contains 43 articles divides into 6 Sections according to the theme of the Conference of the ILA held at Bhubaneswar during 21-

24 Novemeber 1992. It was brought out with salutations to the Father of Library Science in India on his 101st Birthday.

VIJAYKUMAR, P 955

Information technology and the academic libraries in India : The changing scenario, *RDAL*, 111-122.

Describes the development of academic libraries in pre-and post- independent era. States that the dawn of the new era has witnessed severe changes in the attitude and style. Discusses the present situation of library services. Explains development in information technology through NCSI, INSDOC, INDONET, INFLIBNET, ERNET, VSNL, and so on.

VITTAL, N 956

Information technology and management, *Ind Mgmt* 31 (6) Dec 1992: 7-13.

Deals with the versatility of information technology in modern day society. Discusses about its application to the area of management which is deemed to be important from the point of view of overall managerial control of activities and operations.

025.04 (1) Information Systems

BOSE, P C 957

Management of current research information, *STIM*, 16-19.

Outlines the importance of on-going research information system. Gives a description of the system. Explains meeting the user needs of planners, policy makers, decision makers, administrators, managers, individual researchers, information specialists, etc. as the system has the capacity for collecting and storing large quantities of information.

CHANDRAN, D and NAVANEETHAN, R 958

Information systems : Design parameters, *STIM*, 1-5.

Explains the information system design which is more close to library and information system so that timely and accurate exchange of scientific and technical information is made possible. Mentions the steps of a library and information system. Discusses the three major parameters-users, information and technologies-involved in an information system. Concludes to say it is important to study in depth and evaluate all the parameters.

GUPTA, A K 959

Information systems for science and technology: Indian scenario, *ALIS*, V 3, 3-20.

Deals with an indepth analysis of existing information system for S & T in India. Discusses about the information dissemination process, information services, and role of various organizations invovled in the process of information system including NISSAT. Outlines also various plans and projects recently taken up by the government.

IBRAHIM, ABBAS and SHAHJAHAN, ABBAS IBRAHIM 960

RILISAR's CALIBLAN MIS : Management Information Systems for Corporate Secretariat, Library, Hospital, Maintenece Service, Inventory Control, *Rilisar Bull* 8 (2) Apr-June 1993 : 16-21.

Gives the background of development of CALIBLAN MIS. Lists its special features as LAN options, documentation services, placement services, sort, custom made not ready made, circulation service, current awareness bulletin, use profile, future updates, training, maintenance, hardware requirements, etc.

JAIN, H C and GUPTA, B M, *Eds* 961

S & T information management in India : Papers presented at the 10th Annual Convention & Conference of the Society for Information for Information Science, held at RRL, Trivandrum during 17-19 January, 1991, New Delhi : Aditya Prakashan, 1993. viii, 182 p.

Contains 20 papers which were presented at the 10th Annual Convention & Conference of the SIS. Deals with various information system and services in vogue in such areas as Plantation Crops, Food Science and Technology, Iron and Steel Industry, Medicinal and Aromatic Plants, etc. Covers also the networking efforts being made in various sectors and organizations.

KUMAR, S SURESH 962

Information for S & T functions and R & D management, *STIM*, 6-11.

Describes the information system as it applies to the S & T function technicalities. Discusses about R & D management with regard to science technology information, its communication, channels, sources, content, etc. States that in the present times role of information scientist as gatekeeper increases.

NAG, PRITHVISH 963

Role of geographic information system and communication technology in thematic mapping, *ALIS*, V 4, 103-118.

Presents the framework and operational chart of Geographical Information system (GIS). Describes the objectives, need, technology, hardware and software requirements of the Geographical Information Centre. States that the thematic mapping of information is becoming more and more voluminous and it is very difficult to handle this information without using electronic media.

NEGISHI, MASAMITSU and ADACHI, JUN 964

Third International Conference on Japanese Information and ICSTI Symposium, *INICAE*, 11 (1) Mar 1992 : 118-121.

Reports about the Third International Conference held in Naucy, France from 15 to 18 May 1991 and the discussions held particularly to develop systems which enable retireval of Japanese databases in English.

PANDA, S K and NAGABHUSHNAM, A 965

Disease prevention information system, *IJILIS* 6 (3-4) July-Dec 1993: 286-299.

Reports the design of two database schemes in mainframe environs for Disease Prevention Information System. Takes into consideration the Indian conditions. Prescribes a list of possible inputs with important data items and a series of validations. Makes provision for outputs at different time intervals based on statistical calculation, etc.

PARIDA, BAMAN 966

Studies in information system, services and programmes in India and abroad, New Delhi : Ajanta Books International, 1993. 356 p.

Attempts to study and describe the views of prominent authors on the subject in as many as six chapters on Information concept, Theoretical aspects of Information System, Documentation and Information Services at international level and at national level in India, Information system developed at the international level, and growth and development of different types of information systems in India.

PATIL, D B 967

Computerized information retrieval in library and information centres (CIRLIC) : An analysis, *IJILIS* 6 (3-4) July-Dec 1993 : 272-280.

Aims at analysing the information retrieval in library and information centres. States that the coded instruction has been provided through dBASE III Plus to bring out the information retrieval menu.

VINCENT, JOHN D and RATNASAMY, M 968

Books Information Retrieval System (BIRS), *ALIS*, V 4, 141-149.

Emphasises importance of book collection in any type of library. Deals with the experience gained in the creation of computer readable database at IGCAR Library. Describes that BIRS database is accessible through different entry points including Indexterms or Descriptors.

025.04 (1) Information Transfer

HARIHARAN, CHITRA, JAYARAMAN, N and GANAPATHY, T V 969

Technology transfer system and the role of the technology transfer agent, *STIM*, 12-15.

Defines technology transfer. Discusses means and methods of technology transfer. Explains the passive mode and active mode of technology transfer. Lists some of the conclusions about the transfer of technology in public sector drawn by the National Science Foundation Study Group. Concludes that the success of technology transfer is directly related to the enthusiasm and dedication of the technology transfer agent.

OJHA, D C 970

Importance of infomation communication channels in transfer of farm technology - a survey, *ALIS*, 129-139.

Evaluates the existing means of communication for transfer of farm technology using survey techniques. Reveals that out of 18 communiction channels identified for transferring farm technology, posters have been found most popular and effective media for communicating technical know-how. Reveals that transfer of farm technology through pro~~er communication channels has also affected crop production. Suggests for proper coordination among all the existing communication agencies.

025.06 INFORMATION STORAGE AND RETRIEVAL SYSTEM (ISRS)

025.063 ISRS-Social Science

AGRAWAL, S P 971

National information resources for social science in India; mobilisation, dispersal and informational enhancement, New Delhi: Concept Publishing Company, 1992. 191 p (CICIL Series No. 36).

Presents a detialed picture of the national information resources in social sciences in India. Includes 11 chapters in four parts: Part I- Introductory analysis has one chapter; Part II - Abstract also has only one chapter; Part III-Exposition is divided into three sub-parts (5 chapters in all); and Part IV-Linkages has four chapers. Includes 10 useful appendices. Discusses three categories of resources: content, human, and institutional resources.

MEYRIAT, JEAN 972

International cooperation in social science information and documentation : Kaula Endowment Lecture, *INICAE* 11 (2) Sept 1992: 244-251.

Specifies the type of information demanded by users in social science information and documentation. States methodoligical tools and needed infrastructures like equipments, computer hardware, communication and telecommunication networks etc. Discusses problems like universal availability of documents, communication of data, exchange of ideas, joint action plans in promoting international coopetation. Discusses a number of hurdles. Highlights some concrete achievements.

VYAS, S D 973

Library and information scene in India with special reference to social sciences, *IJILIS* 6 (1-2) Jan-June 1993: 1-28.

Deals with the printing technology, printing of periodicals and books, libraries in British period, Ranganathan and libraries. Govt institutions, socio-eco institutes in post-independent India, social science research, various commissions appointed by GOI for the development of research libraries, problems of library cooperation, UGC role in development of libraries, formation of Inter-University Board, and many other vital aspects of scientific research. Offers useful solutions to problems. Gives recommendations about social science.

VYAS, S D 974

Social science information in India; efforts towards bibliographic control, New Delhi : Concept Publishing Company, 1992. 280 p (CICIL Series, No. 41).

Attempts to analyse the development of social sciences in India, and the bibliographical attempts made by individuals and institutions. Evaluates state of bibliographical control of social science. Studies the information gathering habits of social science scholars.

025.06338 ISRS -PLANNING

SEETHARAMA, S and PANDIAN, M PAUL 975

PLANNER : An automated decision support system for planning of libraries and inroamtion centres, *CRL*, 177-195.

Discusses the need for planning and highlights the elements of library planning. Provides details regarding PLANNER which is an automated decision support system for planning of libraries and informtion centres. Gives its limitations also, but it supports decision making.

JAIN, P L 976

Information management system for quality assurance in foundry industries, *CTIT*, 47-60.

Defines quality and quality control for which information management system is required. Discusses about quality policy and quality system ;and its activities in castings. Mentions use of statistical quality control. States that a well organised quality system includes regular reporting procedure.

025.06338 (1) ISRS - Industry

SENDUR CHELVI, K P 977

Industrial management and information systems, *Rilisar Bull* 8 (2) Apr-June 1993 : 1-18.

Discusses management levels for information is a competitive weapon. Gives the information flow, both internal and external. Describes management level and information requirements at each level. Explains major attributes of external informtion flow, ways of obtaining it and methods of achieving it.

TIFAC-CMS-DSIDC Centre for Industry Information, 978
NISSAT Newsletter 12 (3) July-Sept 1993 : 20-21.

Discusses that as an excellent example of maximising cynergistic advantages, TIFAC, CMC Ltd and Delhi State Industrial Development Corporation (DSIDC) have joined hands for a collaborative venture in setting up the Centre for Industry Information in New Delhi, as'one step information shop'. Explains the services planned from the Centre which was inaugurated on August 14, 1993.

025.0634 ISRS - Law

NAVALGUND, C U 979
National Legal Information Centre : A proposal, *LIT*, 203-207.

Explains the need for National Legal Information Centre (NLIC). Gives purpose and broad objectives of NLIC. Describes the features of the information system, functions of the NLIC. Explains organisational structure of NLIC.

PRICE, M KATHLEEN 980
Linking legistative databases into an International Legal Information Network, *Lib Sci sland Docum & Inf Std* 30 (1) Mar 1993 : 36-39.

Discusses the value of legal texts and their usefulness to international legal informtion service. Discusses the resources available in Law Library of Library of Congress. Suggests developments of an International Information System for Legal Information.

025.065 ISRS - Science and Technology

RAMASESH, C P 981
Industrial and Technological Information Bank of UNIDO (INTIB), *Her Lib Sci* 31 (1-2) Jan-Apr 1992 : 9-16.

Mentions activities of UNIDO and establishment of INTIB. Gives sources of information for INTIB and also its functions and activities. Describes services operated by INTIB through its Industrial Inquiry Service, v/s Network system. Describes also INTIB Publication Service, joint patent programme with WIPO.

SECTORAL Centres move into fast lane as NISSAT 982
promotes new S & T information system, *NISSAT Newsletter* 11 (2) Apr-June 1992: 12-22.

Gives the objectives of NISSAT. Explains about the setting of Sectoral Information Centres (now 10 in number) across the country for systematic and orderly growth of a compatible set of information systems. Describes the services available to scientists, academicians, managers, technologists, etc and these include online and SDI services, library networking, computer based information processing, union catalogue, NISSATCARD, document supply service. Discusses also its manpower development programmes, promotion of its activities, products and services, international activities and utility of *NISSAT Newsletter*.

025.0653 (1) ISRS - INSPEC

DIMMOCK, EVA 983
Military systems and equipment; classfication code, *INICAE* 11 (2) Sept 1992 : 262-263.

Discusses abouth the new database introduced in INSPEC in 1988 while revising its classfication scheme dealing specificlly with military systems and equipments. Lists also the relevant thesaurus terms.

025.0654 ISRS -Chemistry

SINGH, R S 984
Chemical information system, *STIM*, 149-170.

Identifies primary publications as major vehicle of chemical informtion. Discusses the role of secondary and tertiary publications also in view of literature growth. Describes databanks, computerised information handling and retrieval, dtabases on chemistry, chemical structure search system, techniques of structure manipulation which helps in designing chemical synthesis.

GUHA BAKSHI, D N 985
National Information Centre for Plant Taxonomy - a case study, *ALIS*, V 3, 239-245.

Describes the establishment, organization, and functions of a NICPLAT. Proposes that it would work in cooperation with the NISSAT. Mentions that the Centre would search, locate, store and disseminate all possible information and data on plant taxonomy at national and international levels.

025.0658 ISRS - Plants

KAMALAVIJAYAN, D 986

Information services on plantation crops in India, with special reference to palm and cocoa, *STIM*, 75-86.

Names some organisations in plantation crops under the Ministry of Agriculture and Ministry of Commerce. States that all R & D agencies provide information services confined to their institutions and there is no central information service as such in the country. Explains the library and information centre and the services of Central Plantation Crops Research Institute. Gives suggestions for organising market information services.

MITRA, R, SRIVASTAVA, A K and SANE, P V 987

Information services in plant science research, *STIM*, 32-48.

Recognises the role of information services as a vital resource to any R & D activity. Explains the need for dissemination of information related to plant sciences, including information services of Botanical Survey of India, Forest Research Institute, PID, National Botanical Research Institute, and so on. Mentions some of the important international informtion services/agencies which cater to the information needs of all user groups of plant science research.

025.06584634 ISRS - Medicinal Plants

INFORMATION Management for medicinal and aromatic 988

plants industry-Workshop, *NISSAT Newsletter* 12 (4) Oct-Dec 1993 : 12-13.

Describes about a three day Workshop on medicinal and aromatic plants was organised by the PID, New Delhi during 12-14 Oct 1993 which was attended by 70 participants from research institutions, government department, etc. Keynote address was delivered by Dr Nitya Nand appreciating the role of PID. Gives several recommendations/suggestions that emerged from the deliberations of Workshop.

JAIN, H C 989

MAPIS : Current status & future prospects, *STIM*, 49-55.

Mentions importance of medicinal plants. States that MAPIS is the creation of specialised information service by PID of CSIR. Discusses information services offered under MAPIS on fee basis. Explains about MAPA, its scope, data collection mechanism, computerisation, etc. Mentions about MAPIS and APINMAP collaboration.

025.066 ISRS - Engineering

JAYARAMAN, N and RAVINDRAN, C C 990

Techinical information services at SERC, Madras, *STIM*, 171-177.

Deals with the services provided by the SERC, Madras, its R & D areas and major facilities. Describes about the technological information services, printing and publications, transfer of technology, public relations, library and documentation activities, reprographic services, etc. Concludes that there is need for setting up a network of information services in structural engineering.

025.06608 ISRS - Patents

RAY, DIPAK KUMAR and CHAUDHURI, ARUN 991

Role of patent information system in the development of Indian society, *IJILIS* 5 (1-2) Jan-June 1992 : 117-125.

Throws light on complications of patent information system in innovative. Highlights present position of patents dissemination in the world, with reference to India. Discusses steps taken by Government of India to ensure patent informtion in every sphere of developmental programme. Gives an exposure of INPADOC and how it has been helping on patent informtion system.

025.661 ISRS - Medicine

FLOWER, M A 992

Libraries without walls : Canadians begin the search for keys to increase access to health sciences information resources, *ML*, 147-152.

Makes a survey of the health science collections and services in Canada in 1986. Presents information on health science libraries with comparison to highlight trends, recommend steps to improve health information services nationwide. Gives methodology, finding, recommendations of the survey.

FOREMAN, JOAN R and FOREMAN, GRET RUDE 993

Smoking cessation programs : Information for decision making, *ML*, 153-155.

Mentions that public health workers in the state of Minnesota have a goal of smoke free environment in the year 2000. Describes that access to and use of information is an integral part of the health professional's planning and implementation of such program. Discusses abouth a survey of employees resulted in smoking cessation services, to provide information.

GUIRGUIS, GEORGE AMIN 994

Health Literature and Information, Services in the WHO Eastern Mediterranean Region, *ML*, 509-512.

Describes the activities of WHO Health Literature Services in EMR and the components as National Focal Point Libraries, regional back up services, utilization of CD ROM technology, Index Medicus for EMR, progress in informatics and support, consultancy and development. Gives also the future prospects.

MARY, G PHILOMINA 995

Key to resources-professional linbrarian's point of view, *ML*, 257-261.

States that medical profession is experiencing a great change and librarians playing a paramount role in selecting the resources and giving services. Describes that the introduction of computer management and retrieval system have combined to challenge the traditional activities. Points out librarians views about the keys to the resources. Discusses specifically the Indian information system.

M'BAISSOUR, PAR BENADJIEL 996

Chad's problems of health and the contribution of medical and sanitary documentation on the information and education for health (IES), *ML*, 31-33.

Describes various health problems in Chad, and small sanitary infrastructure, the Government has set up a program called Information and Education for Health (IES). States the objectives of this program including the creation of a sanitary documentation centre as a national information system, and creation of medical libraries and their activities.

NAIR, M CHANDRAKUMARAN 997

Management of oncology patient information : Application of CD-ROM technology for its optimum use, *ITAH*, 29-38.

Analyses the problems and prospects of the utilisation of vast amount of patient informtion derived from hospital based oncology registry. Mentions the underutilisation of data due to inherent difficulties. States the need for developing a computerised system.

Gives the requirements of the system and its implementation considerations. Points out advantages of CD-ROM based database as vast storage capabilities, high reliability, less experience, quick data transfer, etc.

SCHMALZ, ROCHELLE PERINE 998

Issues and trends in lay health information-a view from the United States, *ML*, 391-397.

Presents the current US health care environs. Describes the significance of providing health information to the lay person. Defines the terms lay / patient / consumer / health information, etc. Gives a description of different models of health information delivery in diocese ways. Discusses issues and trends on the basis of the experience.

SEETHARAMA, S 999

Information consolidation activities and services: Keys to health information, *ML*, 425-429.

Discusses impact of new IT on library and information activities. Highlights the role of new techniques for information management, particularly information analysis and consolidation, catering to different requirements of different users, policy makers/ managers, R & D workers, extension workers, etc. Presents methodology for the development of information consolidation services/products. Discusses some findings and conclusions based on actual experience

SNYDER, LISA ANN 1000

Design and implementation of efficient pathways to health informtion : The Malawi model, *ML*, 453-457.

Discusses the first two years of a project to collect, organise and disseminate health information through a national integrated library system in Malawi, Africa, providing a useful model for other developing countries with limited resources in terms of money, staff and material so as to provide reference materials for health information for clinical diagnosis and treatment. Gives a review of the project, models for collection development, etc.

SRIVASTAVA, DIVYA 1001

Health indicator and sources of information, *ITAH*, 259-263.

Discusses importance of indicators for quantifying medical research. Discusses types of information and the various sources of information which can be used as indirect indicators for quantifying medical research and health status of any society.

SULLIVAN, MARILYN B GOREMAN 1002

Health information for a geriatric education training program, *ML*, 459-462.

Recognises the importance to train health care professionals as to the needs of the elderly in the US, Geriatric Education Centres have been set up. States that the GEC at Missouri provides educational opportunities, and clearing house for citations in the field and stinulates sharing of resources on many levels. Plans for a network linking outlying areas short on resources. Discusses health science libraries as part of these centres.

THAPA, GITA 1003

Health information needs in rural areas, *ML*, 473-478.

Gives general information on existing health informtion services in city areas in Nepal. Makes necessary development to collect and disseminate health information services but there is lack of health information service in rural Nepal. Discusses problems to be faced before the implementation of primary health care. Describes role of the Institure of Medicine in disseminating information. Emphasises on producing literature in the local language. Makes suggestions to improve the situation.

WALKER, CELINE 1004

Contribution of the Advisory Committee for the Co-ordination of Information Systems (ACCIS) to facilitating access by members states to United Nations health information, *ML*, PC 1-6.

Discusses in the Pre-Congress Seminar of the 6th International Congress on Medical Librarianship about the health information from the UN system in support of development through five slides on UNO and its specialised agencies, database and information services in health, sources of information at the country level.

025.0661 (1) ISRS - Biomedical

DACIC, MILUTIN and CRNOBARIC, ANA 1005

The system of Biomedical Scientific Information of Serbia-status and perspectives, *ML*, 105-108.

Describes the significant developments of the System of Biomedical Scientific Information of Serbia with acquisition of new computers, CD-ROM drive, telefax. Gives its current activities including bibliographical database accessible online in Serbia. Mentions the databases acquired as MEDLINE, EXCERPTA MEDICA, DRUG INFORMATION SOURCE ON CD-ROM to give up high quality of information.

DASGUPTA, R K 1006

Biomedical library and informtion network, *IJILIS* 5 (1-2) Jan-Jun 1992 : 88-94.

Reproduces address given at a Seminar on Biomedical Library and Information Network held at the Indian Institute of Chemical Biology on 7 August 1989. Describes about MEDLARS in detail, and tells about its uses and advantages.

MIAH, Md FARID HOSSAIN and KERAMAT ALI, SHAH Md 1007

Sources of biomedical information in Bangladesh : A survey of indigenous biomedial educational resources and their use, *ML*, 263-277.

Describes periodical literature and other publications as primary sources of information for health science professionals. Points out the periodicals of this region being indexed in Index Medicus. Mentions the need for a network of biomedical libraries of Bangladesh.

PATRIKIOS, HELGA 1008

Health service priorities in a developing country : Biomedical and health information support in Zimbabwe, *ML*, 337-342.

Deals with the University of Zimbabwe's Medical Library and centralization and dissemination of health informtion services so as to bridge the gap between fast paced supply of health services and the dearth of medical literature relevant to needs. Outlines steps towards providing the essential health professionals.

ROA, LUCERO ARBOLEDA de 1009

Bibliographic information services in biomedicine : The case of the Dominican Republic, *ML*, 379-384.

Makes an attempt to present the situation of the libraries, documentation centres and information services of the Dominican Republic in the biomedical areas. Establishes a profile of the national biomedical production. Analysis allows the evaluation of the impact of these publications as sources to take informtion and establishes their validity to spread and disseminates the achievements.

SAMPATHA CHARY, K, DEVIDAS, M and RADHAKRISHNA MURTHY, S 1010

Biomedical library and information facilities in Andhra Pradesh : A study, with special reference to nutrition information facilities, *ITAH*, 173-180.

Traces background of medical colleges in India. Gives the present situation where they are giving modest services to their clients. Mentions that inadequate resources and manpower, lower scales are few reasons for the underdevelopment of these libraries. Examines ISR activities in Andhra Pradesh with reference to health and nutrition disciplines. Emphasises need for looking at the problems of information transfer afresh. Highlights ongoing information activities at National Institute of Nutrition, Hyderabad.

SEBASTIANI, BRUNELLA and SALVATORI, GIUSEPPE 1011

Biomedical library as an informtion centre, *ML*, 417-423.

States that information is a resource to be distributed and used. Points out the role of library in this area which has now become a system where the information is distributed and becomes a source for new message. Discusses that the role of biomedical library and librarians has increased and is targeted more on the contents processing to satisfy user needs. States that this has changed the connotation of library to information centre.

025.0661 (1) ISRS - MEDLINE

KIHLBERG, EEVA and NEUVONEN, ULLA 1012

The use of CD-ROM MEDLINE by Finnish dentists and dental students, *ML*, 207-209.

Discusses about the literature search services offered by the Helsinki University Dental Library to every dentist in Finland free of charge. Outlines the volume of and differences between use of CD ROM by the three major user categories of the library : teachers, students, and general dentists. Reveals that CD ROM MEDLINE is an efficient, useful and relatively cheap tool for improving information services.

KOTTAI, A 1013

MEDLINE on CD-ROM A comparison of DIALOG ONDISC and Silver Platter interface, *Lib Sci slant Docum & Inf Std* 30 (1) Mar 1993: 11-16.

Makes a comparison of DIALOG ON DISC and Silver Platter interfaces in relation to MEDLINE. Discusses the CD-ROM technology, hardware requirement, installation procedure, scope, cost, terms, searching the system, displaying and printing search results, documentation and user support.

LANDE, RAGNHILD 1014

Medline on CD-ROM, a user study from a medical library in Norway, *ML*, 231-232.

Deals with the installation of MEDLINE on CD-ROM to enable users to conduct their own searches. Conducts a survey of these users in a Norway medical library told that they used five minutes to three hours on Medline, told abouth the response time, number of references, etc.

REAM, DIANE 1015

Paper chase : A cooperative MEDLINE training project in a US community hospial library, *ML*, 367-370.

Traces the planning, funding, implementation, and evaluation of MEDLINE training project in Miami, Florida in a community hospital setting. Concludes that it has expanded the visibility of the library's role in continuing medical education.

SCHWARTZ, DIANE G and SCHWARTZ, STANLEY A 1016

End-user search training for medical students : Keys to information access, *ML*, 399-416.

Analyses the end-user search training of MDELINE given to third year medical students, on the basis of a questionnaire-based survey. Assesses the value of having unlimited access to MEDLINE on their research work. Concludes that students appreciate the value of having ready access to MEDLINE, the world's most important biomedical database.

025.06616994 ISRS-Cancer

MIIDO, HELIS 1017

Accessing information at the International Agency for Research on Cancer : Coordinating external sources with internal capabilities, *ML*, 279-284.

Describes the setting up of internal information storage and retrieval system using commercial telecommunication programs, internal file transfer, reformatting of external database records, ordering reprints, producing camera ready copy for printing puposes at the IARC. Discusses the practical lessons learned in implementing the above capabilities. Points out the problems.

BORAIYAN, R 1018

Agricultural research information scene in India : An outlook, *IJALIS* 20, 1992: 1-6.

Deals with the infomation resources in agricultural and users or agricultural literature. Narrates the collection development and the transfer of agricultural research information. Mentions organisational sources in India. Identifies the centres and services of agricultural research infomation in India.

HARRIS, SUSAN C 1019

Agricultural information in developing countries, *LT*, 252-308.

Examines the problems of developing world such as diversity of conditions, rate of exchange of informtion work, technology transfer, problems associated with isolation. Looks at the economic situation of agricultural research and information focussing on changes in patterns of interest and funding for agricultural information work in Latin America and Caribbean. Discusses solutions for a variety of libraries and information centres, especially networking and technology-based solutions.

025.0664 (1) ISRS - NICFOS

RANGANATHA, K A 1020

National Information Centre for Food Science and Technology at CFTRI, *STIM*, 25-31.

Discusses the establishment of NICFOS under NISSAT to meet the information needs of the food industries and R & D organisations. Explains the NICFOS information services such as Food Technology Abstracts, Food Digest, Food Patents, and so on. Discusses also the computerised information services of NICFOS such as creation of FTA database, database of CFTRI publications, inhouse computerisation, etc. States that NICFOS is collaborating with International Food Information Science of UK.

025.0668 (1) ISRS - Iron and Steel

JHA, K N, SHARMA, D and SIKKA, G P 1021

Global level information services : A compelling need of R & D in iron and steel industry, *STIM*, 65-74.

Describes the computerisation of library routines and information services available at RDCIS Information and Documentation Centre. Explains the computerisation of centralised acquisition of periodicals and related housekeeping functions as document acquisition system, circulation control, SDI service from Metadex Tapes, Management Information System, Information Services. Concludes that coputerisation of librry routines ensures speed.

025.668 (1) ISRS - Metallurgy

KARTHA, C N and JAPE, K B 1022

Information centre for metallurgy, *ALIS*, V 3, 179-192.

Examines the need for establishing a National Information Centre for Metallurgy. Discusses its planning, determinants of information service, sources of information and explains different phases of implementation. Presents an outline of National Information Network for Metallurgy and its various subfields.

025.1 LIBRARY ADMINISTRATION. LIBRARY MANAGEMENT. LIBRARY ORGANIZATION. INFORMATION RESOURCE MANAGEMENT INFORMATION MANAGEMENT

ARORA, M L 1023

Decision-making process in libraries, *ALE*, 115-119.

Explains what is decision, and why of decision making. Describes implements in decision making such as goal, library system, intution, facts, experience, authority. Discusses the possible alternatives and pre-requisities to choose the best solution. States how to formulate the final solution and the follow up responsibility.

BAKEWELL, K G B 1024

Ranganathan and library management, *PP*, 101-107.

Discusses Ranganathan's contribution to library management which was scientific in nature for effective management of libraries through his Five Laws, book selection, reorganisation, communication, classification, etc. States that Ranganathan was way ahead of his contemporaries in this area.

DILIP, V 1025

Information retrieval system for the management of records, *Lib Sci slant Docum & Inf Std* 30 (4) Dec 1993 : 152-154.

Discusses broadly the importance of records management. Highlights the need for automation in records management for information retrieval system.

ESPERANZA, M (Sister) 1026

Management in Libraries, *LIS*, 33-47

Discusses the role of management in library. Describes characteristics of a good management, administrative qualities of the library manager. Emphasises on role of women in library management. Discusses staff and management expectations, management skills, financial management.

GAUTAM, J N and PANDA, K C 1027

Application of management techniques in modern librarianship : A bird's eyeview, *ILA Bull* 28 (3-4) Oct-Mar 1993 : 74-79.

Defines management and discusses various schools of thought that affect organisation. Deals with the factors making the application of scientific management in libraries and information centres exigent. Lists ingredients of scientific management. Elaborates POSDCORB, and concludes by giving canons of scientific management.

HORTON, FOREST WOODY 1028

The strategic role of information management, *Lib Sci slant Docum & Inf Std* 30 (1) Mar 1993 : 1-5.

Gives background of strategic information management. Defines strategic. Discusses the five guiding principles of strategic information management. Describes the format of the strategic information management planning. Assesses the situation in respect to culture and environment. Examines corporate and departmental strategic issues and concerns, information management issues and concerns. Explains how to develop the information resources baseline.

MANORAMA SRINATH 1029

Impact of organisational climate on personnel management in university librareis, *ALR*, 177-182.

Defines the concept of personnel management in libraries. Identifies some personnel problems with their root cause as three organisational factors making the personnel management as a complex process. These include leadership process, bureaucratic principles, job dissatisfaction and lack of motivation. Calls for developing the appropriate climate for university libaries.

MANORAMA SRINATH 1030

Libraries are ideal bureaucracies, *LIS*, 51-54.

Explains characrteristics of ideal bureaucracy laid down by Max Weber. Discusses the application of bureaucratic principles in libraries. Points out limiatations of bureaucracy. Describes the four tendencies of bureaucracies.

MURGAI, SARLA R 1031

Motivation to manage : A comparative study between male and female Library and Information Science students in the United States of America and India, *Jl Info Sci* 4 (1) Jul-Sept 1993 : 1-24.

Compares in this study management motivations of male and female LIS students in the USA and India basing on the data collected through questionnaire. Applies Ory Pogging Measure of Achievement Motivation and forced choice Licket-type format, with four response alternatives.

NEELAMEGHAN, A 1032

Dimenstions in information management : Ranganathan revisited, *Lib Sci slant Docum & Inf Std* 29 (4) Dec 1992 : 162-182.

Observes that the development in IT, underlying of the role of information in policy and decision making, problem-solving, system-building and in socioeconomic and political development have given new life to the 5th Law. Defines information resource management (IRM). Covers transformations that are happening in physical media for information, in particular, the telematic access, the development of variety of computer based magneto-laser-optico databases, and the emergence of information utilisation culture towards human societal development.

NOVAK, JASMINKA 1033

The use of conceptual models in design and implementation of decision support system, *COP*, 146-159.

Observes four perspectives on the use of computers : the system perspective, the dialogue partner perspective, the tool perspective, and the media perspective. The taxonomy of decision support techniques is put in correlation with these archetypal perspectives. Describes adopted principles for good interface design. Points out need for cognitive compatibility because conceptual models play outstanding role in system design. Discusses use of conceptual model in training as it enables user to form adequate and accurate mental model of the system.

NWALI, L O 1034

Towards maximum utilisation of library and information resources in a developing country, *Int Lib Move* 15(1) Mar 1993 : 1-10.

Describes that in the times of dwindling financial resources for libraries (in Nigeria), it is imperative that libraries in developing countries think of how best to utilize the shrinking budgets. Discusses some of the measures such as organization of library and information resources, user education, ILL, photocopying services, indexing and abstracting services, staffing, library publication, library computerisation, etc.

PARIDA, BAMAN 1035

Fundamentals of library management, 2nd rev ed, Bhubaneswar : Panchashila, 1993. 408p.

Includes twenty chapters on history of library and library science, library organisation, public and academic library systems, library associations, library administration and management, various departments of a library, reprography, changing system, library rules, library finance, annual report and statistics.

PASQUARELLI, MARIA LUIZA RIGO, KRZYANOWSKI, ROSALY FAVERO, IMPERATRIZ, INES MARIA M and AGRAWAL, S P 1036

Integrated library system : Two case studies : Latin America and India, New Delhi : Concept Publishing Company, 1992 (CICIL Series, No. 40). 144p

Makes out a case for an integrated library system in the development of university libraries by citing the case studies of the libraries attaached to leading universities in Brazil and India where intergrated services have been introduced and found effective in providing efficient and modern library services to the students, the faaculty and the reseaarchers has two chapters and three Aappendices.

RAMAIAH, L S and KANKACHARY, M 1037

Motivation and training for the staff in university libraries in India, *ALR*, 171-176.

Discusses about the motivation and training required for the staff working in university libraries so as to update their professional skills in the changing context of the information explosion to deliver the goods and to achieve the goals expected to be performed by them.

RAMASWAMI MUDALIAR, A 1038

Library organisation -a scheme, *LM*, 169-171.

Suggests that Madras Library Association (MALA) should organise the nucleus of circulating library and other local bodies should further organise libraries at different levels.

SAMAL, P K and MISHRA, ASHUTOSH 1039

Information management : Lesson for librarianship, *IJILIS*, 6 (3-4) July-Dec 1993 : 211-218.

Defines information. Explains the concept of information management. Discusses how information can be managed. Explains information management and the harmonization of purpose. Concludes that information management (IM) will lead to the definition of a specialization within the information profession.

SETHI, B and HUKAM SINGH 1040

Productivity measurement for a library, *Ann Lib Sci & Docum* 39 (4) Dec 1992 : 153-159.

Formulates and applies a simple productivity measurement model for a library for better management. The proposed method is called objective matrix, which incorporates participation, motivation and responsibility unlike the traditional output/input models.

SORNAM, ALLY 1041

Information resource management : A challenge, *LIT*, 44-47.

States that there is shift from industrial economy to information economy. Discusses the changing scenario of the information market. Describes the need for information resource management. Asks that who is responsible for IRM and how to accomplish this task ? The library professional should respond to the challenge.

TIAMIYU, MUTAWAKILU ADISA 1042

Pragmatics of developing information resource management systems in government organisations in developing countries, *INICAE* 12 (2) Sept 1993: 201-212.

Refers to the demise of socialist regimes of Eastern Europe and as a result government participation has come down. Describes environment and the issues in the development of information management systems focussing on the institutionalization programme. Streses need for coordination of information resources management systems. States the types of computer-based information technologies and the issues of foreign exchange costs etc. Refers also to the shortage of information specialists and the provision of staff training programmes.

TOMAR, SURENDRA SINGH 1043

Library management, *LIS*, 44-50..

Introduces the subject of management. Gives meaning of management. Distinguishes between administration and management. Explains library management. Describes qualities and functions of a library manager. Mentions basic principles of library management taking into account the aims and goals of a library.

VEERANJANEYULU, K 1044

Quality management in libaries and information centres, *Jl Inf Sci* 3 (2) Oct-Dec 1992 : 81-85.

States that quality being subjective, is difficult to define. Mentions role of management in enhancing quality in library staff, but can't be infused profitably without the active cooperation of library staff. States the need of constantly updating knowledge of library professionals in the changing world of library computerisation so that they can respond postively to new challenges thrown up by growing needs of libary users. Elaborates various aspects of quality improverment in library services including Ranganathan's Five Laws.

025.1 (1) System Analysis

KASHYAP, M M 1045

Library system analysis and design technique, *Jl Lib Inf Sci* 17 (2) Dec 1992 : 128-142.

Considers system analysis and design as a technique of analysing objectives, interrelationships, interdependence that exist among various components of a system. Points out that such a methodology is based on system philosophy and embodies systems approach. Considers a library as an open socio-technical system. Mentions tools and techniques used by an nalyst to systematically collect data. Descraibes steps involved in system analysis and design process.

RAMDAS, JAYSHREE and NAIR, USHA 1046

The system concept as a tool for knowledge reresentation : Understanding the human body, *COP*, 223-241.

Proposes a novel cognitive-developmental framework for modelling knowledge about physiological systems. Makes use of general concept of a system to study students' intutive models of body systems and how these develop with age and teaching. Assumes that 'system' criteria are closely related with cognition about systems, where mental organization of knowledge about any system must depnd on perceiving a collection of objects as an organised whole. Makes a case study of the understanding of the digestive system of school students.

025.1021 Library Management - Statistics

AMBA, S 1047

Use of some tools of inferential statistics in library and information studies, *Lib Sci slant Docum & Inf Std* 30 (3) Sept 1993 : 124-128.

Discusses in detail the applications of books of inferential statistics, like ANOVA (Analysis of Variance) and correlation and regression, used in the library statistics.

BASU, SUJIT K 1048

Use of statistics in library management, In *Papers*, 58th IFLA General Conference, New Delhi, 30 Aug - 5 Sept 1992, pp 6.10.

Highlights the role of and uses and applications of statistics as a tool in the library management. States that it helps in improving the mangerial aspects of the library.

025.11 Library Budget

Library Finance

ABBAS KHAN, A A 1049

Financing of the medical college libraries : A study, *Luck Libn* 23 (2) Apr-June 1991 : 51-55.

Discusses the existing financial resources of six medical college libraries in the Northern part of Karnataka. Examines different sources of finance, and identifies growth rate of the library books, periodicals, back volumes, furniture and equipment, etc.

ABRAHAM, J 1050

Cost accounting in library and information centres and systems, *Lib Prog* (*Int*) 11 (1-2) Jan-Dec 1991 : 16-23.

Attempts to describe the need for cost analysis, the ways for collecting, analysing and controlling costs for the appraisal for library and information services. Analyses costs, methods of costing, cost-effectiveness and cost benefit analysis and the application of cost accounts for the performance appraisal of library and informtion systems and services.

DEVARAJAN, G 1051

Resource allocation in university libraries, New Delhi : Ess Ess Publications, 1993. xii, 187 p.

Includes 9 chapters on survey of realted library, university libraries, and university libraries in Kerala. Discusses about expenditure and revenue of university libraries in Kerala. Makes an evaluation of sources and services of libraries. Examines mainly the state of financing in university libraries in Kerala.

GANPULE, S R and KUMBAR, T S 1052

Effective utilisation of periodicals budget : Some simple and possible methods, *Univ News* 31 (6) Feb 8, 1993: 9-11.

Explains some of the simple and possible to implement methods of effective utilisation of the scarce budget for the periodicals particularly in the times of rising prices of journals almost every year.

JENA, PUSHPANJALI 1053

Zero-base budgeting in library management, *CLIS Observer* 10 (3-4) July-Dec 1993 : 60-61.

Discusses that the genesis of zero-base budgeting lies in the pioneering efforts of E Hieton Young who advocated it in 1924. States that its main purpose is to strike a balance between the needs and resources of a library and achieve optimum utilization of library's resources in terms of its physical plant, reading material and personnel.

KALIA, D R 1054

Libraries without books and books without libraries : A vicious circle, *CLIS Observer* 9 (1-2) Jan-June 1992 : 1-2.

States in this Editorial that the world wide recession has caused a cut down in the library budget and increase in the prices of books and journals by about 25 percent per annum, and the total intake of books has come down, and the future of library profession seems to be bleak.

KAMAIAH, P 1055

Price hike, soaring foreign exchange conversion rates and inelastic funds : Their impact on acq uisition of periodicals - a critical analysis, *CS*, 82-94.

Discusses importance of periodicals in library collection. Points out rise in price of periodical subscription in India and abroad, highlighting factors. Analyses maladies associated with subscription of periodicals in S K University Library, Anantpur (AP). Suggests possible remedial measures to overcome impediments.

KARISIDDAPPA, C R and KUMBHAR, B D 1056

Financing of public libraries in Karnataka, *CS*, 153-162.

Examines the importance of finance, and the provisions for financing of public libraries under the Karnataka Public Libraries Act of 1965 with special reference to State Central Library, City Central Libraries and District Central Libraries. Discusses the existing financial situation and gives suggestions for improving the same.

LOHO, SUGH 1057

The problems and techniques of budget planning for school libraries in developing countries with particular reference to Nigeria, *Int Lib Move* 15 (4) Dec 1993 : 181-196.

Defines various terms such as the school library, library budget, school librarian. Focusses on the problems of and techniques for budget planning for school libraries in Nigeria.

Considers necessary suggestions for solving the problems discovered. Mentions about the National Policy on School Libraries in Nigera.

MEHTA, J H, JOGLEKAR, Y D , JOSHI, M V and KOLEKAR, S 1058

Study of the financial status of health science libraries in Bombay, *ITAH*, 181-189.

Studies the financial status of few health science libraries in Bombay. Discusses that even if standard norms for library financing are adopted, the finances remain inadequate to fulfil library obligations. Describes this situation dwindles the purchasing power of libraries and at times have created a near crisis situation for the medical libraries. Mentions remedial action required.

RAMAIAH, L S 1059

Expanding knowledge-shrinking budgets : Acquisition of foreign books in Indian university libraries, *Univ News* 29 (19) 1991: 9-13.

Discusses the problems of shrinking budget for libraries, and so for the university libraries in India. Explains that how the knowledge-shrinking budgets can be expanded and more foreign books can be procured in libraries to satiate the thirst for information.

RAMAIAH, L S and YADAGIRI REDDY, J 1060

Inelastic budgets and the decline of serials collections in the university libraries in India, *Univ News* 31 (41) Oct 11, 1993 : 9-18.

Describes the problems of decreasing budgetary allocation for libraries telling upon the resource health of university libraries. States that the serial collection of university libraries is declining year after year.

RANA, M S 1061

Funding of university libraries, *Univ News* 30 (25) Aug 31, 1992 : 101-103.

Points out that state university libraries are starved of funds while libraries of central universities and IITs are not. Explains the exising system of funding of state university libraries in the country. Mentions the UGC thinking for the universities to be self-financing. Discusses the norms for funding and book collection. Suggests a functional approach for determining financial needs.

SACHDEVA, D L and DHAWAN, S M 1062

Declining economic health of academic libraries : Whose problem is it any way ?, *Univ News* 30 (35) Aug 31, 1992 : 105-107.

Discusses the magnitude of the problem of rising prices of books and journals supported with data. Mentions the underlying factors causing the situation of crisis. Discusses the options in resource sharing and networking. Concludes that sound economic health is must for reliable access and scholarly communication.

SAROJA, G and PADMINI, K 1063

Impact of rupee devaluation on libraries, *Her Lib Sci* 31 (3-4) July-Oct 1992 : 170-174.

Explores the reaction of the local university and professional librarians of Tirupati towards the impact of rupee devaluation in libraries. Examines increase in the journal subscription in the five university and professional libraries of Tiruptati over the past ten years. Finds out the ways and means to overcome the situation caused by rupee devaluation. Observes the feasibility of setting up a LAN to promote coopeation.

SHANMUGANATHAN, S G and KUMARAVEL, J P S 1064

Limited budgets and survival of the university libraries, *LID*, 70-77.

Gives the present position of university libraries. Identifies problems in acquisition of books and journals due to impact of the rising costs and shrinking funds. Mentions three types of problems in library management : relations with parent organisation, impact on library staff, and impact on library users.

SHARMA, S K 1065

Some measures to reduce the library budget, *Her Lib Sci* 31 (3-4) July-Oct 1992 : 209-211.

Discusses the problems created by the increasing cost of documents in the face of limited allotment of funds. States the measures to meet the situation which include weeding out of unused journals, dependence on ILL, resource sharing, and obtaining microforms.

WALIA, P K 1066

Library finance : A survey of college libraries, *Jl Inf Sci* 3 (2) Oct-Dec 1992 : 99-108.

Mentions that finance plays a crucial role in successful

management of any organization. Discusses role of library finance in providing proper services to users. Attempts to know the situation and sources of finance in college libraries affiliated to Delhi University on the basis of 38 questionnaires received back from 71 distributed. Makes suggestions regarding library finance as got from the respondents.

025.11 (1) Economic Recession

ABRAHAM, J 1067

Economic recession and its impact on libraries and information centres, *CODE*, 1-4.

Explains business cycles or economic fluctuations and their causes. Attempts to provide a general understanding of the economic recession and its impact on libraries and information centres rather than detailed study on different phases and theories and causes of such cyclical functuations in the aggregate economic activities.

BARMAN, R K 1068

Economic recession and its impact on libraries in India : A case study of Gauhati University Library, *CODE*, 9-12.

Discusses the role of university library in teaching and research. Discusses the present trend of library finance in view of economic recession. Attempts to justify with statistical support the need of regular flow of funds to maintain library standards. Discusses factors affecting library economics. Advocates for adequate library budget keeping in view of student enrolment, price rise of books and journals, use of modern gadgets to library operations.

025.12 Reprography. Photocopy Services

GOSWAMEE, BHUPEN 1069

Need of reprographic facilites in university libraries, *LIN*, 59-63.

Points out importance of university library. Defines reprography. Gives usefulness of reprography and its benefits to researchers. Mentions about its use in offering CAS and SDI services. Describes about the reprographic facilities in university libraries in Assam.

PANDA, KRUSHNA C 1070

Photocopying policy in four major university libraries of Orissa: A case, *Univ News* 30 (35) Aug 31, 1992: 145-148.

Defines photocopying. Makes a comparative study of the nature and extent of the photocopying policy that prevails among the four major university libraries in the state of Orissa which determines the scope and extent of its services to their clienteles.

SETH, MOHENDRA KUMAR 1071

Photocopying service in a special library : An analytical study, *Iaslic Bull* 37 (1) Mar 1992 : 39-42.

Provides use of photocopying service in a special library, its importance and problems faced while providing the services to its users. Gives analysis of data on photocopying of different documents in the library of RRL, Bhubaneswar. Suggests few guidelines for the effective utilisation of photocopying service in similar types of Research Laboratories.

025.172 Clippings. Press Clippings

GUPTA, S and SAMAL, P K 1072

Press clipping service at National Documentation Centre, NIHFW: A case study, *Ann Lib Sci & Docum* 40 (3) Sept 1993 : 92-94.

Describes the press clipping service to the scientists and research workers of the National Institute of Health and Family Welfare, provided by its National Documentation Centre. Makes clippings from six English and one Hindi newspapers. Covers the period Jan-June 1992 and prepares 'Press Clipping Index' for the M D students. States that a database of news clippings is created using dBASE III + or Foxplus package.

PANDA, KRUSHNA C and KARISIDDAPAA, C R 1073

Newspapers in university libraries : From curiosity to convention with special reference to Behrampur University Library, *CS*, 75-81.

Highlights the importance of newspapers as a source of information. Provides historical perspectice of newspapers. Discusses need for news libraries. Reports about the newpaper use patterns of users of Behrampur University Central Library.

025.1732 Periodicals. Serials

NOEL-LAMBOT, FRANCOISE and BOLZEE, DENY 1074

Organization of the periodicals section at the new library of the faculty of Medicine of the University of Liege, Belgium, *ML*, 303-308.

States that the library of the Medical Faculty has been set up in 1988 by pooling about 40 odd departmental libraries. Discusses its policy of acquistion, evaluation of the collection, frequency of use of each of the 1000 periodicals, statistics for photocopies requests (ILL), arrangements of the collections on shelves, exploitation of the collections using several methods to facilitate easy access to the collections.

RIAZ, MUHAMMAD 1075

Serials management in libraries, 1992. 199p.

Defines in its chapters serials. Deals with the growth and development of serials, their acquisition problems, processing difficulties, and their management for providing better services to the library users in pursuit of research and development.

025.1747 (1) Slides

SENAPATI, SUSANTA KUMAR 1076

Slide management : A practical approach, *CLIS Observer* 9 (1-2) Jan-June 1992 : 33-38.

Enumerates and defines different types of non-book material and its selection, acquistion, organisaion and retrieval, particularly of the slides. Describes the storage system and equipment needed for effective slide management.

025.1794 Microforms

CHATTERJEE, RANA PRATAP and SEN, SUBIR K 1077

Microform management in Indian libraries : A survey, *Iaslic Bull* 37 (1) Mar 1992 : 31-37.

Surveys 22 speical and academic libraries in and around Calcutta including National Library of India to assess the available microform facilities and their management. States that many important libraries do not have any microform facilittes at all, and except three there are no separate microform sections and microform management is a highly neglected area. Makes some useful suggestions for improvement.

025.196 Management - Special Libraries

CHATTOPADHYAY, AMIT KUMAR 1078

Management of company library : Understanding special characteristics, *Iaslic Bull* 38 (2) June 1993 : 59-65.

Defines company law in the context of special library. Discusses special characteristics of such libraries. Highlights the personal qualities desirable for professionals working in company libraries. Discusses a few points as how to manage a company library well.

025.19772 Management - University Libraries

MAHAJAN, S G 1079

Legal aspects in university library management, *ALR*, 133-151.

Makes a case for knowledge of law on the part of university librarian which may prove very useful for performing his duties effeciently. States that his knowledge about service rules, appointment rules, constitution of India, etc helps him. Mentions some of the court cases regarding students in Poona University. Lists some guidelines, state government decisions, etc.

ROUT, R K 1080

Managerial revolution and unversity libraries, *Univ News* 30 (35) Aug 31, 1992 : 139-144.

Terms the university library as a heart of the university, a dynamic instrument of education. Discusses the impact of management science in modern times. Describes library as the knowledge industry. Discusses evolution of library mangement and application of management techniques in libraries. Distinguishes between library administration and management. Describes the operational management, evaluation and monitoring, design of the operations system. Explains factors which influence performance. Makes a survey of university libraries in Orissa and West Bengal to study the real life situation existing in their operational management. Lists methods of achieving high performance.

ROUT, R K 1081

Operational management of university libraries in India, New Delhi: Reliance Publishing House, 1992. x, 199p.

Divided in eight chapters, attempts to analyse inadequate library environments in India. Makes an attempt for quantifying library services and measuring the satisfactioin of the user through some statistical methods. Discusses some cases of university libraries in Orissa regarding their problems of operational management.

TEJOMURTY, A and SHUKLA, KAUTILYA H 1082

Management of university libraries in Gujrat, *CS*, 54-74.

Discusses in detail the various aspects of the management of university libraries in the state of Gujrat. Highlights the composition and functions of library committee, qualifications, status, faculty relationships, and pay scales of library personnel.

025.2 ACQUISITION. COLLECTION DEVELOPMENT

BANERJEE, SUSHANTA and SEETHARAMA, S 1083

Knowledge and skill required for collection management, *CODE*, 151-156.

Explains collection management. Puts forth that informtion source building is an important function of an informtion centre so it is necessary for information professionals to have necessary knowledge and skill to elicit information requirement from users and build up a core collection based on well formulated document selection and acquisition policies and programmes. Highlights the knowledge and skill required to each step in the collection development programme. Concludes that information professionals should focus on and equip themselves with the requisite knowledge and skill to make them effective collection management librarians.

CHAKRABARTI, B and MAHAPATRA, P K 1084

Library collection : Selection and preservation, Calcutta : World Press, 1992. 200 p.

Attempts to cover all aspects of collection developement that describe a cluster of functions which are given in Part I; while Part II includes chapters on preservation of library materials and the related issues and problems are taken for discussion, with useful suggestions given for improvement.

CHAKRABARTY, BIPUL KUMAR 1085

Knowledge and skill needed for effective collection development, *CODE*, 161-163.

Defines different attributes of collection development (CD)

and the importance of knowledge and skills for developing effective and efficient CD process in library. Highlights the key components of knowledge and skills. States that knowledge and skill for applying the statistical techniques/ES are the basic tools needed for a library, especially, to identify the relevant resources in a library.

CHOUDHURY, B K , PANDA, KRUSHNA C and KARISIDDAPPA, C R 1086

Need for collection development programme : Some parameters, *CODE*, 19-23.

Defines collection development (CD). Enumerates factors affecting CD. Discusses the need for CD, and CD policy. Describes the factors on which the successful implemetation of CD depends. Explains functions of Acquistion Section as allocation of library fund and resource sharing. Describes collection environment, its utility and methods. Mentions the need of weeding the old and outdated material. Identifies problems in CD.

ELDER, NELDA J, HOBROCK, BRICE G, MADSEN, DEBORAL and WIESE, WILLIAM H 1087

Collection development, selection, and acquisition of agricultural materials, *LT*, 116-147.

Deals with collectioin development, selection, and acquisition of agricultural information materials for libraries. Discusses collection planning and evaluation, collection development policies, subject areas of agriculture, cooperative collection development, resource sharing, and preservation. Mentions sources of selection of agricultural materials. Appends a list of general suppliers and vendors.

KEMPARAJU, T D 1088

Knowledge and skill requirements for collection development, *CODE*, 157-160.

Mentions that CD is one of the key activity of librarianship. Brings out that the changing concepts of library profession and application of IT development on CD call for new knowledge and skills. Identifies the knowledge and skill requirements of LIS professionals for the CD in the context of recession management and its impact on LIS education.

MGAYWA, ROBER M 1089

Impartiality or relevancy ? The dilemma of collection development in Third World libraries, *Int Lib Move* 15 (3) Sept 1993 : 133-141.

Discusses about the library philosophy that books and other materials be provided to all. Makes a criticial look at the western promoted doctrine of a neutral 'balanced' and 'impartial' collection development philosophy. Calls for a more realistic and pragmatic approach in this context.

PAL, S S 1090

Electronic publishing : Possibilities for university libraries, *Luck Libn* 24 (1) Jan-Mar 1992 : 11-15.

Highlights the impact of collection development in university libraries on their space requirement and how CD-ROM technology can alleviate the problem with the use of compact disc on various subjects of interest to university libraries. Suggests its effectiveness as an alternative to online searching of international databases and the value for retrospective searches. Calls for introducing CD-ROM in university libraries.

PRASHER, R G 1091

Developing library collection, New Delhi : Medallion, 1993. 251 p.

Deals with the primary task of collection building, an activity of vital importance. Covers all the three facets of the problem: (1) document selection, (2) ordering, and (3) procurement of documents. Divided into 21 chapters, it intends to assist the librarians and information scienctists in the task of collection development so as to develop a need-based, balanced and uptodate collection of all types of documents fit to meet the user needs.

RAMAIAH, L S 1092

Expanding knowledge - shrinking budgets : Acquisition of foreign books in Indian university libraries, *LIS*, 43-49.

Laments that due to lack of appropriate Indian books, our libraries are depending on the imported books in S & T, social sciences, communication, etc. Deals with only three aspects concerning the acquisition of foreign books in Indian universities : (1) escalatioin of prices; (2) increased coversion rates; and (3) inelastic library budgets. Supports them with statistics. Concludes with useful suggestions.

SHAKUNTHALA, K A 1093

Collection development, Ranganathan's APUPA pattern and resource sharing, *CODE*, 13-14.

Discusses about Ranganathan's explanation about the arrangement of books and library collection. Looks at the whole problem of transformation and imapping from the point of view of the reader in context of the APUPA pattern. States that resource sharing will be the best ideal for librarians and CD policies be developed using Ranganathan's APUPA pattern.

SRIDHAR, M S 1094

Problems of document acquisition in science and technology libraries, *ALIS,* V 4, 177-185.

Stresses the importance of acquistion librarian in collection development. Points out general lack of training in librarianship about purchase activities, book trade practices and relevant laws of the land. Enumerates the prevailing circumstances in which document acquisition decisions are made. Discusses selected significant problems of selection and purchasing of books, reports and journals in S & T libraries.

025.2 (1) Collection Development and Computer Acquisition and Computer

DAS, PRADIP 1095

Collection development of library and constraint analysis through Expert System, *CODE*, 105-107.

Discusses the complexities in CD in libraries today in India brought into by economic recession and creates problems. Analyses their issues for solution through a computer-based modelling of different factors. States that more research needs to be done in bibliometric analysis, financial management and computer commuication to develop customer-oriented CD in libraries. Presents a design for ES for modelling data on CD and mentions problems to employ ES.

DESHMUKH, SUBHASH and MEHTA, HARSH 1096

Book acquisition system using CDS/ISIS version 2.3, *Lib Sci slant Docum & Inf Std* 30 (4) Dec 1993 : 160-172.

Describes about a book acquisition system (BAS) designed and developed in CDS/ISIS Version 2.3 using CDS/ISIS Pascal

Interface. States that it is an interactive menu driven and user friendly system used to carry out day to day work of book acquisition activity at the National Council for Cement and Building Material, New Delhi.

MAITY, CHANDANA 1097

Collection development : Technological impact, *CODE*, 166-167.

Explains the concept of CD. Discusses the application of computer in acquisition which speeds up the acquisition process. Describes also the need for cooperation, coordination and sharing in the development and management of collection, and here also the new media speeds up the actual transfer of marterials from one library to another.

025.2 (1) COLLECTION DEVELOPMENT AND ECONOMIC RECESSION

IASLIC, CALCUTTA 1098

Collection development in the context of economic recession : Papers of XIX All India Conference, Calcutta : IASLIC, 1993, iv, 174 p.

Includes 35 articles, and 9 extended abstracts and abstracts on the theme of the Conference held at Birla Institute of Technology, Mesra, Ranchi, during 26-29 December, 1993. Discusses in detail the impact of economic recession and rising prices on the CD in different types of libraries all over the country.

RAMCHANDER, M amd PANDURANGAM, S 1099

Augmentation of collection through institutional linkages, *CODE*, 115-118.

Mentions about the recession in India in all economic activities and price hike of publications lead the libraries and information centres suffer most and can not maintain the level of information storage and supply as the flow of documents is restricted. Attempts to explore unpublished literature in order to complement and supplement the collection. Describes various avenues to mobilise the unpublished literature to meet the information requirements.

SARKAR, KRISHANENDU 1100

Information auditing : An introductory concept towards effective resource utilisation, *CODE*, 103-104.

Purports to encourage a most-effective and a quality intensive approach towards collection building especially for the information centres intrinsic to the S & T institutions/ Laboratores/ Organisations. Explains the concept of 'Information Auditing' which is a device to check the worthless expenditure in the name of CD, regaining user interests with optimum utilisation of resources.

SEWA SINGH 1101

Collection building and economic recession, *CODE*, 5-8.

Explains economic recession as well as collection building. Describes the impact of economic recession on collection building resulting in imbalances in CD as well as library services. Emphasises on generating new sources of revenue for libraries to meet the shrinking budgets by such methods as hike in library fee, increasing library security, book processing fee, and so on. Lays stress on making the library a resource centre leading to optimum utilisation of library resources by organising library work, knowing user needs, reference and information services, marketing of information, user education, resource sharing and networking, etc. Concludes with a Clarion call of duty for professionals to change their attitude.

SHRIVASTAVA, A K and SHRIVASTAVA, MRIDULATA 1102

Selection and procurement of documents in research libraries : A guide for optimum utilization of funds, *Iaslic Bull* 38 (2) June 1993 : 85-88.

Mentions that with rising cost of books and journals and shrinking budget utilising the available funds to the best interest of the clientele is difficult task. Discusses the practices adopted by DRDE, Gwalior such as participative management of the library, with the user and his needs being given the prime importance by the management.

SINGH, A R and SHRIVASTAVA, RAJKUMARI 1103

Archival libraries collection development in the context of economic recession, *CODE*, 85-87.

Aims at reviewing archival CD policies and programmes in

the context of economic recession for devising appropriate strategies at national and state levels to ensure optimum utilisation of archival information. Discusses impact of economic recession on arcival libraries in India. Stresses the need for effective archival collection, keeping in view users' interests and organisations' goals. Suggests cooperation and resource sharing through ILL among archival libraries to minimise the ill effects of economic recession on their CD programmes.

UMMUNNAKWE, U S 1104

Strategies for survival in a depressed economy : Options for Nigerial libraries, *Int Lib Move* 15 (3) Sept 1993 : 146-153.

Gives background to the Nigerian economy austerity. Discusses the problem of collection development and decreasing library role. Gives proposals for adjustments in collection development.

025.2 (1) Collection Development and Users

BALIAR SINGH, R K and MAHAPATRA, M 1105

Public's reading interest in the collection development of public libraries, *CODE*, 99-102.

Assesses the usefulness of the general public's reading interest in the CD of public libraries in the Puri District of Orissa state. Finds that the public library's collection especially in rural areas should not be hampered in the context of the economic recession. Emphasies on the public library to select, collect, and organise need-based literature to suit the public's reading interest.

KURAHATTI, B T and AVASIA, MAYA 1106

Controlling book acquisitions through users' participation : A way to offbeat the impact of economic recession, *CODE*, 139-143.

Gives scope of collection development (CD). States that a research library is to maintain a core collection to support research activities. Describes economic recession and its impact on book trade vis-a-vis on libraries forcing them to be utmost careful in CD. Emphasises the need of user participation in controlling acquisition of published materials in a research library.

SHAH, ANANT A 1107

Collection development by deaf students : A novel experiment, *CODE*, 145-149.

Gives a brief account of collection, services and need of library in special school for the Institute for Deaf, Bhavnagar. Enumerates special collection of documents required by the deaf students, teachers, and parents. Describes a novel experiment carried out by the library of this school in the selection of documents. Records the results of this experiment of participation of users in CD vis-a-vis effect of economic recession and the steps taken to meet the financial crisis.

025.2 (1) Collection Development and Book Reviews

MOHANTA, RABINDRA NATH and BISWAS, SUBAL CHANDRA 1108

Book reviews and collection development, *CODE*, 109-114.

Provides a unique information about the importance of reviews in the CD process with respect to the publisher, place of publication and subject distribution of books reviewed, time lag, etc. Discusses the ways in which book reviews could be effectively utilised for CD. Analyses data compiled from the reviews that have appeared in LIS journals. Highlights whether reviews can be a dependable tool or not as far as selection is concerned.

025.21 Acquisition Policy

ADHAV, ASEEM B and GHOSH, S B 1109

Impact of financial constraints on acquisition policies of libraries, *CODE*, 37-41.

States that budgetary constraints have forced all the libraries to change their acquisition policies considerably. Reports finding of a pilot survey by questionnaire method comprising of libraries, representing cross section of major types of libraries of universities, Govt departments, and R & D organisations to study the impact of financial constraints on the acquisition policies. Studies the various ways they cope up with the situation, including resource sharing, photocopies, etc.

KUMAR, P S G 1110

Towards an acquisition policy for a university library, *ALR*, 79-82.

Gives importance of acquisition. Explains need for

acquisition policy, gives its objectives and aims. Describes the policy statement by identifying critical issues to be involved. Mentions about the formulation of an acquisition policy.

MISHRA, SANJAYA and PARMANAND 1111

Role of policy statement in collection development, *CODE*, 29-31.

Mentions importance of good CD for satisfying users' needs. Defines CD. Discusses the need for policy statement for CD. Elaborates levels and components of a policy statement for this purpose. In the absence of policy statement the collection grows in a haphazard manner affecting the utility of the documents acquired.

PRASAD, H N 1112

Collection development policy for libraries : Some guidelines for its formulation, *CODE*, 25-27.

Examines the nature and content of the CD policy for libraries as essential for building strong collection ensuring maximum satisfaction of users. Suggests that the libraries in India should formulate their CD policy as per the guidelines suggested.

RAINA, ROSHAN, RAJA, M U and GITANJALI, KHURSHID AHMED 1113

Collection development : A policy indicator for IIM Libraries, *CODE*, 33-36.

Discusses that increasing financial constraints have left the IIM Libraries with no option but to go in for acquiring learning resources on cooperative basis. Illustrates this with statistical data from all the four IIM Libraries, it puts forth some broad policy indicators for fine tuning the existing acquisition policies of IIM Libraries.

RAJU, A A N 1114

Government's books acquisition policy: Its impact on collection development in the public library system in Andhra Pradesh, *CODE*, 43-48.

Points out that A P Public Libraries Act, 1960 ushered in the growth of public library services in 4586 libraries. Refers to the creation of Grandhalaya Parishad under the act, which is the highest policy making body. Provides guidelines, under the orders of the Govt, to prepare lists, allocation of book fund to District and Branch

Libraries. Presents briefly the existing set-up for book selection. Discusses delay in bringing out book lists paralyising acquisition collection. Refers to the Ekbote Committee solutions. Concludes that Parishad has to play crucial role to revamp existing policy.

025.2186 Collection Development - Special Libraries

MAHESHWARAPPA, B S and KARISIDDAPPA, C R 1115

Problems of collection development among special libraries in India, *CODE*, 77-80.

Discusses the CD as a systematic approach to building library's collection in the context of economic recession involving community analysis and use studies, development of CD policy, selection, acquisition, and collection management aspects such as weeding, storage, preservation and evaluation of collection in addition to the problems with each of these process as among special libraries in India.

SRIDHAR, M S 1116

Problems of collection development in special libraries, New Delhi : Concept Publishing Company, 1992. 192 p (CICIL Series No., 35).

Takes a holistic look at the collection development in special libraries and at the same time logically shows how CD is related to collection management and evaluation. Gives case studies pointing out lacunae in the system. Puts forth some useful suggestions to overcome these lacunae.

025.21863 Collection Development - Agricultural Libraries

HEMA SUNDER NAIDU, G and GUNJAL, S R 1117

Collection tendency of agricultural libraries in India; a study, *Her Lib Sci* 31 (1-2) Jan-Apr 1992 : 27-32.

Mentions division of agricultural libraries in India in three categories. States that books and journals procured by these libraries are the core collection. Studies collection tendencies on the basis of activities of parent institutions. Observes that books and journals available in the national research institute libraries were found to be very high when compared to other categories.

025.218771 Collection Development-College Libraries

ABBAS KHAN, A A 1118

Collection development in engineering colleges : A case study,

IJILIS 6 (3-4) July-Dec 1993 : 201-210.

Analyses the collection in terms of growth in size, growth of users and compares with the growth of budget. Makes a case study of Muffakham Jah College of Engineering and Technology for the years 1981 to 1990.

BARADOL, A K 1119

Collection development in the Government colleges of Mangalore University, *CODE*, 170-171.

Describes that the Five Laws of Library Science have much to do with the CD by fixing responsibilities on the library staff. States that document collection in colleges is primarily syllabus-oriented, hence textbook collection only. Mentions that most of the colleges do not have non-book materials; and even the document collection is not adequate. Makes suggestions.

RAMAN NAIR, R 1120

Qualitative development of college library collection, *ALE*, 87-101.

Sets out objectives of a college library. Defines the concepts of quality, CD, and qualitative CD. Attempts a qualitiative assessment of the document collections in PG colleges in Kerala. Evaluates the methods followed for CD and their updating in view of the allocation of funds. Suggests measures that can improve the building up and development of college library collections.

025.218772 Collection Development - University Libraries

ARJUN LAL 1121

Book bank scheme : A case study of Rajendra Agricultural University Library, Pusa (Bihar), *IJALIS* 21, 1993 : 41-45.

Defines the purpose of Book bank in a university/college library. Narrates the operation of this scheme at Rajendra Agricultural University, Pusa, its rules, yearwise growth in collection, expenditure incurred, and the services rendered. Offers suggestions for its further development.

CHANDRAIAH, I 1122

Collection development in open university libraries, *Int Lib Move* 15 (3) Sept 1993 : 113-119.

Defines collection development. Mentions role of library in distance education. Describes importance of written policy in planning the collection development. Points out device of material for Open University Library. Gives evaluation of library stock and need for library cooperation.

CHOUDHURY, B K 1123

Collection development in academic libraries of India : A bibliographical study, *ALE*, 102-114.

Explains collection development. Presents a bibliographical study to provide various items of information on collection development by Indian authors, mainly relevant to university and special libraries. Gives abstracts to the items covered in the bibliography. Concludes that it puts together various suggestions made from time to time by various scholars and experts for improving collection development.

HUMANYOON KABIR, S 1124

Collection development : An analysis of Cochin University Library pattern and suggestions for improvement, *RDAL*, 70-76.

Gives background of the Cochin University Library. Defines library collection. Discusses impediments in collection development such as lack of policy, spiralling cost, information explosion, change of media, etc. Offers various suggestions for improvement of collection development.

ISSAH, HALI SADIA 1125

Book donation and exchange as sources of collection development in Nigerian university libraries, University of Lagos Library experience, *Int Lib Move* 14 (2) June 1992 : 57-64.

Describes collection development process. Discusses such methods as gifts and donations for developing collection. Explains donations to Nigerial libraries during 1983-86. Describes donors also. Examines the role of exchange of documents in libraries with reference to University of Lagos Exchange Programme.

LAXMANRAO, N and RATNA RAO, N 1126

Collection development in university libraries, *ALR*, 83-97.

Defines collection development. Discusses that to study collection development in university libraries it is necessary to study users needs, book selection, weeding and storing, evaluation of collection, and contraints about finances, documents and environment. Explains the collection development policy and discusses its external environments.

MAHAJAN, S G 1127

Collection development in university libraries : Some aspects, *ALD*, 54-59.

Explains the concept of self-renewing library in which new collection will be relieved by the withdrawl of obsolete material. Speaks about limiting the size of collection. Discusses problems arising while weeding out in the case of textbooks, theses, dissertations, books beyond repair, question papers and old editions of books.

MEIBALAN, V 1128

Collection development and its problems : A case study of Pondichery University Library, *Univ News* 30 (35) Aug 31, 1992 : 129-137.

Points out goals and functions of unviersity and its library. Discusses the acquisition of books and the policy towards collection development in the Pondichery University Library. Discusses the problem in collection deverlopment and solutions to them.

TAHER, MOHAMMED 1129

Collection in university libraries : A case for balanced development of books, *ALR*, 105-111.

Identifies the essential elements of a balanced collection. Answers the question whether the library's collection is fulfilling its purpose. Points out the absence of a clear cut policy of collection development in university libraries in India. Discusses the neglected area of collection development as it is only based on availability in market and not on institutional research and study.

THAKAR, G S and NAVJEET KAUR 1130

Working of acquisition section in the A C Joshi Library, Panjab University, Chandigarh : A study, *IJILIS* 5 (3-4) July-Dec 1992 : 290-300.

Traces the history of Panjab University Library, which is now known as A C Joshi Library. Discusses the working of the acquisition process, passing the document through various stages, in this University Library.

VENKATESHWAR RAO, K and BHANOT, BHARAT BHUSHAN 1131

Collection development in Indira Gandhi National Open University (IGNOU) Library, *CODE*, 73-76.

Explains the procedure involved in collection building for the IGNOU Library system. Defines CD and mentions factors in CD. Discusses the need for CD. Since IGNOU is offering its programme through distance education mode, innovative techniques need to be adopted in the preparation of course materials. Discusses details pertaining to the procedure adopted in the university library for CD.

025.218772 (1) Collection Development in University Library and Economic Recession

ARJUN SINGH 1132

Declining finances and collection development in university libraries; challenges and strategies : A study based on university libraries of Madhya Pradesh, *CODE*, 53-62.

Presents a review of finances and CD in five selected university libraries in Madhya Pradesh from 1980-81 to 1990-91. Discusses the problems of declining financial resources and their impacts on the process of CD. Suggests stragegies for generating additional revenue by the libraries. Emphasises the use of prevalent IT for resource sharing and networking to form an integrated national system of libraries for meeting challenges posed by various factors related with information dissemination.

DEVENDER and SATYANARAYANA, I 1133

Economic constraints and effective collection development in university libraries in India, *CODE*, 67-71.

Mentions recommendations of the Kothari Commission regarding the role of university libraries. Defines CD. Explains factors due to which it is not easy to achieve book selection objectives. Suggests that resource sharing is perhaps the best way of tackling the problem created by the decreasing buying power of libraries. Mentions purchase of cheaper editions of books as another method of tackling the problem. Concludes that libraries should explore various other methods of CD.

ISAAC, DOROTHY and REDDY, J RUKMINI 1134

University library resources : Need for development, *CODE*, 63-66.

Highlights the importance of the university library resources for providing effective services by the library. Analyses the amount to be allocated to the library from the total university budget. Concludes that the percentage of allocation to the libraries is declining. Recommends the universities in general and the libraries in particular to mobilise their own resources instead of solely depending on the government.

SEHGAL, P C 1135

Collection development and shrinking budgets : An evaluation of textbook sections of Punjabi University Library and Guru Nanak Dev University, *CODE*, 172.

Gives only the abstract. Mentions importance of CD adversely affected by limited book budget, price rise, etc. Makes a comparative study of the Textbook collection of Punjabi University and Guru Nanak Dev University libraries in seven selected subjects. Reveals that the percentage of Textbooks in Guru Nanak Dev University is greater than that of Punjabi University, Patiala.

025.21874 Collection Development -Public Libraries

IJARI, S R and KANNAPPANAVAR, B U 1136

The role of financial resources for collection development in public library system of Karnataka, *CODE*, 172.

Discusses about the importance of CD in public libraries. Describes the provision of funds in the Karnataka Public Libraries Act of 1965 for book purchase in public libraries and their maintenance as per the guideline issued by the Directorate. States that the financial assistance got by public library system for CD at different levels is inadequate to develop a proper collection.

025.233 Libraries and Book Trade

GIRJA KUMAR 1137

Librarians and publishers in dialectical relationship, *ALR*, 57-70.

Discusses about the dialectical relationship between librarians and publishers regarding channels of communication, institutional contacts, environmental constraints, publishing and library scene, dimension of crisis situation, publishing and its dimension, publishing and social relevance defining role for libraries, and common platform.

RAJGOPAL, T R and DURGA DEVI, K 1138

Publisher, bookseller and the librarian : Need for cooperation in acquisition of books and periodicals in the university libraries, *LID*, 59-64.

Deals with the relationship of the publisher, bookseller and the librarian with regard to delay in payments, discount rate. Discusses some constraints in acquisition of periuodicals, role of STC and the time lag of periodicals received by the university library. Brings forth issues for consideration.

THOMAS, P J 1139

The economics of the book trade, *LM*, 73-76.

Makes a case for price discrimination of books so as to suit all pockets, such as expensive edition first followed by cheaper edition just on the analogy of theatre-goers and railway passengers.

025.28 (1) Collection Development-Referenc Sources

CHANDRAN, M R and SUBRAMANYAM, T 1140

Acquisition of current reference sources : Some issues, *CODE*, 168-169.

Attempts to highlight the importance of acquisition of basic reference sources in the times of shrinking budget and rising prices. Discusses about the maintenance of the latest editions of some basic reference sources in the S V University Library, Tirupati. Concludes that rising cost has a bearing on CD programme and answer lies in library cooperation, resource sharing and library networking.

025.28 (1) Collection Development - Art Material

GAKHAR, AP 1141

Collection development and the acquisition of art materials at the Indira Gandhi National Centre for the Arts, *CLIS Observer* 10 (3-4) July-Dec 1993: 77-83.

Mentions the pivotal role of collection development in libraries. Describes that the Reference Library at the Indira Gandhi National Centre for Arts (IGNCA) aims to provide material on all the arts, acquires material in serveral formats such as rare books, private collections, journals, microfilms of Mss, visual resources, video and sound recordings, and in many languages. Hopes that some of the problems being encountered can be resolved by means of contact and cooperation with other art libraries in South and South-East Asia.

025.2832 Acquisition of Serials and Periodicals

ANATONY, REGINA and NEWTON, V 1142

Development of serial collection in Christian Medical College and Hospital, Vellore, *ITAH*, 191-197.

Points out that serials are chief source of information in health science libraries. States that to build serial collection is the most difficult part of serial management. Mentions that librarian is guided by collection development policy. Points out that several sources help the serial librarian in collection development including the users suggestions. Mentions about a core list of serials. Describes about the development of existing collection. Discusses the collection development in the Library of CMC and Hospital, Vellore.

ARAVINDA, P 1143

Periodical literture : Acquisition problems in a university library, *LID*, 65-69.

Attempts to examine various problems involved in acquiring the periodicals, their selection and subscription, registration, binding, etc. Presents a few suggestions to overcome these problems based on experience.

BABY, M D 1144

Subscription of periodicals in Cochin University of Science and Technology Library : An evaluation, *RDAL*, 86-90.

Provides background of Cochin University of Science and Technology and its library. Discusses about the subscription of periodicals through STC, direct subscription, giving statistics about amunt and number of journals received.

DESHPANDE, N J 1145

Effect of financial squeeze on journals subscription, *CODE*, 49-51.

Points out the growth of literature in journals and the low priority of education. Attempts to study the effects of price escalations and inflationary trends on journal budgets in the Jayakar Library, University of Poona. Suggests various remedial measures as purchase of only core journals, resource sharing, use of CD-ROM, donation programme, extra-budgetary support from sources like UNDP.

DHAWAN, S M 1146

Information management within resource constraints, *CODE*, 173-174.

Brings out the problems of rising journal prices in science and technology, declining value of rupee against foreign currencies, stagnating budgets. Identifies possible options to cope with such crisis situations which include cost-effective measures like rationalisation in acquiring, library automating and networking, seek new funding sources, generating additional income, consultancy services, database creation, etc.

KAMAIAH, P 1147

Economic factors ad their impact on acquisition of periodicals -a critical analysis, *LID*, 50-58.

Highlights importance of periodicals and their multiple growth. Attempts to analyse the price rise of periodicals, conversion rates and the slackness in budget allocations. Brings out all feasible remedial measures to solve price hike in periodical subscription in the libraries. Concludes that sharing of resources among the libraries is a viable solution to this porоblem.

LAXMAN RAO, N and PRAFULLA CHANDRA, T V 1148

Rationalisation of periodical subscriptions, *CLIS Observer* 10 (3-4) July-Dec 1993 : 67-72; Also in *Univ News* 31 (12) Mar 22, 1993 : 14-17.

Mentions that library and information centres should have a service oriented approach. States that impact of rising prices on S & T journals is increasing and therefore resource sharing is becoming a must. Discusses about a pragmatic solution for rationalisation of periodical acquisitions to avoid duplication. Mentions about contribution of NISSAT in rationalisation of periodicals subscriptions and resource sharing. Gives a case study of Hyderabad libraries and setting up of HYLIBNET. Offers more suggestions.

MITTAL, REKHA, MAKHIJA, HEM LATA and DHAR, RITA 1149

Acquisition and distribution of serials covered in Index Medicus and Excerpts Medica : An analytical study, *ILA Bull* 27 (4) Jan-Mar 1992 : 150-156.

Reports the results of a quantitative study of NUCSSI

databases on the coverage and distribution of titles of medicine and related fields in Excerpta Medica and Index Medicus all over India. Analyses non-receipt of titles with regards to subject and country. Reveals that 58% of total titles are available in India.

NAGI REDDY, Y and SUSEELA, V JANAKI 1150

Impact of escalating periodical prices on library subscriptions : An analysis of periodical price indices, *ILA Bull* 29 (1-2) Apr-Sept 1993 : 26-34.

Presents the impact of escalating journal prices on periodical subscriptions on the basis of price trends as indicated in the periodical price indices. Indicates that prices increased by more than 20%, foreign exchange by 10-15%, and inflationn by 8% per annum, whereas periodical subscriptions have fallen by 33.33%. Suggests ways and means to overcome the problems.

PANDA, KRUSHNA C 1151

Newspapers in university libraries: From curiosity to convention; with special reference to BUCL, *Luck Libn* 24 (4) Oct-Dec 1992: 154-158.

Traces the history of the origin of newspapers. Describes their role as disseminator of news information to people at large. Stresses the need to establish an integrated Scientific News Information System and a network of newspaper libraries in India. Describes the newspaper collection and its use in the Behrampur University Central Library.

PATAIRIYA, MANOJ KUMAR, OJHA, S R and INDRA SEN 1152

Acquisition of periodicals on exchange : An effective and simple device, *ALIS*, V 3, 229-237.

Presents a case study of the periodicals acquired on exchange basis at PID. Describes its operation based on PID journals with about 200 agencies from over 55 foreign countries and 115 Indian agencies. The practice followed by the PID has proved more economic and upto the entire satisfaction of the participants. Recommends the system for other libraries also.

RAMAIAH, L S 1153

Inelastic budgets and the decline of serials collections in the university libraries in India, *CODE*, 93-97.

Gives importance of university library. Defines serials and

gives their kinds. States that university libraries are suffering with inadequate and inelastic budgets and are virtually begging the State Govts and the UGC for funds to meet their requirements, but decline in budgets is leading to decline of serial collections in the universities. Examines the serial subscription of a few universities in Andhra Pradesh. Suggests ways and means to overcome the financial trauma of the university libraries.

SHAH, A A 1154

Price escalation and its impact on periodical collection development, *CODE*, 15-17.

States that most of the library budget is spent on journal subscription only. Highlights the impact of rising prices and declining budgets on periodical collection development, which in turn severly affects teaching and research in the country. Suggests certain steps for meeting the financial constraints.

VENKATRAMANA, V 1155

Effects of price escalations and inflationary trends on journals budgets, *IJILIS* 6 (1-2) Jan-June 1993 : 93-100.

Portrays the evil effects of the journal price escalations together with the prevailing inflationary tendencies on the budgetary allocations of libraries of university and scientific institutions. Analyses a sample survey of four science disciplines and their prices. Presents the manifestations reflecting adverse effects on information and research endeavours. Suggests assessment of the existing avenues in relation to investments and elimanate the lacunae by the education administrators for exploiting the resources available.

025.2832 (1) Acquisition of Serials and Periodicals - Computerised

LAHIRI, RAMANSU 1156

Serials control system : A critical study, *Jl Lib & Inf Sci* 16 (2) Dec 1991 : 181-198.

Highlights all the primary facets of serials control system. Shows input movements to other subsystem with flowchart. Discusses various decision strategy. Presents a brief case study also. Concludes with the expectations that serials administration in university library system should be given its due importance by considering it as total system and as separate identify for better sarvice.

MANOHAR, M N , *et al* 1157

Computerisation of serials control, *ITAH*, 265-275.

Mentions that Tata Memorial Hospital Library entered into automation programme in 1987. Explains in detail the computerized serials control system for which a software has been developed locally using dBASE III Plus and Clipper. Describes the salient features of this menu-driven programme which is claimed to satisfy the requirements for serials control.

025.28 (1) Collection Development - Manuscripts

VIJAYAN, K 1158

Organising manuscript collections for the library, *PLD*, 60-81.

Defines a Mss which contains wisdom from the ancients. Traces the origins of Mss libraries from the private collections and the royal patronage in Kerala. Discusses the establishment and growth of Oriental Research Institute. Explains collecting Mss and the nature of collection on different writing materials as palm leaves, and other materials. Discusses rich illuminations of Mss, garland like Mss, fan-type Mss, different sizes, layoput and scripts. Lists some important works published by the Institute and the appointment of some great scholars as curators and librarians. States that these give support to research hence they should be tapped well, so much so that the current technology be applied for copying into microfiche, CD-ROM.

025.2832 (1) Acquisition of Reprints

NAVANEETHAN, R 1159

Low-cost collection development method for reprints in special libraries and information centres, *CODE*, 81-83.

Defines reprint. States that reprint collection is an important part of special libraries and information centres. Highlights the role of reprints. Suggests a low-cost method of acquiring reprints using current contents. Touches upon the importance of organising reprints and the future of reprints in the advent of IT.

SHRIVASTAVA, A K and TEWATHIA, ARUN 1160

Reprint of research paper : An effective economical source of primary communication, *ILA Bull* 28 (1-2) Apr-Sept 1992 : 6-9.

Emphasizes need for the reprints as source of current information providing the partial solution to the crisis due to escalating costs of journals and shrinking library budgets. Compares the procurement of copies from INSDOC with that from the authros. Discusses ceontrolized ordering and receipt of reprints procedure of DRDE Library, Gwalior.

SHULA, R K 1161

Reprints collection : A pragmatic approach to cope with the economic recession, *CODE*, 89-92.

Deals with the limited budgetary provision hence alternative course to subscribe to core journals and establish a collection of reprints of useful literature published in peripheral journals. The articles may be selected on the basis of requirements of research workers and engineers. Project profiles may be maintained for the purpose and the search strategy should be designed according to the key words relating to the projects.

025.286 Acquisition of Maps

MITTRA, D K and GHATAK, A K 1162

Map collection of the National Library and its users' pattern, In *Papers*, 58th *IFLA* General Conference, New Delhi, 30 Aug-5 Sept 1992, pp 2.2-2.4.

Gives history of the National Library of India in brief. Discusses the formulation of Map Division, acquisition policy of printed maps and atlases. Describes the type of collection which dates from 16th century onwards. Discusses readers service, users and their orientation, users mainly belong to geography and geology who have only the basic knowledge. The users constitute research scholars, students, miscellaneous group, mountaineers and trekkers, and causual users. Concludes that National Library should establish cooperation with other National libraries.

025.287 Acquisition of Audio Visuals (AVs)

025.287 (1) Acquisition of Motion Pictures

AMJAD ALI 1163

Motion pictures as source of information : The acquisition problems for Indian institutions, *CODE*, 135-137.

Traces the development of writing medium to newer media like photographs to AVs etc and being used for preservation and retrieval of information. Explains the motion pictures as a source of information including the cinematographic films and video recording. Discusses the acquisition of films with educational value. Explains the import policy for such material and other procedural difficulties in their import.

AMJAD ALI 1164

Motion pictures as source of information : The acquisition problems for Indian universities, *Univ News* 31 (22) May 31, 1993: 8-9.

Discusses about the development and importance of motion pictures. Glives its scope. Describes the acquisition of motion pictures, the import policy regarding motion pictures. Concludes that though motion pictures are good source of information, yet hurdles are coming their way in importing them for the academic and research purposes.

025.287 (1) Collection Development- CD-ROM

CHATTOPADHYAY, P S and CHAKRABORTY, PAPIA 1165

Collection development : Utilisation of CD-ROM system - a study, *CODE*, 173.

Explains the collection development programme of IIM Library Calcutta which is a specialised library and is now facing the economic crunch. States that library is taking help of modern technology through CD-ROM to overcome the difficulties, as the disc includes about 800 current publications with new additions to the database. Considers some of its advantages.

DHAKA, R P S , MUNSHI, USHA M and NISHY, P 1166

A technological solution to manage the information resource base of the country, *ILA Bull* 28 (3-4) Oct-Mar 1993 : 80-86.

States that the number of S & T journals being published every year is increasing the world over, but libraries are finding it difficult to procure them for want of funds. Considers 'Optical Disc Technology' as a viable alternative to avoid erosion of information base in India.

MOHANDAS, M K and SHET, K C 1167

Technological impact of CD-ROM : A new media in collection development, *CODE*, 131-133.

Mentions about fast growing literature and usefulness of CD-ROM. Modern, new media like CD-ROM offers a viable alternative for library collection development in the context of escalating prices and declining grants. Evaluates CD-ROM technology in the light of its compatibility with the Indian libraries. Discusses maintenance, economic and related issues. Concludes that CD-ROM is now available in Indian libraries also

THAKUR, RANJAN SINHA and PRASAD, A R D 1168

CD-ROMs in collection development, *CODE*, 125-129.

Begins with the premise that CD-technology is a major breakthrough document production. Gives a brief discussion of the importance and the growth in Compact Discs (CD) in various types of documents like reference, CAI materials, etc. Presents various criteria in choosing software and hardware and the information available on CDs. Discusses also the role of CDs in library collection development. Concludes with a brief scenario of the future libraries.

025.287 (1) Collection Development - Databases

GOPINATH, M A and SIVACHINDABRAM, S 1169

New databases products and their economic value in collection development, *CODE*, 119-123.

Discusses the developments that have emerged in new database products technology. Mentions that emergence of more than 5000 secondary journals in the form of CD-ROM databases have given scope for establishing bibliographic information centre through online networks. Describes that this would reduce the cost of subscription in periodicals budget which could effectively be used for buying print-on-paper primary periodicals.

025.29 Collection Development - Area Studies

SUDARSANA REDDY, D 1170

Tirumala Tirupati Studies : An area studies approach to the study of local history collection, *Her Lib Sci* 31 (1-2) Jan-Apr 1992 : 32-39.

Discusses the facets constituting Tirmula Tirupati Studies, its meaning, scope and significance. Mentions local history collections and approach to the study of local history. Provides a model for estbalihsing Tirumala Tirupati Studies Research Centre (TTRC) to fulfil the objectives. Suggests certain activities for consideration in promoting the use of local history materials.

025.3 BIBLIOGRAPHIC ANALYSIS

GOPINATH, M A 1171

Typology of structural relations for information analysis and consolidation process, *Lib Sci slant Docum & Inf Std* 29 (3) Sept 1992 : 139-142.

Defines the information analysis and consolidation process. Discusses the static and dynamic aspects of organisation of information. Presents a typology of relations for structural relations and consolidation processes.

025.3 BIBLIOGRAPHIC CONTROL BIBLIOGRAPHIC ORGANISATION

ANANTHARAMAIAH, R L 1172

Bibliographic control in Kannada, *DAB*, 234-242.

Describes about bibliographic control of books published in Kannada. Mentions about the problems coming in the way of collecting relevant material. States that most of the publishers violate the Delivery of Books Act. Makes suggestions to overcome the problems and books be collected on behalf of the National Library. Describes some bibliographic tools being published in Kannada.

BISWAS, S C 1173

Bibliographic control in South Asia, *In* McIlwaine, I C (Ed), Standards for the international exchange of bibliographic information, London : Library Association, 1991

States that since Ranganathan's demise little progress has been made on cataloguing standards until the present time, but now the situation is becoming more hopeful.

CANO, V 1174

Periodicals from developing countries : Bibliographic control and visiblity, *INICAE* 12 (2) Sept 1993 :143-165.

Evaluates level of bibliographic control and the consequent international visibility of periodical publication. Discusses commercially produced international reference sources on periodical publications based on evolution of CD-ROM version of Serials Directory (1990). Studies of a sample of 604 periodicals vis-a-vis bibliographic control indicators. Reveals that India has established a consistent policy of bibliographic control in S & T periodicals. Suggests improvements.

DESHPANDE, K S 1175

Bibliographic organisation of Commonwealth literature in the humanities : A case for the establishment of a Commonwealth Studies Research Institute in India, *DAB*, 83-98.

Traces the historical development of bibliographic control and organisation in humanities in the Commonwealth countries. Describes the post-independence attempts including that of the INB, Library of Congress Accession List, Bibliography of Asian Studies, etc. Gives reasons of the problem and neglect of the humanites, lack of finances, etc. Discusses the solution of the problems.

GAUTAM, J N 1176

Exponential and quantitiative growth of universe of knowledge and bibliographical control for literature search, *IJILIS*, 6 (1-2) Jan-June 1993 : 29-48.

Highlights impotance of knowledge. Deals with the social origin and growth of universe of knowledge, exponential and quantitative growth of knowledge, its structure and development. Discusses about growth of journals and research materials. Explains the need for bibliographic control of vast literature in order to tackle with locating, searching and ascertaining the material. Describes various types of bibliographical tools needed in libraries as effective aids.

ISAAC, DOROTHY 1177

Problems of bibliographic control in the study of philosophy, *DAB*, 126-132.

Outlines the importance of philosophy. Discusses sources of information as essential tools for information retrieval in research. Describes information services in India, particularly with reference to Indian Council of Philosophical Research. Makes a case for a national information system for philosophic and religious instructions so as to develop sharing of resources and provide access to these resources. Gives suggestions for a National Information System in Humanities on the lines of NISSAT.

KRISHAN KUMAR 1178

Bibliographic control in Indology : Scope and importance of the humanities, *DAB*, 99-103.

Mentions importance and scope of the humanities. Discusses about the origin of the indological libraries set up in India starting with Mss libraries but donot provide free access to Mss. Describes some of the leading bibliographic tools about India. Makes a case for the setting up an Indian Council of Humanities Research.

KUMARAPPA, G 1179

Bibliographic control of periodical literature in Indian languages, DAB, 243-249.

Mentions importance of periodicals in information dissemination. Shows in a table number of periodcials in humanities in each language. Discusses the obstacles in having bibliographic control such as language, proliferation, periodicity, lack of proper tools, postal delays and missing issues, etc. Mentions the need for retrospective bibliographic control. States that bibliographic control and bibliographic organisation can be achieved by library cooperation.

SUDARSHAN RAO, S 1180

Recorded communication in Telugu and bibliographic control, *SPLS*, 29-38.

Defines bibliographical control. Discusses the need for bibliographic control. Mentions the materials to be controlled. Gives data about publishing in India. Discusses tools for bibliographic control of Telugu publications at national, and at local/state levels.

TAHER, MOHAMED 1181

Bibliographic control of Islamic literature in India : Trends & prospects, *DAB*, 116-125.

Intends to portray the state of the art of bibliographic control of Islamic studies literature in India. Gives a bird's eye view of the existing situation of the resources available for access and control. Discusses the problems of access and control of Islamic literature. Offers solutions to the problems, and gives suggestions.

THOMAS, SARAH E 1182

Bibliographic control and agriculture, *LT*, 216-235.

Defines bibliographic control. Points out that the process of bibliographic description and analysis is still labour intensive, new technology notwithstanding. Although several cooperative efforts are underway to minimise duplication in establishing bibliographic control over agriculture material, yet overlap between and among agricultural databases will continue for the near future.

VYAS, S D 1183

Bibliographic control of American/English literature in India, *DAB*, 104-115.

Explains bibliographical control. Discusses need of bibliographic control. Identifies boundaries of humanities. Discusses information seeking behaviour of humanists in consulting primary and secondary resources. Describes various documentation activities in India of American literature including the role of ASRC services.

025.3 CATALOGUING

BILESANMI, S A 1184

Cataloguing and classification of library materials : A necessary or luxury, *Int Lib Move* 14 (3) Sept 1992 : 140-145.

Discusses the advantages and disadvantages of cataloguing to the library users. Makes a case for its justification in spite of huge amount of money spent on the preparation of a catalogue cards.

VED PRAKASH 1185

Cataloguing practice : For library and information science students, officers librarians & documentalists, 1993.

Deals with the various cataloguing practices useful for library and information science students, library officers, librarians, and documentalists in order to achieve standardisation in rendering different entries.

025.3 (1) Computerised Cataloguing

CHOFRA, H R 1186

Automation in library cataloguing, *Jl Inf Sci* 3 (1) July-Sept 1992 : 25-30.

Mentions that automation in cataloguing needs special thrust in India considering rapid development in the field in other developed countries. Discusses automation in library cataloguing comprehensively, from unit record system to online system.

NAGARAJARAO, K and VARMA, P K 1187

Catalouing services : Computerized application, *STIM*, 113-117.

Describes the computerised catalogue service system integrating three oprations, viz., catalogue card producation, publication of new additions bulletin, and search services. Gives an overview of cataloguing system describing all the three functions. States that with computerisation of this system a lot of human effort is saved.

025.3 (1) Cataloguing, Pre-Natal

LAXMAN RAO, N and PRAFULLA CHANDRA, T V 1188

Ranganathan's concept of pre-natal cataloguing : A precursor to cataloguing-in-publication, *IJILIS* 5 (3-4) July-Dec 1992 : 258-265.

States that the concept of centralised cataloguing became popular after Ranganathan propounded his ideas on pre-natal cataloguing and resulted ultimately in the present CIP, and now CIS. Discusses its implications on ISBN, CIS, CIP. Concludes with the suggestion that in the birth centenary year of Ranganathan CIP should be introduced for Indian publications in various disciplines and languages.

025.3 (1) ISBN

MUDHOL, M V and ROUT, R K 1189

Standardization with a special reference to ISBN : An implication for computer education in the library system, *Jl Inf Sci* 3 (1) July-Sept 1992 : 3-9.

Gives concept of standardization and opines the computer as the instrument of standardization. Describes the role of standardization in libraries and its services. Deals with ISBN and its importance in library acquisition and cataloguing system. Streases the need for computer education in Indian universities for LIS students and library users.

025.313 Card Catalogue

OGUNROMBI, S A 1190

Book availability and user failures in the medical library of the University of Ilorin, *Int Lib Move* 14 (4) Dec 1992 : 190-197.

Aims at finding out the extent to which the medical students are finding books sought through the use of card catalouge; factors responsible for both the avaialability and non-avaialability of books in the library and ; options open to patrons when they fail to either locate books in the card catalogue or on the shelf.

025.3132 OPAC (Online Catalogue)

SHABAHAT HUSSAIN and O'BRIEN, ANN 1191

Recent trends in subject access to OPACs : An evaluation, *Int Classif* 19 (3) 1992 : 140-145.

States that research in 80's has shown subject access as one of the most dominant approaches in OPACs. Investigates problems and finds solutions in improving search methods. More recent research indicates that the real answer to the question of 'precision without sacrificing recall' lies in developing user friendly interfaces and also in designing 'knowledge based systems'. Visualises evolving trends of research vis-a-vis their future prospects as possible solutions.

SUKIASYAN, EDWARD 1192

Homo quarerens (The seeking man) : On the problems of development of the readers's cognitive capacities in the searching process, *COP*, 15-22.

Analyses the process of search of bibliographical information through the catalogue search is a function of the user, who works with the catalogue. Discusses language of the catalogue, the electronic cataalogue (OPAC). Describes additional potentials of classification-based, element-by-element search and shows their ties with the development of the users's cognitive power Concludes that search and cognitive activities of the user are closely connected and interdependent.

MAJUMDAR, UMA 1193

Implementation of UNIMARC at India's National Library, *Int Cat & Biblio Cont* 21 (2) Apr-June 1992 : 19-24.

Discusses the reasons of developing MARC and selecting UNIMARC for the National Library, Calcutta. Describes the programmes of automation at the National Library. Explains in details the UNIMARC/MINISIS interface, tagging structure of MARC, creating a MARC format for the National Library. Discusses the creation of a MARC Table and MARC databases for National Library. Explain how Indian language materials are handled by computer. Mentions about the training programmes for this purpose.

025.317 Conversion of Records

ANAND, LATIKA, LAKSHMI, V V and VERMA, R K 1194

Creation & conversion of bibliographic record of monographs and development of catalouge management software at NSL, *LIT*, 126-135.

Discusses various problems and issues in the project of INSDOC of converting manual data into machine readable form. Highlights main features of a software package developed by NSL for catalogue management. Touches upon some of the future developments.

025.317 (1) CCF

NAVALGUND, C U and HARINARAYANA, N S 1195

Adoption of Common Communication Format for a legal bibliographic information system : An experience at the National School of India University, *LIT*, 142-150.

Highlights the efforts made at the National Law School of India University, Bangalore in designing a legal bibliographic information system. Gives the future plans of this University Library.

SHARMA, KAMINI and SUNDER SINGH, B G 1196

Design and creation of faceted databses using CCF (F) : UNESCO-NISSAT experts meet on factual databases, *NISSAT News* 12 (3) July-Sept 1993 : 3-7.

Reports about this two week Experts Meet on Design and Creation of Factual Databases using CCF (F) during April 19-30, 1993 at Technology Bhavan, New Delhi. Gives its objectives, resource persons, proceedings, and comments. Gives the recommendations made at this meeting.

SUNDER SINGH, B G and SHARMA, KAMINI 1197

CCF: The Common Communication Format, Edition 3 (1992), *NISSAT News* 12 (3) July - Sept 1993 : 13-14.

Describes abouth the 3rd edition of CCF brought out by PGI/ UNESCO in two volumes : Volumes 1 is the CCF (B) : The CCF (Bibliographic); and Volume 2 is actually de novo CCF (F) helpful in designing and developing databases on individuals, organisations and projects.

SUR, S N and CHOWDHURY, G G 1198

A prototype design of a bibliographic database based on CCF using Micro CDS/ISIS, *Iaslic Bull* 38 (1) Mar 1993 : 17-37.

States that design aspect of bibliographic databases are important for effective resource sharing and better information retrieval services. Standard formats like CCF may be adopted. Mentions that modifications to the CCF format may be more useful for data manipulation. Proposes design of a bibliogrpahic databases based on CCF for use in Micro CDS-ISIS. Mentions addition of a few new fields for better results. Provides sample catalogue entries to demonstrate how the proposed design help perform various information retrievl operation in libraries.

UNESCO / PGI, PARIS 1199

International exchange formt, *INICAE* 11 (1) Mar 1992 : 109-112.

Explains need for standars to facilitate exchange of information in all sectors of information. Discusses such attempts as MARC, CCF, international meeting for the development of CCF. Application of CCF, computer software and format conversion, estension of format. Mentions training and promotion for CCF

025.32 AACR-2

DASGUPTA, ARJUN 1200

What is new in AACR -2 ; with special reference to choice of access points and description, Calcutta : Ratna Prakashan, 1991, ii, 126 p.

Attempts to show the vital difference and comparative study between the 1967 British Edition and that of 1978 Edition of AACR. Gives some new features of AACR -2. Provides a rule-by-rule study of this international cataloguing code.

SEHGAL, R L 1201

Cataloguing manual, AACR II, New Delhi : Ess Ess Publications, 1993. v, 350 p.

Discusses in Section A (Chapters 1-18) about the theoretical concepts of catalouging and AACR - II. Describes in Section B (Chapters 1-9) about the various rules meant for practice according to AACR - II.

025.32 (1) CCC (Classified Catalogue Code)

SHARMA, C D and DAVE, MEENAKSHI 1202

Classfied Catalogue Code in theory and practice, rev and enl ed, Jodhpur : Scientific Publishers, 1993.

Assists in understanding and application of the CCC itself. Describes the various catalouging problems, viz, entries and their recording, rendering of various sections in the Main Entry, Construction of the cross-reference and Book Index Entries, cataloguing treatment to the corporate, multi-volumed, composite books, and periodical publications.

025.3432 Cataloguing of Serials

VASHISHTH, C P 1203

Cataloguing of serials using AACR 2, *Lib Her* 30 (1) Apr 1991 : 38-47.

Gives the main features of AACR-2. States that the new rules provide for three recommended levels giving options to the agency of cataloguing to choose any level as per its requirements. Identifies the problems encountered in cataloguing serial publications and provides necessary rules for each of these idiosyncracies.

025.4028 (1) Abstracting Services

KHAN, M M 1204

Abstracting in conservation of cultural property, *Iaslic Bull* 38 (3) Sept 1993 : 139-140.

Defines the term 'cultural property'. Describes about the unique collection of books, journals and other information sources on conservation at the National Research Laboratory for Conservation of Cultural Property Library in Lucknow. Points out the library has been preparing abstracts from book and relevant journal articles regularly, and inputs to the abstracting journal Art and Archaeology Technical Abstracts published from USA.

SALES - PONTES, A H 1205

Mapping the way through English literature and language-indexing and abstracting services, *DAB*, 183-202.

States that English literature and language are the most developed among humanities and researchers need to know how to find out literature. Aims at concentrating on some select existing indeing and abstrating publications and other specifies aids avaialble in the field of English language and literature.

025.42 LIBRARY CLASSIFICATION

KNOWLEDGE ORGANIZATION

DAHLBERG, INGRETRAT 1206

The network of knowledge fields : Conceptual systematization in action, *COP*, 323-333.

Uses congnitive approach in understanding how a network of knowledge fields composed of knowledge units/concepts can be generated and put into action. Explains Information Coding Classfication as being constructed on the guiding knowledge units gained from the catagories of objects and activities arranged according to integrative level theory. Explains dynamic character of ICC system. Shows that new findings of classification theory are based on sound cognitive paradigms for knowledge organisation.

DAS, MAMOTA 1207

Learning teaching cognitive paradigms in knowledge organisation, *COP*, 362-371.

States that education should help in furthering growth and use of knowledge, and learning and teaching are connected. The cognitive view is : learning is an active, constructive and purposive process dependent on mental activities. Explains congnitive learning theories and principles, giving schema theory as an explantion for cognitive learning. Mentions future directions of learning-teaching cognitive paradigms.

GOPINATH, M A 1208

Creativity and knowledge organisation : A cognitive interpretation, *COP*, 390-400.

States that creativity is a complex of processes of active thinking. It guides a mind to intuitively comprehend sublimated knowledge and intellectually analyse, synthesize, disseminate knowledge which helps problem solving. To be productive, knowledge resulting from such processes have to be cumulated into systems. Gives features of knowledge organisation. Discusses role of classification as a thread of knowledge, and provides a structure for learning. Concludes that knowledge of classification enhances the productivity of a creative person. Points out S R Ranganathan's contribution in this regard.

NEELAMEGHAN, A , GOPINATH, M A , RAGHAVAN, K S and SANKRALINGAM, P, *Eds* 1209

Cognitive paradigms in knowledge organisation ; Second International ISKO Conference, Bangalore : Sarada Ranganathan Endowment for Library Science, 1992. 466 p.

Contains 38 articles presented and discussed at the Second International ISKO Conference held at Madras during 26-28 August 1992 to mark the Birth Centenary Year of Dr S R Ranganathan. Includes articles by authors from different countries on eight areas of the conference.

NEELAMEGHAN, A , GOPINATH, M A , RAGHAVAN, K S and SANKRALINGAM, P 1210

Introduction, *COP*, xii-xvi.

Explains that cognitive paradigms indicate the knowledge seeking behaviour of individuals and groups of individuals. Gives the scope of cognitive science and attempts to identify structure of knowledge and its components. States that ISKO organised a Conference for discussion on eight areas of cognitive paradigms.

PARTHASARATHY, S 1211

Preface, *COP*, v.

States that knowledge organisation was one of the areas in which S R Ranganathan was deeply interested, hence ISKO organised its Second International Conference in Madras as part of the Birth Centenary Celebrations of S R Ranganathan. Mentions that in all, 38 papers included in 8 areas in this publication.

PERREAULT, J M 1212

Not even the voice of a ghost : Epistemology as a bridge from our bibliographical past to a new paradigm, *COP*, 51-64.

Describes that all culturally purposive activities including the searching of bibliographical files on pages, card-files, and on a CRT dependent on an OPAC, rely on an implicit epistemology. Traces the development from pre-OPAC, OCLC, etc. Points out the usefulness of APUPA arrangement in this connection.

SATIJA, M P 1213

Classification and indexing in India : A state-of-the-art, In *Papers*, 58th IFLA General Conference, New Delhi, 30 Alug-5 Sept 1992 : 4.26-4.29.

Explains the real beginning with Ranganathan as the

mechanism of CC, and his contribution to library classification. Discusses DRTC and Sarada Ranganathan Endowment contribution to library classification, India's contribution to classification terminology, classification practice in India, classfication teaching, research and literature, classification organisation, and conferences.

SATIJA, M P 1214

A deserted bastion : Classification and indexing in India; a state of the art, *Int Cat & Bib Cont* 22 (3) July-Sept 1993 : 51-54.

Presented at the 58th IFLA General Conference, New Delhi (1992) gives short account of S R Ranganathan. Discusses contribution of DRTC, Sarada Ranganathan Endowment. Explains India's contribution to subject cataloguing, classification terminoloyg, classfication practices.

SEKHAR, M and EKBOTE, E R 1215

Cognitive skills of conceptualisation process and types of concepts, *COP*, 23-34.

Defines knowledge. Identifies cognitive skills involved in conceptualisation process. Evolves a new concept classification to facilitate learning and teaching. Classfies the concepts into six categories based upon their attributes and attributes relations. A specific 'Concept Analysis Ability' tool is also developed to measure the concept analysis ability of secondary school teachers.

SHABAHAT HUSSAIN 1216

Library classification : Facets and analyses, New Delhi : Tata McGraw-Hill Publishing Company, 1993. 367 p.

Presents various facets of library classification after defining and giving need, purpose, etc, right down from their origins to the latest developments therein. Discusses in detail the latest editions of DDC, CC, and UDC. Covers also recent trends in classification including work of CRG, BSO, computer genrated classification schemes, classification in online systems with emphasis on DDC and LC.

SHRIVASTAVA, R K 1217

Knowledge generation process : A conceptual model in ecosystematic framework, *COP*, 432-441.

Deals with knowledge generating process speically to develop conceputal framework for a General System of Knowledge Organisation (GKO) Interprets knowledge base in individual experts' cognitive process participating in knowledge generation in ecosystematic confederation with other similar experts around a event structure, defined as ecosystem, ie, articulated knowledge base (AKB). Uses various notions of second generation Expert System in ecosystematic base rather than traditional man-machine interaction.

SRIVASTAVA, A P 1218

Theory of knowledge classification for librarian, rev and enl ed, assisted by M P Satija, R Padmanabhan and Anil Srivastava, New Delhi : The Learning Laboratory, 1992. 115 p.

Divided into 7 chapters, it deals with knowledge classification, Fundamental Categories, terminilogy, and notation, patterns and tools in classification, document number. Also includes lasting impact of Ranganathan. Gives some practical examples and a glossary at the end.

SVENONIOUS, EVAINE 1219

The impact of computer technology on knowledge representation, *COP*, 1-14.

Explains knowledge representation. Focusses on the use of three computerbased knowledge representation of potential relevance for information retrieval : hypertext systems, cluster analysis and knowledge representations accommodating rule-based reasoning. Considers research that might be persued to inform the development of knowledge representations for information retrieval.

UMARANI, ASHA 1220

Knowledge classification : A permanent structure for dynamic knowledge, *COP*, 211-222.

Explains that a true library classification system came into existence with DDC followed by many more general schemes, and an elaborate theory. Though analytico-synthetic scheme of S R Ranganathan solved many problems, growth of knowledge after WW II changed the framework of knowledge, rejection of theory and turning to word indexing for IR, and rejection of classification when computers came. Stresses that Ranganathan tried but could not find the basis for dividing the universe of knowledge into main divisions comprising the first array. But the problem of laying down principles and tests for deeming a subject to be a (BS) remains unsolved.

WAHLIN, EJNAR 1221

A universal system without ordering codes, *COP*, 205-210.

States that well known universal systems are characterized by a collection of areas of knowledge ordered according to codes in the form of figures or letters. Discusses a system in which knowledge are denoted by letters not in alphabetical order but the names of the respective subjects. Suggests internal replacement so that a contact is made between material sciences and technologies.

025.42(1) RANGANATHAN'S CONTRIBUTION TO LIBRARY CLASSIFICATION/KNOWLEDGE ORGANISATION

AMAN, MOHAMMED M 1222

Ranganathan the classificationist, *RAW*, 1-9.

Describes the importance of the Five Laws of Ranganathan which had international appeal. Discusses in detail his contribution to classification, to terminology, development of scientific method, general theories, deep analysis and synthesis, etc. Describes his Colon Classification, contribution to facet analysis, contribution to cataloguing. Concludes that he had international impact as a classificationist and true library scientist.

BATTY, C D 1223

The influence of Ranganathan on the structural design of index languages, *PP*, 47-59.

Traces the origins of classification from Aristotle to Melvil Dewey. Discusses the beginning of synthesis in classification from Dewey. Describes in detail the contribution of Ranganathan to the discipline of classification. Discusses Ranganathan's development of facet analysis. Explains Ranganathan's fundamental contribution to classification in England and the USA. Mentions also about Artificial Intelligence systems.

COMAROMI, JOHN P 1224

Ranganathan's influence on American librarianship, *PP*, 123-129. Relates how Ranganathan's ideas entered US via UK where they did not stir much initially and had no immediate effect on library classification. States that Ranganathan provided a rationale and a vocabulary for classification construction such as facet analysis. Describes about the influence of Ranganathan on DDC.

CURRAS, EMILLIA 1225

Ranganathan's classification theories under the systems science postulates, *Jl Lib & Inf Sci* 17 (1) June 1992 : 45-65.

Describes the basic ideas about systems science. Discusses Ranganathan's ideas about concept of 'universe of ideas', 'universe of science', 'universe of knowledge, 'universe of classification'. Examines principles, canons and postualtes underlying Colon Classification. Discusses structure of Colon Classification. Points out that the ideas of Ranganathan conform to the concept of 'unity of science'. Concludes that the principles of systems science or system thinking are helpful in understanding theory of classification.

DHYANI, P 1226

Ranganathan's normative principles and Dewey Decimal Classification, *PP*, 61-69.

Discusses normative principles of Ranganathan and its application to DDC because it is being used in 70% of Indian libraries. Explains individualisation of clubbed isolates, Add device, relocation, etc.

GOPINATH, M A 1227

General system theory vis-a-vis classification theory of Ranganathan, *CPT*, 114-121.

Discusses general systems theory and its laws. Hightlights application of these laws to the development of a theory of classificaion. Evaluates research done in classification in India and Britain. Redefines PMEST in terms of systems theory. Formulates rules on the basis of principles derived from systems law for the development of schedules for classification and procedures for classifying of documents for collection formation.

GOPINATH, M A 1228

Science of classification: Ranganathan's contribution to classification, *Jl Lib & Inf Sci* 17 (1) June 1992: 66-70.

Identifies the contribution of Ranganathan towards scientific basis for classification. Discusses the values in developing theory and practice of classification in the current day inter-disciplinary subjects in library and information science.

GOPINATH, M A 1229

Towards a scientific approach to classificationa and cataloguing: Contributions of S R Ranganathan, *Lib Sci slant Docum & Inf Std* 29 (2) June 1992: 85-89.

States that development of scientific approach to classification and cataloguing were initiated by S R Ranganathan. He provided a theoretical framework for the development of these intensely practical techniques in library science. Points out that such theoretical framework in the form of a hierarchy of normative principles are capable of guiding the contextual situations arising out of the new developments in the field of library and information services.

HUNTER, ERIC J 1230

Ranganathan UK: The influence of Ranganathan's work on the development of classification and indexing in the United Kingdom, *PP*, 77-91.

Narrates importance of faceted classification in computer which finds its origin to Ranganathan. States that Ranganathan's theories went to West because of Bernard I Palmer (a close friend of Ranganathan), and then A J Wells through chain indexing in British National Bibliography. Describes role of Classification Research Group in spreading Ranganathan's classificatory ideas, and production of special classification schemes based on faceted principles, the thesaurofacets, Bibliographic Classification-2, Broad System of Ordering, etc.

INGWERSEN, PETER and WORMELL, IRENE 1231

Ranganathan in the perspective of advanced information retrieval, *Libri* 42 (3) July-Sept 1992: 184-201.

Examines S R Ranganathan's approach to knowledge organisation and its relevance to "intellectual accessibility" in libraries. Discusses current and future development of his methodology and theories in knowledge-based systems. Elaborates usefulness and applications of analytico-synthetic methodology and establishes parallel with case-frame theory in techniques of information retrieval. Concludes that his helpful sequence and other methodology may have limitation in other fields, but in cognitive modelling his principles for knowledge organisation and faceted methodology find applications.

KRISHAN KUMAR 1232

Distinctive contribution of Ranganathan to library classification, *Jl Lib & Inf Sci* 17 (2) Dec 1992: 116-127.

Discusses Ranganathan's distinctive contributions to library classifcatin such as normative principles, three plane model of work, freely faceted classification, postulational approach, Fundamental Categories, certain notational devices like sector device, group notation device, emptying digit device, and seminal mnemonic device. Considers 7th Edition of Colon Classification as the best example of application of all these ideas of the truly great scholar.

KUMAR, P S G 1233

Ranganathan through classification, *PP*, 1-5.

Attempts to throw light on his qualities through classification approach in that looking at his universe of knowledge, his attributes, his characteristics, his arrays and chains, and phases and facets, and fundamental categories, in terms of life span, space, etc.

LANGRIDGE, D W 1234

My debt to Ranganathan, *PP*, 7-11.

Describes author's meetings and discussions with Ranganathan particularly on classification, among others. Discusses about the benefits derived from Ranganathan's work and contribution in clssification. Pays tribute to Dr S R Ranganathan during the Birth centenary celebrations and expresses his debt to the great man.

MCILWAINE, I C 1235

Ranganathan and classification in Britain, *PP*, 93-100.

Speaks of Ranganathan's days at the School of Library, Archives and Information Studies at the University College, London in 1924-25. Discusses about the papers Ranganathan wrote in examinations and score he got, the teaching methods followed then. Discusses about Ranganathan's contribution in classification and his influence in Britian particularly through Classification Research Group (UK).

RAJU, A A N 1236

Ranganathan: The propounder of dynamic theory of library classification, *DL*, 81-87.

Explains the emergence of dynamic theory of classification and the basic work of S R Ranganathan. Gives its ingredients, normative principles, impact of dynamic theory of Ranganathan on Dorking Conference held in 1957, on British Classification Reserah Group, on American students, etc.

RAJU, A A N 1237

Ranganathan: The propounder of dynamic theory of subject classification, *Her Lib Sci* 32 (1-2) Jan-Apr 1993: 17-21.

States the early work on classification through descriptive theory. Describes early emergence and application of dynamic theory of classifcation propounded by Ranganathan. Discusses the basic work on dynamic theory through the work of Classification Research Group (UK) and through the outcome of Dorking Conference.

RANGANATHAN and classification: A chronology, 1924-1992, *CC*, 194-205. 1238

Provides in chronological order, the conception and developments of Colon Classification of Dr S R Ranganathan. Puts the chronology for the benefit of the readers, in an Appendix A.

SATIJA, M P 1239

Ranganathan and classification: A chronology 1924-1992: *Int Classif* 19 (1) 1992: 3-6.

Identifies some sources on which is based this chronology giving Ranganathan's development in the field of library classification with a short description of the impact and significance of the dates. The chronology which has been structured according to some periods of his life determined mostly by location lists. Mentions also some post mortem events.

205.42 (1) Classificationa and Computers

RAM KUMAR and SHARMA, JAIDEEP 1240

Development of Export System in classification: Some theoretical aspects, *Lib Her* 31 (1-2) Apr-Sep 1992: 13-23.

Attempts to provide in brief the features and characteristics of an ES. Reviews breifly existing ES in library classification. Describes the actual process of developing an ES in library classification and then building class numbers automatically. Discusses anticipated problems while developing such an ES.

025.42 (1) Call Number

McGARRY, DOROTHY 1241

Displays of bibliographic records in call number: Functions of the displays and data elements needed, *COP*, 65-80.

States that online displays of bibliographic records in call number order can serve various functions. A literature search showed no papers on this topic. Examines various displays from online catalogues available via the INTERNET, but they were uninformative. Makes suggestins of useful data elements to be included in displays of bibliographic recrods in call number order for such functions as shelflisting, cataloguing, catalogue manitainance, reference, public searches, collection development and inventory control. Makes recommendations or inclusion of such data elements in call number displays: entire call number as a sequencing element; main entry; entire title proper; and the date.

025.42 (1) Classification - Common Subdivisions

ASUNDI, A Y and GUNJAL, S R 1242

A review of research on common subdivisions, *CRL*, 30-46.

Makes a review of comparison of six categories of common subdividions in four general classification schemes to study compatibility in their structural and verbal plane. Based on the findings a general theory for common subdivisions has been formulated.

025.42014 Classification Terminology

D'ALOISI, DANIELA 1243

Knowledge representation in human-computer interaction: A terminological representation, *COP*, 192-204.

Describes a hybrid system, KRAM, and one of its applications in human-computer interaction area. Focusses on terminological component, TERM-KRAM that offers expression representation language. Discusses functions of TERM-KRAM. Explains the implementation of KRAM with example.

PRASAD, K N 1244

Development of terminology in library classification: A case study, *CRL*, 1-16.

Highlights the importance of standardizing terminology. Presents evloution of terms in Library Classification and the Indian contribution to the study of terminoogy in library classification. Analyses rate of growth of terms - studies principles for absorption of new terms into the systems and updating mechanism.

025.428 Book Numbers

SATIJA, M P and AGRAWAL, S P 1245

Book number in the new Edition, *CC*, 131-140.

Describes the book numbering system as followed in Colon Classification of Ranganathan, Points out problems arising out of this system. Mentions some of the advantages of this book number developed by Ranganathan.

SATIJA, M P and COMAROMI, JOHN P 1246

Beyond classification: Book numbers, New Delhi: Ess Ess Publications, 1992. 115p.

Discusses about the various Book numbering systems available at presents. Defines book numbers, and gives their history. Favours chronological book numbers and gives their advantages. Ends with a chronology of book numbers and a useful bibliography.

025.43 General Classification Systems.

Comparative Classification

GIRJA KUMAR 1247

Classic classifications, *Frontline* 9 (17) Aug 15-28, 1992: 62.

Gives a brief about some of the classification systems deemed to be classic such as those of British Museum, Bibliogheque Nationale (Paris), Dewey Decimal Classification, Library of Congress Classification, Universal Decimal Classification, Bibliographic Classification, and Colon Classification of Dr S R Ranganathan.

RAJU, A A N 1248

Fine arts: Scope and treatment in the Universal Decimal Classification and Colon Classification. *DAB*, 55-65.

Mentions importance of humanities as a branch of universe of knowledge. Gives definition and scope of humanities. Points out the Indian tradition of classification of arts and Western influence on it. Deals with treatment of Fine Arts in UDC and CC with regard to their branches. Discusses problems of classification regarding individual artists and their works, schools, styles, and periods.

Discusses various devices, auxiliaries, etc. Concludes that UDC has an edge over CC in this subject.

SEHGAL, R L 1249

Number building in Dewey Decimal Classification, Universal Decimal Classification and Colon Classification, New Delhi: Ess Ess Publication, 1993. 280+266+78 p.

Describes the three schemes of library classification in three Sections of this book: Section A - has 21 chapters on Dewey Decimal Classification discussing its practical aspects supported with examples. Section B - has 9 chapters on Universal Decimal Classifiation, and its examples; while Section C describes the rules and practice of Colon Classification.

025.432 Universal Decimal Classification (UDC)

GOUD, M G 1250

Evaluation of Universal Decimal Classification - chipless working/metal forming depth schedule: Problems faced by Central Metal Forming Institute (CMFI), *IR*, 96.

Discusses chipless working/metal forming. Explains how metal forming discipline as such is recognised as a Basic Class of Mechanicl Engineering. Studies the possibiligy of grouping together related subject fields. Suggests a cooperative effort for the development of schedules of metal forming technology literature.

025.435 COLON CLASSIFICATION

CHATERJEE, AMITABHA 1251

Making of Colon Classification: The inside story, *Coll Lib* 8(1-2) 1992: 22-25.

Relates the interesting story as to how the idea of the Colon Classification was first conceived and given shape by S R Ranganathan since 1924. Identifies the various problems he faced during its preparation, and the soloutions found by him. States that it helped Ranganathan to lay a strong foundation for the magnificent edifice of the Colon Classification, the most outstanding contribution from his fertile mind.

GOPINATH, M A 1252

Colon Classification: Its theory and practice, *CC*, 68-98.

Presents the developments in PMEST, new developments in Colon Classification as primary Basic Subjects (BS), Systems,

Environmmented Basic Subjects, Specials, Secondary Basic Subjects, Compoud Subjects, Schedules of Common Property isolates, Matter Property isolates, Energy isolates, Space isolates, Language isolates, Phase Relation indicators, Anteriorising Common Isolates (ACI), etc.

SEHGAL, R L 1253

Handbook on Colon Classification, New Delhi: Ess Ess Publications, 1993. xii, 285 p.

Discusses the theory of CC in the first nine chapters Describes the rules and practice for the various Main Classes from 'a' Generalia Bibliography to Z Law on number building. Gives graded examples to help the users. Includes also 'Things to do' and at the end gives Answers to exercises.

VERMA, JITENDER 1254

Colon thesaurus of social science terms, New Delhi: Khanna Publishers, 1992. xv, 150 p.

Explains the construction and design of thesaurus based on the principles of the theoretical developments of CC, for the subjects of social sciences. Describes its usefulness in information retrieval process.

025.435 (1) COLON CLASSIFICATION -EDITION 1

KRISHAN KUMAR 1255

Historical roots of Ranganathan's Colon Classification (Edition 1), *Jl Lib & Inf Sci* 17 (1) June 1992: 71-81.

Describes Ranganathan's contribuitons to library and information science in general. Mentions about his library education at London and influence of Berwick Sayers. Describes the seeds of Colon Classification, Edition 1, and its salient features. Brings out Ranganathan's indebtedness to Melvil Dewey, influence of Universal Decimal Classification on Colon Classification - Ed 1. Discusses the growth of the concept of 'categories'. Mentions the influence of Hulme, Biscoe, and others. Concludes that he possessed an amazing degree of ingenuity to apply old ideas so as to look original.

025.435 (1) COLON CLASSIFICATION - EDITION 7

ASUNDI, A Y 1256

Common isolates in Colon Classification with emphasis on Edition 7, *CC*, 107-115.

Discusses about the common isolates as introdced in Colon Classification right from the beginnig, ie, its first edition. Defines common isolates. Gives canons of common isolates, and enumerates changes in common isolates from Edition 1 of Colon Classification to its Edition 7.

CHATTERJEE, AMITABHA and CHOWDURY, G G 1257

CC 7: An evaluation of its development in three planes, *CC*, 25-67.

Gives a detailed account of Colon Classifiation - Edition 7 discussing all the salient features, additions made, modifications efffected, new concepts incorporated within the purview of the three planes of work as propounded by S R Ranganathan.

DHYANI, P 1258

Colon Classification - Edition 7, *CC*, 1-10.

Discsses the structure of Colon Classification - Edition 7, Vol 1. Describes additions and modifications made with regard to Language Isolates, Time Isolates, Space Isolates, Phase Relations, special isolates, and notational system. Concludes that publication of CC-7 is a positive development made by the Editor.

KUMAR, P S G 1259

Notational developments in the CC with special reference to Edition 7, *CC*, 124-130.

Discusses the notation of Colon Classification of S R Ranganathan with regard to zones in main classes of Colon Classification - Edition 6 and Colon Classification - Edition 7. Discusses its other features such as modes of formation of subjects, compound subjects, complex subjects, etc.

SATIJA, M P 1260

Colon Classifiation, 7th Edition, 1966-1991: A literature analysis, *CC*, 206-215.

Provides a literature analysis of what has been published on Colon Classification during 1966-1991. Gives a list of 59 references published during the period of 26 years, with yearly average of 2.27 publications.

SATIJA, M P, *Ed.* 1261

Colon Classification 7th edition: Some perspectives, New Delhi: Sterling Publishers, 1993. xx, 220 p.

Includes 12 essays on the various aspects of Colon Classification - 7th Edition of Dr S R Ranganathan, and edited by M A Gopinath. Covers such topics as descriptive, theoretical, and individual aspects in this publication. Also includes two Appendices including a bibliography on CC-7.

SATIJA, M P 1262

A critical introduction to the 7th Edition (1987) of the Colon Classification, *Luck Libn* 24 (1) Jan-Mar 1992: 32-41.

Reviews the schedule of CC-7 publiched in 1987. Describes its structure, new features in the Idea and Verbal plane. Highlights merits and defects. Illustrates its practical application. Suggests a quick revision of CC-7 to rectify the inconsistencies and correct the misprints.

SATIJA, M P 1263

Use of Colon Classification, *CC*, 180-193.

Gives a brief account of Colon Classification of Ranganathan. Discusses sources for studies on the use of Colon Classification system. Presents some statistics based on these sources. Points out that the future use of Colon Classifiation is difficult to predict.

SATIJA, M P and GUPTA, O P 1264

Colon Classification, 7th Edition (1987). A concise introduction, *CC*, 99-106.

Provides a brief introduction of the 7th Edition of Colon Classification of Ranganathan, touching all the salient fearutes. Discusses about all other changes made in this new edition of CC.

SETHI, A R 1265

CC 7: Some preliminary observations, *CC*, 11-24.

Brings forth the association of Jawaharlal Nehru University Library and Colon Classification - Edition 7. Presents an evaluative account of CC-7 giving its salient features, changes in three planes of work, Environmental divisions, common isolates, special isolates, etc. Gives examples of adhocism, complexity, etc giving difficulties in its use in Jawaharlal Nehru University Library.

SEWA SINGH 1266

Time and space isolates in CC-7: A study, *ILA Bull* 27 (4) Jan-Mar 1992: 168-177.

Makes a comparative study of the Space and Time isolates schedules fo Colon Classifiction Edition 6 and Edition 7. Discusses in detail the Space and Time isolates in the 7th Edition of CC. Opines that provisions of CC-7 have made the numbers and number building process rather complicated and complex by increasing the number of digits in a Class Number.

SHABAHAT HUSSAIN 1267

A theoretcal basis for the accommodation of new subjects in Colon Classification Edition 7, *CC*, 141-158.

Investigates how Colon Classification Edition 7, with its strong theoretical base, deals with the problem of a growing universe of subjects. Discusses the work in the Idea Plane, formation of new dubjects, and work in the Notational Plane to accommodate them suitably.

025.435016 Colon Classification - Bibliographies

SEWA SING and SUKHBIR SINGH 1268

Colon Classification; a select bibliography. New Delhi: Ess Ess Publications. 1992. xvii, 86 p.

Covers 701 entries in this select bibliography on Colon Classification. States that the material has been taken from various primary and secondary sources. Arranged in classified order according to the subject headings such as General Classification, Colon Classification. More headings include Design, Depth classification, automatic classification, uses of classification, Canons, Common Isolates, postulates, Fundamental Categories, and so on. Entries are further arranged in alphabetical order by author under each heading. Claims not to be comprehensive in coverage.

025.435 (1) Facet Analysis

CIGANIK, MAREK 1269

Modular faceted marker passing in textual data, *Lib Sci slant Docum & Inf Std* 29 (1) Mar 1992: 32-40.

Outlines the problem of the automatic text analysis. The starting point is Ranganathan's full title creation and analysis. Elaborates the faceted marker passing theory. Applies information flow principle in a semantic network-like structure based in inforation nuclei. The underlying model is an algebric model of (FC) formulated as a complex semantic relational model of text.

FOSKETT, D J 1270

Ranganathan and "user friendliness", *Libri* 42 (3) July-Sept 1992: 227-234.

Defines 'user-friendliness'. States that Ranganathan's Five Laws place the user as the focus of library and information services and exphasize the need to understand the user. Describes that facet analysis helps the information specialist to undertand and interpret the subject of user's enquiry which contributes to user-friendliness. Mentions that facet analysis reflects a natural way of thinking and can be introduced into computerized systems.

FRIIS - HANSEN, JENS B 1271

Facets and clusters, *PP*, 71-75.

States that Dewey Decimal Classification was established as a shelving system, hence enumerative. Mentions that new concepts of facets etc were developed in Colon classification of Ranganathan which is the foundation of whole system. Describes faceting as ideal technique for representing subject content, and searching aid. says that clusters help in searchng particularly in Danish libraries.

GOPINATH, M A 1272

Ranganathan's theory of facet analysis and knowledge representation, *DESIDOC Bull* 12 (5) Sept 1992: 16-20.

Presents the basis of Rangnathan's theory of facet analysis and identifies its application to the analysis of knowledge. Discusses its value in knowledge representation in different contexts. Gives examples from design database for public finance.

IYER, HEMLATA 1273

Facet analysis and information retrieval, *CC*, 116-123.

Deals with the empirical testing of Ranganathan's facet structure, especially in on-line environment. Establishes the meausure of concreteness of the categories.

KWASNIK, BARBARA H 1274

The legacy of facet analysis, *RAW*, 98-111.

Discusses role of classification and facet analysis against a backdrop of classification theory in general. Describes three applications of faceted schemes: (1) The Art and Architecture Thesaurus, (2) a classification scheme for sensable software components, and (3) the use of facet analysis in describing and organising research results.

SEETHARAMA, S 1275

Cognitive approach in information consolidation, *COP*, 286-292.

Provides operational definitions of some of the technical terms used as 'paradigm', etc. Mentions the usefulness of Ranganathan's facet model. Demonstrates with an example how such a cognitive model can be used in information/knowledge representation in an information consolidation product. Concludes that the generalised facet model and the postulates and priciples proposed by Ranganathan in the framework of general theiry of classification are relevant even today - whether it is for creation of databses, user needs study, classification and indexing, and/or for information consolidation.

025.435 (I) Fundamental Categories

FOSKETT, D J 1276

More on the personality facet, *Jl Lib & Inf Sci* 17 (I) June 1992 : 39-44.

Mentions use of notationl synthesis or number building in different classification schemes. Points out the use of facet analysis by S R Ranganathan is an exact parallel with the central notion of General Systems Theory. Explains that Ranganathan's concept of 'Personality' facet seems to correspond closely with 'whole', 'wholeness' of General Systems Theory. Concludes that none has yet attempted an alternative term ot 'personality' which so accurately mirrors the central concept of General Systems Theory.

GOPINATH, M A 1277

Problem in the recognition of PMEST; a sematic analysis, *CRL*, 47-51.

Presents a sematic analysis of the problems in the recognition of the five (FC) postulated by Ranganathan. Discusses the problems that a classification and classifier would encounter in their recognition. Identifies four casual factors, namely, Qualification, Multiconnation, Heterogerneity, and a combination of Age, Literature and Professional Aspects.

025.435 (I) POSTULATES

IYER, HEMLATA 1278

Subject representation and entropy, *Int Classif* 19 (I) 1992: 5-18.

Examines the systems approach to subject structuring. Presents an overview of empirical studies undertaken to test the postulates relating to subject sturcturing. Discusses Ranganathan's categories and absolute syntax. Says that entropy provides a disorganization in a system. Structured subject representation are considered as systems. Studies empirical validation of Ranganathan's postulaties, concretencess of categories, bond strenght, etc.

NEELAMEGHAN, A 1279

Application of Ranganathan's general theory of knowledge classification in designing specialized databases, *Libri* 42 (3) July-Sept 1992: 202-226.

Discusses some practical applications of the postulates, principles and techniques of Ranganathan within the framework of his general theory of knowledge classification in the design and developmnet of specialized databases. Highlights usefulness of postulational approach, helpful sequence, etc. Illustarates application of mnemonics in designing intergrated databases. States that interaction between system designers and end usere is essential to understand users' perception of reality and their information requirements.

NEELAMEGHAN, A 1280

Application of S R Ranganathan's postulates and principles of the general theory of knowledge classification to database design and information retrieval, In *Papers*, 58th IFLA General Conference, New Delhi, 30 Aug-5 Sept 1992, pp 4.20 -4.25.

Mentions that Ranganathan's postulates and principles of the general theory of knowledge classification can be applied in structuring knowledge bases and object-oriented databases, designing schemes of classification, vocabulary control tools. Demonstrates enhancement of user-friendliness of information retrieval by interfacing facet anlyses query terms with thesaurus terms. Mentions usefulness of Ranganathan's generalised subject structure conforming to the analytico-synthetic freely faceted model.

NEELAMEGHAN, A 1281

Application of S R Ranganathan's postulates and principles of the general theory of knowledge classification to databases design and information retrieval, *Int Cat and Biblio Control* 22 (3) July-Sept 1993: 46-50.

Describes Ranganathan's holistice integrative apporoach. Explains application of analytico-synthetice methodology. Considers this and the related postulates and principles of his General Theory of Knowledge Classification to the design and development of databases, in particular, specialised and object-oriented databases and in information retrieval. Demonstrates improved user-friendliness of information system resulting from interfacing facet-analyses query terms with thesaursus terms.

025.435 (I) Phase Relation

CHATTERJEE, AMITABHA 1282

Concept of phase relation in CC and its impact on BC, *Iaslic Bull* 37 (3) Sept 1992: 163-170.

States that though the idea of Phase Relation was first initiated by Universal Decimal Classification, most of the other schemes either ignored it or tried by enumeration. Explains that only Ranganathan developed the idea to a finer degree and gave it a concrete shape in his Colon Classification. Mentions that though Bliss followed enumeration in BC-1, but BC-2 adopted analytico-synthetic method for phase relation. Attempts to establish the impact of CC on BC in this regard.

025.435 (1) MNEMONICS

MANDAL, SATYANANDA 1283

Seminal mnemonics in classification system and Prof Ranganathan, *Coll Lib* 8 (1-2) 1992: 14-16.

Makes an attempt to trace the origin of the concept of seminal mnemonic, a concept which is absent in other classificatory languages. Discusses Ranganathan's thought about non sensual perception and cognition beyond sense organs. States that as seminal mnemonics has its special flavour in classificatory environment, that Ranganathan discussed Indian pholosophy, Indian classics,and tried to assimilate and absorb it into knowledge organising systems.

025.435 (1) NOTATION

RANGANATHAN, S R 1284

Zone analysis and mixed notation, *Iaslic Bull* 37 (3) Sept 1992 : 101-106.

Reporduced from Iaslic Bulletin 1 (2) Dec 1956: 44-47, in view of its relevance, under the heading 'Thus wrote Ranganathan'. Gives history of mixed notation with the use of the connecting symbols needed in an analyticohsynthetic classification suited to the needs of depth classification. Points out advantages of zone formation in an array, with mixed notation, to accommodate new classes, islates of a facet, telescoped facet. Points out the vast amount of routine saearh to be done and the economics of zone abalysis.

SHABAHAT HUSSAIN 1285

Calculating the capacity of notational systems : Some new formulae, *Int Forum Info & Docum* 16 (1) 1991: 22-27.

Investigates the ways and means to evaluate the capacity of different types of notational systems so that a designer may decide about the nature of the classification and the variety of degits needed to build pure or mixed notational system of the scheme concerned. Discusses the parameters for the capacity of notational systems and the formulae used of calculate it.

025.435 (1) MODES OF SUBJECTS

BINWAL, J C 1286

Modes of formation of subjects : A model for knowledge representation, *JL Lib & Inf Sci* 17 (1) June 1992 : 82-88.

Discusses the concept of social knowledge. Describes the criterion for distinguishing different kinds of social knowledge. Enumerates the attributes of a subject and concept of formation of subjects. Describes empirical study carried out to test the model prepared by S R Ranganathan. Concludes that this model is a powerful tool for knowledge representation in information retrieval.

NEELAMEGHAN, A 1287

Ranganathan's generalised model of subject structure and modes of formation of subjects, *In* A Neelameghan, M A Gopinath, et al (Eds), *Cognitive paradigms in knowledge organisation*, Bangalore : Sarada Ranganathan Endowment for Library Science, 1992, pp 269-285.

Recaptulates postulates of modes of Formation of subjects. Discusses Ranganathan's conceptual model of subject structure and its usefulness in the organisation of subjects.

025.46 (I) Design of Special Classification

MAHAPATRA, M 1288

Design of special classification schedules based on the principles of Colon Classification, *CC*, 159-179.

Describes the basic steps required for the design of special classification schedules on the Idea Plane and Verbal Plane, as followed by the Documentation Research and Training Centre for designing the depth classification of Colon Classification.

025.461 Classification - Humanities

KANKACHARY, M 1289

The humanities : Conceptualization, classification and clarification, *DAB*, 43-51.

Traces the origin and development of the concept 'humanities' from the ancient past to the present. Gives some important definitions of humanities like that of Socrates, Plato, Aristotle, etc and its inter- and multi- disciplinary nature by way of classification. Gives classification of the term humanities in the division of univers of knowledge. Mentions subjects included in the humanities.

025.463 Classification - Social Sciences

UPADHYAY, PRATIBHA 1290

A 'path model' in social and behavioural research, *COP*, 173-191.

Illustrates the path analysis. Shows the ways in which a path model can be of help in dealing with complex causal network in social and behavioural sciences; the way it generates information for analysis of phenomena. The path model is developed heuristically to study the effects of background factors on the academic performance of schools. Gives caution while using this path analysis as a tool.

025.4634 Classification - Law

RAO, SUNEETI 1291

Representing knowledge through legal concepts, *COP*, 334-343.

Deals with the semantic aspects of legal knowledge, both tacit or non-verbal knowledge as well as verbal or explicit knowledge. Knowledge represeting through machines is still restricted to verbal knowledge only. Legal knowledge is of two kinds - legislative materials and precedents. Artificial Intelligence researchers have been attracted to the domain of law because of the several characteristic features of this domain. Concentrates on the working of the legal language. Applies scematic analysis to legal language with a view to better understanding of the legal domain.

025.465 Classification - Science

NEGRINI, GILIOLA 1292

Systematization of science and technology research, *COP*, 293-307.

Defines the term science. Discusses about dichotomy between science and knowledge, philosophical knowledge and scientific knowledge. Describes shift in the viewpoint of 'science' over the years and its use in science policy. Defines the term 'research', its use in science research, technology research as a system which can replace the system of classification. Defines system and describes system principles to know the external and internal structure. Discusses systematization of research, the content of particular aspects, interaction of research. Concludes with emphasis on the flexibility of the systematifier as an expression of the simultaneous duality of formula and guide.

025.46548 Classification - Crystallography

POWNIKAR, SHRINIWAS SHARADRAO 1293

Crystallography: Subject and its classification, *CRL*, 52-66.

Traces the development of crystallography as a subject giving its nature and status. Discusses about the need for depth classification for crystallography. Gives schedule of isolates with allocation of Sectors. Supports it with examples. States that the Schedule given is not exhaustive in its listing of concepts,

025.46608 Classification - Patents

HIRWADE, ANIL W 1294

International patent classification, *Jl Inf Sci* 3 (4) Apr-June 1993: 187-193.

Provides general information about Internationl Patent Classification, its sturcture, editions various schedules, application and use of International Patent Classification in the patent classification.

025.4661 Classification - Medical Sciences

GANGEMI, ALSO, GALANTI, MARIO, GALEAZZI, ELENA and MORI ANGELO ROSSI 1295

A compositional approach to acquire and represent knowledge from medical coding system, *COP*, 308-322.

Lays down the basis for a compositional model of medical semantics that starts from the analysis of the available coding system. Discusses the basic medical concepts which may be releted to the semantic space, thereby overcoming the limits of conventional coding systems. Enables computers to process terminological knowledge in order to compare, cluster, and validate terms.

SEETHARAMA, S 1296

Compatibility among classification systems, *CRL*, 17-29.

Studies compatibility among medical classification systems at the nearnseminal level by the application of normative principles of the General Theory of Classification, and at phenomenal level by classification a set of few hunderd cardio-vascular pathological conditions. Gives major findings and influence based on the study.

SIVAREDDY, K and VARALAKSHMI, R S R 1297

Organisation of knowledge in neurological sciences-a comparative studey of secondary sources, *COP*, 242-259.

Studies the conceptual organization of neurological sciences in various secondary sources which endeavour to assist medical professionals in locating pertinent information. Makes a comparison of the organisation of concepts and establishement of their relation in secondary sources such as *Index Medicus, Excerpta Medica,* and *Biologival Abstracts.* Compares such parameters as indexing language, conceptual organisation, sequence of ideas, relationships between concepts, hospitality to new and changed concepts, etc.

025.4678 Classification - Music

KRISHNAMOORTHY, C S 1298

Use of paradigm in classification of melodic- scales, *COP*, 357-361

Gives the importance of music. Explains the 72 'Mela'

scheme of diatomic melody scales suggested by the musicologist Venkatamahin in 1635 and composed with nomenclature in later century by Govindachrya provided a useful paradigm of melody-scales. It paved way for a systematic growth and understanding of melody based scheme of ragh and its ramifications.

025.46891 Classification - Indological Literature

SHARMA, NARINDER KUMAR 1299

Depth classification for Indological literature: Compulsions, *DAB*, 66-80.

Makes a critical appraisal of the attempts so far made either to develop an independent separate scheme for Indology or to accommodate Indology in DDC or CC as such assessing the compulsions for the designing of depth schduels. Discusses the classification schemes with regard to general structure, notation, syntax, layout, class numbers, etc.

025.469 Classification - History

BUSCH, JOSEPH A 1300

Use of a relational database system to model the variability of historical source information, *COP,* 372-389.

Suggests ways to modify the conventional IR model to accommodate an ambiguous IR response from historical resources. Reviews recent research on the cognitive process of inquiry and method used by historians to organise information. Uses a retrospective system analysis to describe and generalise the Gatty System data model for Gatty Art History Program.

025.48 INDEXING. SUBJECT INDEXING

BATTY, C D 1301

The influence of Ranganathan on the structural design of index languages, *PP*. 47-59.

Traces the origin of classification from Aristotle to Dewey. Discusses the beginniges of synthesis in classification from Dewey. Describes in detail the contribution of Ranganathan to the discipline of classification. Discusses Ranganathan's development of facet analysis. Expalains Ranganathan's fundamental contribution to classfication in England and the USA. Mentions also about Artifical Intelligence systems.

BHATTACHARYYA, G 1302

A new trend in the evolution of subject indexing languages, *CRL*, 67-76.

Discusses the trends set in the field of subject indexing languages alongwith their pactical implications. Discusses a new trend that has emerged out of the evolution of subject indexing languages leading to the developmnt of a General Theory of subject indexing languages. Describes POPSI and Clausrus.

BINWAL, J C 1303

Modes of formation of subjects: Formation-head of concept organisation in indexing languages, *Jl Lib & Info Sci* 18 (1) Jan 1993: 32-42.

Points out conceptual foundations of indexing relationships are discernible in canons, postulates and principles development by S R Ranganathan and their source lies in his modes of formation of subjects. Concludes that canons, postulates and principles of indexing language are deducible from modes of formation of subjects representing typology of relations.

CRAVEN, TIMOTHY C 1304

Three-dimensional displays of concept relation structures, *Lib Sci slant Docum & Inf Std* 29 (1) Mar 1992 : 1-14.

Makes special reference to the possible use of automatically generated displays as an aid to abstrators. Outlines some advantages of three dimensional displays with experimental and result confirming their reduced distortion of concept space. Notes features that may set three- demensional representation of concept spaces off from other kinds. Describes features of a propotype system operating on a micro- computer with VGA display.

DEVADASON, F J 1305

Deep structure indexing system: Comuter generation of different types of subject index entries based on deep structure of subject indexing languages, *CRL*, 77-102

Describes that deep structure indexing system is based on a set of postulated elementary catagories of the elements fit to form components of names of subjects; a set of syntex rules; a vocabulary controal tool; a set of indicator digits; a set of codes. Names of subjects formulated on the above mentioned basis are iuput to a set of computer programs to gererate several different types of subject index entries.

OWOLABI, O 1306

Dictionary organizations for efficient similarity retrieval, *Jl Lib & Info Sci* 18 (1) Jun 1993: 1-11.

Points out that searching dictionaries for exact match to a given input string can be done very efficiently, performance degrades when inexact matches have to be located. Examines some methods of dictionary organization that could lead to improved performance. Concludes that a two-level indexing method combining two partitioning criteria performs reasonably well.

SOMA RAJU, P 1307

Subject indexing in university libraries: An evaluative study, *IR*, 98-99.

Evaluates subject indexing part of library catalogue. Reveals effectiveness of information retrieval system to users. Identifies the latest subject concepts in 'Psychology' and test their coverage in the subject index of Andhra University Library Catalogue as a case study. Appears gap between the subject terminology included in the catalogue and those found in the latest documents. Suggests to reduce the gap so as to make IRS more effective.

VICKEEY, B C 1308

Ranganathan's contribution to indexing, *SRR*. 8-10.

Describes the background when Ranganathan gave his ideas on indexing. Discusses that his ideas have penetrated the theory and practice of indexing in the form of the principles of synthesis, the principle of symbiosis between classification and cataloguing of index.

025.48 (1) Book Indexes

RAMESH BABU, B 1309

Some thoughts on book indexing, *LIS*, 79-94.

Mentions the importance of a book index. Gives qualities and characteristic of good index. States four agents who prepare index: author, professional indexer, someone in the publisher's editorial staff, and author in collaboration with editor. Gives qualities of indexer and his collaboration with editor. Gives qualities of indexer and his ethical responsibilities. Indetifies some studies on book indexes. Points out status of book indexing in India.

RAMESH BABU, B 1310

Some thoughts on requirements for a good index to a book, *Luck Libn* 23 (2) June 1991: 56-62.

Explains meaning of 'book index' and need for a good index'. discusses characteristics of a good index such as exhaustiveness, indexing scheme, depth of index, locators, physical appearance, etc. Highlights current situation of indexing practices. Enumerates qualities and ethical responsibilities of indexing.

RAMESH BABU, B 1311

Use of preferences for indexes in philosophical books: A survey, *Libr Rev* 41 (1) 1992:47-55.

Describes the importance of book indexes in location of suitable information. Explains how to prepare indexes to philosophical books, and reports the findings of a survey made for the purpose.

025.48 (1) LIBRAMETRY

RAVICHANDRA RAO, I K 1312

Librametry to bibliometrics to informetrics... Guest Editorial, *Lib Sci slant Docum & Inf Std* 30 (2) June 1993: i-ii.

Traces history of bibliometrics which was called as librametry by Dr S R Ranganathan. Explains the scope of librametry and bibliometrics which suggests to examine the statistical distribution of processes relating to the utilisation of documents. States that since mid 1980s this subject is popularly known as Infometrics. Mentions its scope and trends which is mostly towards discovery of theory and /or generalised mathematical model of library/ information use phenomenon.

SANGAM, S L 1313

Librametrics, *DL*, 267-278.

Gives genesis of the term 'Librametry'. Gives its meaning and definition. Mentions scope of librametrics. Discusses application of the librametrics according to Ranganathan in the various areas of library and information activities. Concludes that librametric studies are a good indicator for measuring various activities of librariaship.

SUBBA RAO, CV 1314

Librametry case studies; science of measurment of library activites, resourece and output phenomena, New Delhi: ABC Publishing

House, 1992.

Deals with librametry as a tool to analyse library routines, work out staff formula, use of resources, users habits, etc. Traces the history of librametry. Advocates close association of statisticians with library and information scientists.

SUBBA RAO, C V and RAMASUBRAMANIAN, S 1315

Certain aspects of editing and writing, *Her Lib Sci* 31 (3-4) July-Oct 1992: 211-217.

Mentions the experience in analysing books and articles and the development of librametry. Discusses the case studies in librametry, repetition of matter in several books of an author and reproduction of the matter in different articles without acknowledgement or specifying the source. Suggests careful editing of seminar papers to avoid such situations.

025.48(1) Ranganathan's Contribution to Librametry/ Bibliometrics

GOPINATH, M A 1316

Ranaganathan : A profile in realation to librametry, *Her Lib Sci* 32 (1-2) Jan-Apr 1993: 7-11.

Discusses the contribution of S R Ranganathan with emphasis on use and quatitative measures of library operations leading to use of the term "Librametry". Discusses further these quantitative measures in relation to all library operations such as classification, cataloguing, library advertisement, library services, etc.

LANCASTER, FW, ZETER, MARY JO and METZLER, LAURA 1317

Ranganathan's influence examined bibliometricaly, *Libri* 42 (3) July Sept 1992 : 268-281.

Studies through a bibliometric analysis of the citation to Ranganathan's writings over the period 1956-1990, using Social Science Citation Index and Science Citation Index that this influence has not diminished over the years. States that his books are more frequently cited than his articles. Mentions that citations to Prolegomena (95), Colon Classification (69), Classified Catalogue Code (32), Five Laws (28) account for more than a third of the total of 630 citations.

MAHAPATRA, GAYATRI 1318

Post Ranganathan era: A bibliometric analysis of Ranganathan's contributions, *Iaslic Bull* 37 (3) Sept 1992 : 177-182.

Measures degree of influence of Ranganathan's work on Indian library and information science literature by analysing the references provided in the articles of journals. Reveals that Ranganathan's works were highly cited even long after his expiry. States that classificaton and cataloguing are influenced most by Ranganathan's contributions.

RAVICHANDRA RAO, I K and NEELAMEGHAN, A 1319

From librametry to informetrics : An overview and Ranganathan's contributions, *Libri* 42 (3) July-Sept 1992 : 242-257.

Traces the development of the application of quantitative methods in library and information science. Discusses briefly contributions of Ranganathan to quantification in library work and service, making the services more user-frinedly and enhancing efficiency of library and information management.

025.48(1) BIBLIOMETRICS. BIBLIOMETRIC STUDIES

ARJUN LAL 1320

Most important journals from the point of view of Indian soil scientists : A bibliometric study, *Iaslic Bull* 38 (3) Sept 1993 : 123-131.

Analyses 6273 references contained in *Journal of Indian Society of Soil Sci,* Vols 33-36, 1985-88. Prepares a ranked list of 50 most important jounals representing 83.42% of the total citations. Reveals that 58.43% journal citations relate to only 6 journals out of the most important 50. Gives countrywise distribution of the journals in the ranked list and chronological distribution of all references. Shows use of different kinds of documents by research workers in soil science.

ASUNDI, A Y 1321

Bibliometric study of national bibliographies : Implication for the surrogates of library classsification, *Timeless Fellowship* 15, 1993: 69-83.

Defines the term bibliographic analysis. States certain bibliometric characteristics. Discusses the absolute interrelationship betwwen bibliometric and classification. Selects BNB and INB as text sources. Highlights results of a pragmatic analysis of documentary sources. Concludes that some recurrent concepts of classifictaion shows that their behaviour is invariably the same in all systems.

BANKAPUR, M B and KUMBAR, MALLINATH 1322

Bibliometrics and scientimetric tools for measurements of productivity in agricultural research, *IJILIS* 6 (3-4) July- Dec 1993 : 169-178.

Mentions that data which is scattered in a variety of sources is required for technology transfer, R & D, planning, etc. States that by using bibliometrics and scientometrics tools for measuring the productivity in any discipline. States its impact in agricultural research.

BARUA, DIPAK KUMAR 1323

Biblometrics and Dr Indra Narayana Sengupta: An evaluation, *IJILIS* 5 (1-2) 1992:1-22.

Describes the concept of bibliometrics from its origin to the present. Gives biodata of Dr I N Sengupta. Explains scholarly contribution of Sengupta. Tells that a committee is constituted to publish a Festschrift volume in his honour and a seminar was also organised. States that utility of bibliometrics can no longer be ignored.

BURRELL, QUENTIN L 1324

The dynamic nature of bibliometric process: A case study, *INFO*, 97-129 b.

Reports an empirical case study of a bibliography compiled continuously over time which reveals how the distribution of references over journals does indeed change with time. Illustrates these chages graphically by using Bradford and Leimkuhler curves. Compares some observed features with those given by a theoretical stochastic model. considers the problem of predicting the number of additional journals in the compilation of a certain subject bibliography when extended in time.

DELGADO, HECTOR and RUSSEL, JANE M 1325

Bibliometrical analysis of medical articles published in the international literature during the eighties by research institutes in the Mexican Republic, *INFO*, 130-147.

Analyses a total of 5296 articles published in 675 medical journals by scanning SCI CD ROMs for 1980-89, by Mexican authors and coauthors affiliation. States that about 22.8% were published in three journals edited in Mexico; the yearly production in non- Mexican SCI journals increased steadily. Of the 4077 articles published in foreign journals, they were in neuroscience, pharmaceutical, biochemistry, molecular biology. Half of these were written in collaboration with foreign institutions, particularly in USA and Europe.

HUMAYOON, KABIR, S 1326

World literature on bibliometrics : Authorship and growth pattern, *ILA Bull* 28 (3-4) Oct-Mar 1993: 87-94.

Investigates characteristics of biblometrics literature by analysing *LISA*, 1964-90. Studies reveal that single authorship pattern dominates with 65% of the total. Poins out that exponential growth of literature on biblometrics is doubling every ten years. English, Journals, and Articles on LIS studies dominate language, format and subject respectively.

LANCASTER, F W 1327

Bibliometric methods in assessing productivity and impact of reasarch, Bangalore: Sarada Ranganathan Endowment for Library Science, 1993. xi, 52 p.

Expalins in detail about the different bibliomtric methods followed by scholars for various studies made by them for making assessment of the literature production and its impact on their research activities.

MUNDHE, BT 1328

Publication trend in veterinary research : A bibliometric study, *IJALS* 20, 1992: 14-19.

Analyses 1686 Indian veterinary science contribution to find out subject-wise, year-wise, state-wise distribution. Authorship analysis reveals the growing importance of collaborative research. The growth paramater of the subject literature would be useful to the Indian veterinary scientists while designing their research projects in veterinary science.

NELSON, MICHAEL J 1329

Modelling the tail of bibliometric distributions, *INFO*, 343-357

States that the traditional bilbiometic distribtions of Bradford, Lotka and Zipf are all concerned with modelling a set of source generating articles, authors and words. Discusses two basic apporaches to organising this type of data. Investigates a model where the data is split into two portions.

PARVATHAMMA, N 1330

Bibliometrics - its origin and applications, *CS,* 163-183.

Presents various definitions of the term 'Bibliometrics' Discusses various application/techniques of bibliometics including growth rate of literature, scientific productivity of authors, collaborative trend among authors, and core journal. Reviews important studies undertaken so far in each of these categories.

PATEL, D R 1331

Bibliometrics, citation study, selective dessemination of information (SDI) service using SCI CD-ROM, *Jl Lib & Inf Sci* 16 (2) Dec 1991 : 113-128.

Provides defintions and descriptors about Bibloimetrics, its laws and scope, Impact Factor of journals, citation analysis and bibliometrics, etc. Describes improtance of SCI, Jouranl Citation Reports (JCR) and their various parts. Discusses the methodology used to retrieve information using SCI CD-ROM and elucidate the various search carried out.

RAVICHANDRA RAO, I K 1332

Quantitative methods in library and information sciencne, *CRL*, 133-148.

Discusses the origin of the term 'Bibliometrics'. Explains the characteristics of Bibliometric laws - Zipf's law, Lotka's law, and Bradford's law. Discusses citation analysis, and use studies which fall withint the scope of bibliometrics. Suggests areas in bibliometrics where further research is needed.

ROUSSEAU, RONALD 1333

Determination of a core of bibliography, *Iaslic Bull* 38 (2) June 1993: 49-57.

States that documentalists have always attached great importance to the determination of a group of core journals. Proposes to utilise concentration measure for the determination of a group of a core journals as this method is completely reproducible and can be applied to any bibliography, whether or not this bibliographty can be described by one of the so called informetics laws.

SARASWATI, MORE, RAJAGOPAL, B and KANKACHARY, M 1334

Bibliometric study of tribal linguistics in India, *Int Lib Move* 15 (1) Mar 1993 : 17-25.

Aims at finding out different analyses quantitatively of the recorded knowledge which includes the study of books, periodicals, government reports, book reviews, conference/seminar proceedings, research dissertations. Also aims to know the growth of literature in tribal linguistics, authorship pattern, etc.

SEN, SUBIR K, CHATTERJEE, SUNIL K and GAN, SHYAMAL K 1335

Making bibliographic scattering studies useful: Significance of zero-item (empty) and sigle-item sourecs, *INFO*, 426-446.

Derives bibliographic populations from bibliographies where there is no scope of enumerating or estimating the sources having zero-items. Shows empiricaly and theoretically that the zero-item sources are to be estimated in the same sequence of geometric progression apparent for the source in the population of the bibliography. Argues that scattering of bibliographic items among sources takes place over sources.

SEWA SINGH 1336

Literature on library and information science manpower problems, *Ann Lib Sci & Docum* 40 (3) Sept 1993 : 95-103.

Analyses literature on various aspects of L & I manpower published in Indian sources such as journals, books, anthologies, monographs, seminar papers, etc contributed by librarians, LIS teachers, researchers, etc. Divides literature under 13 subject headings with analysis to find out chronological scatter, conceptual / subject scatter, artical scatter, and authorship pattern. Reveals that literature on this subject has been growting since 1989. Makes some useful suggestions.

SHAILENDRA, K and GARG, B S 1337

Measurement of bibliographic information: A review, *ILA Bull* 28 (1-2) Jan-Apr 1991: 48-54.

Makes a survey of literature in the area of measuremnt of bibliographic studeis carried out so far in this area during 1970-92.

SHARDA, B A 1338

Bibliometric studies in linguistics and bibliometric laws, *Lib Sci slant Docume & Inf Std* 30 (2) June 1993 : 71-75.

States that the three laws of bibliometrics formulated by Bradford, Lotka and Zipf are the three mile stones in the field of Information Science. Examines their feasibility in various studies conducted in Humanities and Social Sciences. Examines the results obtained from bibliometric studies conducted on the corpus of Linguistics.

SHARMA, PRAVEEN and GARG, K C 1339

Bibliometrics of solar power research in Indian, *Iaslic Bull* 38 (4) Dec 1993 : 155-160.

Analyses 536 papers published in journals and presented at conferences/seminars in the field of solar power. Indicates that Indian scientists publish their findings in jouranls published from scientifically advanced countries. States that most of the papers have been published in low impact journals. Reveals that academic institutions are the major contributor and the prolific single authors are negligible as compared to co-authors.

SINHA, SURESH CHANDRA 1340

Individual profile of building research scientists - a bibliometric studies and anylysis of their articles through Science Citation Index (SCI) *Int Lib Move* 14 (1) Mar 1992: 45-52.

Attempts to measure the impact of Indian building research scientists by studying their citations with the help of SCI. Concludes that India's contribution of new knowledge in building science is limited.

SINHA, S C and FURQUANULLAH, M 1341

A bibliometric study of articles published & paprer presented by scientists of Central Building Research Instituted, 1980-90, *Jl Inf Sci* 3 (3) Jan-Mar 1993 : 129-150.

Presents a bibliometric study of the research parers contributed by the scientists of CBRI, Roorkee in the form of articles published in foreign journals and papers presented in national and international conferences during 1980-90. Finds out the impact factor for the journals of interest to CBRI. Makes analysis of research output in tabulated form. Prepares a list of journals with ranking, impact factor and immdiacy index.

SUBRAMANIAN, R and NAVANEETHAN, R 1342

Library Science with a slant to Documentation and Information

Studies, 1981-1990: A bibliometric study, *Lib Sci slant Docum & Inf Std* 29 (3) Sept 1992: 157-162.

Discusses the various features of the issues of the Library Science with a slant to Documentation & Information Studies during 1981-1990. Identifies the variations in content analysis which emphasies in IT and quatitiative studies, volume of papers, review articles, research in progress, etc,. to enhance the periodicals coverage.

TAHER, MOHAMMED 1343

Indian contribution to the field of bibliometrics, *Int Lib Move* 14 (2) June 1992: 79-81.

Enumerates various writings in the field of bibliometrics contributed by Indian authors from Dr S R Rangangathan to date.

VAISHANV, AA 1344

Journal of Marketing - a bibliographic studey *CLIS Observer* 9 (3-4) July-Dec 1992: 71-73.

Analyses the contents of the ' Journal of Marketing' published by the American Marketing Association. Determines the extent of its coverage, audits its objectives, indentifies the emerging and decaying subjects dealt with in the Journal. Evaluates authoritativeness of the authors and highlights the findings.

WALI, M L 1345

Concept of bibliometrics and its impacts on dissemination of information, *ALE*, 60-65.

Discusses bibliometrics. Gives its definitions. Mentions its coverage and limitations in the study of literature and features of documents. Discusses bibliometircs techniques and their mathematical relationship. Mentions its uses to library and information professionals. Concludes that students may use it for conducting various studies and assessing their usefulness.

WHITNEY, GRETCHEN 1346

Asian authorship in major international bibliographic databases: Trends for 1970-1990, *INFO*, 506-526.

Examines Asian authorship patterns in 16 major scientific and technical bibliographic databases on DIALOG information system for works published between 1970-1989. States that most heavily represented countries were Japan, India, Israerl, China and Korea;

three databases BIOSIS, INSPEC, MEDLINE showed increases but Chemical Abstracts showed fewest number of countries Reveals trends in authorship, ranking of countries, etc.

WU YISHAN, *et al* 1347

Bibliometric studies in China and ISTIC's approach, *INFO*, 527-548.

Gives in brief general retrospect on the crescent development of China's bibliometics studies. Focusses on the activities of ISTIC's working group with the aim to provide bibliometric information to decision makers in S.&T. Analyses data from 1200 titles of Chinese scientific and engineering journals and entered into databasee; data also collected from four international indexes: SCI, EI, ISTP, ISR to make comparison between China and other countries in terms of quality of scientific publications.

025.48 (1) CITATION ANALYSIS. CITATION INDEXING

ARJUN LAL 1348

Literature contribution in Indian Journal of Genetics and Plant Breeding : A citation analysis, *Ann Lib Sci & Docum* 40 (2) June 1993: 65-76.

Analyses 4136 citations from the Indian Journal of Genetics and Plant Breeding from 1985 to 1989 and prepares a rank list of 60 most cited primary jounals representing 66.86% of citations. Reveals that literature on genetics and plant breeding was scattered in 574 journal of which 505 citations are covered by only 20 journal. Gives authorship pattern also.

BAROOAH, PK 1349

Pattern of information use by Indian entomologists, *Ann Lib Sci & Docum* 40 (3) Sept 1993 : 104-114.

Discusses the pattern of information use by entomologists by citation analysis of *Indian Journal of Entomology* for 1989. Indentifies the various sources of information and their country of origin. Gives a ranked list of Indian journals, another joint list of journals. Mentions also the obsolescence of literature in entomology.

BAROOAH, P K and BHUYAN, B R 1350

An approach for selection of journals in libraries of R & D institutions, *Ann Lib Sci & Docum* 40 (3) Sept 1993 : 115-124.

Reports a use- based selection process which seems to be more systematic and cost effective for R&D organizations, considering the conventional approach for selection of journals based on ranking through bibliographical countings not entirely suitable for these libraries.

DHARMAPURIKAR, R G 1351

Citation analysis : An important tool for knowledge organization, *COP*, 108-111.

Gives the value of citation analysis as an important research tool for the understanding of science, scientific contirbutions of publications. States the aims and purpse of citation analysis. Examines through citation analysis of *Herald of Library Science*, type of documents cited; ranking of cited authors ; ranking of journals, frequency of use of periodicals; and purpose of citations. It is thus helpful in mapping knowledge in library science.

GOPINATH, M A 1352

Across the frontiers: Impact of foreign journals in library science in India: A citation analysis, *Lib Sci slant Docum & Inf Std* 30 (1) Mar 1993: 17-24.

Presents a citation analysis of foreign LIS journals by the Indian LIS authors. Indicates that the USA being the largest publisher of LIS literature, have the largest impact, followed by the UK. The data is gathered out of a cross-section of publication, published during the last five years.

GOPINATH, M A 1353

Across the frontiers: Impact of foreign journals in library science in India : A citation analysis, In *Papers*, 58th IFLA General Conference, New Delhi, 30 August- 5 Sept 1992.

Gives a citation analysis of foreign LIS journals by the Indian LIS authors. Indicates that the USA is the largest publisher of the LIS literature. Tells about its impact, followed next by the UK. Gathers data out of a cross section publications published during the last five years.

GUPTA, DAVENDRA K 1354

Author productivity patterns: Geoscientific literaute of Nigerai for the period 1904-1979, *Lib Sci slant Docum & Inf Std* 30 (2) June 1993: 76-89.

Analyses a bibliography of geoscientific literature of Nigeria for 1904-1979 containing 1,005 items to test the applicability of

Lotka's law and the negative binomial distribution model to author productivity distribution patterns. Applies chi-squatre, and K-S statistical tests to find out significance level. Negative binomial distribution were found fitting better than Lotka distribution.

GUPTA, DAVENDRA K 1355

Collaborative research trends in exploration geophysics, *Ann Lib Sci & Docum* 40 (2) June 1993: 46-55.

Analyses a comprehensive database, the cumulative index for 1936-85 to study collaborative and authorship trends in exploration geophysics. Reveals through analysis that like in any other discipline in sciences, collaboration in exploration geophysics research has been increasing over the period of time.

HUKAM SINGH and SAXENA, S K 1355

Application of biotechnology in mass health care - literature trend, *Ann Lib Sci & Docum* 39 (1) Mar 1992: 19-25.

Analyses 3199 references collected in the areas of ' Mass Health Care' published in Derwent Biotechnology Abstracts, 1983-87. Reveals that the reseach work carried out in the area of antibiotics is more than that done on other pharmaceutical products. Researchers from Japan have contributed about 35% followed by USA. Private companies play a significant role. Gives a rank list of journals.

HUMAYOON KABIR, S 1357

Citation in world bibliometrics research: An analysis, *Lib Sci slant Docum & Inf Std* 30 (4) Dec 1993: 155-159.

Analyses 1372 citations from LISA (1964-90) in order to determine the most frequently cited journals in bibliometrics, such as Scientometcrics, Journal of ASIS, Nauch Tech Inf Seriya, Journal of Documentation, Annals of Libreary Science and Documentation, International Library Review, College and Research Libraries, and so on.

KALYANE, V L and VIDYASAGAR RAO, K 1358

Collaboration trends in sugarcane reserach - a case study, *Ann Lib Sci & Docum* 39 (1) Mar 1992: 9-11.

Undertakes a case study with the help of publications from Sugarcane Breeding Institute, Coimbatore during 1948-87 in order to find out the collaboration trends. Calculates disciplinewise collaboration coefficient (CC) and Average Authorship per Paper

(AAP). Notices that both CC and AAP increased steadily over a period of time. The relationship between these two factors indicates positive direction.

KARANDE, A G and BORLE, U M 1359

Literature use pattern in cytogenetics and plant breeding: A citation analysis of these, *Ind Jl Agric Lib Inf Sci* 18, 1991: 32-41.

Analyses references on the subject of cytogenetics and plant breeding to find out the literature use pattern made by the researchers, authorship pattern, group of core journals, etc.

KARISIDDAPPA, C R, SANGAM, S L and MAHESWARAPPA, B S 1360

Information use pattern of Indian historians, *DAB*, 157-165.

Makes a study to determine the different information sources used by Indian historians, various apporaches used for locating information, problems faced in the use of information, and awareness and usefulness of information services of NASSDOC to the Indian historians, on the basis of a survey. Presents the results and discussion.

KAUL, RAMA and MAHAPATRA, GAYATRI 1361

Self-citation behaviour of Indian plant taxonomists, *Jl Inf Sci* 3 (4) Apr-June 1993: 171-180.

Analyses 649 articles publshed in the Journal of Economic and Taxconomic Botany during 1987-1990. Reveals that about 505 of the articles were having self citations, but rate is not so high in comparison to other subjects. Analyses extent of self-citation practised by taxonomists. Concludes that Indian taxonomists mostly carry out independent research in new fields of plant taxonomy.

KOCHHAR, V B, SUBBA RAO, A, ARORA, A M and ELHANCE, D 1362

Materials research in India : A quantitative analysis of publications output in scientific journals, *Jl Lib & Infor Sci* 17 (2) Dec 1992: 198-207.

Highlights certain observations resulting from the statistical sample from two secondary sources Indain Science Abstarcts and Science Citation Idex (CD-ROM), while creating a database of Indian literature output in materials science research in India for a period of ten years from periodicals.

KRETSCHEMER, HILDRUN 1363

Significance of the logaritham of number of publications for the measurement of social stratification in coauthorship networks, *INICAE* 12 (1) Mar 1993: 63-84.

Discusses the theory of startification of referring to general social psychological theory, measuremnt of social stratification in sciencne. Explains methods and hypotheses in describing normal counts procedure in authorship. Applies statisitical procedure in analysing scientometirc data. Applies various methods of data retrieval. Makes analysis of elements in relation to collaborating authors. Investigates logs if the numer of publications as a measure of stratification.

KUMBAR, T S 1364

Most frequently cited journals in the field of fluid mechanices *INICAE* 11 (2) Sept 1992: 197-209.

Explains citation analysis methodology and its application in examining 302 articles published in the Journal of Fluid Mechanics, 1985/86. Makes analysis of articles and 6,370 citations published. Presents formwise distribution, country wise scattering, language wise distribution, and chronological scattering of citations. Ranks also the most frequently citted journals.

MACIAS-CHAPULA, CESAR A 1365

Citation analysis of the Panamerican Health Organization's medical eduction jouranl "Eduation Media Y Salud", *ML*, 237-245.

Reports on a research in progress related to the content and citation analysis of PAHO's journal ofmedical education. Finds multiple authoriship and the use of books and grey literature. Mentions the use of the scientific journal as a cited source. Analyses cited journals and confirms Bradford's law. Finds that among Latin American countries, there exists an important information transder in the field. Mentions further research lines.

MAHAPATRA, G and KAUL, R 1367

Citation characteristics of Indian sericulturue literaute, *CS*, 184-220.

Analyses references collected from the Indian Journal of Sericultrue for 1962-85 to determine the citation characteristics of sericulture literature, to test whether the data fits with Bradford's Law of Distribution or not. Concludes that the journal articles are cited more freuqently than any other type of documents. Gives core list of jounal, self -citation pattern, obsolescence factor, utility factor, etc.

MAHESWARAPPA, B S and NINGOJI, M M 1368

Growth of literature in the field of applied sciences in India (1965-89). *INICAE* 12 (2) Sept 1993: 191-200.

Studies the growth of literature in Applied Sciences in India based on the Indian Science Abstarats from 1966 to 1989. States that mean relative growth rate of literature has consistently declined and the doubling time of literature has gone up. Concludes that data had to be fitted to test with other growth models.

MAHESWARAPPA, B S and NINGOJI, M M 1369

Growth of literature in the field of science and technology in India, *INICAE* 11 (2) Sept 1992: 186-197.

Studies the relative growth rates and doubling time of literature in the field of S & T in Inida during 1965-89. Fits data with modified exponential, logistic and linear corves. Concludes that the data does not fit with the modified exponential, logistic and linear pattern.

MAHESWARPPA, B S and NINGOJI, M M 1370

A study of the growth of biological science literature in India from 1965-89,. *ILA Bull* 29 (1-2) Apr-Sept 1993: 47-55.

Studies the growth of biological science literature in India based on the data collected from Indian Science Abstracts, 1965-89. States that relative growth rate of biological science literture has consistently declined, while the mean reletive growth rate has increased. Reports about the doubling time of biological literature. Concludes that the growth of biological literature in India follows neither modified exponential, logistic nor the linear pattern.

MAHESWARAPPA, B S and SAVADATTI, S G 1371

Multiple authorship trends and collaborative reasearch in entomology literature (1970-80), *CS*, 258-266.

Studies the collaborative research and multiple authorship trends in entomology based on Entomology Abstrcts for 1970-80. Shows decline in single authorship papers over the period and increase in multi-authored papers.

MANDAL, AKHILESH and SAIN, CHITTARANJAN 1372

Collaborative research by the sicentists of a particular country vis-a-vis by the scientists of different countries in the field of geo-science, *Iaslic Bull* 38 (3) Sept 1993: 137-138.

Studies the collaborative research work between scientists of different counties and between scientists of a particular country in the filed of Geoscience based on the data collected from Journal of the Geological Society of India, 1987-1991. Calculates the degree of collaboration between scientists of different countries as .099 as against. 554 of collaborative research by the scientists of a particular country.

MANDAL, B R, DATTA, SUBRATA and DEY, S K 1373

Collection development in biomedical science: New media, *CODE*, 174.

Considers citation analysis of cited journal articles as an authentic tool for the collection development of journals according to their degree of importance on the basis of IICB, Calcutta in their publishedd articles during 1988-89 to 1992-93. Prepares a list of 75 core journals on the basis of 9400 citations.

MISHRA, SANJAY and MISHRA, MANOJ K 1374

Collaborative research in medicinal in aromatic plants, *Lib Her* 30 (1) Apr 1991: 30-34.

Studies the authorship pattern and research collaborations in the field of medicinal and aromatic plants based on the data collected from the Medicinal and Aromatic Plants Abstracts (1979-89). Reveals that papers with two and three authors constitute a major part. Depicts that the average number of authors per paper has remained almost consistent.

MOHANTA, RABINDRA NATH 1375

Information use pattern of Indian library and information scintists; a citation study, *Her Lib Sci* 31 (3-4) July- Oct 1992: 217-224.

Analyses citations appeard in five Indian LIS periodicals to know the number of references, bibliographical formats of cited documents, self citations, etc. Determines life of LIS periodicals, books on the basis of citations, core periodicals for LIS. Observes that *Annals* ranks first among the cited periodicals.

MUJOO-MUNSHI, USHA and KARANJAI, ARUNA 1376

Influence of island effect on the citation behaviour: A comparative study, *ALE*, 44-59.

Gives importance of citing earlier works. States that new literature gains more citations and that Indian researchers cite compartively older literature as compared to their Western counterparts because information service there is better organised. Analyses recency of cited references in Chemistry and Chemical Technology to find out the pattern of literature usage by Indian scientists, and whether the place of work and availbility of literature has any influence on literature usage as reflected in the references quoted.

MUNSHI, USHA MUJOO and VASHISHTH, C P 1377

Recency of citations, *Jl Lib & Infor Sci* 18 (1) Jun 1993: 25-31.

Finds out patterns of literature usage by Indian agricultural scientists. Indentifies top ten journals based on the number of papers published by agricultural scientists and studies the citation pattern for 1990. Concludes that general trend is to quote references from the last decade and earlier period. Points out their less exposure to latest developments in their field and have limited access to CAS.

MUNSHI, USHA M, VASHISHTHA, C P and GAUTAM, J N 1378

Journal preferences in agricultrual sciences, *ILA Bull* 29 (1-2) Apr-Sept 1993: 1-13.

Attempts to trace out the publishing habits of Indian agricultural scientists based on data collected from six agricultural universities for a period of 5 years covering 8100 papers published in journals. Concludes that national journals are preferred. Gives lists of journals, top 15 journals, journals in which papers are communicated, etc.

MUNSHI, USHA M, VASHISHTHA, CP and GAUTAM, J N 1379

Resource collabroation in agricultural sciences, *ILA Bull* 28 (3-4) Oct-Mar 1993: 57-60.

Finds out the pattern of research from amongst the scientists working in six agricultural universities of India. Determines degree of collaboration in quantitative terms using a formula developed by K Subramanyam. Points out also local/international collaboration.

PARVATHAMMA, N, GUNJAL, S R and
NIJAGUNAPPA, R 1380

Growth pattern of literature and scientific productivity of authors in Indian earth science (1978-88) : A bibliometric study, *Lib Sci slant Docum & Inf Std* 30 (2) June 1993: 54-64.

Detrmines rate of growth of Indian earth science literature by calculating relative growth rates and doubling time for total number of all types of publications for 1978-88. Shows mean relative growth in a declining trend. States that mean doubling time for Indian earth science literature is slightly less than the groth rate of earth science literature as a whole. Finds the scientific productivity of authors conforming to Lotka's Law.

PERITZ, BLUMA C 1381

The use of meta analysis for citation studies: An illustrative exmples, *INFO*, 358-376.

Proposes to make use of these data in order to study the association between citations and various characteristics of these studies with the ultimate purpose of evaluating citation frequencies as measures of a paper's worth. Presents an example of small data which shows that meaningful conclusions can be drawn regarding the relationship between citations and the methodological quality of the study.

PICHAPPAN, P 1382

Ranking of journals: Its techniques and validity, *DL*, 307-317.

Defines ranking. Gives its values in journals. Discusses ranking techniques and the need to rank. Describes the methods used including the citation studies to measure the standing of a journal. States that user perception of journals is also important.

PODDER, ASHOKE KUMAR and ROY,
SATYABRATA 1383

Status of periodical collection in major medical libraries of Calcutta: An informative evaluation, *ITAH*, 199-212.

Attempts to study about the bibliographical references appended to the articles in five Indian medical journals from 1988 to 1990. Prepares a rank list of cited journals. Finds out how many of them are available in the major medical libraries of Calcutta. Shows also whetehr these libraries are subscribing less relevant journals according to the present financial constraints.

PURKYASTHA, PRADIPTO DAS 1384

Social change: a study of Indian periodical literature, *Int Lib Move* 15 (4) Dec 1993: 175-180.

Makes a study of Indian periodical literature on social change to find out the extent of single and multiple authorship; the extent of Indian and foreign contribution; the proportion of keywords to total words in titles of articles; the number of pages devoted to articles, reviews, etc and the extent the authors refer to Indian and foreign journals and other documents.

RAVICHANDRA RAO, I K 1385

Growth and obsolescence of literature: An empirical study, *INFO*, 377-394.

Studies a relation between growth and obsolescence. Observes that faster the growth of literature quicker the obsolescence as well as less the halflife. Aslo it has been re-confirmed that age distribution of cited journals follows log normal distribution. Studies pattern of obseolescence of literature.

SANGAM, S L 1386

Obsolescence of literature in different disciplines of social sciences: A comparative study, *CS*, 221-257.

Attempts to identify and compare the obsolescence factors such as annual aging factor, half-life, mean-life, utility factor, and corrected obsolescence factor for journal literature and books cited in the doctoral theses of different disciplines of social science.

SANGAM, S L 1387

Ranking of periodicals in geography: Citation study of PhD dissertations accepted by Karnataka University, Dharwad, duing 1964 to 1982, *CRL*, 149-156.

Gives the importance of citation analysis. Finds out the core jounals and ranks them as to their respective use for the purpose of evaluating the selection policy in the field of geography by refering to the Ph D theses submitted to Karnataka University during 1964-82.

SHARMA, R M and SINGH, S N 1388

Ascertaining principal bibliographic form and core journals in soil science, *IJALIS* 20, 1992: 33-36

Attempts to ascertain principal bibliographic form and core journals in soil science research in India by using citation analysis technique. Reveals periodicals as the principal form followed quite distantly by books. Finds that only first 26 journals meet apporximately 70% periodical information needs.

SHARMA, R M and SINGH, S N 1389

Strategy to build up sound information base and service in soil science, *IJALIS* 21, 1993: 49-55.

Studies through citation analysis doctoral theses submitted to BHU during 1983-87. Finds that immediately past 30 years literature was most useful. Subject dispersion shows that soil science alone contributed 36.68% of the total periodical literature. India produced maximum literature followed by USA. English was the principal language used to communicate information. Finds only first 36 authors contributed substantially to periodical literature.

SINHA, S C 1390

Indian contribution on the literature of building science: A quantitative analysis, *ALIS*, V 4, 187-203.

Quantifies the Indian research acitivities in the areas of building sciences as seen from Building Science Abstracts. Evaluates its impact on the world's literature which was found to be merly 2% as analysed from Science Citation Index. Makes comments on coverge of SCI which appears to be not as good as in the areas of technology in general and building science in partucular as compared to comprehensive coverage in the area of pure sciences.

SINHA, SC and FURQANULLAH, M 1391

Citation profile of Dr V S Ramachandran a - bibliometric analysis of his highly cited articles and books in the area of cement and concrete chemistry, *Ann Lib Sci & Docum* 40 (1) Mar 1993: 21-31.

Studies the citation pattern of the citation recieved by the works of Dr V S Ramachandran with special reference to his highest cited articles and books, based on a citation counts for 49 articles published in the learned journals.

SINHA, S C and FURQANULLAH, M 1392

Eleven year of CBRI research output, 1980-90: A bibliometric study, *Ann Lib Sci & Docum* 40 (3) Sept 1993: 77-91.

Analyses 822 research papers published by the scientists of CBRI during Jan 1980 to Mar 1990 in Indian and foreign journals and presented at national and international conferences. Indicates downward trend of the Institute's research output. Finds out impact factor of journals of interest to CBRI. Makes suggestions to improve the situation by taking more R & D projects in future. Gives a list of suggested journals with their rankings, impact factor, and immediacy index.

SINHA, S C and FURQANULLAH, M 1393

Ten years of CBRI research output, 1980-90: A bibliometric study, *IJILIS* 6 (3-4) July-Dec 1993: 179-200.

Makes a bibliometric analysis of the papers produced as a result of the research activity carried out at CBRI, Roorkee, during 1980-90. Indicates the downward trend of its research output. Makes suggestions to improve the research by taking more R & D projects. Gives a list of suggested journals.

TALWAR, V G 1394

Profile of semi conductor device technology specialists, *CRL*, 120-132.

Analyses literature on semiconductor device technology in relation to author associated characteristics, geographical distribution, subject specialisation, institutional affiliation, productivity, multiple authorship, mobility of specialists, etc. Presents findings of the study.

VAISHANV, AA and DEO, V N 1395

Literature of computerised library and information services: A bibliometric study, *Lib Sci slant Docum & Info Std* 30 (2) June 1993: 45-53.

Analyses 26,669 items to study the growth of literature, subjectwise growth, oulets, journal literature, its distribution and application of Bradford's Law. Finds that maximum literature published in computerised information storage and retrieval, cataloguing, information services, etc while financial management and classification are evolving subjects and computerised citation indexes, printed catalogues, etc are decaying. States team work is becoming popular.

VERMA, A K and VERMA, MAYA 1396

Study of age distribution of journal citation in the American Economic Review, *ILA Bull* 29 (1-2) Apr-Sept 1993: 14-20.

Examines the characteristics of age distribution of journals cited in American Economic Review using citation analysis. Studies form of publication, country of publication, language of distribution of citations. States that journal citations accounted 58%, and 64% journals are from USA, and English language sources are most frequently cited. Mentions that Pearsonian coefficient of skewness is positive.

025.48 (1) INFORMETRICS

BONZI, SUSAN 1397

Variables affecting productivity among senior faculty, *INFO*, 79-96.

Looks into long term trends in scholarly productivity, as measured by publication rate, among faculty at Syracuse University (USA). Studies such factors as acdemic discipline, sex, acdemic rank, date of terminal degree. Reveals that more productive faculty tend to hold higther rank, males excelling females, science and mathematics are more productive and publish in journals than others who publish in books. Indicates that in some disciplines productivity exhibited during the early years in the profession may not continue after tenure is granted.

BOOKSTEIN, A 1398

Theoretical properties of the informetric distributors: Some open questions, *INFO*, 17-35.

States that informetrics is a broad fiels, and informetric regualieslie at its heart. Presents a coherent inerpretationof these regfularities. Begins with and interperetationof the variables of interest. Gives a model describing how the type of data analysed by these regularities is genrated. Discusses the problem of ambiguity and the im;ocations Third International Conference on Informetrics - 91.

EGGHE, LEO 1399

Qualitative analysis of the recall procision relationship in informaton retrieval, *INFO*, 148-174.

Investigates the mathematical relationship between recall and precision in IR based on the notion of the relevance dansity function. Studies recall precision relationship as a fucation of time as well as their mutual relation. Disproves the 'classical' as well as 'hyperbolic' type relation. concludes with a recall fallout relation study.

GLANREL, W and SCHUBERT, A 1400

Predictive aspects of a stochastic model for citation processes, *INFO*, 175,207.

Presents a statistical model for citation processes as a particular version of a non-homogeneous pure birth process with immigration. Records the citation rate for papers published in 1980 in the period 1980-1989 in three science fields, illustrated with examples.

GOPAL RAJ, N 1401

Informatrics for libraries, *The Hindu*, Madras, 14 August, 1991.

Reports the views of various scholars, international and Indian about the value of informetrics in increasing the information use, as also the increasing fields to which this technique can be applied. Those who expressed their opinions include Dr Michael E D Koening (USA), Ms Jean Tague-Sutcliffe (Canada). S Parthasarathy, I K Ravichandra Rao, S Arunachalam.

IYENGAR, S S, RAO, S V A and KRAFT, D H 1402

The Multiple Attribute Tree as an index structure for large bibliographic files, *INFO*, 208-260.

Employs computerised bibliographic information systems in a number of applications. The operational success of these systems in interactive environs critically hinges on the response time, which in turn depends on the underlying storage and retrieval structure. Multiple Attribut Tree is shown to a very efficient index structure for the retrieval of multi-dimensional information. Defines MAT and explains it in detail in relation to I R system.

KALYANE, V L 1403

Informetrics on neem research in India, *Lib Sci slant Docum & Inf Std* 30 (4) Dec 1993: 139-145.

Research on use of Neem plant products for control of insect pests. Nematodea, fungus, and virus have gained improtance in Inda, Analyses yearwise and domainwise publications and their scattering.

KOENIG, MICHAEL E D 1404

The information environment and the productivity of research, *INFO*, 261-288.

Examines the relationship between the R & D productivity of major US pharmaceutical companies and the information environment of those companies. Defines R & D productivity. States that productivity among large pharmaceutical companies differs quite dramatically. Analyses data on the informaton environment of the companies colleted through questionnaires distributed to individual researchers.

KRETSCHMER, HILDRUN 1405

Significance of the logaritham of number of publications for the measurement of social stratification in coauthorship networks, *INFO*, 289-331.

Mentions that there is a generalised psychological theory of stratification. Investigates whether the structure of coauthorship networks was in line with the social psychological theory. Tests empirically whether the log of the number of publications is better measure for the social rank than the number of publications per se.

KURTZE, DOUGLAS, SNYDER, HERBERT and NEWBY, GREGORY B 1406

An investigation of chaos in computer mediated communictaion, *INFO*, 332-342.

Submits agruments for applying bibliometric techniques to computer-mediated communication. Analyses a sample space consisting of the entire message traffic of a computer network discussion group. Adapts from physics a standard technique for examining time sequence data for patterns of non-linear dynamics. Discusses future prospects for applicability of chaos to bibliometric research.

RAVICHANDRA RAO, I K 1407

A brief report of the Third International Conference on Informetrics, 9-12 August 1991, *INFO*, 549-575.

Reports about the Third International Conference on Informetrics held in Bangalore to herald the Birth Centenary celebration of Dr S R Ranganathan in which more than 100 delegates from about 14 countries participated. Mentions that it was inaugurated by A Neelameghan, Keynote address by A Bookstein, welcome by I K Ravichandra Rao, and vote of thanbks from G Bhattacharyya. Reports about the Technical Sessions in which 32 papers were presented and discussed. The Panel discussion inclued F W Lancaster, Bluma Peritz, S Parthasarathy, Susan Bonzi with M A Gopinath as moderator. Appends a list of 102 participants and also the programme.

RAVICHANDRA RAO, I K 1408

A compendium of selected papers of bibliometrics and informetrics, Bangalore: Sarada Ranganathan Endowment for Library Science, 1992. ix, 580 p.

Includes only a few selected papers presented at the Third International Conference on Informetircs held during 9-12 August, 1991 in Bangalore to herald the Birth Centenary celebration of Dr S R Ranganathan. This is published in the "Rangannathan Centenary Series" as number 4.

RAVICHANDRA RAO, I K 1409

Guest Editorial: Informetric models *Lib Sci slant Docum & Inf Std* 30 (3) Sept 1993: i-ii.

Mentions in this Guest Editoral about a few classic works in the field of informetrics with their contexts. Gives their features, laws, and other aspects of interest to the experts in the field of informetrics.

RAVICHANDRA RAO, I K 1410

Welcome address, *INFO*, 1-8.

Welcomes the delegates from different countries including India to the Third International Conference on Informetrics held during 9-12 Aug, 1991 in Bangalore, as a part of the Centenary year programme of the late Dr S R Ranganathan, an eminent librarian, teacher, Father of Library Movement in Inda, and who coined the most meaningful term 'Librametry' for the first time in 1948.

ROUSSEAU, RONALD 1411

Pielou's axiom and n-dependent concentration measures, *INICAE* 11(1)Mar 1992:43-63.

Considers two requirements adapted from Pielou's axioms and one by Dalton to investigate which requirements concentration measures must in the case of a varying number of sources. Reveals that no measure can meet these. Divides them into two groups of measures: concentration measures of the first kind; and concentration measures of the secon kind. Concentrates on the ascond group.

ROUSSEAU, RONALD 1412

Pileau's axions and independent conecntration measures, *INFO*, 395-425

Investigates requirements concentration measures. Considers two requirements adapted from Pilou's axioms and one originated by Dalton. Makes out distinction between two groups of concentration measures. Demonstrates special properties of this new class of concentration measures using the reference list of ınformetrics.

SHAH, KANUBHAI L 1413

Interpreting readership data: A new multi variated approach through visualizaion, *Lib Sci slant Docum & Inf Std* 30 (3) Sept 1993: 103-117.

States that multivariate anaysis is a fresh wave of data

analysis in informetrics. Applies this method in readership data. Reports the results in tabulated from for more visualization.

TAGUE-SUTCLIFE, JEAN 1414

How good is a model? Explicativity as a goodness-of-fit measure, *INFO*, 484-505.

Attempts to answer the question: What do informetric models really represent? Gives explanation of earlier models of Bradford, Lotka, Zipf and later researchers : as Burell, etc. Stakes that never statistical concepts provide a more approximate paradigm for informetric investigations, as explicativity. Illustrates this by model development for two informetric databases.

025.48(1) SCIENTOMETRICS

GUPTA, D K 1415

Scientometric study of exploration geophysics - author productivity trends, *Ann Lib Sci & Docum* 39 (4) Dec 1992: 145-152.

Analyses cumulative index of "Geophysical Prospecting". and "Geophysics", two important journals in this area for 1936-85 for author productivity trends which were tested for the application of Lotka's Law by applying K S statistical test.

KALYANE, V L and KALYANE, S V 1416

Scientometric portrait of Vinodini Reddy, *Jl Infor Sci* 4(1) Jul-Sep 1993: 25-48.

Analyses quantitatively research publications of Dr Vinodini Reddy, a role model medical scientist, by year, authorship pattern, collaboration coefficient, journal wise countribution, and keywords from titles of the articles.

KORENNOI, A A 1417

Scientometrics classification of research groups, *INICAE* 11 (1) Mar 1992: 13-25.

Presents a method of classification of research groups. States that the method is based on determination of the subect similarity of research reports. Takes into account the users requests. Fulfills the hierarchic cluster analysis of classification on the base of the fuzzy binary relations of similarity between objects.

Mc DONALD, LILIANA 1418

A communication model of the scientific school, *Lib Sci slant Docum & Inf Std* 30 (2) June 1993: 65-70.

Application of scientometric methods combined with sociological procedures and analysis of the discovered information links yielded five types of links: Tutorship links, Co-authorship links, reference links, informal direct information links. Shows that combined with other procedures, scientometirc methods are useful in establishing the membership and structure of a scientific school and tracing its development in history.

SHAILENDRA, K 1419

Information sources in history of science in India: A scientometric study of periodical literature - a prologee, *Lib Her* 31- (1-2) Apr-Sep 1992: 72-75.

Explores the information sources in History of science in India from the selected research journals. Analyses them with the aid of suitable scientometric techniques to identify significant scientometric indicators such as growth of subject, authorship pattern, highly productive authors, content analysis, citation pattern. Reports the summary of PhD thesis of the author submitted to University of Rajasthan, Jaipur.

SINGH, U N and ARUNACHALAM, S 1420

Profile of laser research in middle-level countries: A scienctometric analysis of publication productivity and citation impact, *INFO*, 447-483.

Analyses 5933 citations to 644 journals on laser collected from Physics Abstracts, 1976-1987 to identify the geographicl orgin, the prominent institutions, language and journal-wise distibution of the articles, their citedness, their distribution as a time series for the highly cited papers. Reveals that laser data is on the rise and share of China is rising fast; the share of English language journal articles is also rising. States that the USA leads followed by UK in laser publications.

025.48 (1) BRADFORD'S LAW

BASU, APARNA 1421

On the theoretical foundations of Bradford's law, *INFO*, 51-69.

Explains Bradford's law. Gives theoretical expression for the distribution of articles in journals. Attempts to obtain the law from fairly general statistical premises, using a model of a strictly hierarchical, random partitioning of unit line. Seeks an over-arching law that incorporates the characteristics of both Bradford's and Lotka's laws.

VENUGOPAL, M V and YADGIRI REDDY, J 1422

Use paradigm and the LCD statistical model of distribution in the evaluation of existing collections and acquisitions, *Luck Libn* 23 (2) Apr-June 1991: 73-78.

Outlines in brief the analytical methods available and used in LIS studies. Describes the method of determining the distribution based on Bradford phenomena to indentify the core collection. Offers suggestions.

025.48 (1) IMPACT FACTOR

ARORA, KAMLESH and SEN, B K 1423

Use of impact factor as a valid measure for evaluating the performance of scientific papers, *INFO*, 36-50.

Gives importance of citation of papers. Defines impact factor. Mentions that this technique was used for evaluation of research papers of CSIR scientists for 1986 and repeated for analysis of CSIR research output of 1987, 1988 and 1989. Tests the validity of using the impact factor in place of citation for the purpose of evaluation by consolidating the data for 1986-90 for each paper.

KARANJAI, A, MUNSHI, U M and SEN, B K 1424

Are the JCR impact factor of India S & T journals reliable? *Ann Lib Sci & Docum* 39 (1) Mar 1992: 26-30.

Mentions that though SCI Includes about 3,000 S & T journals in its database every year, it does not show a good coverage of journals from the developing countries. In 1988 only 11 Indian journals were covered in SCI. Shows that the impact factor of Indian journals obtained from JCR are not probably ture reflections of the quality of Indain journals.

MUNSHI, USHA M 1425

Concept of normalised impact factor socre, *ILA Bull* 28 (3-4) Oct-Mar 1993: 128-129.

Gives method to work out the highest impact factor in different subjects and journals belonging to the same subject.

MUNSHI, USHA MUJOO and VASHISHTH, C P 1426

Impact factor of Indian agricultural journals *Lib Her* 31 (1-2) Apr-Sep 1992: 1-12.

Discusses the citation behaviour of Indian agricultural scientists. Finds out the Impact factor using Science Citation Index. Suggests the measures to enhance the image and reputation of Indian agricultural journals.

SEN, B K 1427

Normalised impact factor, *Jl of Docum* 48 (3) Sept 1992: 318-325.

Describes how the data of normalised impact factor came into existence and the method of its determination. Describes properties of normalised impact factor. Observes that the ranking of a journal in its own category is better revealed by the normalised impact factor and the average normalised impact factor seems to provide better indication of the comparative performance of a set of laboratories engaged in different areas of research.

025.48 (1) Bibliographic Coupling

SHARDA, B A and SHARMA, J S 1428

A study of bibliographic coupling in linguistic research, *Ann Lib Sci & Docum* 40 (4) Dec 1993: 125-137.

Discusses the concept of bibliographic coupling in the area of citation analysis and its applicability to linguistic research. The coupling indexes are computed on the basis of sample articles from socio-linguistics and grammar published in the journals *Indian Linguistics* and *Language*.

025.48 (1) Visibility Index

MUJOO-MUNSHI, USHA and VASHISHTH, C P 1429

Visibility index, *ILA Bull* 28 (1-) Apr-Sept 1992: 1-5.

Deals with an asynchronous time-frame method devloped for documents with delayed publication to provide a more reliable short response-intensity score for publication emanating from the developing countries. Studies the method using asynchronous time-frame which gives more chance for journals with longer publishing time.

025.482 PRECIS

SHARMA, A K and KANKACHARY, M 1430

Preserved Context Indexing System, *Lib Prog (Int)* 11 (1-) Jan-Dec 1991: 9-15.

Presents the state-of-the-art report of PRECIS from 1971 to 1989. Deals with various aspects particularly its application to different media. language, institutions at regional and global level. Provides suitable examples wherever required in its opereation. Concludes that it is the best system of subject indexing from amongst the existing systems at present.

025.486 Title Indexing. Keyword Indexing

SRIDHAR, APARNA and SREELATHA, G 1431

Generation of descriptors for the text of a technical paper : A case study, *Lib Sci slant Docum & Inf Std* 30 (1) Mar 1992: 25-38.

Discusses an experiment with an article in an established journal, using single-term automatic indexing methods, title, abstract and text of article were indexed. Finds out the expressiveness of the title and abstract, and whether the paper follows APUPA pattern of information flow.

YITZHAKI, MOSHE 1432

The variation in informativity of reseach papers with time and field, *COP*, 401-418.

States that titles constitute the most concise statement of a document's contents, and heavily used in IR systems. The more informative the title, the more effectively they serve their functions. Assesses the long-range trend during the past 50 years, concerning the number of substantive works in journal articles titles in the humanities, social science, sciences.

025.486 (1) KWIC Index

VYASMOORTHY, P 1433

KWIC Index program, *INICAE* 11 (1) Mar 1992: 72-80

Mentions the making of KWIC Index. States the steps involved in its production. Based on sample output, states Index Entry components. Specifies use of Index and its progamme. Discusses the complete programme of the Index and its further developments. Specifies copy left policy containing the KWIC package.

025.486 (1) Keyword Indexing and CDS/ISIS

KANJILAL, APURBA 1434

Permuted Keyword Index using CDS/ISIS - a tutorial, *Ialsic Bull* 37 (2) June 1992 : 83-88.

Describes a step-by-step tutorial to create the necessary databases, program file and compile it with the help of the utility program which generate a permuted Keyword index from a CDS/ ISIS database. Lists also the program and a sample output.

025.49 Subject Headings

CHATTERJEE, AMITABHA 1435

Information retrieval languges: Attributes and vocabularly-a comparative study, *IR*, 15-18.

Defines information retrieval (IR) and IR language. Brings out the differences between a natural language and an IR language and the attributes of IR language in the light of those differences. Emphasises role of controlled vocabulary in IR. Makes a comparative study of the various types of controlled vocabularies. Discusses also the measures to guage the effectiveness of a controlled vocabulary.

CHOWDHURY, G G 1436

Natural language processing of chemical patent information, *IR*, 19-30

Describes concept of natural language processing (NLP).

Mentions different areas of IR where NLP could be useful. Describes briefly nature of chemical patent information. Discusses different techniques of NLP adopted in the prototype system developed for semi-automatic translation of chemical patent abstracts. Reports preliminary study of automatic extraction of useful information from full-texts of chemical patents.

McCRAY, ALEXA T 1437

Natural language research program, *INICAE* 11 (2) Sept 1992: 256-258.

Describes about the Natural Language Systems (NLS) Program of the Lister Hill National Centre for Biomedical Communications conducting research in natural language processing to improve access to biomedical information stored in computerised form.

VYAS, S D 1438

Use of subject headings in Indian libraries, *IJILIS* 5 (3-4) July-Dec 1992: 273-281.

Discusses the use and purpose of subject headings. Analyses the concept of subject headings and the characteristics of the *Sears List, Library of Congress Subject Headings* and chain procedure. Concludes with a need to translate these lists in Indian languages. Suggests need for internship programme.

025.49 (1) Library of Congress Subject Headings (LCSH)

IFFIDON, BETTY I 1439

Library of Congress Subject Heading List: A study in practice, *ALD*, 11-21.

Discusses the importance of subject cataloguing. Defines subject cataloguing and mentions various subject headings lists. Examines uses and abuses of subject headings lists in relation to the LCSH. Describes features of LCSH list such as classification, symbols and subject subdivisions. Mentions the practical utilisation of the list. Suggests to study the list in detail and recommend areas that require modifications according to local circumstances.

SUDARSHAN RAO, S 1440

Lists of subject headings as aids for information retrieval: A brief stury od Library of Congress Subject Headings (LCSH), *IR*, 97-98.

Gives meaning of subject headings and IR. Explains need for a standard and exhaustive list of subject headings for content represenation of documentary collectiuons. Makes a study of LCSH 13 (1990) as regards to its format, headings, cross-references, class numbers, scope notes, etc. Concludes that LCSH 13 is an exhaustive list of subject headings that can be used by any type of library. Gives some useful suggestions.

025.49 (1) Medical Subject Headings (MeSH)

BARBIERI, CARLA, CAVAZZA, LAURA, IORI, RITA and SARTO, TERESA 1441

The subject entries of the Library of Centro Studi ... Balogna (Italy): A work based on MeSH,*ML*, 35-40.

Mentions about the complete reorganisation of the Library of Centro Studi witnessed a painstaking work on subject entries. Describes the application of MeSH for cataloguing required researching and control view of users needs. Discusses the methodology followed. Mentions the results and problems. Lists the advantages of the new subject index. Gives also the disadvantages.

025.49 (1) Thesaurus

HUMPHREYS, BETSY 1442

Metathesaurus and semantic network, *INICAE* 11 (1) Mar 1992: 115-118.

Announces the development of Unified Medical Language System (UMLS) as a knowledge source by NLM. Describes the UMLS Project and participants, Meta-1 and the semantic network, and its availability.

KARISIDDAPPA, C R and PRASAD, A R D 1443

Declarative programming and thesaurus construction, *Iaslic Bull* 38 (4) Dec 1993: 161-165.

Discusses the emergence of the new concepts in programming languages. Presents a brief history and features of one topic programming language, viz., Prolog. Demonstrates the procedures and advanages of declarative paradigm in the construction of thesauri.

RAGHAVAN, K S and SANKARALINGAM, P 1444

Multiple subject representations and cognitive searches, *COP*, 130-138.

States that the conventional thesaurus displays a limited

number of inter relationships between terms/concepts, and may be semantically inadequate to formulate an effective search. Discusses searching OPAC, and thesaurus relations. States that the contents of the 'subject rich' subject representation fields in bibliographic records can be effectively used to extend a thesaurus that will enable formulation of more effective searches.

RAHMSTORF, GERHARD 1445

Conceptual representation based on natural language phrases, *COP*, 344-356.

Analyses semantically meanings of phrases defining technical terms, represented by conceptual structures which constitute thesaurus. Describes the phrase analysis method for improving IR. Nouns, verbs and adjectives in the phrase are interpreted as concepts. Prepositions and grammatical morphems are represented as binary conceptual relations. Discusses some of the linguistic problems associated with the analysis of term definitions.

YOSHIDA, SANTOSHI 1446

Construction of library and information science thesaurus, *INICAE* 12 (2) Sept 1993: 166-172.

States the application of monolingual thesaurus in Japanese to some data bases or periodical indexes. Mentions bibliographical sources and the principles of construction of thesaurus. Discusses the need and type of thesaurus attempted since 1969. Lays down the relationships of the terms used, the process of construction and the systematic display which is a detailed faceted classification process and consisted of ten facets.

025.5 SERVICE TO USERS

LIBRARY SERVICES

BOHLMANN, IRENE L 1447

Service - an overlooked high technological aspect of the library, *ML*, 55-57.

States the library as primarily a custromer-oriented business, one where the product, ie, information, does not automatically structure the workload. Mentions that without service, no product exists. Without service and without a system for giving employees complete responsibility and authority for implementing a service - action, library experiences may cause customer dissatisfaction.

TAGORE, RABINDRANATH 1448

What makes a library big, *LM* ,1-4.

States that large number of books doesnot make the library big, it is rather the use of books and journals, the ability of librarian to get the books read, the hospitality that makes the library big. Suggests that library must compile a list of interesting articles and circulating them.

VIJAYLAKSHMI, K 1449

Socio-economic change and library services in a developing society, *LID*, 26-31.

Mentions library as an agency for disseminating knowledge for use. Discusses how information is helpful in socio-economic transformation of society. Describes major issues in providing and improving library services. Concludes with the summary of the main findings and its policy implications.

025.52 REFERENCE AND INFORMATION SERVICES

ABDUL RAHMAN 1450

Reference service in action, *Lib Sci slant Docum & Inf Std* 29 (3) Sept 1992: 148-156.

Discusses in detail the reference service in relation to the Five Laws of Library Science giving suitable examples from public library, sheding light on the catalogue room, stack room, reference librarian etc, university library, industrial library. Provides suitable case studies wherever possible.

AMUDHAVALLI, A 1451

Reference librarian as a communicator, *Jl Inf Sci* 3 (1) July-Sept 1992: 31-36.

Deals with regard to the communication skills needed for the reference librarian to offer effective information services. Suggests that library schools should incorporate packages on communication skills as part of their overall educational programme.

BANERJEE, MRINAL KANTI 1452

Reference service: Views of Dr Ranganathan, *RAT*, 38-43.

Explains the views of Dr S.R. Ranganathan on reference service with regard to Five Laws of Library Science. Introduces the concept of short range reference service and long range reference service. Describes how information explosion and interdisciplinary research have created new techniques as current awareness service, selective dissemination of information. Discusses Ranganathan's views about National Library also.

BHATIA, K K and GUPTA, S P 1453

In the footsteps of the great master: Some innovative information services at CRRL, *AGLIS Jl* 9, 1993 (Abstract only).

Describes about providing some of the innovative information services as 'Emerging Terminology', 'Global Development', 'Technological Development', etc. in the footsteps of Dr S R Ranganathan.

FISHER, RITA C and KINCH, MICHAEL P 1454

Agricultural reference service, *LT*, 71-88.

Surveys the variety of libraries and information centres in which agricultural reference service is given to show how reference varies in each, and indicates what trends in reference service are occuring. Highlights only the major issues and trends encountered by agricultural reference librarians such as those affecting user education, bibliographic searching, communications, collection, and staffing. Concludes that technological advancements have greatly improved the accessibility of the broad range of information relevant for agriculture.

GHANCHI, D A 1455

Library and information services as a multi-learning resources in higher education, *Univ News* Feb 4, 1991: 6-9.

Explains how library and information services turn out to be multi-learning resources in the contexct of higher education in colleges and universities where students and other scholars rub shoulders with the scholars of the past through their writings of immortal valve.

GOPINATH, M A 1456

Humanising library and information services: Role of the library profession, *Lib Sci slant Docum & Inf Std* 29 (4) Dec 1992: 203-212.

Analyses the factors that call for humanising the library and information activities. Identifies the various aspects of information technology, information service, and information service that call for human knowledge. Presents Ranganathan's approach to these aspects of library service which is called Energising Library Service.

IYENGAR, T K S 1457

Science & technology: Information services for Third World countries, *ALIS*, V 3,21-30.

Highlights importance of information and information services in Third World countries. Identifies areas of information and different categories of users, their information seeking behaviour patterns. Discusses the problems of economics of information regarding cost effectiveness of information systems. Discusses India as one sample in Third World countries regarding information systems.

KUMAR, SUSEELA 1458

From reference service to information retrieval: Guest editorial, *Lib Sci slant Docum & Inf Std* 29 (4) Dec 1992: 165-168.

States that for Ranganathan reference service was the core of all library work. Mentions that with computers around it seems that machines will do it all but it is not true as human intervention will continue to be needed in new information technology. Gives advantages and disadvantages of computer, illustrating with manual and machine search studies. Concludes that no technology can beat the highly developed skill of information personnel who can analyse an information problem.

LAHIRI, A 1459

Why can't we hit the international market?, *NISSAT Newsletter* 12 (3) July-Sept 1993: 1.

Explains the need of information products and service and databases of information on India to be marketed either with collaborative arrangements or for unadultrated and solely Indian brand of information products and services.

MALHOTRA, NIRMAL 1460

Information services and user response, *Univ News* 31 (2) Jan 11, 1993: 12-13.

Mentions importance of information these days. Studies the users' reactions in the light of information users' problems and information providers efforts. States that under-utilization of information should be eliminated through user education. Lists some of the problems of users as ignorance, information explosion.

MISHRA, SANJAY 1461

Library and information services for disabled individuals, In *Papers*, 58th IFLA General Conference, New Delhi, 30 Aug - 5 Sept 1992, pp 0.39-0.40.

Defines the term 'disabled'. Discusses the need for library and information services to disabled individuals. Enumerates the need for special 'E & T' of librarians. Makes out a case for 'National Policy' on L & I system.

MOHANTA, RABINDRA NATH 1462

Reference and documentation service in India's National Library: Present status and some proposals in the light of Dr S R Ranganathan's views, *RAT*, 30-37.

Defines reference service. Discusses its type as short range reference service and long range reference service. Defines documentation. Mentions its facts. Discusses documentation service. Points out National Library as a documentation and bibliographic centre. Describes the present status of National Library with regard to reference service, documentation service, reprographic service, special bibliographic service as printed catalogues. Suggests some proposals for National Library as user education programme, arrangement of reference collection, compilation of union catalogue, CAS, users' survey, etc.

NEELAMEGHAN, A 1463

Libraries and information services in Third World countries, *In* F W Lancaster (Ed): *Libraries and the future: Essays on the library in the twenty-first century*, New York: Haworth Press, 1993.

Indicates that there are wide differences in development in Third World countries and there is a range of development agencies offering informatics support. Gives a brief description of regional alliances, IT which will enhance the usefulness and image of the library in the community it seeks to serve. Presents to achieve a unified perspective.

RANGANATHAN, S R 1464

Information service and imported confusion number one, *Iaslic Bull* 37 (3) Sept 1992: 107-117.

Reprinted from *IASLIC Bulletin* 2 (1-2) Dec 1957: 9-16, in view of its relevance, under the heading: 'Thus wrote Ranganathan'. Describes that information officers were appointed after independence without a clear understanding of their functions. Explains that information service presents documentation service, aggressive reference service, precis service, and dissemination service necessary to increase indusdtrial productivity. Wishes that library profession in India should excel and reach international level in research and service.

REYAZ, RUFAI 1465

The scope of a specific "Area study" as a discipline: A reference framework for information service professionals, *IJILIS* 6(3-4) July-Dec 1993: 240-267.

Defines the scope of a specific area study as a discipline, in terms of a reference framework: and it is meant priority for the use of information service professionals. For the purpose of concretising the issues involved in this process, the discipline "Central Asian Studies" has been taken up as an example.

SEETHARAMA, S 1466

Role of classification in information services generation, *Lib Sci slant Docum & Inf Std* 29 (2) June 1992: 109-118.

Mentions areas of application of the postulates and principles of Ranganathan's general theory of knowledge classification. Indicates that classification in the sense of organising concepts is involved in the generation, storage, retrieval, and dissemination of information, especially in designing databases, construction of user interest profile, subject description of document, arrangements and presentation of information, etc. Demonstrates with examples, the application of Ranganathan's postulates and principles of classification in the preparation of an information analysis and consolidation product.

SEWA SINGH 1467

From reference to information services : Impact of Ranganathan, *Timeless Fellowship* 15, 1993: 1-8.

Defines reference service. Gives developments of reference service. Describes the four categorisation of reference service, viz., initiation, general help to general readers, Ready reference service, and Long range reference service. Highlights Dr S R Ranganathan's unique contribution of reference service. Discusses its relationship with humanism. Presesnts analysis of reference work and service. Shows the symbiosis of reference service and classification. Concludes that Ranganathan was already out of scene when the new technology came in.

SEWA SINGH 1468

From reference to information services: A study on impact of Ranganathan, *IASLIC Bull* 37 (3) Sept 1992: 171-176.

States that like everything else in library and information science, Ranganathan made a mark in reference service also, by putting forth novel ideas and actual case studies. Discusses development and categories of reference service into initiation, general help, ready reference and long range reference. Analyses mechanics of reference work and service to come up with a holistic view. Stresses upon humanistic side and symbiotic relationship with classification of knowledge. Discusses that Ranganathan could not foresee the tremendous advancement in information technology to revolutionize all types of information service including reference.

SEWA SINGH 1469

Ranganathan and reference service, *CLIS Observer* 9 (1-2) Jan-June 1992: 16-22.

Discusses the concept of reference service as defined by S R Ranganathan in his writings. Traces the development of reference service. Gives various categories of reference service, differentiating between the short range and long range reference services. Pressents analysis of reference work and service as far as preparation, service and assimilation are concerned. Gives Ranganathan's unique contribution to reference service from humanistic point of view, symbiosis of reference service and classification. Mentions relevence of Ranganathan's contribution in today's environs.

SEWA SINGH 1470

Ranganathan and reference service, *DL*, 43-58.

Explains Ranganathan's contribution to reference service while giving its definition, development, categories, etc. Discusses relationship of reference service with humanism, classification, etc. Mentions reference librarian and his flair. Describes the place of Ranganathan's reference service and its impact in the Western countries.

SHARMA, P N and CHAUDHURY, ARUP RAY 1471

Meeting information needs in an industrial house: A case study, *STIM*, 87-100.

Gives a brief about the Thapar Group and the Thapar Corporate R & D Centre (TCRDC), Patiala. Explains the library and information services of the Dept of Library & Information Services, such as CAS, SDI, retrospective searches, state-of-the-art reports, technical enquiries. Discusses about public relations, staff, etc. Gives observations and conclusions about the S & T information work. Gives useful annextures.

SINGH, SONAL 1472

Reference service: Humanism in practice, *LIS*, 95-101.

Discusses the need for a human agency in a library in view of the phenomenal growth of literature. Describes objects of reference service to fulfil the aims of a library. Gives importance of reference department and reference sources essential to provide reference service. Points out the need of reference librarian, his qualifications, etc. States that reference service is essentially humanism in practice.

VISHWAMOHAN, V and CHANDRAMOHAN, V 1473

Ranganathan and reference and information service, *DL*, 36 - 43.

Discusses S R Ranganathan's contribution to reference service giving its conceptual framework/theoretical base. Points out achievement of post/s of reference librarian (s) in university libraries. Identifies the items of literature Ranganathan published on reference service. Mentions about the moral strength and courage the fresh librarians receive from his words and deeds. Concludes that he had a great foresight about the new technology.

025.524 Information Search and Retrieval

BAISYA, K N 1474

Information retrieval need of today and tomorrow for North East India, *LIN*, 47-58.

Mentions importance of information and its transfer. States that I R is a vital part of new discipline information science. Describes the role and importance of system analysis. Discusses about information arrangement and its handling. Explains the use of electronic device and computer in IR from one part of the world to another. Explaine the NE Region profile and its impact on disseminating information, role of public librasry act and North East Region Information Documentation Centre. Concludes that it is desirable to switch over gradually to uptodate I R network.

BANERJEE, BIMAL KUMAR 1475

Impact of 'generality' on retrieval effectiveness of large collection, *IR*, 95.

Assesses the effectiveness of retrieval performance of large document collections. Assesses effect of 'generality' in retrieval system evaluation and depicts evaluation results by collection comparison through generality over.

BEZSONOFF, D 1476

The value of bibliographical retrieval in biomedicine depends on the expertise in the use of medical language and bibliographical vocabularies, *ML*, 41-45.

States in spite of new technologies the documentary resources are underused. Observes system publications bibliography is not obsolete. Discusses reliability of biobliographical retrieval for biomedical publications rests on knowledge of biomedical language and controlled vocabularies.

CHATTERJEE, AMITABHA, SEN, SUBIR K and
KAPOOR, S K, *Eds* 1477

Information retrieval: Models and techniques; Papers of 15th National Seminar, 26-29 Decembezr, 1992, Annamalai University, Annamalainagar, Calcutta: IASLIC, 1992. iv, 100 p (Special Publication, number 32).

Contains 14 full-text papers as well as extended abstracts and abstracts of 19 more papers presented at the 15th National Seminar of IASLIC by LIS authors from around the country with a couple of them from abroad on theme of information retrieval.

GOPINATH, M A 1478

Descriptors and their role in information retrieval, *Lib Sci slant Docum & Inf Std* 30 (3) Sept 1993: 118-123.

Describes a descriptor. Gives its definition. Discusses methods of generating descriptors from the text, their correlation to classification schemes, their ability as substantive linkages in providing dues to individual users of IR. Points out that the variety of controlling devices that can be operated in modulating. Descriptors too moderate roles in IR.

GOPINATH, M A 1479

Information retrieval: A confluence of models, techniques and tools into a process: *Iaslic Bull* 37 (4) Dec 1992: 251-257.

Enumerates the requirements of basic premises, components, search characteristics, user interfaces, design models, design features, etc of information retrieval. Previews the present and future research areas, trends and possibilities. Engineers integrated development of IR. Presented at the 15th IASLIC National Seminar held at Annamalai University, 26-29 Dec 1992.

GOPINATH, M A 1480

Information retrieval-a modelling process: Guest Editorial *Lib Sci slant Docum & Inf Std* 30 (1) Mar 1993: i-iii.

Defines information retrieval (IR). Mentions three basic components in a computer based I R services: the Database, the Information Seeker, and the Repporteur of tools, techniques, models and processes. Explains the Database and storage and retrieval of information from it. Mentions kinds of data stored in a database. Describes how to search these. Discusses the problems that begin with a searcher. Mentions how to meet them in a conducive way. States that quality in retrieval of information is the motto of all these efforts.

GOPINATH, M A 1481

Information retrieval and knowledge base, *DL*, 253-266.

Defines information retrieval system. Mentions its basic features. States that IR can be made efficient by adopting an information processing language. Discusses the facet analytic approach and its application to design database for motor vehicle engineering. Describes knowledge representation systems and development of decision support system for information retrieval.

GOPINATH, M A 1482

Information retrieval, ontological model and Ranganathan's contribution, *IR*, 9-14.

Discusses the analytico-synthetic model designed by S R Ranganathan with application of categories and the knowledge representation schemes used in KBS. Identifies the analogical approaches in both the systems and finds global ontological approach to organisation of knowledge. Provides a cognitive basis among users of knowledge.

GOPINATH, M A 1483

Object-modelling in information retrieval, *ALR*, 207-215.

Aims to analyse the concept modelling aspects of informastion retrieval. Gives basic features of IRS where information retrieval can be made effective by adopting information processing language. Adopts the fact analysis approach in concept modelling. Discusses its application to the field of 'Automobile Engineering'. Describes the development of decision support system for IR with knowledge representation system.

GOSWAMI, SAJAL KANTI 1484

Graphic information retrieval system, *IR*, 96.

Explains the concept of graphic search by which we can visualise the information at a glance and also explains how to organise the thematic information on distinct planning maps. States that the advent of digital mapping system has enhanced the efficiency of graphic retrieval system.

HASHMI, ABUZAR 1485

Ranganathan on non-conventional methods in document retrieval, *RAT*, 44-49.

Describes about the introduction of the non-conventional methods in information retrieval in the second half of twentieth century. Discusses only application of computers in document/ retrieval and contribution of Ranganathan in computerised information retrieval, Colon Classification, and the computer CIRS in National Library of India and role of Ranganathan. Mentions about the databases developed in the National Library and the future plans.

IIVONEN, MIRJA 1486

Factors affecting the analysis of requests and the formulation of query statements, *COP*, 112-129.

Considers factors affecting the analysis of requests and the information of query statements and reports on the results of study in which 32 searchers analysed 12 requests and formulated query statements for a search from a particular database. Calculates consistency of the first and second search. Establishes connections between specificity, complexity and clarity. Discusses the intersearcher and intrasearcher consisting in formulating query statements.

MYTHILI RAMAN, T 1487

Search strategy in the process of information retrieval, *IR*, 97.

Deals with the need for a search and defines search strategy. Explains pre-requisites before search opeartion begins in the process of retrieval. Describes steps involved in search formulation, suggests certain retrieval approaches and mentions causes for search failures.

RAVICHANDRA RAO, I K 1488

An overview of information retrieval: Issues for consideration, *IR* 1-7.

Explains IR. Discusses characteristics and differnt functional approaches to an IR system. Mentions issues pertaining to design, development and implementation of IR system in Indian context. Points out recent research done in IR. Concludes with some useful propositions on the basis of the discussions and issues.

SATISH, N and YADAGIRI REDDY, J 1489

Information storage and retrieval in a university library system: Problems and prospects, *IR*, 99-100.

Explains information needs of various user groups of university libraries. Argues that organisation of library materials by classifying and cataloguing provides access to macro documents only and not to micro documents and articles contained in composite books. Explains that secondary information sources are helpful to a limited extent. Concludes with suggestions.

SEN, SUBIR K 1490

Some issues in information retrieval and fuzzy information retrieval: Accounting for information loss, *IR*, 100.

Defines an information retrieval system as a four-component system and an IR process in nine steps. Defines 'conflation'. Introduces fuzzy-logical ideas as compared to other weighted matching procedures in IR. Prepars information loss account at various stages on the basis of which a measure of efficiency as distint from measure effectiveness has been suggested. Discusses relation between efficiency and effectiveness.

SHAH, G A, DESAI, A T and NAGARKAR, SA 1491

Search strategies: Their importance in IR process, *IR*, 31-34.

Discusses how the users' questions should be analysed and appropriated search strategies should be formulated with a view to enhancing capabilities of a system in retrieval of the most relevant information with a high degree of precision.

SHAH, PC 1492

Information retrieval for developing countries through secondary periodicals in the field of textile and allied subjects, *Lib Prog (Int)* 13 (1-2) Jan- Dec 1993: 16-24.

Mentions about early period of ATIRA and setting up of NICTAS. States objectives of NICTAS. Discusses about computerization of NICTAS, and starting of TEXICON on the basis of a comprehensive survey of informaton needs of textile industry. Describes production and publication of TEXICON, marketing and publicity efforts to make the service popular.

SHARMA, S K and VINDO KUMAR 1493

Search of information in science and technology, *Lib Prog (Int)* 13 (1-2) Jan-Dec 1993: 31-36.

Gives importance of information. Mentions way of spreading information. Explains media of scientific and technical information as journals, theses, conferrence proceedings, reports, patents, standards, trade literature, etc. Discusses about searching in the abstracts and indexes of getting information. Describes ways of keeping with current information.

SINGH, A R and SRIVASTAVA, RAJKUMARI 1494

Information retrieval in archives and archival libraries in India: Models and techniques, *IR*, 99.

Deals with the difficulties of traditional archival information services coping with the situation, hence required to be replaced by modern techniques and models of IR. Makes a case for modernisation and application of automated information methods. States that automation is not expensive vis-a-vis manual systems.

SRINIVASAN, PADMINI 1495

Knowledge organisation for information retrieval, *COP*, 81-94.

Defines knowledge. Examines the role of knowledge in information retrieval systems which are sytems designed to retrieve items from text databases. Focuses on current research on knowledge-based information retrieval systems. Looks at representation of knowledge and then acquisition of knowledge. Discusses the depth of knowledge reuqired for IR. Concludes by indetifyng key issues and open research issues in the area of knowledge based IR.

025.525 Selective Dissemination of Information (SDI)

BARADOL A K 1496

SDI services, *IR*, 95.

Emphasises that the success of SDI service depends on the strategy for creating the user profile and its matching with the database.

MUSOKE, MARIA G 1497

The dissemination of health information at grassroot level with special refernce to women keys to information at the grassroot level: Layman's point of view, *ML*, 295-298.

Discusses some factors affecting the availbility and accessibility of information at grassroot level in Uganda. Indicates what needs to be done to remedy the situation that health information, like other meterial resoureces, reaches the grassroot people who form majority of the population.

RAO, M M 1498

Selective Dissemination of Information (SDI): A case study of Central Water and Power Research Station (CWPRS), *Ann Lib Sci & Docum* 40 (4) Dec 1993: 146-154.

Discusses the information needs of the CWPRS. Describes a computer based SDI service rendered at the CWPRS, Pune using HP 3000/ Series 58 computer and MINISIS software. The user feedback service indicates that by and large the service is catering to the information needs of CWPRS scientists and engineers.

025.525 (1) SDI - Computerised

ARORA, J and SHARANPAL KAUR 1499

Recent information technologies and their impact on dissemination of information, *Ann, Lib Sci & Docum* 39 (1) Mar 1992: 12-18.

Points out the importance of the development of IT as it has opened up new possibilities in dealing with the problems of collecting, organising and disseminating a vast amount of scientific and technical information. Highlights the use of computers for ISR and traces its history. Discusses its advangaages in the dissemination of information.

KRISHNA, K M and SINGH, Y K 1500

Computer-based retrospective SDI service and its imlication in academic libraries of India, *IJILIS* 6 (3-4) July-Dec 1993: 268-271.

Discusses the need, method of preparation and imporatance of computer-based retrospective SDI service. Highlights its implications in academic libraries with special reference to India.

VAISHNAV, A A and BAPAT, N G 1501

Computerised SDI service: A case study, *LIS*, 144-152.

Describes the information services provided by the Marathawada University Library which includes the CAS, location service, Reference service and Backup service. Explains the steps in computerization of SDI service given on a prepared menu driven, user friendly software package.

025.525 (1) Current Awareness Service (CAS)

KANKACHARY, M and PRABHAKAR, S S 1502

Current awareness service in CIEFL Library, *ALD*, 46-55.

Defines CAS on the basis of views of various authors. Gives goals and need of CAS in CIEFL Library such as compilation of bibliographies, checklists, indexes, reference sources. Enumerates also the bibliographies in progress. Concludes by way of offering suggestions.

VARMA, A K 1503

Current awareness services in libraries, *LIS*, 102-113.

Points out explosion of knowledge. Discusses psychological theory of awareness. Mentions the current approach in CAS. Defines CAS, gives its characteristics, levels, etc. Explains CAS in India. Mentions the measures to promote CAS in view of its usefulness.

025.5276 Reference and Information Services-Special Libraries

SAMPATHA CHARY, K 1504

A Study of information services in nutrition science with special reference to India, *ML*, 385-390.

Coves an historical method of investigation and the modus operandi of the IR activities in human nutrition, abroad and in the country. Suggests a model for setting up a National Information Facility in Nutrition and Allied Sciences at NIN, Hyderabad.

Concludes that India will fulfil the targets of WHO's call "HFA-2000 AD" by improving information of nutrition science.

025.52772 Reference and Information Services-University Libraries

GAUTAM, ANIL KUMAR 1505

Modern information technology and reader's services in university libraries in India and abroad, *LIT*, 188-195.

Mentions importance of IT and IT devices. Explains concept of reader's services and the services as developed under this concept. Because the status of library sevices in university libraries in India is low, therefore there is need to use some IT and the level can be enhanced to the level in the UK and the USA.

GOZO, AGNES JOYES 1506

Health professionals' evaluation of the services provided by the University of Zimbabwe Medical School Library, *ML*, 177-186.

Attempts to determine how the health professionals in Harare evaluate the services provided by the University of Zimbabwe Medical Library. Makes a questionnaire survey to evaluate specific library services as well as overall evaluation of the whole library. Reveals that though the response rate was low (26.10%) the survey results indicate areas which need further examination.

KUMAR, P S G 1507

Organising reader services in university libraries, *Univ News* 30 (35) Aug 31, 1992 : 99-100.

Discusses users and their types; services and their categories. Describes the situation of reader services in Indain universities. Makes suggestions to the UGC, and to the university libraries for improvement.

MAHESWARAPPA, B S and KARKUN, S G 1508

Awareness and usefulness of information services of INSDOC and National Centre for Science Information (NCSI Bangalore) among the biological and physical scientists in a university environment, *DL*, 213-220.

Surveys the awareness and usefulness of information services of INSDOC and NCSI among the biological and physical scientists working in Karnataka University on the basis of a questionnairre.

Concludes that most of the scientists are aware of the services of INSDOC and NCSI and make use of them.

025.56 BIBLIOGGRAPHIC INSTRUCTION. LIBRARY ORIENTATION. USER EDUCATION USER INSTRUCTION

PATEL, JASHU 1509

Ethnic bibliographic instruction: Yesterday, today and tomorrow, *Jl Lib & Infor Sci* 18 (1) Jun 1993: 12-24.

Mentions that students, scholars, researchers etc face library problems in the US, UK and other countries as no bibliographic instructions are given for ethnic materials. Believes if bibliographic instruction provided it will save time, energy and frustration of international students and researchers. Outlines bibliographic instruction programme for ethnic materials.

025.56 (1) User Educaton for Distance Learning

CHANDRASEKHAR RAO, V and SUJATHA, G 1510

Designing user education programmes for distance learners, *ALR*, 295-301.

Gives nature of distance teaching and learning for library facilities. Points out limitations of library use by distance learners. Defines user eduction. Focusses on the aspects relating to designing of user education programmes for distance learners by giving objectives and methods to be used.

025.5661 User Education - Medical Libraries

EATON, ELIZABETH K and RICHARDSON, ELIZABETH J 1511

Librarian instructors in the core medical school curriculum: Database searcbing - a key to resources and information management, now and in the future, *ML*, 139-146

Discusses the involvement of librarians in the Problem Based Learning (PBL) Programe at the Tufts University School of Medicine with in a traditional medical curriculum as a key to the students learning about information learning resources and the skills to obtain this knowledge.

025.5674 User Education - Public Libraries

SHARMA, R C 1512

User orientation in public libraires, *PLD*, 120-125.

Gives definition of user orientation. Mentions its types. States objectives of orientation. Explains user orientation methods such as lecture and other methods. Gives orietation programme, and how to design a new programme, and where care of new technology has to be taken.

025.5677 User Education - Acdemic Libraries

GADDAGIMATH, RAVI B 1513

User instruction programme in academic libraries, *CS*, 292-303.

Discusses the need, goals and objectives, interpretation of the objectives, curriculum planning, programme content, teaching methods and aids, and evaluation of the user instruction programme in academic libraries. Mentions about the information management skills programmes developed at NAARM.

MISHRA, SANJAY 1514

Teaching of bibliographic instructiion at undergraduate level : A proposal, *Luck Libn* 24 (3) July-Sept 1992: 114-117.

Deifines ' Bibliographic Instruction'. Discusses the need and objectives of Bibliographic Instruction. Proposes a plan to introduce Bibliographic Instruction as a foundation course paper at the undergraduate level. Provides the syllabus and suggests teaching method

RATHORE, JAGMOHAN SINGH 1515

User education programme in academic libraries, *Luck Libn* 24 (3) July-Sept 1992: 104-107.

Describes the goals and objectives of user education. Maentions categories of users. Discusses different stages of user education programme, different methods of instruction and aids in user education. Concludes that user education is one of the few dependable tools to make users library conscious.

VARMA, A K 1516

User orientationin academic libraries, *LIS*, 73-78.

Explains the need and purpose of user orientation. Discusses its objectives also. Mentions four classes of usere as under-graduates, post-graduates, researchers and scholars, and academic staff. Gives course contents with the user categories. Mentions direct and indirect methods of orientation.

025.56772 User Eduaction- University Libraries

GOSWAMI, D D and GOSWAMI, R C 1517

Users education and library orientataion in Assam Agricultural University Library, *LIN*, 75-79.

Explains need for user education (UE). Discusses bibliographic instruction with objectives. Describes the library orientation in Assam Agricultural University Library as it carries out teaching, research and extension activities on agricultural education. Puts forth the various suggestions for further improvement of library oreintation. Concludes that a proper understanding of UE in the beginning of session is essential.

MOHAMMAD YUSUF and KHAN, JABIR HASAN 1518

Planning of user education programme (UEP) in universtiy libraries, *ILA Bull* 29(1-2) Apr-Sep 1993: 35-38.

Gives meaning of the concept of user education. Highlights various aspects of UE as need and objectives. Discusses planning of UE programme. Explains the strategies to achieve the objectives of the UEP in a university library.

SEWA SINGH 1519

User education in university libraries: What, why and how?, *ALE*, 66-70.

Explains what is UE. Discusses factors which neccessitate the introduction of UE programme in university libraties. Describes objectives of UE. Discusses the role of university libraries in view of the need and objectives of UE in undetaking such programmes at under-graduate level, research scholar level, faculty level. States that it is a continous feature of university libraries. Mentions the importance of feedback in the success of UE. Concludes that it should be made an integral part of university libraries in India by setting up a UE Dapartment.

VISHWA MOHAN, V and CHANDRA MOHAN, V 1520

User education in university libraries, *ALR*, 287-294.

Explains the concept of user education. Discusses need for user education. Describes planning and designing the user education programmes which include such aspects as contents, methods of instruction, instruction packages, equipment, resource persons, scheduling and execution of the programme.

025.56 (1) INFORMATION NEEDS

USER NEEDS

AMBA, S and IYER, HEMLATHA 1521

Contextual information needs: Retrieval techniques and the reserarch process, *COP*, 95-107.

Discusses about the information needs of users. Defines infrormation needs, and the organisationof information and the development of various techniques to retrieve it. Discusses the information needs and IR system design with cognitive models developed by various scholars. Describes the information needs of scientists in relation to IRS design. Mentions discussion about retrieval techniques. Concludes that there are different stages in the research process; several retrieval strategies; IR systems that have modeled some of these techniques and cognitive models applied to domain knowledge; world knowldege and user knowledge structures.

DAHAL, LEELA 1522

Access to basic health documents, *ML*, 109-115.

Enhances the satisfied crossmatching access to wanted information hidden within the bibliographic world and their tracing methods. Views users' information needs, bibliographic worlds and guides to the access points as the triangular structure.

DEVARAJAN, G 1523

Information needs and use pattern of humanities scholars, *DAB*, 166-173

Gives importance of information. Discusses the definition and scope of humanities. Makes a study of the information needs, information gathering behaviour and use pattern of information of the humanities scholars based at Kerala University.

DIXIT, R P 1524

Assessment of health literature/information needs of medical scientists, *Lib Her* 31 (1-2) Apr-Sep 1992: 76-91.

Examines the extent of availability of services and resources fulfilling users' needs through questionnaire of 1032 respondents. Studies on the basis of responses the use of library, evaluation of library collection and resources organisation of materials, loan of books and journals, reference service, photocopying facilities, ILL, documentation list, MEDLARS/MEDLINE search service, literature search request, SDI, microfilming, slide making, and translation of foreign language papers.

FRENCH, BEVERLEE A 1525

User needs and library services in agricultural services, *LT*, 89-115.

Profiles users of agricultural information. Describes their information needs and behaviour. Reviews trends in agriculture and information delivery and implications for users and for the relationship between information professionals and users. Suggests roles which librarian can assume in order to meet agricultural information needs.

FROHMANN, BERND 1526

Cognitive paradigms and user needs, *COP*, 35-50.

States that the recent LIS literature has in cognitive models of knowledge organisation, the promise of a new and fruitful paradigm for the discipline. Aims to investigate the claim that cognitive paradigms effect a shift from system needs to user needs; but it is open to criticism. Criticism suggests the hypothesis that the paradigm might be understood as the ideological expression of the histroriacl shift from large system of knowledge organisation to a new commercial sector aimed at sale of database systems.

GUPTA, R C 1527

Information and communication needs of structural engineering researchers, *ALIS*, V 4, 119-127.

Enumerates need for information system in scientific research. States that the users are most important component in the whole process and their needs be identified to design the appropriate and essential information services to yield the research results faster. Lists the library and information services provided to the researchers in structural engineering.

JOSEPH, ROSAMMA 1528

Information requirements of journalists in Kerala, *CS*,. 284-291.

Surveys the information needs for 297 journalists working in the eight major newspapers in Kerala. Studies in detail the purpose of visit to the library by journalists, the purpose for which the information is obtained from the library. Concludes that they visit the library for some background material, etc used for writing/ editing a news item and writing features.

KAPOOR, MALTI 1529

Meeting information needs of slow, average and gifted learners, In *Papers*, 58th IFLA General Conference, New Delhi, 30 Aug-5 Sept 1992, pp 3.14-3.16.

Points out that the school library serves as a laboratory for effective reading. Describes that there are some slow learners, some average and some gifted learners which require educational and psychological care, and accordingly reading material should be given to them.

MANSINGH, LAXMI 1530

Integration users needs with retrieval and dissemination at the medical library of the University of the West Indies, *ML*, 253-256.

Explains the development of innovative strategies for introducing contemporary services for the users in the University of the West Indies Medical Library. Discusses the Caribbean Health Information Project (CHIP) for providing service to every category of users.

NGOZI, I S 1531

Public participation in urban planning, planning laws and information needs in Tanzania, *Int Lib Move* 14(4) Dec 1992: 198-204.

Focuses on public participation and planning laws in their relation to information for urban planning and research in Tanzania. Gives suggestion to ensure information flow so that urban planning process could me made better to solve the peoples problems.

PETER, K M and PETER, SUSY 1532

Information needs of small scale industries: A projected study for industries in Bangalore, *Iaslic Bull* 38 (4) Dec 1993: 167-168.

Describes that technical information is a vital ingredient for the small scale industries for solving many of its problems. Mentions that unlike the heavy industries, the information infrastructure of the small scale industries are rather very poor and their information needs are slightly different in nature.

PRASAD, H N 1533

Information needs and users, Varanasi: Indian Bibliographic Centre, 1992. 165 p.

Presents a clear exposition of the fundamental elements of information needs and users. Defines information as the basic resource. Divided into 7 chapters on information, information and its users, information needs, information use and user needs, user study, methodology of user studies. Gives account of some user studies.

RAMAIAH, L S and PRAFULLA CHANDRA, T V 1534

Information needs and resources in linguistices: A case study, *DAB*, 250.258.

Explains the need to study language and linguistics in India. States that volume of informations growing fast. Describes the online services in linguistics, abstracting and indexing services, bibliographies, institutions and associations, periodicals and newsletters, current awareness bulletins. Concludes that neither a database nor a network is available at national level hence a gap between information available and information use exists in linguistics.

RAMESH, D B and KARISIDDAPPA, C R 1535

Information needs of engineering scientists of Regional Research laboratory, Bhubaneswar - a case study, *CTIT*, 95-108.

Explains the objectives of study to find out information needs of scientists, frequently used information sources, usefulness of library collection, etc. Analyses data collected through questionnaire form 57 engineering scientists of RRL, Bhubaneswar. Tabulates the data and lists the findings.

SENGUPTA, I N 1536

Assessment of information needs of scientists of Third World countries, *ML*, 431-434.

Mentions importance of information and role of library/ information centre in a research set up in collection and provision of information Describes the need for assessing information needs of users. Explains effective pathways for dissemination of information with reference to Third World countries.

TEJOMURTY, A 1537

Information requirements of and information services to the engineers in Dewas: A case study, *IJILIS*, 5 (1-2) Jan-June 1992: 55-71.

Defines information. Attempts to find out the information needs and requirements of engineers employed in various industrial units of Dewas city near Ujjain (MP), based on a survey with questionnaire method. Mentions their sources of information and scope of information required. Suggests that there should be a library in all industries and users be trained in the use of library and library resources.

025.56 (1) Information Satisfaction

Users Satisfaction

JOSEPH, ROSAMMA 1538

An assessment of user satisfaction with collection and services :A study of the Calicut University Library, *RDAL*, 60—69.

Gives a brief profile of Calicut University Library to assess the satisfaction of users regarding collection and services, to assess the use of library facilities by readers and to offer suggestions for improvement of the situation.

JOSEPH, ROSAMMA 1539

An evaluative study of services provided by the Calicut University Library and departmental libraries, *IJILIS* 6 (3-4) July-Dec 1993: 231-239.

Makes a survey to ascertain users satisfaction with the library services and facilities provided by the Calicut University Library and its departmental libraries. Reports the results of survey and expects that it would enable the library administration to channalise its services effectively for bringing maximum satisfaction to users.

KAPASI, HEERA 1540

Librarian in pursuit of the simple truth - Users' satisfaction, *Iaslic Bull* 37 (4) Dec 1992: 247-250.

States the ultimate goal of library and information services is to provide access to information to the maximum satisfaction of users. Mentions that Ranganathan sensitised the library professional to the needs of the users. Describes that the new technology should be utilised as infrastructural facilities for service and user satisfaction. Discusses that librarians should act as gatekeepers and guides to the electronic culture and information supermarkets. Presented as Presidential Address at the 15th IASLIC National Seminar held at Annamalai University during 26 to 29 Dec 1992.

NAGIREDDY, Y, UMA, V and TALPASAI, G 1541

Assessment of faculty satisfaction with periodical collection: A case study, *Luck Libn* 25 (1-2) Mar-Jun 1993: 25-31.

Surveys the information needs of the faculty of the University of Hyderabad and the extent of satisfaction. Concludes that because the periodical collection is not uptodate it is unable to satisfy the needs due to which research is delayed or is not possible in micro and interdisciplinary areas, and international standards can't be maintained. Gives useful suggestions.

SAHA, KARUNA 1542

Influence on usres' satisfaction other than library parameters: A study in users' behaviour, *ALE*, 71-81.

Discusses the roles assigned to library and librarians. Mentions that users' satisfaction depends on the quality of services provided by the library. Describes how to measure the quality service by library dimensions, users background etc. Studies 15 special and academic libraries of Delhi and 200 users to get their response. Analyses data thus collected to know the psychology and users satisfaction.

025.56 (1) Information Seeking Habits

GUHA, B 1543

Information seeking and communication behaviour of Indian scientists-NISSAT Study, *NISSAT Newsletter* 12 (1) Jan-Mar 1993: 18-22.

Reports about the summary of the study conducted by the Institute of Social Analysis and Communication under the sponsorship of DSIR in 1992. Mentions the sample of study, pattern of library use, keeping abreast of current developments, relative importance of types of documents, finding relevant documents in specific topics, tools used for obtaining data type information. Mentions steps taken to obtain copies of documents, use of INSDOC services, use of online facilities, publication rate of scientists in the sample, time allocation for information gathering activities, and information through invisible college.

INFORMATION SEEKING and Communication behaviour of Indian scientists: NISSAT study, *CLIS Observer* 10 (3-) July-Dec 1993: 54-59. 1544

Reports about the study conducted by the Institute of Social Analysis and Communication under the sponsorship of DSIR, Govt of India. Presents a summary of the study about the information seeking behaviour of Indian scientists including library use pattern, getting documents and information in them, language barrier, etc. Based on 148 respondents from six research and research-cum-teaching institutions in Delhi.

JAGGA RAO, N V and KANKACHARY, M 1545

Information seeking behaviour of the humanists, *DAB*, 174-179.

Defines the concepts 'humanist' and ' information seeking behaviour'. Makes a literature review about the symbiosis between humanists and information seeking behaviour. Suggests that computer applications will have to be made to the field of humanities.

NISSAT, NEW DELHI 1546

Information seeking and communication behaviour of Indian scientists, *CLIS Observer* 10 (3-4) July-Dec 1993: 54-59.

Reports about the NISSAT study made to ascertain the information seeking as well information communication behaviour among the Indian scientists working in different organisations, therby revealing interesting results about them, in collecting data and information and in publishing their papers, etc.

NWEKE, KEN M C 1547

Information-seeking habits of human and veterinary medical scientists (HVMS) in Borno Sate, Nigeria, *ML*, 309-312.

Gives the concept of information seeking habit. Discusses patterns of ways HVMS in Borno State use to get information. Discusses reasons for the ways they use information. Describes problems of the ways they use to get information. Gives the methodology a combination of questionnaire and interview. Provides the results and discussions.

PANGANNAY, N B and RAMAKRISHANANA RAO, N 1548

Information gathering habits of R & D personnel of selected large scale industries, *INICAE* 12 (1) Mar 1993: 25-42.

Presents data/information pertaining to information gathering habits of R & D personnel of industries. Examines factors which may have some bearing on information gathering habits. Highlights certain factors requiring consideration and suggests ways and means for improvement of industrial library units in respect of staff, collections and services.

025.58 USER STUDIES/SURVEYS
INFORMATION USE PATTERN
LIBRARY USE STUDIES

AHLAWAT, S 1549

Increasing efficiency and effectiveness of library usage : Report of the Seminar, *Her Lib Sci* 32 (3-4) July-Dec 1993: 242-245.

Reports about the Seminar held at BBK DAV College for Women, Amritsar on 3 April, 1993 with Keynote Address by P N Kaula, and presidential remarks by Bakshish Singh. Mentions that the Business Sessions were chaired by Prof AP Srivastava and P N Kaula, while the former also deliverd an address to the assembly on how to increase the library use.

KAWATRA, P S 1550

Library user studies: A manual for librarians and information scientists, Bombay : Jaico, 1992. ix, 301 p.

Divided into 11 chapters, deals with need and importance of user studies. Describes about user behavior user needs and UE, Collection development and user studies. Explains methods and technique of user studies. Reviews user Studies conducted in India and abroad. Gives useful appendices.

KOGANURMATH, M M and KARISIDDAPPA, C R 1551

Importance of information/user need studies for the planning and design of a technical institute library, *Jl Inf Sci* 3 (2) Oct-Dec 1992: 57-71.

Introduces the information management. Gives definition and objectives of user need studies. Reviews research made in technical planning and development. Discusses role of user need studies in planning design with justification. Outlines user needs and behaviours studies done in the Karnataka Regional Engg College Library, Surthkal, keeping in view the planning and management. Concludes with benefits of such studies.

PURKAYASTHA, PRADIPTO DAS 1552

Information use pattern and analysis of literature in the field of social action, *Iaslic Bull* 38 (3) Sept 1993: 133-136.

Studies the authorship pattern, geographical distribution of authors, information use pattern and obsolescence rate of literature based on the data from journal *Social Action*, vol 39, 1989. Shows that single authorship is more prevalent, and majority of authors are affiliated to institutions, and in India, Delhi concentration. Shows citing of 12 documents on average by Indian social activist, depending heavily on Indian publications and book literature. Reveals that 10 journals contain more than 61% of the relevant information.

SADASIVAMURTHY, P, SIDDAMALLAIAH, H S and BHANUMATHI YADAV, B R 1553

User-based evaluation of library and information system in day-to-day work, *Luck Libn* 25 (1-2) Mar-Jun 1993: 1-5.

Describes that regular evaluation plays and important role in the development of a library and information system and evaluation can be integrated in the routine activity of the library service. Explains how the system can be evaluated through user interaction. Indicates how direct or indirect users can be utilised for evaluation.

SHARMA, PANDEY S K 1554

Library user studies: A manual for libraries, New Delhi: Ess Ess Publications, 1992. 301 p.

Deals with the subject of library use studies, their usefulness for the librarians to know about their users so that their information requirements could be met with the latest literature available. Makes emphasis on the point that librarians must conduct user studies.

SUBBAIAH, R 1555

User oriented libraries and information centres : A necessity of the day, *ALIS*, V 4, 167-176.

Describes the importance of user and user studies as a functional component of a library/information centre. Portrays user identification, user needs assessment, organization of library and information services on the basis of user information needs and user education for the use of library system and services are key factors in conducting user studies and equipping the library user-oriented. Reports the important findings of a user need assessment study conducted of agriculture scientists of India.

025.585 User Studies - S & T Libraries

SRIDHAR, M S 1556

Review of Indian user studies in science and technology, *ALIS*, V 3, 31-55.

Explains the primacy of information and communication to research and industry. Discusses need for sound, comprehensive and localised user-research industry in India. Presents overview of quantitative and geographical distribution of user research, Puts forth conceptual frameworks and theoretical background for user research, analysis. Reviews selected Indian user studies. Concludes by pointing out the void in nature of user-research in India, need for meta-analysis of literature on user-research and need for systematic study of information behaviour of Indian engineers, technologists and technicians.

025.5861 User Studies - Medical Libraries

SIVAREDDY, K and VARALAKSHMI, R S R 1557

Use pattern of Index Medicus, Excerpta Medica and Biological Abstracts by health professionals - a study, *ML*, 371-377.

Covers use of bibliographical tools by faculty members, practitioners and researchers working in health science institutions in Andhra Preadesh. Examines the use of printed version of Index Medicus, Excerpta Medica and Biological Abstracts from the point of view of their access, knowledge of how to use these sources, need for orientation in the use, most used source, level of satisfaction on the basis of data collected through questionnaire and personal interviews.

025.5875 User Studies - Government Libraries

GUPTA, ANURADHA 1558

Measurement of performance in government libraries: Users view point, *AGLIS Jl* 9, 1993: 31-36.

Highlights need for performance evaluation of libraries. Enumerates various measures for evaluation of libraries with special reference to Government of Indian libraries. Presents an evaluation study of selected GOI libraries on the basis of a sample survey conducted on group of gazetted government officials.

025.5875 User Studies - National Libraries

AINA, JOSEPH O 1559

Use of government publications at the Illorin Branch of the National Library of Nigeria, *Int Lib Move* 15 (3) Sept 1993: 142-145.

Reports about the usage pattern of government publication that form a part of information materials needed by the users of Illorin Branch of the National Library of Nigeria. Finds out the categories of users of resources.

025.5877 User Studies - Academic Libraries

GUHA, B 1560

Use of scientific and technical secondary periodicals in research and academic libraries in Delhi –Summary report, NISSAT News II(I) Jan-Mar 1992 : 15-17.

Reports about the :tudy conducted recently of the Institute of Social Analysis and Communication, Delhi, sponsored by the DSIR on the use of abstracting/indexing periodicals in nine selected Delhi libraries. Gives a brief resume of the finding, giving information about the most preferred abstracting/indexing periodicals, use of other libraries, approach to secondary periodicals, use of advance series, level of satisfaction, maintenance of personal files, need for more abstracting/indexing periodicals, attitude towards sheering. Points out obsequation in libraries and librarians' response.

025.58772 User Studies - University Libraries

BEGUM, KHAISER JAHAN and MUBEEN, M AKHTAR 1561

Catalogue use study in an academic library: A case study of Mangalore University Library, *LID*, 127-141.

Lists objectives of this study as to identify frequency of use of library catalogue and dependence upon it, purpose of using catalogue, and predominant approach to the catalogue. Interprets data collected through questionnaire, observation and informal interviews of the users. Analyses data with regard to frequency of library visit, frequency of catalogue use, sources of search in the catalogue, approach for documents, source of guidance to use library catalogue, type of catalogue preferred, etc. Discusses also about the computerisation of library catalogue.

HARPAL KAUR 1562

The relationship between the academic achievement and library use by post-graduated students in two agricultural universities, *IJALIS* 21, 1993: 33-40.

Studies the relationship of academic achievements of the PG students and the quantum of daily library use on the basis of two samples from Hayana Agriculture University, Hisar and Punjab Agriculture University,Luhiana. Calculates Spearman's Rank Correlation Coefficient for the two different sample groups and their results compared.

JASMER SINGH and HARI SINGH 1563

Needs and expectations of users from a university library, *IJILIS* 6 (3-4) July-Dec 1993: 219-230.

Makes a survey to assess the needs and expectations of users of Panjab University Library, Chandigrah on the basis of a questionnaire delivered to 250 post-graduate students, researchers and teachers. Analyses and tabulates data regarding use pattern, reasons for using library, familiarity with services, satisfaction with lending, reference services, journals, catalogue facility. Gives suggestions.

KIRAN KUMARI, A K RUTH and CHANDRAN, D 1564

Attitude of women users towards library services in Sri Venkataswaran University Library: A study, *LID*, 142-151.

Brings forth importance of user studies. Gives objectives of user studies. Mentions need for user studies. Reports about the objcetvies of the present study as to know the attitude of women users, awareness of women users, and to what extent they are utilising the library services offered at S V University. Gives the results and discussion regarding purpose of visiting library, book collection, circulation, technical services, ILL, CAS, reference service. Offers suggestions.

MALLAIAH, T Y and BADAMI, K K 1565

Library and information service facilities in Mangalore University Library from the research scholar's point of view: A survey, *Ann Lib Sci & Docum* 40 (4) Dec 1993: 155-165.

Describes the relevance and dependability of user study. Attempts to elicit opinions from the research scholars as the users of the Mangalore University Library on the basis of a questionnaire.

Analyses data thus collected covering the use of library collections, library catalogue library service facilities, and the information needs of the users of the library. Highlights suggestions made by the research scholars for the future planning of the library.

MGAYWA, ROBERT M 1566

The use of foreign language journals by social science faculty of the University of Dar-es Salaam, *Int Lib Move* 15 (1) Mar 1993: 26-32.

Finds out the actual use of one segment of library stock - social science foreign langauge serials- so as to find out a rational way of building up the serail collection. Based on a survey carried out in 1991 at University of Dar-es-Salaam.

OYELEKAN, GBADEBO O 1567

Under graduates, utilization of services in Nigerian University libraries: The case of University of Maiduguri Library, *Int Lib Move* 14 (4) Dec 1992: 205-216.

Studies the role of audio visual materials as these are becoming essential part of information provision and dissemination in the University of Maidugury Library. Gives collection of Avs. Makes study on the basis of data collected in 1991-92 from students and faculty about media awareness and materials preferred. Gives adequacy of AVs.

SATYANARAYANA, M 1568

Utility of periodicals in the Andhra University Library: A case study, *Ann Lib Sci & Docum* 40 (2) June 1993: 59-63.

Studies the use made of periodicals by the faculty of Andhra University by using survey research method. Covers users who visited the Library during February to March 1989. Presents analysis of data in tabulated form. Suggests methods to enhance use of periodicals.

025.6 CIRCULTION SERVICES

MISHRA, SANJAY 1569

Charging system: A new approach, *Luck Libn* 23 (2) Apr-June 1991: 63-67.

Gives an account of the necessity of charging systems. Discusses the difficulties faced in the present systems of charging. Describes a new methodology in this respect with its material requirements, charging and discharging procedures, and advantages.

025.6 (1) Circulation and Computers

CHOWDHURY, S and CHOWDHURY, G G 1570

CIRC: A prototype circulation control system using micro- CDS/ ISIS, *Iaslic Bull* 37 (2) June 1992: 73-81.

Provides background information about CDS/ISIS, its system restrictions and major applications. Discusses a prototype circulation control system 'CIRC' which can perform the functions related to circulation control. Describes the desired features of a circulation control system and discusses function of 'CIRC'

GANPULE, S R and WAYDANE, H S 1571

Using barcode for circulation in the Central Library of IIT Bombay, *Ann Lib Sci & Docum* 40 (1) Mar 1993: 12-20.

Explains the introduction of Barcode technology in IIT Bombay. Describes the Barcode system and its implementation. Discusses the pilot project of 500 books in library and information science and 70 library staff members as readers. Gives the alternative strategies for implementing the technology. Mentions about generating Barcode for readers. Mentions the need to design and handling the project.

PALANIYANDY, M V and RAVICHANDRA RAO, I K 1572

Automated circular control system, *Lib Sci slant Docum & Inf Std* 29 (4) Dec 1992: 183-202.

Discusses the importance of the circulation section and the need for the automation of this section. Describes in detail the various databases created and how the program is to be executed for its efficient functioning.

025.6 (1) Overdue Charges

UDOFIA, UDOFIA ITON 1573

Fines on overdue materials in academic libraries: Benefits and abuses, *Int Lib Move* 14 (2) June 1992: 92-95.

Describes what is fine. Discusses the benefits and abuses of overdue fines on library materials in the Nigerian situation. Gives some useful suggestions.

025.62 Inter library Loans (ILL)

HEMA SUNDER NAIDU, G and GUNJAL, S R 1574

Inter library loan service in agricultural libraries in India, Ann *Lib Sci & Docum* 39 (4) Dec 1992: 134-138.

Stresses importance of ILL. Studies ILL relations of the agricultural libraries based on a questionnaire collecting information from 65% of the 152 agricultural libraries. Discusses the type and number of documents borrowed including the response. Suggests certain steps for effective ILL service.

SREEPATHY NAIDU, R 1575

Library cooperation with special reference to ILL (inter library loan), *SPLS,* 26-28.

Recognises the need for ILL and library cooperation. Describes that the public libraries can enter into cooperation with the university libraries. States that the Andhra Pradesh public libraries can organise a systematic library cooperation.

025.62 (1) Document Delivery System

Document Supply System

CORNISH, GRAHAM P 1576

The conflict between copyright and document supply: Real or imagined? *Jl Lib & Inf Sci* 16 (2) Dec 1991:102-112.

Brings forth the conflict between copyright of publishers. authors and document supply systems to make documents more widely accessible. Explains in detail the owners' view regarding undermining sales, depriving authors of income, reward according to use, reward according to value. Gives also users view regarding freedom of access, improved intellectual activity, economic use of resources. Concludes that the conflict is more imagined than real.

DITZLER, CAROL J, LEFEBVRE, VERONICA
and THOMPSON, BARBARA G 1577

Agricultural document delivery: Strategies for the future, *LT*, 51-70.

Deals with the changes in document delivery and ILL in recent times from original document to providing a photocopy, telefacsimile, etc. Discusses on going new technology projects which may influence document delivery, as CD-ROM, online catalogue and database, OCLC, AGRICOLA, ADONIS, communication networks, ES, hypermedia, etc. States that successful libraries will embrace future by incorporating new technology in daily routines.

LAHIRI, A 1578

Established institutions watch out, *NISSAT Newsletter* 12 (1) Jan-Mar 1993: 1.

Speaks in this Editorial about the slackness of a few large institution in the area of document supply services as these have been on no-profit no loss basis. States that because of their slow service many fee-based but efficient supply sources entered the market. Points out that the old sellers' market is gradually giving way to open and competitive real world market environs.

LAHIRI, A 1579

The problem of a document supply: A look at Indian sources and NLA-ASTINFO facility, *CLIS Observer* 10 (1-2) Jan-June 1993: 30-36.

Examines questions relating the finding of a document, locating the right source, etc in detail. Considers the effectiveness of Indian sources and looks at the status of NLA-ASTINFO facility while making some helpful comments and suggestions.

LAHIRI, A 1580

The problem of document supply: A look at Indian sources and NLA-ASTINFO facility, *NISSAT Newsletter* 11 (1) Jan-Mar 1992: 18-22.

Examines some important questions regarding finding a document easily, speedily, right source, time, cost, involved etc. Considers effectiveness of Indian sources and looks at the status of NLA-ASTINFO facility. Discusses it in relation to document supply system of INSDOC. Mentions nodal institution handling NLA-ASTINFO facility.

RAMAIAH, L S and PRAFULLA CHANDRA, T V 1581

Document delivery: A case of NHDC, *DAB*, 304-314.

Gives definition of humanities. Explains information needs of humanities scholars. Mentions humanities research in India with 26% PhDs and highest research projects. Discusses need for document delivery humanities citing examples. Examines the present status of document delivery in humanities in India. Points out need for a national Humanities Documentation Centre. Mentions its function. Concludes with emphasis on resource sharing.

VARALAKSHMI, R S R 1582

Access to medical literature need for a document supply centre: A proposal, *Timeless Fellowship* 15, 1993: 20-27.

States that access to primary information has to be given adequate attention in the era of knowledge explosion . Studies access to medical information sources provided in India by NML, Delhi. Indicates that access to world medical literature is meagre which deprives the user of his rightful access to information. Mentions non-availability of sources as a major drawback. Makes suggestions to start a Document Supply Centre at NML, Delhi.

025.62 (1) British Library Document Supply Centre (BLDCS)

SAHNI, NEERA 1583

British Library Document Supply Centre (BLDSC), In *Souvenir* of CLA, 1992.

Describes the BLDSC, Boston Spa as a centralised source of documents, and gives its collection development. Explains the significance of BLDSC which is indispensable national and world asset with storage area of 160 Kms of shelving and 27,000 Kms of microfilms with 2 lakh journal titles, 30 lakh reports, 5 lakh conferences and 30 lakh books.

025.62 (1) Electronic Transfer

DHAKA, R P and MUJOO-MUNSHI, USHA 1584

Electronic transfer of documents, *Ann Lib Sci & Docum* 40 (2) June 1993: 41-47.

Discusses document transfer options, such as fax and E-mail. Describes the transmission time and the problem to reduce it by reduction in the size of file and increasing rate of data transfer by using right speed modems. Mentions the hardware and software requirements of the purpose.

025.62. (1) Universal Access to Information

MGAYWA, ROBERT M and CHAKRABARTY, SWAPNA 1585

Universal Access to Information: Problems and prospects, *ILA Bull* 27 (4) Jan-Mar 1992: 143-149.

Describes information explosion problem. Explains efforts towards achieving UAI. Discusses that its realization depends upon a set of interrelated factors as availability of information, programs established, goodwill etc. States that though some progress towards UAI has been made there is long way to go.

025.62 (1) Universal Availability of Publications (UAP)

MANDAL, SATYANANDA 1586

Universal Availability of Publications and comprehensive collection- making in India, *Coll Lib* 7 (1-4) 1991: 18-20.

States concept, scope, and development of UAP programme, Discusses the comprehensive collection development, one of the problems with regard to UAP at national level in India. Makes suggestive conclusion.

025.8 Maintenance and Preservation of Collections

025.82 THEFT, LOSS, MUTILATION AND OTHER HAZARDS

MSUYA, JANGAWE 1587

Serials mutilation hazard: The situation at the University of Dar-es-Salaam Library in Tanzania, *Int Lib Move* 15 (2) June 1993: 71-76.

Highlights the findings of the survey of mutilation of journals at the University of Dar-es-Salaam Library. Includes factors which have led to mutilation. Suggests comprehensive measures to be taken in order to remedy the situation.

RAJA RAMMOHUN ROY LIBRARY FOUNDATION, RESEARCH COMMITTEE, CALCUTTA 1588

Loss of books in libraries and remedial measures, *Granthana* 3 (2) July 1992: 143-160.

Reports about the norms of book loss, detecting loss, accountability of librarians and their staff causes of loss of books in libraries, prevailing security arrangements in India, etc. Concludes that mutilation and loss is a human weakness, to some extent it is inevitable which may be written off, and librarian should not be penalised. Report with recommendations submitted to the Dept of Culture, Ministry of Human resource Development, Govt of India in Sept 1992.

SEWA SINGH 1589

Mutilation, theft and misplacement of reading materials in libraries, *IJILIS* 5 (1-2) Jan- June 1992: 48-54.

Describes library as a social institution. States that all

libraries-academic, special and public - are suffering from the debilitating disease of mutilation, theft, and misplacement of library materals. Explains the terms mutilation, theft and misplacement. Discusses their reasons, and identifies issues for consideration. Makes a plea that librarian should not be made responsible for any loss. Points out need for research in this area..

025.82 (1) Stocktaking. Stock Verification

REVATHI, V and RUKMINI REDDY, J 1590

Stock verification in university libraries: Problems and prospects; a case study of O U Library, *ALR*, 197-204.

Defines stock verification. Gives its advantages. Discusses various methods of stock verification. Makes a case study of stock verification. undertaken in the Osmania University Library in the faculties of Public Administration and Biology. Offers various suggestions on the shelf rectification and stock verification. Gives an Annexture of GOC Guidelines for Library Stock Verification.

025.84 Preservation and Conservation

BISWAS, S C 1591

Conservation of manuscripts in Indian libraries, *DAB*, 133-143.

States that the form of book is ever changing, and Mss collections are scattered all over India. Describes various users of the Mss for whom knowledge of classical languages help, but less interest in these languages is contributing to the deteriorating conditions of Mss in libraries. Raises the question of conservation of the scattered Mss all over the country and for this purpose staff need to be given training. Discusses the need for physical amenities for conservation of Mss.

ONWUBIKO, M C 1592

Causes of the deterioration of library and archival material in Nigeria, *Int Lib Move* 14 (3) Sept 1992: 146-151.

Concerns with the causes only of the deterioration of library and archival materals in Nigeria. Does not discuss preservation/ conservation and restoration of bibliographic resources. Gives definition of some terms, and paper manufacture. Suggests some measures for paper house-keeping, storage facilities, temperature, etc.

SENAPATI, SUSANTA KUMAR 1593

Education in preservation and conservation of library materials in India, *ILA Bull* 29 (1-2) Apr-Sept 1993: 39-46.

Defines preservation and conservation (PAC). Discusses needs of education in PAC on library materials. Highlights present international scenario on education in PAC. Elaborates course of study and nature of training of different organizations to contribute and familiarize PAC programmes in India. Makes suggestions and recommendations for awareness and popularization of PAC programmes among library professional in India.

SINGH, R S 1594

Conservation of documents in libraries, archives and museums, New Delhi: 1993.

Deals with the preservation and conservation of documents in libraries, archives and museums, which is so important for the cultural legacy. Discusses the various methods to be followed for this purpose.

025.84 (1) Weeding

BACHALAPUR, M M 1595

Weeding out of books, *CODE*, 165-166.

Deals with weeding out of old and less used collection. Identifies criteria for weeding out of books which includes out of date and obsolescence of literature, change in the curriculum, change in educational policy, etc. Makes some useful suggestions helpful for making a policy of weeding.

ROY, RADHA KANTA 1596

Weeding : A solution of space problems to libraries, *Coll Lib* 9 (1-4) 1993: 21-24.

Provides meaning of weeding. Mentions pre-requisites of weeding. Discusses some normative principles to be followed. Gives some recommendations for weeding including those of UGC, Govt of India, etc. Concludes that it is a difficult task to perform.

SUBRAMONI, T K 1597

Discarding library collections, *ILA Bull* 27 (4) Jan-Mar 1992: 157-160.

Discusses basic issues relating to discarding or weeding of books in libraries in general Discusses why books are discarded, why some are not used. Describes systematic method of discarding, who should decide, and the probable risks of discarding.

026 SPECIAL LIBRARIES

SAHA, KARUNA 1598

Critical issues in measuring and assessing library organisation: A study based on special and academic libraries in India, *ALIS*, V 3, 269-283.

Gives characteristics of service organisations. Finds out factors that can be adopted as a measure of effectiveness in library organisations and factors that contribute to their effectiveness on the basis for data collected from employers, users, supervisors from 15 libraries in Delhi.

SAHA ,KARUNA 1599

Functioning of special librarians, *ALIS*, V 3, 193-214.

Deals with role of structural factors such as size of organization, degree of specialisation, etc in the functioning of special libraries. Measures effectiveness by criteria variables as user satisfaction, employee job satisfaction, group performance, rate of growth, on the basis of data collected from employees, users, supervisers from 15 libraries in Delhi. Indicates that the size of organisation and degree of specialisation are negatively related in special libraries.

SHARMA, RAVINDER KUMAR 1600

New and innovative measures in special libraries, *LIT*, 55-62.

Mentions that the socio-economic development of a nation depends on special librairs. Traces the growth of libraries and library techniques. Discusses the use of IT, computers and online access facilities to databases. Describes computing infrastructure and network development, new technologies of CD-ROM. Mentions hurdles and their removal in implementing IT for which trained human resources are needed.

026.000954 Special Libraries - India

SENGUPTA, I N 1601

Research library scenario in India, *Her Lib Sci* 31 (3-4) July-Oct 1992: 163-169.

Explains the concept of a research library. Discusses some basic problems faced by Indian research libraries including literature explosion, trends in multidisciplinary research, increase in the number of users, lack of manpower and resource, lack of coordination and cooperation, lack of research aptitude among librarian, non-availability of modern technologies, etc. Presents the current status of research libraries and makes suggestions to overcome the problems.

026.0009669 Special Libraries-Nigeria

NWEKE, KEN M C 1602

Providing information services for rural mobilisation in special libraries for national development in Nigeria, *Ann Lib Sci & Docum* 40 (1) Mar 1993: 1-5.

Reports the results of a study of Nigerial special libraries revealing features and shows that available services in the libraries are too sophisticated for rural Nigerians. Discusses information services for rural mobilisation as well as specialised information needs of ruralites. Proposes extension services of the Nigerians special libraries at the community or grass level identified as community information services.

026.02 (1) Special Libraries Standards

BAHL, A K and VIJ, V P 1603

Bureau of Indian Standards: Information services, *STIM*, 56-64.

Discusses about the services of the technical library of BIS which has growth into Information Services Department with three units: Library, ISONET Centre, and GATT Enqury Point. Describes the reference and enquiry services about the latest technological developments. Discusses bibliographic and database services, information builtin and translation services.

026.070172 Newspaper Libraries

JOSEPH, ROSAMMA 1604

Library of newspapers in Kerala: A survey, *Int Lib Rev* 23 (4) 1991: 333-343.

Records a study undertaken on the basis of a questionnaire with the objective of assessing the present state of newspaper libraries in Kerala with respect to their administrative set up, organizational efficiency, library collection, technical processing, services, personnel, and physical facilitates. Reveals that book collecting is inadequate in newspaper libraries and these are not procured regulary; that newspapers mangements do not seem to be enthusiastic about developing library collection. Points out inadequacy of staff, no clipping service, problem of space, and so on.

026.294 (1) Mosque Libraries

TAHER, MOHAMMED and ABIDEEN, MOHAMMEJD ZAINUL 1606

Library services to the people from mosques, *PLD*, 149-155.

Discusses functions of mosque. States that literature on mosque library is still a rarity. Describes the existence of Mecca Masjid Library at Hyderabad. Describes its collection orgenisation, users, etc on the basis of a survey of 48 users of this library. Reports the findings of the study. Makes suggestions for its future possibilities. Gives in Appendix the traditional scheme of classification adopted in Muslim libraries.

026.38454 Radio Libraries

JOSHI, H M 1607

Sound archives in All India Radio, In *Papers*, 58th IFLA General Conference, New Delhi, 30 Aug- 5 Sept 1992, pp, 6.3-6.6.

Outlines the status of present sound Archives in All India Radio. Describes plans for the proposed permanent set-up. States that in the preservation of sound documents, technique plays an important role. Mentions the factors to be taken into consideration while selecting the technique and medium for preservation of aural documents for posterity.

026.4 Language Libraries

BALASUBRAMANI AYYAR, K 1608

The need for a library in Indian languages, *LM*, 147-150.

Explains the need for setting up libraries at all convenient centres in Indian languages, which will provide a potent agency for education of masses. Mentions that these libraries will also preserve the glorious literature for future.

MURTHY, SULOCHANA S 1609

The Central Institute of Indian Languages: Library and documentation activities, *DAB*, 265-277.

Lists objectives of CIIL and its various units to help organise research activities. Discusses computer facilities and applications in the Institute. Describes six Regional Languages Centres. Explains the resources and documentations activities of CIIL including bibliographic services, CAS, catalogue of periodical holdings, preservation of theses, dissertations newspapers reprographic service. Gives future plans and programmes of having NICIIL. Gives its objectives, need. functions and services. Makes a case for linking CIIL with INFLIBNET.

026.5 SCIENTIFIC LIBRARIES

BORIYAN, R 1610

Referential skills - library as a source of learning skills, *Jl Info Sci* 4 (2) Oct-Dec 1993: 58-68.

Deals with the structure of scientific and technical literature. Describes role of scientific and technical library in information transfer cycle. States the use of card catalogue, classification system in referential skills. Guides researchers.

CHAWLA, MOHINDRA 1611

Science, library science and libraries in perspectives, *Univ News* 30 (35) Aug 31, 1992: 33-36.

Describes the perspectives of active researches and university professions about librarians and the reference, university and research libraries in India with special reference to certain science and technical libraries in Delhi. States that computerisation, somehow, has not been successful in India. Points out how to streamline library operations. Emphasises on current awareness services in consultation with the faculty. Suggests an alternative in students/researchers, efficient reprographic services, ILL, etc and called for improvement of quality of interpersonal relation to make library a place of scholarship.

RAMESH, D B 1612

CSIR: Library & information services, *STIM*, 20-24.

Provides brief introduction about the CSIR. Analyses information collected through questionnaire from 15 out of 40 laboratories, in terms of manpower, budget, collection, services, reprographic facilities, computer application, online information retrieval services. Reveals that all libraries offer CAS.

SRIDHAR, M S 1613

Features of contemporary special libraries particularly science and technology libraries in India, *ALIS*, V 3, 255-267.

Enumerates types of special libraries. Discusses characteristic features of special libraries vis-a-vis objectives, users, services, tools and techniques, acquisition, collection, ways of lending and staff of special libraries. Lays emphasis on typical Indian science and technology libraries.

026.59 Wildlife Libraries

RANA, M S 1614

Changing face of the WII Library, WII *Newsletter* 78 (3-4) July-Dec 1992: 20-25.

Mentions the objectives of the library and documentation centre of the Wildlife Institute of India, Dehradun. Points out the reasons for not functioning effectively in the past. Gives its organisational plan, and the layout with circulation section, computer terminates for online catalogue, general and reference collection, current journals, photocopying, reading area, etxc. Mentions about the computerisations. Discusses about the services rendered such as reference and ILL, abstracting and indexing, bibliographic compilation, literature search, press clipping service, FAS, etc. Gives the future planning for online access to international databases, library networking, etc.

026.61 HEALTH SCIENCE LIBRARIES

MEDICAL LIBRARIES

AVRIEL, DEBORAH 1615

Role of health information professionals in the design of new information products, *ML*, PC 35-38.

Identifies information problems in developing countries. Brings out that due to new technologies, new processes and products are now being created and there is a new role for the librarian to play in the production of CD-ROM and Expert Systems.

AVRIEL, DEBORAH 1616

World Health Organisation Health Literature Services programme in a changing world, the librarian as health communicator, *ML*, 495-501.

Deals with WHO programme, its targets, new strategies, WHO information, R&D, integration in resource centres, creation of multisectorial networks, partners in search of solutions in view of global changes.

BOILARD, DAVID W, GELLER, JACK M, ETTL, LORRAINE and ALTOBELLI, JOYCE 1617

Rural health information resources and the library: An interdisciplinary perspective by the health professional, *ML*, 59-63.

States the true nature of rural health information is interdisciplinary as some related literature is found ouside of medical literature. Advocates an intergrated, interdisciplinary and crossdisciplinary literature database for indentifying topics appropriate to rural health care. Discusses the various efforts of the Centre for Rural Service at the University of North Dakota in indetifying appropriate interdisciplinary access points to the current literature and creating a selective relevant bibliogrphy. Also indentifies non-clinical subject headings pertinent to rural health.

SUNYAN, LINDA, LUTZ, EVELYN, and DUMONT, ROSEMARY 1618

Application of the "sense making" model in designing library services for nurses, *ML*, 65-69.

States that medical librarians education preparation focuses on serving information needs of the physicians and not nurses. Describes sense-making model related to information seeking behaviour. Addresses how nurses and librarians can make sense of their shared work situation within situational and contextual constraints. Concludes through survey that nurses may have positive attitude towards libraries.

CHAUDHARY, BIRENDRA KUMAR 1619

Health information in Kala-azar-professional point for view, *ML*, 77-79.

Describes Kala-azar disease trasmitted from man to man. Deals with the source of information and the relevant documents Kala-azar which can help health information. Discusses that health information services equipped with modern, uptodate and scientific components have to play vital role in relation to scientific communication pin pointedly, expeditiously and efficiently. Mentions about the sources available.

DHONGADE, P L 1620

Knowledge on health is everyone's right, *ML*, 117-123.

Mentions on literacy rate in India and awareness about health. Traces history of health. Discusses existing health facilities in India regarding number of colleges and number of doctors in different systems of medicine. States that to provide education to people about health for all by 2000 AD a National Policy on Health is needed. Discusses that health science libraries can lay a leading role to provide relevant literature to achieve all that.

DIXIT, R P 1621

Assessment of health literature information services in Indian health science libraries, *Intl Inf & Lib Rev* 25 (3) Sept 1993: 165-182.

Describes succintly the historical development of Indian health science libraries. Illustrates outcome of study conducted for assessing the strengths and weaknesses of prevalent health literature, information services such as bibliographical, CAS, SDI, MEDLARS/MEDLINE, indexing and abstracting, translation and reprographic of 240 medical libraries belonging to modern medicine. Recommends suitable steps to be undertaken to optimise the utilization of available resources and services.

DIXIT, R P 1622

Information management in health libraries in India, New Delhi: Concept Publishing Company, 1992.

Elaborates the emergence of various systems of medicine and their impact on the development of health science libraries in India. Traces history of health science libraries. Provides information about the existing manpower, their qualifications, health science information resources and their management, the financial aspect, infrastructural facilities and services of 240 health science libraries.

KARIM, S A 1623

Status of health science libraries and librarians in India, *ITAH*, 143-147.

Sketches brief development of medical education in India. Discusses present position and status of the medical libraries attached to the various medical institutions in terms of collection, staff and services and role of MCI in the development of library services and reasons for its inability to play its role as a watchdog body for the balanced growth of medical libraries.

KUMAR, R P 1624

An evaluation of library and information services provided by a medical library, *Lib Prog* (*Int*) 11 (1-2) Jan-Dec 1991: 25-32.

Gives background of AIIMS Library. Lists the services it provides to its users. Reports the results of a survey of the information services conducted through a questionnaire given to 200 users with 88% response. Analyses the collection, photocopying service, use of information services, usefulness of library service. Concludes that feedback will help to improve the existing services

LAW, DEREK G 1625

Modern health science libraries at the cross reads, *ML*, 15-19.

Discusses about the various challenges to the libraries including the one presented by technology in delivery of information to the end user. Explains the challenges at the crossroads, the technology affects medium in which information is presented, development of satellite communication, and the biggest challenge of moving from being a repository of information to winning acceptance of the user for gathering right information for them and telling them how to develop their own information skills

LEMKAU, HENRY L 1626

Management of biomedical media production as an integral component of an academic health science library, *ML*, 233-236.

Describes the broadened role of the Dept of Library & Biomedical Communication from the traditional responsibilities of acquisition, organisation, storage and dissemination of information to include production of information as well. Discusses about the marketing and networking computerized graphics as new opportunities, new knowledge and new technologies.

MARIAPPAN, N 1627

Status of medical libraries and librarians in India, *ITAH*, 149-152.

Describes the historical aspects of medical librarianship in India. discusses comparative status of medical librarians in India vis-a-vis other developed countries. Explains the problems faced by medical librarians with respect to their status. Makes suggestions for existing problems which can be solved with a united front, cooperation and devotion of Medical Library Association of India and other professional bodies.

MEDICAL LIBRARIES: Keys to health information: 1628

Proceedings of the 6th International Congress on Medical Librarianship, and Pre-Congress Seminar on 'Health Information: Impact of Technology Development on its Production, Analysis, Distribution and Consumption', 24-25 September 1990, New Delhi, New Delhi: Medical Library Association, 1992. 2 volumes, 794 p.

Volume I includes all the papers presented at the Congress. Volume II includes Pre-Congress Seminar; Report and recommendation about the inaugural; session, ten plenary sessions and concurrent sessions, and the concluding session.

MEDICAL LIBRARIES: Keys to information: 1629

Proceeding of the 6th International Congress on Medical Librarianship, and Pre-Congress Seminar on 'Health Information: Impact of technology Development on its Production, Analysis, Distribution and Consumption', 24-25 september 1990, New Delhi, New Delhi: Medical Library Association of India, 1992. 2 volumes.

Volume I includes 81 papers presented at the Congress, and Volume II includes the report and the proceedings.

MWAPWELE, DICK W K 1630

Tanzania medical libraries-keys to health information, *ML*, 299-302.

Gives background of medical libraries in Tanzania. Discusses about a survey conducted to study the situation and devise an infrastructure to link all medical libraries and other health information centres into a cooperative network based on the recommendations proposed at the Arusha workshop. Includes major findings that the recognition of the role medical libraries can play is based on the dynamic functioning of the medical libraries as key to health information.

OBAKA, DANIEL NEWTON 1631

The challenge of medical librarianship in Africa, *ML*, 313-318.

Gives origin of medical activities in Africa. Explains the growth and development of medical libraries in Africa. Mentions about the biomedical literature explosion. Points out about the central place of the medical library and information services, the socio-economic dilemma, information on biomedical research in Africa, education of medical librarians. Gives conclusions and recommendations.

PALANIYANDY, M V 1632

Automation of Aravinda Eye Hospital Library using CDS/ISIS, *ITAH*, 67-69.

Explains how the library and information centre of Aravinda Eye Hospital, Madurai, is catering to the needs of its users which include doctors, students, research workers, visitors, para medical staff, and tells the details of various databases available in CDS/ISIS.

PATHAN, A MAJID and KARISIDDAPPA, C R 1633

The health sciences libraries in Karnataka : An overview, *ML*, 331-336.

Points out that hospital treatment is possible through efficient and effective utilization of current biomedical information and through qualitative and timely library services. Mentions that Karnataka has 70 plus health care institutions imparting both graduate and PG education. Presents an overview through a survey of libraries of the pathetic situation in these cathedras of learning.

PESKA, JAN 1634

The impact of medical libraries and health information centres on the future development of public health biomedical sciences in the Czechoslovak Republic, *ML,* 343-347.

Describes main features of information infrastructure in Czechoslovak public health and life sciences together with proposals for further improvement of users access to relevant information. Explains the goals of Institute for Medical Information and of the corresponding network of information centres and medical libraries.

PRASANNA KUMARI, R 1635

Keys to health information: Problems and prospects with special reference to medical libraries in Kerala, *ML*, 355-361.

Observes the scope of medical sciences under the astounding changes brought by medical technology, consequent growth of medical education and research, proliferating medical literature output and achievements in bibliographic control and significance of information and communication technology in providing better keys to the resources of medical information through networks. Considers plight of Indian medical libraries in the light of the above. Proposes for setting up a network of Resource Sharing through national and international databases.

RAY, SIDHARTHA SHANKER 1636

Medical libraries in Third World countries: Their role in awareness, services and research on health and biomedical sciences, *ML*, 365-366.

Discuses 'three-in-one' role of a medical library in a Third World country as more important and vital for health. Highlights the aspects on which a medical library can assist. Discusses three way activities. Provides for major problems in relation to manpower, language, finance, resources and services with reference to Third World countries.

SAHA, S K 1637

User's view of a modern medical library, *Iaslic Bull* 38 (4) Dec 1993: 181-182.

Narrates his experience of libraries during his student days in Calcutta in fifties. Expresses his view of a modern medical library with the coming of new media of CD and online searches. Views the medical librarian as clinical librarian who works as consultant whose services will be utilised for access to medical literature.

SAMUEL, N M and RAJAN, B P 1638

Medical informatics centers at the Tamilnadu Dr MGR Medical University, *Univ News* 31 (49) Dec 6, 1993: 5-7.

Deals with the establishment,activities and services offered by the medical informatics centres at the Medical University in Tamilnadu. Points out its potentials in expanding the information services and fulfilling information requirements of the specialist users.

SUNDARAMMAL, R 1639

Goals and objectives of medical libraries in the information age, *ML*, 463-465.

Observes that health for all by 2000 A D can be achieved if the specialist keeps abreast of current developments in the ocean of medical literature in this information age. Deals with the needs of an efficient information searcher which can be unlocked by a medical librarian who is specially trained in IT and library organization, planning, direction, contract and operation to meet the goals. Concludes how efficiently medical librarian should interact with specialist, students and patients to give right information in right time by using appropriate technology.

VARALAKSHMI, R S R 1640

Information services in medical college libraries, New Delhi: Ess Ess Publications, 1993, xii, 238 p.

Includes six chapters on the subject of medical librarianship. Studies to ascertain the information dissemination in mechanism of medical college libraries. Identifies lacunae in the existing system of medical college libraries in rendering efficient services. Suggests the need for quality library services. Based on a Ph D thesis includes three Appendices, bibliography, etc.

VARALAKSHMI, R S R 1641

Medical college libraries of Andhra Pradesh - a comparative study with standards, *ITAH*, 161-171.

Examines how far the medical college libraries of AP have been fulfilling their objectives of meeting the information needs of users. Compares the date with availiable standards/norms collected through questionnaire. Reveals that holdings and services of the subject libraries are very inadequate due to financial constraints and lack of manpower. States that the existing collection and staff are not at all meeting the required standards.

VIVEKANANDAN, VASANTHA 1642

Characteristics and successful library services at CMC Library, Vellore, *ITAH*, 219-233.

Mentions growth of the library regarding space, budget, collection, users, manpower, searches, etc. Explores how the CMC Library, Vellore provides its services to relate as closely as possible to the goals, strategies and activities of the parent body to the institution population as well as to the growing number of external users in spite of the environmental changes, economic climate and other competitive forces.

WALIA, P K 1643

Health science libraries: Growth and development, *ITAH*, 133-141.

Traces growth and development of health science libraries in India. Discusses the findings of survey carried out to study the prevailing situation regarding library buildings, finance, collection, library staff, organisation of documents and services provided by health science libraries in Chandigarh. Data was collected through questionnaire, personal visits and interviews. Gives suggestions for improvement.

026.61 (1) Medical Libraries and IT

CAMPANILO, ANNA MARIA and FAZIO, ANNUZIATA 1644

Biomedical libraries in Rome: Networks, keys to access, keys to health information, *ML,* 71-76.

Gives importance of libraries and information. States that exponential growth of medical literature and speed with which information is outdated requires librarian to acquire new skills as soon as possible. Describes the creation of computerised library network with the sharing of information resources at two levels of cooperation. Discusses the role of MEDLARS in providing online information

CRAWFORD, SUSAN 1645

Developing the electronic library: The Washington University Library and Biomedical Communication Centre, *ML*, 97-103.

States that in this era of rapid technological and socio-economic changes, health science libraries are challenged by the whole range of new technologies, changes in environs of libraries, computer based systems, and financial problems. Describes the conceptualisation of the Library of Biomedical Communication Centre, Washington University which is a mode in a telecommunication network, and thus mentions evolution of electronic library and the architectural summary.

GUPTA, S P, SRIVASTAVA, DIVYA, SIDDIQUI, A M and KUMAR, R P, *Eds* 1646

Information technology and health science libraries: Papers presented at the National convention and Workshop, New Delhi, Oct 1993, New Delhi : Medical Library Association, 1993. x, 279 p.

Discusses some of the issues concerning health science libraries. Contains 29 papers presented at the MLAI-93, National Convention and Workshop, Oct 13-16,1993, contributed by eminent professionals in LIS. Divided into two parts: Part I deals with application of IT in health science libraries covering the state-of-the-art and practical applications; and Part II deals with growth and development in health science libraries in India and their status with respect to budget, manpower, collections and services vis-a-vis application of modern technologies.

KALIYAPERUMAL, K and THANDAVAMOORTHY, K 1647

A survey of modern technological developments in health care libraries in Madras, *ITAH,* 71-78.

Attempts to find out the usage of modern technologies in health care libraries in Madras, eg, online services, CD-ROM, photocopier, microfilming, AVs, library automation such as MARC, automated circulation control, serial control, acquisition control, etc. Identifies problems in adopting the modern technologies. Makes a survey carried out to find out the various aspects on the basis of questionnaire and personal visit to various health care libraries in Madras.

KUMAR, R P 1648

Application of modern technologies in health science libraries in India: A survey, *Aslib Proc* 45 (3) Mar 1993: 63-67.

Examines in detail the use of modern technologies in health science libraries on the basis of a survey of 54 libraries in Delhi. These technologies are telecommunication, photocopying, micrographics AV, computer applications, online, and CD-ROMs, etc. Aims also to pin-point the need for development of these modern technologies appropriately. Makes some suggestions.

PAI, DAYANANDA and BHAT, K SHIVANANDA 1649

Modern technologies and health science libraries, *ITAH,* 39-47.

Explains that modern technologies play important role in dissemination of health information to researchers, teachers, and students, health care workers, health administrators planners, and public. States that health science libraries are undergoing radical changes with the advent of new IT. Explains objectives of modern information technology and its impact on health science libraries.

026.61 (1) AIIMS Library

KUMAR, R P and KHOSLA, SANTOSH 1650

Database search facility in AIIMS Library: A case study, *ITAH*, 1-7

Describes all the modern facilities as photocopying, microfilming, AVs, computer, E-mail and CD ROM in the AIIMS Library. States that CD-NET workstation became operational in Jan 1993. Describes the operational know how and modus operandi of the CD-NET and analyses users comments. States that different databases available in the Library are MEDLINE, POPLINE,

CANCER, and PSYCHIATRY. Reports about a survey done about users of database search facility.

026.61 (1) Nurses Libraries

PARR, LINDA J 1651

Recent developments in libraries for nurses in Britain, *ML*, 327-330.

Mentions that libraries for nurses have been slow to develop for several reasons. Discusses changes in recent years such as computerisation of library services. Describes the position of library staff in nursing libraries as inadequate and libraries are not being given high priority

026.63 AGRICULTURAL LIBRARIES

BORAIYAN, R 1652

Changing nature of agricultural librarianship: Organisational and managerial aspects, *IJILIS* 5 (1-2) Jan-June 1992: 78-87.

Defines agricultural librarianship. Describes goals and objectives, organisational responsibility of agricultural libraries. States the ethical relations with users, administration and suppliers of information. Sketches the pressure for more services and the application of computers and communication in its activities.

FRIERSON, ELEANOR and LINDSEY, GEORG 1653

Computers and communication: Technologies for the management of international agricultrual information, *LT*, 148-171.

Gives historical basis of today's scientific information explosion. Examines changing paradigm of information retrieval. Focuses on the shift from point of view of codifiers to that of the end users. Examines four key technologies: telecommunications, optical media, data conservation technology, and ES and AI. Describes each technically with evaluation. Highlights the ways in which libraries and information resource centres can employ these new technologies to increase their ability to respond users.

GESSESSE, KEBEDE 1654

Agricultural library and information development in Botswana, *ALD*, 31-34.

Provides a profile of the agricultural library and information development in a Sub-Saharan African country, Botswans. Explains the various aspects of four agricultural libraries under the Ministry of Agriculture. Gives also a profile of the southern African Centre for cooperation in Agricultural Research (SACCAR) in the national and regional agricultural information systems.

KENNEDY - OLSEN, JAN 1655

Management of trends in agricultural libraries, *LT,* 24-50.

Gives purpose of agricultural libraries. Reviews agricultural library trends of the time. Includes those trends, among others, which have deep land permanent impact on agricultural libraries. Describes about the considerable significance for change in US agricultural libraries, and therefore, for their management. Discusses about a new paradigm of librarianship, impact of new IT on these libraries including CD-ROM, computer files, electronic data, etc.

LIVINGSTONE, E D and NARASIMHA RAJU, G V S L 1656

Agricultural library services in Guntur district: An evaluation, *Ialsic Bull* 37 (2) June 1992: 67-72.

Surveys the library and information resources and services for agriculture in Guntur district, Andhra Pradesh. Points out the inadequacies of library facilities. Proposes effective utilization of information resources through library cooperation and networking to support research and education in the field of agriculture.

PASSKOFF, BETH M 1657

History and characteristics of agricultural libraries and information in the United States, *LT,* 5-53.

Traces history of agricultural information coming of America from Europe. Discusses that the earliest U S agricultural libraries were those in professional associations and scholarly societies, and created to serve government agencies. Describes the establishment and development of the National Agricultural Library, one of the most significant libraries in the world. Explains the support given to research and extension work by academic libraries. Discusses about the variety of information services provided by various types of libraries in agricultural sector.

PRASHER, R G 1658

Agricultural libraries for scientists and farmers, *IJALIS* 21, 1993: 1-8.

Points out constraints in agricultural productions in India. States that transfer of technology to farmers is way out to meet the food requirements. Explains that the library must become partner in agricultural production not only for the scientists but also for the farmers through rural library services. Mentions that the Government should support libraries with liberal grants, enactment of library legislation and formulating a national policy on information.

RUSSEL, KEITH W and PISA , MARIA G 1659

Introducation, *LT*, 1-4.

Provides introductory overview of the articles covered in the book on agricultural libraries and information services as a result of the reprint of the *Library Trends*, volume 38, No, 3, 1990. Attempts to find a common ground by covering a full range of topics on agricultural libraries and information services world wide reflecting the state of the art, future trends, and direction.

RUSSELL, KEITH W and PISA, MARIA G, *Eds* 1660

Library trends: Agricultural libraries and information, Jodhpur: Scientific Publishers, 1992. 312 p.

Designed to serve as a handbook for agricultural and other science librarians. Covers articles on acquisition, management, and dissemination of agricultural information of all types and in all formats, as well as the infrastructure of agricultural information world wide. Includes 13 articles from authors from across the world.

SOMASHEKAR, K T 1661

Development of agricultural education and libraries: Indian scene, *IJALIS* 21, 1993: 9-15

Traces the development of agriculture as a government department in India. Mentions the importance of agricultural education and factors responsible for the establishment of agricultural universities. Presents a bird's eye view of the agricultural libraries engaged in establishing databases for their use.

026.63016 Agricultural Libraries- Bibliographies

BIRD, JAMES E and SMITH, JESSIE C 1662

A selected annotated bibliography of agricultural information, *LT*, 191-215.

Emphasises on resources which discuss current and future trends in agricultural information and libraries, user needs, issues facing developing countries, technological advance, and special problems. Provides a framework for understanding the current and future status of agricultural information and agricultural libraries. Divided into 12 sections, and within each section documents are listed alphabetically by first author.

026.64 (1) Nutrition Libraries

MURTHI, S RADHAKRISHNA 1663

Scientific publication and information services at Nutrition Library, *ALD*, 75-80.

Describes in detail the main sources of information for scientists such as periodicals, technical reports, conference/ seminars, news digests/ newsletters. Points out need for scientific information. Mentions use and habits. Discusses services provided to the National Institute of Nutrition, Hyderabad scientists which include bibliographies, catalogues, CAS, information bulletin, press clippings, and so on.

026.665 Petroleum Libraries

TEYAGI, S R 1664

National Convention of Petroleum Librarians, *Her Lib Sci* (3-4) July-Oct 1992: 245-247.

Reports about the Convention of libraries in the petroleum sector in India organised by the Oil Corporation Limited during April 9-10, 1992 to chalk out a plan for the sharing of the resources available. Lists the recommendations made at the Convention.

026.677 (1) NIFT Library

SANJEEV KUMAR and MISHRA, SANJAYA 1665

Use of National Institute of Fashion Technology: A survey, *ILA Bull* 28 (3-4) Oct-Mar 1993: 116-123.

Presents analysis of response of National Institute of Fashion Technology (NIFT) Library users to a questionnaire, regarding the suitability of library opening hours, frequency of library visits, information requirements, information search strategy, most frequently used services and periodicals.

026.77 (1) Film Libraries
Video Libraries

PATEL, CHITRA 1666

Computerised information and management system of stock shots in a video library, *Iaslic Bull* 38 (4) Dec 1993: 175-179.

Defines stock shots as video shots kept in stock of future use whenever necessary as a documentary evidence. Planning of computerised stock shot system was taken up on successful completions of Computerised Information System of Video Library (VILCIX). The system will be user friendly, menu designed. Users can select the different access options and get output in "View" or "Print" mode, depending on the need.

027 GENERAL LIBRARIES

LIBRARY DEVELOPMENT

NAUTA, PAUL 1667

Libraries today: In 60's, not 90's, *In* Ravi, N (Ed), *The Hindu speaks on libraries*, Madras: Kasturi & Sons, 1992, pp 288-289.

Reports about an interview of Paul Nauta, IFLA General Secretary held on 7 Feb 1992. Nauta describes Indian libraries still not doing much good as far as services are concerned, and the libraries are in 1960s and not in 1990s. Outlines certain measures to increase more and more services to the readers. These include telling them about literature, photocopy services, ILL, and for this they may have AVs, computer, etc.

027 (1) Libraries of Future

LANCASTER, F W 1668

Libraries in the year 2001, *Her Lib Sci* 32 (3-4) July-Oct 1993: 163-171.

Refers to the print on paper era and shift to an electronic society. Discusses the advent of computer and its applications to libraries and publishing. Examines implications of transitional phase. Highlights capabilities of electronic system. Evaluates the growth of electronic communication, online services, SDI, etc. Forecasts advent of electronic library and electronic librarian, decline in the use of present day libraries. Puts forth the enhanced role of librarian in the new situation.

MAHAWAR, K L 1669

Information handling in libraries in the 21st century, *LIS*, 135-143.

Traces growth of IT. Describes the application of new IT in order to visualise the future of the library. Explains its applications such as telecommunications, networks, online services, electronic publishing, and microforms. Discusses the state of libraries in the 21st century and the concept of E-mail.

RING, K 1670

The path to a tele-library through knowledge management services, *Lib Sci slant Docum & Inf Std* 29 (3) Sept 1992 : 143-147.

Based on a lecture delivered as the Annual Lecture on Informatics at New Delhi on 8th Feb 1992, states that development of communication facilities helps libraries to give access to people beyond its four walls and help delivery of information at the point of use. Mentions still the need for a library as the principal facilitator of knowledge providing relaxed and recreative reading, self education, etc. Defines tele library. Mentions teleaccess as one more part of library services in addition to all the other traditional services.

SUBBA RAO, A and RAJALAKSHMI, V 1671

Libraries in 21st century in India, *Ann Lib Sci & Docum* 39 (3) Sept 1992: 89-93.

Mentions about the change in the meaning of the word 'Library' in recent times. Describes the present state of libraries in India. Discusses some of the centres such as INSDOC, DESIDOC, etc which are providing state-of-art information services. Discusses future of libraries in India which may have less of printed materials.

027 (1) ARCHIVES

AINA, JOSEPH OLUFEMI 1672

Administration and arrangement of archival materials : Surveys of the process of five national archives in Nigeria, *Int Lib Move* 15 (4) Dec 1993: 169-174.

Discusses the methodology followed to carry out the survey on the basis of questionnaire. Analyses the findings of each of the five archives on the parameters of administration, arrangement, use and users, and library. Gives a summary of the findings.

PAL, S S 1673

International organizational effort for the preservation and management of recorded resources, *Int Lib Move* 15 (3) Sept 1993: 154-160.

Describes such international organization as UNESCO, IFLA, SAA (Society for American Archives), and their effort towards preservation and management of archival sources. Calls for inter-professional organization.

027.00901 Libraries - Ancient India

KRISHNASWAMI AYYANGAR, S 1674

Libraries in ancient India, *LM*, 63-68.

Traces the history and establishment of libraries in ancient India. States that it had university libraries all over, libraries set up by Muslims, and so on.

027.00902 Libraries - Medieval Period

SHARMA, A K and SHARMA, S N 1675

A historical survey of the library of some Muslim kings in Medieval period, *Lib Prog (Int)* 12 (1-2) Jan-Dec 1992: 26-30.

States that Mughal kings being lovers of books, paid much attention to the development of education as well as libraries during their period. Describes the contribution of Babur, Humayun, Akbar, Jahangir, Lal Begh, Shah Jahan, Aurangzeb, towards their libraries which had collection of books and other materials of concerned period.

027.00903 Libraries - Mughal Period

CHOPRA, H S 1676

Imperial Library of the Mughal emperors, *Luck Libn* 24 (4) Oct-Dec 1992 : 149-153.

Describes the growth and development of art, literature and music during Mughal period in Indian history. Mentions that Mughal emperors like Babur, Humayin, Akbar were fond of books and libraries. Describes how the Imperial Library was developed by the Mughal emperors.

PRASAD RAO, T V S 1677

Development of libraries under Akbar's patronage, *Lib Today* 15 (10) Oct 1993: 1-3.

Discusses about the growth and development of libraries and literature under the partronage of Akbar the great as he was a great lover of art, literature and books

027.054 Libraries - India

Library Development - India

VISWANATHAN, C G 1678

Indian libraries have really made the grade, *In* Ravi, N (Ed), *The Hindu speaks on libraries*, Madras : Kasturi & Sons, 1992, pp 290-294.

Reports about the views of Paul Nauta, and responds that standards and norms of library services be related to quality and not quantity, and an effuluent society like the US has failed to meet the standards. Even in the absence of national standards for public libraries,Indian libraries have launched data transmission networks throughout the country. States the difficulties of depleted finance, rising prices, etc. Concludes that Indian libraries are not in the sixties, but they have made the grade.

027.05413 Library Development - Orissa

MAHARANA, SARAT CHANDRA and BARDHAN, NIRMAL CH 1679

Libraries of pre-independent Orissa : Brief history of the Fakir Mohan Memorial Library, Balasore, *IJILIS* 6(1-2) Jan-Dec 1993: 148.

Describes briefly the setting up of a small library in 1922 after the name of a well known poet Fakir Mohan and managed by students, and also it served to some extent as a public library in Balasore town. Mentions how it was later donated to the Zilla School where it is kept as the Fakir Mohan section.

MOHANTY, K P 1680

Progress of libraries in Orissa from 1912-1936, In *Souvenir*, 38th All India Library Conference, 21-24 Nov 1992, Bhubaneswar, pp 37-39.

Explains the library development in Orissa since 1912 such as school, college, public and village libraries. Outlines the difficulties faced by these libraries in the state.

PARIDA, BAMAN 1681

Libraries in Bhubaneswar, In *Souvenir*, 38th All India Library Conference, 21-24 Nov 1992, Bhubaneswar, pp 11-20.

Explains the setting up and activities of academic libraries, public libraries, departmental libraries, special/research libraries.

Concludes that public library service in the city is very poor. Gives list of libraries in the city of Bhubaneswara.

027.0514 Library Development -West Bengal

MUKHERJEE, NIRMAL 1682

Development of library services in the state of West Bengal, *Granthana* 4 (1-2) Jan-July 1993: 113-116.

Traces briefly the history of public library development in West Bengal upto the major part of 7th Plan. Describes also the present administrative set up, book deposit, training programme, library services rendered and assistance received from Raja Rammohun Roy Library Foundation.

027.05414 (1) Library Development - Calcutta

OHDEDER, A K 1683

Library development in Calcutta, 1700-1900, *Iaslic Bull* 37 (1) Mar 1992: 1-14.

Traces library development in Calcutta during four distinctive phases spanning the period 1700-1757, 1758-1800, 1800-1857, and 1858-1900. Some of the important libraries set up during this period were The Asiatic Society (1764), Calcutta Public Library (1836), Fort William College (1800), Sanskrit College (1824), Hindu College (1836), Bangiyo Sahitya Parishad (1895). Mentions several other public libraries and reading rooms set up during this period. Presented at the 200th Iaslic Study Circle, Calcutta.

027.05456 Library Development - Delhi

KRISHNA ANANT, V 1684

Il l-equipped for research and reference, *The Hindu,* New Delhi, Sunday, Aug 30, 1992, Special feature, A.

Gives a critical look at some of the important libraries in Delhi such as those attached to the IIT, CSIR, ICSSR, ICHR which are handicapped by collection, space, funds, staff, etc. Points out Nehru Memorial Museum and Library as an exception, and is one of the leading libraries in the world today. Suggests large scale reorientation of the library network.

027.0678 Library Development - Tanzania

NGOZI, I S 1685

Libraries, education, creativity and the reading habits in Tanzania, *Int Lib Move* 14 (4) Dec 1992: 161-174.

Takes a general look at the condition of Tanzania's education system and library scene. Looks at different organs and professions that should work together to achieve the desired goal. Discusses various problems such as lack of educational set up, lack of appropriate books in libraries, lack of creative imagination. Suggests ways of arresting the situation.

027.06894 Library Development - Zambia

CHISANGA, CHILESHE J J 1686

Factors affecting utility of keys to resources in Zambia: A professional librarian's point of view, *ML*, 81-84.

Analyses the factors such as human resources, financial resources, IT, printed materials, networking, affecting the utility of keys to resources from a Zambian professional librarian's point of view. Gives the impact of the availability of keys to resources on library users and personnel.

027.0669 Library Development - Nigeria

IWE, J I 1687

Libraries and information in national development - the case of Nigeria, *Int Lib Move* 15 (2) June 1993: 87-100.

Attempts to analyses the role of libraries and information services in the development of Nigeria from the eve of independence to the present day. Examines the possibility of a National Information Network System in Nigeria. Points out what could constitute problems in the realization of such a venture.

027.1 PRIVATE LIBRARIES
PERSONAL LIBRARIES

ALLAUDDIN, SHAIK and ROUT, R K 1688

The library of Tipu Sultan, *CS*, 31-38.

Provides a detailed profile of the library of Tipu Sultan in which were kept books collected from far and wide which were classified. Gives also the arrangement of the catalogue prepared by the Britishers.

027.4 PUBLIC LIBRARIES

GOPALA MENON, C 1689

Public libraries, *LM*, 114-115.

Discusses the utility of public libraries as instrument of education. States the need to stack them with good books on art, literature, industry, commerce, religion, sociology, science, and so on.

GOPINATH, M A 1690

Community information services for public library system, *Lib Sci slant Docum & Inf Std* 29 (1) Mar 1992: 26-31.

Observes that public library system in India is still in the mould of the 19th century scholarship, as it has been slow to respond to the contemporary needs. Analyses a case study for developing community information services in public library system. Presents the inputs, with details, needed to be put into information policy perspectives.

JAGGA RAO, N V and PRAFULLA CHANDRA, T V 1691

Role of public libraries in community information service, *SPLS*, 14-17.

States that community information centres will be a major step towards effective dissemination of information to the masses in rural areas. Proposes a Community Information Network (COMNET), a multi-tier structure with a national centre, regional centres, state centres, district centres, local centres. Highlights role of public libraries in community information programmes.

KRISHNASWAMI AYYAR, CV 1692

On public libraries, *LM*, 77-81.

Makes a case for libraries, and good books, such as classics, should be kept in them including books on all subjects as geography, history, popular science. politics, economics, all the Puranas and religious books, agriculture, etc. Points out about their arrangement, binding, and create proper environment. Mentions of library tax to finance the public libraries.

MOORE, NICK 1693

Measuring the performance of public libraries: A draft manual, *Granthana* 3 (1) Jan 1992: 57-85.

Prepared for Unesco, this manual attempts to identify that

pattern of coordinated measures. Discusses in detail, the eight basic principles according to which it is compiled. Explains measures of resources, as bookstock and other materials, staff resources, building. Gives the measures of outputs also.

MOORE, NICK 1964

Measuring the performance of public libraries: A draft manual, *Granthana* 3 (2) July 1992: 161-205.

Prepared under contract to IFLA and published by UNESCO in 1989, explains about the consumer opinion, adapting the measures, interpreting the results, bibliography, glossary of terms, and so on. Continued from *Granthana*, 3 (1) January 1992.

NAIDU, G HEMA SUNDER 1695

User services in modern public libraries towards improving readership, *SPLS,* 5.1-5.6

States the role of libraries. Defines a library user. Gives aims and objectives of public libraries. Outlines the user services like document services, information services, CAS, reference service, computer service, etc, to improve the readership of the modern public libraries. Studies the District Central Libraries for this purpose.

ODUSANNYA O K 1696

Development at the grassroot level: The strategic role of the library, *Int Lib Move* 14 (1) Mar 1992: 39-44.

Looks into the library as a factor of development in rural areas. States that school library can perform this function of the public library in rural areas. Both school and public libraries should function in coordination and cooperation for promoting learning and use of libraries for independent study.

PANTULU, V RAMDAS 1697

The library and nation building, *LM*, 12-14.

Describes the purpose of a public library which is now an integral part of public education. States that library should be given more publicity so as to reach it to far flung areas. Mentions about the features of public library movement;

PATIL, L M 1698

Wanted: A public libraries network: Tribute to Dr S R Ranganathan, *Bhavan's JI* 39 (20) May 31, 1993: 23-25.

Pays tribute to Dr S R Ranganathan in his Birth Centenary year. Describes his contribution particularly in getting the public library network which unfortunately could not be accomplished even after 46 years of independence. Makes an appeal to the Government of India to initiate uniform legislation for making public library services obligatory.

PAWAR, S S 1699

Public libraries role and eradication of illiteracy: A conceptual framework, *IPLA Souvenir*, No. 16, 5 p.

Discusses eradication of illiteracy through libraries. Proposes that a useful approach to combating illiteracy is to find reading material at the right stage of difficulty. Mentions various efforts made by the Govt of India, and other agencies to eradicate illiteracy including NAEP. Proposes a public library structure. Makes suggestions.

PUBLIC LIBRARY system in West Bengal: 1700

Ranganathan Birth Centenary Workshop, 11-13 September, 1992, Calcutta, Organised by the Directorate of Library Services, Government of West Bengal in collaboration with the RRRLF, Bengal Library Association and the West Bengal Public Library Employees Association.

Includes papers on four topics set for the Workshop, namely 'Actual picture of the libraries in West Bengal...', 'Public Library service in West Bengal... and 'The role of library in the movement of literacy, science and culture.

RAMAIAH, L S 1701

Public libraries and public finances in India: A critical perspective, *Her Lib Sci* 32(3-4) July-Oct 1993: 171-180.

Describes information as important resource hence information infrastructure be developed. Stresses importance of public libraries in transfer of knowledge to people. States that public libraries require mandate of law and adequate finances for their efficient functioning. Discusses various aspects of financial provisions. Suggests a proportional method providing a certain percentage either of the education budget or of state budget for public libraries.

RAMAN NAIR, R 1702

Public library purpose, *PLD*, 6-17.

Points out the origin of the concept of public library which is based on the free access for the people. Traces history of libraries and the quality of library services in ancient India. Discusses the modern definition of public library giving its objectives as mentioned by Ranganathan and ALA. States that for continuous personality development, human adjustment, spread of education, political awareness, social development, economic development etc, public library service is essential. Summarises the possible future situations in the changed social context.

RAMAN NAIR, R 1703

S R Ranganathan and the public library system *Her Lib Sci* 32 (1-2) Jan-Apr 1993: 21-29.

Discusses the work of Ranganathan in achieving functions and objectives of public libraries. Evaluates Model Public Library Act, 1930, model library bills and plans of Union Library Bill and library legislation in various states. Also discusses National Library Policy of 1986. Concludes that government should give priority to public library system legislation.

RANGANATHAN, S R 1704

Philosophy of 'Free book service for all', *Lib Sci slant Docum & Inf Std* 29 (3) Sept 1992: 119-126.

Reprinted from 'Free book service for all-an international survey', published in 1968. Defines the term 'All'. Gives the beginnings of free book service for all. Discusses social forces leading to free book service for all. Describes agencies for promotion of free book service for all. Mentions need for legislation for this commitment. Points out need for training of personnel to give such a service. Discusses the financial position for this purpose. Gives standards for viability.

RANGANATHAN, S R 1705

Rural library service in the West, *In* Madras Library Association: *The library movement: A collection of essays* by divers hands, Madras: MALA, 1929; Reprinted by Government Press. 1992, pp 122-124.

Discusses about the rural library service in the West that aims at providing literature to increase the value of school education, and its basis is the formation of a central collection of books. Talks about mobile library system also.

RANGANATHAN, S R 1706

A typical municipal library of the West, *In* Madras Library Association: *The library movement: A collection of essays* by diverse hands, Madras: MALA, 1929; Reprinted by Government Press, 1992, pp 143-146.

Describes in detail the library system of a Municipality of the West which consists of a central library and several branches and delivery stations. Mentions that a library has seven departments: lending, reference, magazine room, news room, children, local collection, technical department.

TREHAN, G L 1707

Public library movement and public library system - a dream conversation with Ranganathan, *In* G L Trehan and Girja Kumar: *Ranganathan Birth Centenary Monograph,* Chandigarh: Chandigarh Library Study Circle, 1993, pp 24-26.

Reports the conversation the author had with Dr S R Ranganathan at a night about the public library problems and setting up of an integrated system so as to provide efficient service, free of charges, to all.

027.4 (1) Mobile Libraries. Bookmobiles

SRINIVAS AYYANGAR, V V 1708

A library at every door and in every house, *LM*, 43-45.

Gives the importance of printed book, as the essence of life and thought of greatmen. Points out the importance of reading habit. States that library movement is conceived to wake the nation of book lovers. Emphasises the importance of mobile library to take books to the door of everyman.

027.4 (1) Rural/Village Library

Community Libraries/Information Centres

GUPTA, SUSHMA 1709

Community library; an approach to rural development in developing countries, *Int Lib Move* 14 (3) Sept 1992: 110-117.

Outlines the problems of the developing countries. Discusses importance of community library. Makes a case for setting up a community library. Describes components of community library, media resources centre, extension services. Discusses its need for Nigeria and recommends that Govt should take this task seriously.

MANORAMA SRINATH 1710

Eradication of illiteracy and community service by part time libraries in Tamil Nadu - a model plan, *SPLS*, 2.1-2.4

Treats public library as one of the most important agencies of mass education. Gives the importance of Community Information Services in satisfying daily information requirements of a common citizen - literate and illiterate as sometimes libraries also fail here. Presents a model plan for Community Information Service and eradication of illiteracy in Tamil Nadu through part-time libraries.

RAMASWAMI SASTRI, R S 1711

The rural library as the main basis of rural reconstruction, *LM*, 46-49.

Describes the ways and means of rural reconstruction, and lays emphasis on the role of rural library in educating the masses. Discusses that books and libraries can change the life of peasants as a library is the people's university. The rural libraries be stocked with good books and even mobile libraries be started.

RANGANATHAN, S R 1712

Public library service in the West, *LM*, 122-124.

Discusses about the rural library service in the West that aims at providing literature to increase the value of school education, and its basis is the formation of a central collection of books. Talks about mobile library system also.

SITARAMMAYYA, PATABI 1713

Libraries - a factor in village reconstruction, *LM*, 24-25.

Describes how village libraries were set up in Andhra, but soon movement shifted to Madras. Points out that gradually the rural libraries in Andhra became the victim of party squabbles.

SIVARAJA PILLAI, K N 1714

Villabe libraries, *LM*, 136-137.

States that the area of library movement and library development has been neglected so far. Suggests that a District committee be given the responsibility of founding village libraries which will spread knolwledge and remove illiteracy. Mentions that these village libraries should have books in Indian languages.

SWAMINATHAN AYYAR, R 1715

Libraries as an aid to popular education, *LM*, 127-129.

States the importance of rural libraries to remove illiteracy. Mentions that to every rural school a library should be attached and made accessible to villagers.

VENKATAPPAIAH, V and PRAFULLA CHANDRA, T V 1716

Community information centres in the developing countries with special reference to India, In *Papers,* 58th IFLA General Conference, New Delhi, 30 Aug - 5 Sept 1992, pp 0.31-0.33.

States that information poor are unable to take advantage of the social welfare programmes. Describes that the feudal landed gentry, vested political leaders and business communities are sabotaging the development programmes and economic reforms. Suggests that establishment of Community Information Centres (CICs) will be a major step towards effective and efficient dissemination of development communication to the masses in rural areas.

VENKATASUBBAIYA, V 1717

Village library in Alamuru area, *LM*, 125-126.

Discusses that in Alamuru area, the village libraries have played important part in rural reconstruction alongwith cooperative societies.

VISHWAMOHAN, V 1718

Rural libraries for rural development in AP, *ILS*, 2 p.

Mentions importance of information in modern day society. Describes need for rural library services and mentions that many libraries in AP have been rendering services to the rural areas.

027.4 (1) Circulation Libraries

CHANDRAIAH, I 1719

Circulation libraries: A study, *Granthana* 4 (1-2) Jan-July 1993: 37-40.

Studies the nature of circulation libraries that exist in Tirupati town. Examines kind of users, financial and literary status, profitability and their modus operandi. Concludes with the observation that till the public libraries are developed in India, circulation libraries will have to be around to meet the reading demands of the public.

027.454 Public Libraries - India

ANDHRA PRADESH LIBRARY ASSOCIATION 1720

Seminar on public library system at crossroads, organised on the occasion of 36th Andhra Pradesh Library Conference, held at Vijaywada during 11-12 Jan 1992. Hyderabad: Andhra Pradesh Library Association, 1992. Various pagings.

Contains 13 articles in English and 13 articles in Telugu presented at the 36th Andhra Pradesh Library Conference held in Jan 1992, and cover different facets of public librarianship.

DASGUPTA, KALPANA 1721

Role of public libraries as communication centre for socio-economic development, *TDF*, 83-87.

Defines role for public library according to Unesco. Explains need for information in a developing society. Outlines different kinds of communications such as oral, documentary, AV, films, TV, traditional media. Explains the role of public library as a communication centre, particularly in Indian context with a need to activate all developmental activities.

INDIAN PUBLIC LIBRARY ASSOCIATION, HYDERABAD 1722

Souvenir of All India Public Library Conference, Hyderabad, The Author, 1992,

Contains 19 articles in English, and each article with separate pagings. Brought out on the occasion of the Conference held during 25-28 Feb 1992 at Guntur, and organised by Indian Public Library Association.

KALIA, D R, BISWAS, S C, KRISHAN KUMAR and BARUA, B P 1723

Guidelines for public library systems and services, *TDF*, 15-57.

Mentions need for guidelines, definitions, library standards, Indian public library through the plans. Discusses objectives and functions of public library, categories of public libraries. Explains public library system, its need, model, role of SCL and other libraries. Discusses structure and administration of public library services, library finance, reading material, library personnel, physical facilities. Organisation of materials, library records and statistics, application of IT, planning public library system at various levels.

KAULA, P N 1724

Keynote address: An evaluation of public library policy and development, *IPLA Souvenir*, 12 p.

Mentions his association with A P Public Libraries Association. Defines a public library. Mentions its purpose. Narrates the story of public library movement in India since 1910. Laments that NPE did not specify the role of each type of library. Describes in detail the National Policy on Library and Information System of RRRLF. Points out lacunae in the policy document and suggests the outline on the analogy of the US. Identifies issues for consideration such as Union Library Bill, National grid of libraries, structure and linkages of public libraries, planning and development of libraries, public library extension activities, aided libraries, and public library standards.

KHANNA, S N 1725

Public library system at state level vis-a-vis the national public library system, *IPLA Souvenir*, No, 19, 10 p.

Gives data of literacy in India. States library and aid to education. Discusses functions of a national library. Reviews the efforts made so far in the field of public library development at national level in our country from 1931 Model Library Act to various State Library Acts. Gives the present scenario. Proposes national public library system.

MAJEED KHAN, M A 1726

Role of public libraries in India: Structural and functional approach, *IPLA Souvenir*, 5 p.

Traces the historical development of public library movement in India during the 20th century. Mentions that structures of integrated public library system is linked with legal base, and the importance of National Policy for Public Library System in India depends upon understanding of democracy.

MUKHERJI, BARUN KUMAR 1727

Multi-faceted approach towards development of public libraries in India, *TDF*, 78-82.

States that RRR Library Foundation has been striving for years for inplementation of a national policy for public library development in India. Mentions on the basis of user survey that public libraries are not being used by all classes of society; however the scene is changing gradually. Mentions types of public library services, NAPLIS, Unesco recommendations for public libraries, introduction of community information service as a challenge.

NARASIMHA SASTRY, S V 1728

Public library movement in India, *LM*, 31-34.

Examines the role of public library movement in disseminating knowledge and culture throughout the country. States that the scope and extent of public libraries be made widely known through propaganda; all libraries be organised to strengthen and consolidate them so that library movement could grow.

RAGHAVAIAH, A 1729

Public libraries and national policy, *IPLA Souvenir*, 4 p.

Explains the role of public libraries as institutions of popular and perpetual education. Traces the origin of information service. Stresses the need for uniform public library system in all states. Gives a brief account on the National Policy for public library and information services. Appeals for encouragement to library associations.

RAMAIAH, L S 1730

The state of public libraries in India: The need for alternative public finances to the library cess, *TDF*, 58-66.

Explains the relationship between society and information, state and information. Defines public library. Describes public libraries in Indian context. Discusses the state of library legislation, and the financial provision in the public libraries acts. Argues the case against the library cess and gives alternative public finance. Makes some useful suggestions. Appends a list of recognised public libraries in India.

RAMAN NAIR, R, *Ed* 1731

Public library development, New Delhi: Ess Ess Publications, 1993. xi, 178 p.

This is published as Dr S R Ranganathan Centenary Volume for the remembrance of his contribution to the development of public library system in India. Includes 16 articles on different aspects of public library system including one on the life and work of Dr S R Ranganathan, another on National Library of India.

RAMESH BABU, B 1732

All India Public Libraries Conference: A report, *Her Lib Sci* 31 (1-2) Jan-Apr 1992: 62-65.

Reports about the Conference on 'National Policy for Public Library System in India' organised by Indian Public Library Association (IPLA) during 25-28 Feb 1992 with 180 delegates at Guntur. After Inaugural Session, there were four business sessions of the Seminar directed by P N Kaula, in which 24 papers were presented. Gives also the resolutions adopted at the Conference.

RAMESH BABU, B 1733

An analysis of public libraries system in the legislation-based states in India: Need for national policy, *IPLA Souvenir*, 9 p.

Mentions need for an effective public library system. Highlights the provisions in the 'NAPLIS' on legislation giving overview of library legislation in India. Presents a comparative analysis of the public library system in the states where library acts are in force. Stresses need for National Policy for Public Library System. Outlines future course for the successful implementation of National Policy.

SATHIKUMAR, C S 1734

Public library development in India, *PLD*, 18-30.

Gives a prelude of libraries in ancient India, including the British impact of their growth. Discusses library movement in the states. Explains the eight states with library legislation, thereby making a brief survey of library movement in the various states and UTs. Suggests that centre should bring out an Indian Library Act which provides for coordination of state library and information system at national level.

SEMINAR REPORT "Right to Information, Democracy and Role of Public Libraries," June 13-15, 1992, *Luck Libn* 24 (4) Oct-Dec 1992: 165-168. 1735

Reports about the National seminar organised by the UP Library Association on the "Right to Information, Democracy and Role of Public Libraries" during June 13-15, 1992 at Narendra Dev University of Agriculture and Technology, Faizabad. Prof P N Kaula delivered the Keynote Address. In all, 20 papers were presented in four sessions.

SHARMA, S K and VINOD KUMAR 1736

Need for establishment of National Library and a network of public libraries in Garhwal Himalayas, *Lib Prog (Int)* 12 (1-2) Jan-Dec 1992: 1-5.

Gives physiography and background of libraries in Garhwal Himalayas. Discusses need for a library network in Garhwal area. Describes place and shape of a National Library in Garhwal Suggests a few points of consideration at appropriate level of library system in removing illiteracy from the masses of the region.

THOMAS, V K 1737

Census 1991 and its implications on public library development, *Granthana* 3 (1) Jan 1992: 41-56.

Details the census report 1991 with critical comments in Part 1. Part 2 is a study of the implications of the census figures with respect to the per capita expenditure on public library service, urbanization, sex ratio, literacy rate, etc. Touches also on the direct contribution of the census to public library service.

TREHAN, G L 1738

Public library movement and public library system - a dream conversation with Ranganathan, *In* his: *Ranganathan Birth Centenary Monograph*, pp 24-26.

Reports the conversation the author had with S R Ranganathan at a night about the public library problems and setting up of an integrated system of public libraries in the country.

TRIPATHI, TRIDIB and BARUA, P 1739

Need for public library planning in the developing countries with special reference to India, *LID*, 16-25.

Explains the role of public library as per Unesco manifesto including its educational role, informational role, receational, and cultural role. Discusses the need for public library planning. Describes the phases of planning of public libraries. Highlights public library planning in India with regard to information needs of illiterates, women, children and ruralites. Concludes that public library planning be done according to the needs of each country.

VARALAKSHMI, R S R 1740

Open learning and public libraries, *ILA Bull* 28 (1-2) Apr-Sept 1992: 10-15.

Presents an overview of open learning programme undertaken

in different countries. Mentions about nature of participants in open learning programme and methods of delivery. Discusses in detail the role of public libraries in open learning. Describes the Indian requirements that can be met by public libraries.

VENUGOPAL, M V 1741

Librarianship in India: Reflections on the state-of-the-art with reference to public libraries. *LID*, 32-39.

Mentions characteristics of librarianship in developing countries, and India. Explains need for national library policy. Mentions few barriers also. Describes the provision of public library service as a local effort which fails with state imposition of legislation, because of the problem of funding it. Discusses other factors of vital concern which also hold the progress, as lack of proper training, lack of active association, impoverished collections of public libraries, absence of non-book materials. Points out the need for a network. Gives few useful suggestions.

027.4541 Public Libraries - Northern India

SEWA SINGH 1742

An assessment of public library development in Northern India, *Lib Prog (Int)* 13 (1-2) Jan-Dec 1993: 8-15.

Defines a public library with Unesco's manifesto. Gives purposes of a public library. Highlights the role of library legislation in public library development. Discusses public library services in Northern India. Reports about the surveys already made by a newspaper and discusses the findings in view of the current situation. Makes some suggestions which may help in the establishment of new libraries and maintenance of the existing one.

027.45412 Public libraries - Bihar

027.45412 (1) Khuda Baksh Library, Patna

CHAUDHURI, KALYAN 1743

A treasure-trove: The Khunda Baksh Library, *Frontline* 9 (17) Aug 15-28, 1992: 63-68.

Describes about the stock of valuable and vast collection of Manuscripts - over 18,000 in Urdu, Persian, and Arabic - in the Khuda Baksh Oriental Public Library in Patna set up in 1891. Besides, it also has over 95,000 old and rare printed books, and over 2,000 original paintings of the Mughal, Rajput, Iranian and Turkish schools.

027.45413 Public Libraries - Orissa

CHOUDHURY, N B 1744

Public library movement in Orissa and Dr B B Shukla, *IJILIS* 5(3-4) July-Dec 1992: 235-244.

Gives basic facts about Orissa. Defines public library. Discusses strategies for development of library acts. Discusses library movement in Orissa during 19th century and 20th century. Mentions role of Dr B B Shukla during the last two decades in furthering the library movement in Orissa.

DAS, G N 1745

Public library movement and the development of public library system in Orissa, *IJILIS* 6(1-2) Jan-June 1993: 125-147.

Discusses the development of libraries in Orissa during ancient period, medieval period and in 16th to 19th centuries and their role for mass education. Describes library movement in Orissa during 20th century, vigorous library movement in Orissa from 1973 and Dr B B Shukla's role in it. Describes also the existing library network in Orissa. Suggests for the implementation of public library legislation in the state. Appends the Draft Bill of Orissa Public Library Act.

PANDA, B D 1746

Development of public libraries in Orissa, Volume 1: Analytical aspects, Delhi: Pratibha Prakashan, 1992, xiv, 262 p.

Deals with the development of public library service in Orissa since ancient times to the present. Discusses every conceivable aspect of the public library development in the state with emphasis on the analytical aspects. Describes also about the efforts made for library legislation in the state.

PANDA, B D 1747

Public library organisation with reference to the Department of Culture, Govt of Orissa, Bhubaneswar, *IPLA Souvenir*, 3 p.

Describes the total picture of public library organisation in the state of Orissa. States that the Dept of Culture, Govt of Orissa is looking to the administration for the public library contemplates to bring out a law in the coming session of Assembly and bring out a new Directorate of Public Libraries.

PATRA, BHAGIRATHI, BEHURIA, R K, MISHRA, ASHUTOSH and JENA, A K 1748

Two decades of public library movement in Orissa (1973-1993) and Dr B B Shukla, *IJILIS* 5 (3-4) July-Dec 1992: 161-220.

Traces the history of public library movement in Orissa. Gives the concept of public library movement. Discusses library movement at the national level and role of Dr B B Shukla in arousing library awareness among people. Describes in detail library legislation in Orissa and Dr Shukla's efforts. Also discusses other phases of library movement and Dr Shukla's role in getting the UGC pay scales for Orissa librarians.

SRICHANDRAN, G K 1749

Public library service in Orissa - a status report, *Granthana* 4 (1-2) Jan-July 1993: 79-82.

Describes public libraries at various levels like HKM State Library, District Libraries, Subdivisional Libraries, Ex-district Board Libraries, Integrated and Memorial Libraries and Rural Libraries. Touches briefly on financing of public libraries from 1990-91 to 1992-93.

027.45414 Public Libraries - West Bengal

BOSE, SUBRATA and SIRKHEL, INDRA NATH 1750

Ranking position of different public libraries in Bally policy station aresa, *ILA Bull* 27 (4) Jan-Mar 1992: 178-181.

Evaluates the services of seven public libraries falling in the Bally police station area of Calcutta. Makes a suggestion to the West Bengal Govt to enhance the amount of grant-in-aid for the improvement of services and activities.

PUBLIC LIBRARY system in West Bengal : Ranganathan 1751

Birth Centenary Workship. 11-13 September, 1992, Calcutta, Organised by the Directorate of Library Services, Govt of West Bengal in collaboration with R R R L F, Bengal Library Association and West Bengal Public Library Employees Association.

Includes papers on four topics set for the Workshop, namely 'Actual picture of the libraries in West Bengal...', Public Library service in West Bengal..., Review of West Bengal Public Libraries Act..., and The role of library in the movement of literacy, science and culture.

027.45415 Public Libraries - Tripura

GUPTA, B B 1752

Status report on development of public libraries in Tripura, *Granthana* 4 (1-2) Jan-July 1993: 99-106.

Traces history of public library in Tripura during pre - and post-independence period. Details the prevailing administrative structure, staffing pattern, financial resources, collection development, training and services. Dwells on assistance received from R R R L F during 1985 to 1988. Concludes by delineating gaps and deficiencies in the public library system.

027.454162 Public Libraries - Assam

HAZARIKA, B 1753

Status report on the public library development in Assam, *Granthana* 4 (1-2) Jan-July 1993: 41-44.

Traces beginning of public library in Assam. Narrates briefly history of public library development of Assam. Elaborates on present conditions and services available. Dwells also on training facilities available, RRRLF assistance received, etc

027.4541666 Public Libraries - Mizoram

LIANZAMA, C 1754

Status report of public library development in Mizoram, *Granthana* 4 (1-2) Jan-July 1993: 75-78.

Gives an account of staffing pattern, administrative structure financial resources and collection development of public libraries in Mizoram. Comments briefly on RRRLF assistance. Narrates problems of library development in Mizoram. Highlights difficulties faced by the landlocked states.

027.45417 Public Libraries - Manipur

SINGH, KHOMDON 1755

Public library development in Manipur, *PLD* 126-132.

States the need for public library in the country to make democracy real. Lists important objectives as given in Unesco Manifesto and IFLA Public Library Section. Outlines land and people of Manipur from ancient past to present. Explains library movement in Manipur and need for re-organising the library system. Discusses role of Manipur Library Association and people's involvement to get the Library Act enacted.

SINGH, P ACHOUBA 1756

Public library development in Manipur, *Granthana* 4 (1-2) Jan-July 1993: 69-74.

Explains the administrative structure, staff pattern and financial resources of public library system in Manipur. Presents a comprehensive statement of book collection development during 1984-85 to 1988-89. Highlights the various public library services and training facilities. Touches briefly on RRRLF assistance received and gaps and deficiencies in the development of public libraries.

027.4544 Public Libraries - Rajasthan

BHARADWAJ, C B 1757

Public library system in Rajasthan - a bird's eyeview, *Granthana* 4 (1-2) Jan-July 1993: 83-87.

Discusses briefly about the administration of public libraries, their financing, services and staffing. Presents also an agenda of action for future, and mentions about the efforts put up to prepare library legislation.

027.45452 Public Libraries - Himachal Pradesh

JUSTA, H R 1758

Development of public libraries in Himachal Pradesh, *Granthana* 4 (1-2) Jan-July 1993: 57-60.

Discusses administrative structure of public libraries, staffing pattern, financing, library service, and training. Deals also with RRRLF assistance to Himachal Pradesh and the areas where RRRLF could play greater role in the development of public libraries.

THAKAR, G S, ASHA MARKAN and SHARMA, NEELAM 1759

Growth and development of libraries in Himachal Pradesh with special reference to public library system, *IPLA Souvenir*, 8 p.

Mentions about education, libraries and literacy in Himachal Pradesh. Describes the development of libraries and gives public libraries scenario in the state. Explains a conceptual framework of public library system in H P. Makes useful suggestions.

027.45455 (1) Public Libraries-Chandigarh

RAMOLA, K C 1760

Chandigarh public library system, *Granthana* 4 (1-2) Jan-July 1993: 121-126.

Elaborates on the services rendered by the Central State Library, Chandigarh, various branch/village libraries, mobile libraries, model village library, integrated library centres, etc hence appears to be quite developed system. Mentions that Central State Library, Chandigarh is also the first library in India connected with the General Information Service Terminal - National Information Centre (GISTNIC) Service.

027.4542 Public Libraries - UP

MEHROTRA, R K 1761

Public library development in Uttar Pradesh, *Granthana* 4 (1-2) Jan-July 1993: 107-111.

Traces the history and development of public libraries in UP during the Five Year Plans. Enumerates the proposed development plans during the Seventh Plan and Eighth Plan. Gives also the budget provision for public library development for the period 1980-81 to 1989-90.

027.4543 Public Libraries - Madhya Pradesh

TOMAR, SURENDRA SINGH 1762

Public library system in Madhya Pradesh, *Lib Her* 31 (1-2) Apr-Sep 1992: 45-51.

Defines a public library. Describes briefly the historical development as well as present state of public libraries in Madhya Pradesh. Suggests library legislation for better development of public libraries in the state.

027.45456 Public Libraries - Delhi

027.45456 (1) Delhi Public Library

BALBIR SINGH 1763

Delhi Public Library system: Present status and future plans, *AGLIS JI* 9, 1993: 23-30.

Traces history of Delhi Public Library (DPL). Gives its organisational set up and services being rendered such as reference service, children service, social education service, extension service, prison house service, service for tourists. Describes library branches servicing various zones. Envisages need for modernization of DPL system, networking for resource sharing, and General Information Service Terminal (GISTNIC) under NIC.

027.454558 Public Libraries - Haryana

RATTA, W D 1764

Status report on development of public libraries in Haryana, *Granthana* 4 (1-2) Jan-July 1993: 49-55.

Describes development of public libraries in Haryana and their progress under 7th Five Year Plan, but have not yet reached rural areas. Discusses staffing of libraries, budget provisions, library legislation, etc. Discusses an action plan for implementation of National Policy on Library and Information System including modernisation of library services and libraries' role in formal/adult/ distance education.

027.454799 Public Libraries - Goa

RODRIGUES, PIA DE MENEZES 1765

Development of public library services in Goa, *Granthana* 4 (1-2) Jan-July 1993: 45-48.

Traces history of public libraries in Goa. Describes in detail the present status, financial resources, collection developments and services, etc. Touches also on efforts made in the enactment of library legislation.

027.45482 Public Libraries-Tamil Nadu

RANGANATHAN, G 1766

Public libraries: Tamil Nadu, *Granthana* 4 (1-2) Jan-July 1993: 89-98.

Describes the public library scene of Tamil Nadu, functioning of the Department of Public Libraries and financial assistance received fro RRRLF during 1990 to 1993. Gives detailed picture of various innovative programmes being implemented such as acquisition of free sites adoption of library by institutions, enrolment of every educated person as a member of a library, enrolment of patrons, etc.

027.45483 Public Libraries - Kerala

SUKUMARAN NAIR, N 1767

Public libraries in Kerala - origin and development, *Granthana* 4 (1-2) 1993: 61-67.

Traces the development of public libraries in Kerala with special emphasis on Kerala Granthasala Sanghom's pivotal role. Deals with structure of public library system in Kerala and financing of public libraries during 1985-86 to 1988-89. Highlights the RRRLF assistance to the Kerala library scene.

027.45484 Public Libraries - Andhra Pradesh

INAMDAR, N B 1768

Development of public libraries in Andhra Pradesh, *Granthana* 3 (2) 1992: 115-131.

Studies the development of public libraries in Andhra Pradesh under three periods: pre-independence, post-independence upto 1960, and since 1960. Dwells deeply on development since 1960. Covers structure of AP Public library system, etc. Mentions about low per capita expenditure, poor coverage of rural areas and limited role.

JANARDHAN REDDY, P 1769

Network of public library services in twin cities, *ILS*, 3 p.

Describes the public library services, mobile libraries, branch libraries in the twin cities of Hyderabad and Secundrabad extended through the Hyderabad City Grandhayaya Samstha, an autonomous statutory body under the AP Public Libraries Act, 1960.

LIVINGSTONE, E D and HEMASUNDER NAIDU, G 1770

Modern public libraries - their collection and services to meet the changing need, *SPLS,* 18-22.

Mentions that there is a change in the organisation of library and information services at various levels including public libraries. Describes that public libraries in AP will have to undertake many more programmes for the literate population and adult education. Discusses in detail the District Central Libraries/Branch Libraries in AP with regard to their resources and services.

RAJU, A A N 1771

A look into the problems of public library service in Andhra Pradesh, *LID*, 165-173.

Describes the present structure of public library set up in AP listing the number of different types of libraries. Gives total book stock, periodicals, personnel, library service. Enumerates various problems faced by the 'System' under the Act, include non-remittance of library cess, ban on recruitment, new libraries sans books, lopsided book selection policy, ban on expenditure, etc. Points out unsatisfactory performance of Govt libraries, and non-utilisation of matching book assistance of RRRLF.

RAMESH BABU, B 1772

Towards better public library services in Andhra Pradesh: A proposal, *SPLS*, 6-13.

Makes an attempt to present the state of library services in AP, and emphasises the need for changing the traditional understanding of the concept of public library system. Proposes an ideal plan for the provision of better public library services.

SARADA, K 1773

Public library system of Andhra Pradesh and community information services, *SPLS*, 1-5.

Gives the total number of government libraries, libraries functioning under the jurisdiction of Zilla Grandhalays Samstha, and aided libraries in A P. Explains their administrative set up, growth and expansion, development of library services. Makes a proposal for the introduction of Community Information Services in the public library system of A P.

SATISH, N and BHOOPATHI RAO, S 1774

Critical analysis of the organizational structure of the public library system in Andhra Pradesh, *Luck Libn* 23 (2) Apr-June 1991: 68-72.

Attempts to identify and analyse the organizational factors responsible for creating hurdles in the smooth functioning of the public library system in A P. Suggests possible solutions on the basis of the data collected mainly through observation method. Gives a critical study of the A P Public Libraries Act, 1960.

027.45484 (1) State Central Library, Hyderabad

PAWAR, MANJULA 1775

State Central Library, Hyderabad, *IPLA Souvenir*, 2 p.

Deals with the establishment, growth and development, building, etc of the State Central Library. Explains its various sections giving their unique features.

027.45487 Public Libraries - Karnataka

BARADOL, A K 1776

The role of library in the literacy programme of a district, *LID*, 158-164.

Mentions the role of libraries in post-literacy programme. Discusses the existing library facilities in the district of Dakshina Kannada (Karnataka). Explains the role of public libraries in the district including the mobile library. Discusses also the role of academic libraries, role of newspaper libraries. Makes some useful suggestions for improving the educational level of people.

KARISIDDAPPA, C R, SANGAM, S L and KONNUR, P V 1777

Karnataka State Central Reference Library services: Problems and prospects, *LID*, 152-157.

Makes an attempt to ascertain the Karnataka State Central Reference Library. Mentions present status of services rendered by the SCR Library. Outlines reasons for poor performance by the S C R L. Offers suggestions for improvement.

MALLESHAPPA, T 1778

Public library in Karnataka, *Granthana* 3 (2) July 1992: 133-142.

Touches upon almost all aspects of public libraries in Karnataka, like the Library Act, public library system, library resources, training facilities. Gives information on books purchased, periodicals subscribed to, number of members enrolled. Emphsises on the scope for more diversified activities in public library field.

027.45487 (1) District Central Library, Kodagu

RAJENDRA KUMAR, P Y 1779

District Central Library, Kodagu at Madikeri, Karnataka State: A status report, *CLIS Observer* 9 (3-4) July-Dec 1992: 74-77.

Studies the background establishment of the Library. Evaluates books, building, staff, budget, periodicals, extension activities, donations, thus giving nature and scope of a well organised District Central Library.

027.45488 Public Libraries - Andaman & Nicobar

ADAK, TAPAN 1780

Development of public libraries in Andaman & Nicobar Islands, *Granthana* 4 (1-2) Jan-July 1993: 117-119.

Delineates the public library system in Andaman & Nicobar Islands which had no public library before Independence. Presents the current status report. Gives the assistance rendered by R R R L F during 1986 to 1988.

027.46 Public Libraries - Africa

KEDEM, KOSI A 1781

Libraries as partners in the fight to eradicate illiteracy in Sub-saharan Africa, *Jl Lib & Inf Sci* 16 (2) Dec 1991: 87-101.

Examines situation and causes of adult illiteracy in Africa. Argues that traditional public libraries have not succeeded to eradicate adult illiteracy. Suggests therefore the establishment of special Adult Literacy Libraries. Stresses the importance of stocking these libraries with suitable and adequate reading materials, made easily accessible to rural community.

027.4669 Public Libraries-Nigeria

AINA, JOSEPH O 1782

Children's literature in Yoruba with particular reference to Kwara State Public Library, *Int Lib Move* 14 (3) Sept 1992: 118-126.

Studies children's literature in Yoruba (Nigeria) at the Kwara State Public Library. Regards all persons under 16 as children. Defines children library as an integrated part of public library. Describes availability and use of reading material in the Library including Acs.

027.5 GOVERNMENT LIBRARIES

027.554 GOVERNMENT LIBRARIES - INDIA

GUPTA, ANURADHA 1783

Relevance of Chattopadhyaya Committee Report for betterment of Government of India libraries, *Lib Her* 31 (1-2) Apr-Sep 1992: 52-64.

Presents briefly status report of the Government of India

libraries. Explains the highlights of the Chattopadhyaya Committee Report for the betterment of these libraries regarding their salaries, status, services, etc.

GUPTA, O P 1784

Indian government libraries and information centres: An overview, *AGLIS Jl* 9, 1993: 19-22.

Presents an overview of the government departmental libraries and the information centres in India with reference to modern science such as IT, computer and communication systems, etc. and their impact on the traditional services. Reviews the developments in this area.

JAIN, M K 1785

Government of India libraries and new pay structure of librarians, *AGLIS Jl* 9, 1993: 9-18.

Gives historical background and growth of Govt of India libraries. Discusses recommendations of the Govt of India about the new pay structure and the formula for categorization of libraries. Explains anamolies and the librarians' resentment. Makes suggestions to bring these recommendation to the notice of all librarians so that they can get the benefit of the formula for upgradation of their libraries. Makes comparison of payscales of library staff with other posts with similar pay scales in Govt of India.

JAIN, M K 1786

Government libraries in India: An overview, In *Papers*, 58th IFLA General Conference, New Delhi, 30 Aug-5 Sept 1992, pp 2.1-2.2.

Gives historical background of government libraries in India. States that in spite of lacking facilities like accommodation, adequate funds, latest equipments, they are still imparting efficient reference service. Mentions that some big libraries have their separate buildings and bring out their publications. Mentions that pay scales have been revised. Concludes that the application of computers to various library services is the latest trend.

KAULA, P N 1787

Status of Government of India libraries and the challenging tasks of their development, *Her Lib Sci* 32 (3-4) July-Oct 1993: 203-213.

Discusses structure for government libraries and their character and dimensions. States the challenging tasks of librarians and their new role caused by new technologies. Highlights new activities and services, and application of new technology resulting in automated information systems. Discusses the image and status raised by S R Ranganathan specifying the role of reference librarians. Points out the attitude of librarians after gaining the status.

027.5 NATIONAL LIBRARIES

027.554 NATIIONAL LIBRARY - INDIA

BANDYOPADHYAY, BALLARI 1788

Ranganathan and the role of the National Library, *RAT*, 16-20.

Describes how Dr S R Ranganathan's recommendations in connection with the functioning of the National Library of India have been made effective within the constraints of the system. Discusses about the various National Library services including the automated information services, reprographic services, information network by database communication.

DASGUPTA, KALPANA 1789

The National Library of India, *PLD*, 42-59.

Traces the origin of the National Library from Calcutta Public Library giving the access to people, development of collections, organization of materials and its becoming the Imperial Library by Lord Curzon through an Act to this effect. Discusses the aims and objectives of the National Library housed in its own building, and a nine-storey annexe. Explains the functional set up of the National Library with its professional divisions, conservation divisions, and administrative divisions. Gives the present collevtion as more than 3mn units. Mentions also about special collections. Describes its readers' services. Outlines the modernisation schemes as computerisation, databases and standardisation of diacritical marks. Points out the future plans of the National Library.

DASGUPTA, KALPANA 1790

The role of National Library as a bibliographic centre in a multi-lingual situation: The Indian context, In *Papers*, 58th IFLA General Conference, New Delhi, 30 Aug-5 Sept 1992, pp 1.7-1.9.

Gives background to the present National Library in India. Describes the acquisition policy for collection development. Discusses the Delivery of Books and Newspapers (Public Libraries) Act, 1954. Mentions collection through cultural exchange programme. Discusses the role of National Library as a bibliographic centre. Describes the present bibliographic services including general and retrospective bibliographic services, bibliographic activities of the Indian languages, union catalogue of Indian resources pointing out the problems. Concludes that the National Library must develop linkages and alone can not play the role of the National Bibliographic Centre effectively.

DASGUPTA, R K 1791

National and public libraries of the 1990s, *Granthana* 3 (1) Jan 1992: 1-6.

States the shape of the National Library of India will be determined largely by the shape of the public library system. Exmaines in this context the role of RRRLF in building up a national library policy. Stresses the improtance of creating an intellectual atmosphere necessary for improvement of libraeis. Suggests that rural and semi-rural libraries should be attractive community centres.

HUMPHREY, K W 1792

Ranganathan: National and university libraries, *RAW*, 42-49.

Brings out Ranganathan's contribution to National Library of India on the model of the former National Central Library, London. Discusses his contribution to the setting up of university libraries particularly with the reports he prepared and norms provided for it.

ISLAM, S MAZHARUL 1793

Buhar collection in the National Library: Important information sources in humanities, *DAB*, 144-153.

Gives scope of humanities. Deals with personal collection of books and Mss pertaining to the medieval period available in the National Library of India. Discusses about the Buhar collection in Arabic, Persian and Urdu. Appends a list of them.

KUMAR, P S G 1794

National libraries as carriers of culture, *CS*, 24-30.

Traces the origin of national libraries. Outlines the functions of national libraries. Elaborates the systems of national libraries. Discusses the role played by national libraries. States the goals to be achieved by these libraries in the near future.

THE NATIONAL Library of India, Calcutta: National Library, 1993. 23 p. 1795

This brochure was brought out on the occasion of the 58th General IFLA Conference held in commemoration of Birth Centenary of Prof S R Ranganathan in New Delhi during 30 August - 5 September, 1992. Discusses about the functions, activities, services, and publications of the National Library of India.

STANLEY, M K 1796

Indian National Agricultural Library, *IJALIS* 21, 1993: 26-32.

Emphasises the importance of agricultural libraries. Gives characteristics of a national library. Traces the history of the endeavous to establish a National Agricultural Library in India. Discusses about the IARI Library, its building, collection, users, regional stations, documentation services, user education, and librarians.

SUBBA RAO, C V 1797

National Central Library of India: Proposal for establishment, *Her Lib Sci* 32 (3-4) July-Oct 1993: 181-190.

Discusses the state of libraries where unification of interlinking or coordination among libraries is absent. Though discusseions made at the professional conferences, resolutions passed but not implemented. States that efficient funding, equipment and furniture, staff, services are absent hence the governements donot get the returns they should. Discusses present structure of libraries in the national information system. Mentions functions of NCL. Suggests that Central Secretariat Library can function as NCL as suggested by S R Ranganathan.

027.56894 National Libraries - Zambia

LUNGU, CHARLES B M 1798

University of Zambia Library as the National Reference Library of Zambia, *ALD*, 1-10.

Describes that Zambia Univesity Library has been playing the role of the National Reference Library alongwith three more institutions. Explains the designation and significance of the National Reference Library as the Univesity of Zambia Library deserves the status of the National Reference Library. Describes the reflections on future development of this Library.

027.6 LIBRARIES/LIBRARY SERVICES FOR SPECIAL GROUPS

027.625 LIBRARIES FOR CHILDREN CHILDREN LIBRARIES

RAO, MOHINI 1799

Children's books and libraries in India, In *Papers*, 58th IFLA General Conference, New Delhi, 30 Aug-5 Sept 1992, pp 3.11-3.14.

Gives the present status of children's books in India after 1947 which is uncertain. Describes the efforts of Children Book Trust, National Book Trust, NCERT, and the publishers' problems when there is high prices and low purchasing power, low literacy rate, undeveloped reading habits, adult apathy. States that it is necessary in India to promote reading habits among children through mass media, open more libraries for children. The government and other agencies should play a key role.

027.65 Parliament Libraries

BORAH, BHADRA 1800

Reference and research section in Parliament Library, *LIN*, 17-22.

Traces the genesis of the research and reference section in Parliament Library. Describes the creation of research and reference section. Discusses about 'study Boxes' as an innovation of Parliament Library. Describes the services being prepared and given to MPs, such as background materials, brochures, etc. Mentions about the help regarding the anticipated enquiries of the members.

JAIN, C K 1801

Parliament of India and information management, In *Papers*, 58th IFLA General Conference, New Delhi, 30 Aug-5 Sept 1992, pp

Discusses about the Parliament Library of India, its collection, and services to the Members of Parliament. Stresses on the information management aspect so as to render more effective services to its important users.

MALHOTRA, G C 1802

Library and reference, research, documentation and information services to Members of Parliament in India, In *Papers*, 58th IFLA General Conference, New Delhi, 30 Aug -5 Sept 1992, pp

Describes about the various types of services given to the Members of Parliament which include such sersvices as reference and documentation services, research and information services, and so on.

027.65 (1) Legislative Assembly Libraries

DEBNATH, SATISH 1803

Tripura Legislative Assembly Library: A study, In *Papers*, 58th IFLA General Conference, New Delhi, 30 Aug - 5 Sept 1992, pp

Examines the utility of the library of the Tripura Legislative Assembly. Describes about its collection, the users, the variety of services given to the members of the Assembly.

RAJAMANI, S 1804

Library and information services in Andhra Pradesh Legislative Assembly In *Papers*, 58th IFLA General Conference, New Delhi, 30 Aut - 5 Sept 1992, pp

Discusses about the library and information services being rendered by the Legislative Assembly Library to the legislators in Andhra Pradesh. Mentions about the need to further improve these services so as to improve the efficiency of the members.

027.663 Libraries for Blind. Libraries for Visually Handicapped

PARIDA, BAMAN 1805

Library services for the blind in India, *PLD*, 113-119.

States that in a democratic country, library and information centres play a vital role for formal and non-formal education, hence there is right to library services, as provided in our constitution. Describes that for the social upliftment of people, welfare of the disabled, library services be set up, as the National Institute for the Visually Handicapped which gives services to the visually handicapped. Mentions the need for standards, need for resource sharing networks for the country as a whole.

027.663 (1) Libraries for Handicapped /Disabled Persons

AITUFF, T A 1806

Library services to the handicaped, *PLD*, 99-112.

Defines handicapped. States that they have right to information. Mentions that Parliament Acts in Nigeria and elsewhere provide for facilities to them. Examines implications of managing handicapped libraries in terms of stock and services. Evaluates the efforts made by Govt of Nigeria towards the provision of library services to the handicapped. Makes suggestions also.

MISHRA, SANJAYA 1807

Library and information services for disabled individuals, *Luck Libn* 25 (1-2) Mar-June 1993: 40-44.

Defines the term 'disabled'. Discusses the need for and barriers to quality library and information services for the disabled. Emphasises the need for special education and training of librarians. Makes out a case for a National Policy on Library and Information System.

027.665 Prison Libraries

WOMBOH, S H BENKI 1808

The provision of library and information resources in Nigerian prisons: Status and needs, *Int Lib Move* 14 (3) Sept 1992: 127-139.

Studies the provision of the prison library services in Nigeria, based on the questionnaire using random sampling method. Discovers that Nigeria has libraries in almost every prison, large, medium, small. Gives information about stock, services. Concludes that quality of resources is bad, while the quantity is grossly inadequate.

027.68 Libraries for Learned Societies

027.68 (1) American Studies Research Centre

IYENGAR, SREENIDHI and SATISH, N G 1809

American Studies Research Centre: Resources and services in humanities, *DAB*, 285-294.

Mentions the establishment of American Studies Research Centre (ASRC). Describes the library and information activities of ASRC with its holdings. Discusses library services, the traditional library services. Gives details about its humanities collection and highlights them giving some important sources available in the library. Mentions about other facilities available.

027.68 (1) Royal Commonwealth Society Library

INGRAM, DEREK 1810

A great library is dying, *The Tribune*, Sunday Reading, Feb 28, 1993, p 2.

Discusses the history of the Royal Commonwealth Society Library, London founded in 1868. Describes its rich collection about the history of the British Empire, today's Commonwealth, old and new reports. Finds difficulty of funds, space, etc to house 350,000 books, more Mss, 70,000 photographs, and so on.

027.69 Business Libraries
Industrial Libraries

DESHMUKH, P P 1811

Information support for industrial development, *ALIS*, v 3, 247-254.

Describes the need for information support for the speedy growth of industries at higher, middle and lower level industrial operations. Discusses the ways to synthesize the information and the use of modern technology for its proper dissemination. States in-house documentation and CAS are the essential part of the industrial development of India.

EDOKA, B EZIUKWU 1812

Informaion for industrial development, *Iaslic Bull* 38 (3) Sept 1993: 107-111.

Provides overview of the role of industry in the economy of Nigeria. Focuses on importance of information for industrial growth and need for industrial information service. Offers a robust conception of industrial information potential and proffers realistic actions that would lead to integration of an organised information system with overall industrial development effort.

NEELAMEGHAN, A 1813

Information for small enterprises, Bangalore: Sarada Ranganathan Endowment for Library Science, 1992, 165 p.

Aims at specialised training and guidance of information personnel to cater to the needs of the small and prospective enterprises. Brought out as the first publication of the newly started "Ranganathan Centenary Series"

THAKUR, RANJEET S 1814

Consumption of information in a textile manufacturing unit, *ALIS*, v3, 91-94.

Describes importance of textile industries in economic development of the country and also need for information in the growth of textile industries. Explains role of libraries and information centres in providing information by way of newspaper clippings, periodical scanning and information capsules. Discusses how the information stored collected by different international and national sources is being consumed by the managers and engineers.

TIFAC-CMC-DSIDC Centre for Industry Information, 1815

NISSAT Newsletter 12 (3) July-Sept 1993: 20-21.

Deals with the activities of the TIFAC-CMC-DSIDC Centre for Industry Information. Mentions about its achievement in this area of importance in agreement with CMC.

027.7 ACADEMIC LIBRARIES

DEVARAJAN, G , GOPALAKRISHANAN NAIR, P and KUNJUA, M AHMED, *Eds* 1816

Resource development in academic libraries, New Delhi: Ess Ess Publications, 1992. xii, 124 p.

Covers 16 papers dealing with various aspects of the resource development in school, college and university libraries. This book marks the occasion of the completion of 20 years of the Kerala Library Association, doing well for the cause of the profession.

ESPERANZA, M (SISTER) 1817

Library development through information, *ALD*, 84-86.

Considers the importance of information in our lives and need to start efficient information dissemination services. States the need to build academic information section in view of the courses of study, support to higher studies. Explains the role of information in vocational courses. Mentions tools for collecting information in academic libraries where user participation is becoming important.

GARDE, ASHA 1818

Quality of higher education, a library perspective, *Univ News* 12 Aug 1991: 17-20.

Deals with the poor quality of higher education in Indian context. Supports the idea of a strong library rich in resources with effective services to raise the quality of higher education.

GOPALAKRISHANAN NAIR, P 1819

Resource development in academic libraries: Some practical considerations, *RDAL*, 8-15.

Gives data about the educational system in terms of schools, colleges and universities in India, and the school libraries. Discusses importance of academic libraries and recource development in them. Describes various impediments, such as finance and manpower, to resource development.

ISAAC, DOROTHY, RAJU, A A N and RAMAIAH, L S, *Eds* 1820

Academic libraries: Role in national development: Festschrift volume in honour of Prof N B Inamdar. Associate Editor: D Ramchander Rao, Madras: T R Publications, 1993. xx, 304 p.

Contains 30 articles written by eminent and experienced teachers of LIS and experienced practising librarians, contributed in honour of Prof NB Inamdar who recently retired as Librarian of Osmania University, Hyderabad. Arranges in six Sections: 1-Academic Libraries and their Role (5 articles); 2-Collection Development (6 articles); 3-Management (9 articles); 4-Services (3articles) 5-Resource Sharing and Networking (2 articles); 6-Education & Technology (5 articles).

JENA (DHAL), PUSHPANJALI 1821

University and college libraries of Orissa, In *Souvenir*, 38th All India Library Conference, Bhubaneswar, 21-24 November 1992, pp 26-29.

Describes historical development of university and college libraries of Orissa. Discusses the types, growth of collection, status and qualification of librarians. Gives some suggestions to improve the present state fo the art.

KRISHNA, K M 1822

Need of information principles and their importance in academic libraries of India, *IJILIS* 6 (3-4) July-Dec 1993: 281-285.

Describes the need of information principles in academic libraries of India. Highlights the salient freatures of five information principles. Concludes with their importance in the academic libraries.

KRISHNAMURTHY, M 1823

Library in an academic institute, *LIS*, 29-32.

Describes the Library of the Indian Statistical Institute, Bangalore centre focussing on Statistics, Mathematics, Economic Analysis, Documentation and information science subjects. Discusses its collection, services such as circulation, reference service, documentation service, ILL, reprographic services, CAS, IT, technical processing, periodicals, etc.

RAJASEKHARAN, K and RAMAN NAIR, R, *Eds* 1824

Academic library development, New Delhi: Ess Ess Publications, 1991. 92 p. (Perspectives in Academic Librarianship Series, 1).

Includes 12 papers by Indian and foreign authors on different aspects of academic librarianship such as collection management, CAS, networking, new challenges, national libraries, in-service training, agriculture libraries, and their changing roles as a result of technological developments.

RAMAN NAIR, R and RAJASEKHARAN, K, Eds 1825

Academic library effectiveness, New Delhi: Ess Ess Publications, 1992. viii, 123 p (Perspectives in Academic Librarianship Series, 2).

Includes 12 papaers on the various aspectes of academic librariaship and explains the methods that can assess and improve academic library effectiveness. Discusses about IT, market segmentation concept, citation analysis, bibliometric techniques, user education, and user satisfaction.

RISWADKAR, M R 1826

Evaluation of academic library services, *ALR*, 71-78.

Explains meaning and scope of evaluation in LIS regarding library services. States that total evaluation of library will cover such factors as acquisition, classification, indexing, circulation, reference service, staff. Describes some evaluation studies made as that of Carl White, Cranfield Project, and so on.

SEWA SINGH and AMUDHAVALLI, A 1827

Challanges for academic librarianship, *ALD*, 87-90.

Mentions about the importance of information and information society in which we are now chasing information. Deals with the increasing role of academic libraries in providing access to knowledge. Describes that in view of the changing information needs academic librarians ought to be user-oriented and for this LIS schools should play their key role.

SEWA SINGH and AMUDHAVALLI, A 1828

Challenges for academic librarianship, *CS*, 47-53.

Discusses the changing pattern in academic world and its impact on and the challenges for academic librarianship. Mentions also the professional development of manpower both in the LIS schools and as continuing education programmes.

027.7 (1) Academic Staff Colleges

ASLAM MEHDI 1829

UGC Acadmic Staff Colleges and Refresher programme in India, *Her Lib Sci* 31 (3-4) July-Oct 1992: 225-230.

Describes the need, aims and objectives of Academic Staff Colleges set up by the UGC in selected universities. Explains various Refresher programmes conducted at Aligarh Muslim University. Discusses the subject oriented Refresher courses in LIS conducted by the Dept of Library & Information Science and Aligarh Muslim University. Gives also some suggestions.

027.70954 Academic Libraries - India

ARUN KUMAR 1830

Higher education and role of libraries in India, *Univ News* 30 (35) Aug 31, 1992: 23-26.

Talks about the hard economic times in recent years. Describes importance of libraries in higher education but also discusses the non-performance of libraries. Points out links between the new economic policies and education and the impact of budget cuts on libraries, but states that to maintain education standards allocations for libraries need to be increased and libraries be made the focus of higher education.

027.7095413 Academic Libraries - Orissa

PANDA, B D 1831

The growth of academic library system, New Delhi: Anmol Publications, 1992. vii, 247.

Focuses in the historical development of academic library system in Orissa state since ancient times. Divided into 7 chapters, it assets the attention from ancient, medieval and modern times, and brings facts and figures on libraries of Mathas, Monasteries, schools, colleges and universities.

027.71 COLLEGE LIBRARIES

ARAVAMUDA AYYANGAR, A 1832

College libraries, *LM*, 116-119.

Mentions importance of books and libraries in colleges and universities. Discusses that good libraries shoud be well used and create taste for wide reading. Suggests to have 'open access' in spite of its evils; and that colege library may also be open to the public. Suggests for its proper care and good staff.

KHWAJA ALI 1833

United theological college library, *Inside Outside* 106, Nov 1993: 14-22.

Deals with the activities, functions, and services of United theological college library for the students of theological studies.

SEWA SINGH 1834

Seminar on college librarianship, *Her Lib Sci* (3-4) July-Oct 1993: 240-242.

Reports about the seminar on 'College Librarianship' organised at Guru Nanak Dev University, Amritsar in January 1993 in commemoration with the Ranganathan Birth Centenary. It was inaugurated by the Vice Chancellor of the University, while Dr Sewa Singh gave the introductory and welcome remarks. Mentions that 5 papers were presented at the Seminar. Technical Session was followed by Discussion Session with a Panel of educationists.

SWAROOP RANI, B S 1835

College library effectiveness, *ALE*, 82-87.

Identifies the problems the college librarians face for effective functioning and the barriers to academic library effectiveness. Makes suggestions for improvement by overcoming the barriers. Concludes that in this age of information, communication and distribution of information is a challenging task for librarians.

027.710218 College Libraries - Standards

KONNUR, M B 1836

Standards for college libraries, *RDAL*, 53-59.

Discusses functions of a college library. Gives problems and prospects of college library in India. Explains earlier attempts to devise standards for college library. Discusses standards for collection, library staff, library finance, library services to readers. Hopes that authorities will give due attention to the standards.

027.7154 College Libraries - India

ABDUL KAREEM, S 1837

State of college libraries, *Univ News* 30 (35) Aug 31, 1992: 121-123.

Speaks of inadequate grants from funding sources for collection development. Mentions that the staffing pattern of the college library is hardly adequate. Advises the teachers to make teaching library-centred rather than class room-centred, and let them learn of their own. States that librarians must improve their qualifications to keep with the items. Cites the example of resource creating for clollege library. Exphasises on the need of networking and thus should assume the status of information market.

AMUDHAVALLI, A and STEPHEN, LAWYED 1838

College library facilities in Madras city: A survey and analysis, *RDAL*, 30-34.

Studies to assess the college library facilities in Madras city, and the changes and impacts of an earlier study. Based on a questionnaire, examines the changes in 20 college library facilities over 10 years under three heads: (1) Physical facilities, (2) Resource availability, and (3) Service availability. Indicates no positive trend, hence college libraries are failing to adopt to rapid changes in practice.

BANSAL, G C 1839

A new challenge for the college library in India, *Jl Inf Sci* 3(2) Oct-Dec 1992: 87-92.

States that library services are still considered a low priority area in most of the colleges in India, as there is always dearth of space, staff, funds. Points out that libraries need to be taken as an important area to cater to the needs for knowledge and reading material. Discusses the deteriorating state of acedemic libraries and need for reorganisation of services have been felt.

CHINDHADE, SHIRISH V 1840

The state of our college libraries, *Univ News* 30 (35) Aug 31, 1992: 119-120.

Relates how society is changing from 'reading' to 'viewing'

with TV, VCR, taperecorder, around. Describes the state of college libraries in India for want of a vicious circle of numbers. Laments upon the enormity of declining reading habits among those for whom books are the be-all and the end-all.

INAMDAR, N B 1841

Revitalising the college libraries, *Her Lib Sci* 31 (3-4) July-Oct 1992: 180-191.

Describes the Action Plan of the National Education Policy and the place of college library in education. Discusses factors that bring vitiality to college library which include physical facilities, reading resources, library personnel, teaching and evaluation methods, scientific management and modernisation of work, etc. Puts forth some suggestions for improvement of college libraries.

JANAK RAJ and VERMA, RAMA 1842

Engineering college libraries in India: A survey, *ILA Bull* 28 (1-2) Apr-Sept 1992: 16-34.

Examines the status of engineering college libraries in India in terms of collection, finances, staff, services, and organization, etc. based on data collected through a questionnaire. Gives in Appendix the Questionnarie used as a tool for study.

SEWA SINGH 1843

Ranganathan Centenary Seminar on College Librarianship: A report, *IJILIS* 6(1-2) Jan-June 1993: 156-158.

Reports about a one-day seminar organised by the Guru Nanak Dev University in commemoration with the Ranganathan Birth Centenary, on 15 January 1993. About 70 librarians from all over Punjab participated in the Seminar, directed by the author, and inaugurated by the Vice Chancellor of the University. Discusses about the Technical Session and presentation of papers, the Discussion Session, and vote of thanks.

VERMA, I B 1844

College libraries in Chandigarh - a survey, In *Souvenir* of Chandigarh Library Association, 1992.

Reports the survey of college libraries in Chandigarh which play the key role in the educational institutions. Describes their collection, membership, staffing pattern, building, pilferage and mutilation, extension services, librarian versus assisting staff, etc.

027.715412 College Libraries - Bihar

SINGH, VIRENDRA PRAKASH and SINGH, SANJAY KUMAR 1845

Agricultural college libraries in Bihar; a sample survey, *IJALIS* 21, 1993: 56-61

Studies the status of five out of eight agricultural college libraries in Bihar on the basis of a questionnaire. Describes them in terms of building, book collection and journals, circulation, calaloguing and classification systems, budget, services offered to users. Mentions future plans. Gives useful suggestions.

027.715414 College Libraries - West Bengal

BOSE, SREEKANTA 1846

Library centred education system: A new horizon to the college libraries & librarians of West Bengal, *Coll Lib* 9 (1-4) Jan-Dec 1993: 25-27.

Mentions that library centred education system (LCES)is not a new idea. Explains what is library centred education system. Discusses bad effect of present education system such as private tuition, notes-oriented study, and lack of self-study. Describes programme of LCES as initiation to library knowledge, library hour, library period, individual assignement, etc. Explains the LCES and status of the librarian with reference to the situation in West Bengal. Seeks cooperation of the teachers.

EDITORIAL, *Coll Lib* 9(1-4) 1993: 1. 1847

Describes the present scene of college libraries in West Bengal which is stated to be alarming as in most cases college libraries are ornamental adjuncts of the academic institutions. Mentions about growth without planning, lack of adequate furniture/equipments and manpower.

027.71542 College Libraries - U P

CHATURVEDI, D D 1848

College libraries in Uttar Pradesh, *Lib Prog* (*Int*) 13 (1-2) Jan-Dec 1993: 38-43.

Provides history of college libraries in India. Describes in detail the college libraries in UP pointing out the method of teaching and evaluation, status of college librarian, qualifications and salary scales, merit promotion sceme, membership of teachers association, etc. Makes suggestions for consideration of the college librarians.

027.715483 College Libraries - Kerala

LALITHA BAI, K K and DEVARAJAN, G 1849

Resources in the college libraries in Kerala: Some basic issues, *RDAL*, 22-29.

Highlights importance of college libraries but states that they exist as non-functional appendages today. Offers the prospective solutions to the problems such as lack of library-centred teaching and learning, lack of right books, scientific book selection policy, escalating cost of books, inadequate funds, staff, services, lack of library awareness. Gives some useful suggestions.

027.72 UNIVERSITY LIBRARIES

ADISESHIAH, MALCOLM S 1850

Role of the library in the university, *Univ News* 30 (35) Aug- 31, 1992: 13-14.

Discusses the main function of the library in university education. Gives qualities of library staff for quick retrieval of documents and information. Establishes relation between library and the process of learning so that it is a centre of learning. Mentions means of making the scholar library conscious. Suggests a periodic study of and discussion on the library in its academic bodies.

INAMDAR, N B and RAMAIAH, L S 1851

Inadequacies in the working of university libraries, *The Hindu*, Madras, Feb 12, 1991.

Describes that in their 100-year existence university libraries in India have suffered from inadequate funds and lopsided planning. Examines the various recommendations made regarding the allocation of funds to university libraries since Independence. A comparative statement of norms recommended shows a wide variation. Discusses the two methods of allocation of funds. Makes a case for 20 % of the total expenditure of the university for its library as it is essential tc procure latest books and journals.

ISAAC, K A 1852

Centralised versus decentralised library organisation in a university, *ALR*, 115-120.

Deals with the centralised v/s decentralised library organisation with other models in a university. Explains each organisational set up as with one central library, operational centralisation and service decentralisation, central library and departmental libraries as parallel units, departmental libraries with no central library, subject divisional library set up.

RAMA DEVI, V 1853

Academic research: Role of the university library, *ALR*, 47-54.

Defines research. Gives kinds of research. Describes functions of the universities and libraries support to the functions of the universities. Discusses research function of university library and factors affecting it. Concludes that library plays an important role in higher education and research.

RAMAMURTI, S V 1854

Intellectual conscription, *LM*, 15-20.

Describes the two functions of a university research and teaching and their importance in imparting knowledge. Suggests to have universal compulsory education for fair distribution of knowledge and libraries will serve the purpose. Suggests diffusion of knowledge by graduate students by wandering from village to village.

SETHI, A R 1855

Sustainable development & university libraries, *Univ News* 30 (35) Aug 31, 1992: 69-71.

Describes the situation of economic difficulties and budget cuts for the university libraries which have to sustain. Speaks of information growth, information packages, complexity of damand on libraries. Talks of the times of sustainable librarianship based on better, not more; dependence no, participation yes; global thinking, local action; etc. Establishes relations between the Five Laws and sustainable librarianship and meet the challenge.

027.72 (1) Libraries in Open Universities

NEELA JAGANNATHAN 1856

Libraries in open universities in India: Issues & Problems, *Univ News* 30 (35) Aug 31, 1992: 109-117.

Describes genesis and development of distance education in India. Gives reflections of distance education in NEP, 1986. Provides organisational structure of the open universities. Discusses role of library in Open universities listing the basic objectives of

IGNOU. Describes the network of libraries of Open universities. Discusses the collection development for Open university libraries giving users analysis, selection policies, acquisition, management policies, staffing, resoruce sharing, participation in networks, weeding, collection evaluation. Explains library services to users in Open university libraries. Discusses problems faced by these libraries in providing library services and offers solutions.

027.72 (1) University Data Archives

PAL, S S 1857

University information: Need for building up data archives, *Her Lib Sci* 31 (1-2) Jan-Apr 1992: 39-44.

Explains the need for building up data archives as information support to decision making and evaluation of performance of universities, especially in the context of the National Education Policy. Suggests areas in which computer files can be created for the management of academic data.

027.720218 University Libraries - Standards

GAUTAM, ANIL KUMAR 1858

Need for standardization in a university library system with special reference to University of Rajasthan, Jaipur, *Lib Prog (Int)* 12(1-2) Jan-Dec 1992: 7-16.

Discusses the meaning and benefits of standardisation in a university library system. Evaluates critically the need for standardization in classification and cataloguing practices in reference to the University of Rajasthan Libraries by a random sample survey and personal interviews. Makes some suggestions.

027.7254 University Libraries - India

AMRIK SINGH 1859

Libraries and the academic process, *Univ News* 30 (35) Aug 31,1992: 27-30.

Traces the development and growth of university libraries in India since 1947. Discusses some problems of funds, breach of norms set up by the UGC. Describes college libraries did not receive as much attention as those in university. Studies the role of the UGC and as a result 50% of university libraries do not have a properly appointed person. Raises other issues such as resource sharing and the efforts being made for it.

GHANCHI, D A 1860

The library in the university, *Univ News* 30 (35) Aug 31, 1992: 19-22.

Points out that the university in modern India has to perform six functiions of conservation, transmission, promotion, development, proaction and revolutional functions. States that stress should be shifted from direct teaching to indirect learning through library, as it is a multi-faceted learning centre. And for this there should be a purposeful unison of classroom and the library.

GIRJA KUMAR 1861

Decadence in academic libraries, *The Hindu*, New Delhi, Sunday, Aug 31, 1992, Special feature, D.

Reproduced from *University News,* August 31, 1992, wherein it recalls the glorious past of the university libraries which now are in crisis. Mentions about the environmental deterioration, further deepening the crises, as even the authorities kare also not paying any attention. Blames the librarians as the quality of their training is also deteriorating.

GIRJA KUMAR 1862

Decline and fall of the academic library, *Univ News* 30 (35) Aug 31, 1992: 47-51; Also in *CLIS Observer* 9 (3-4) July-Dec 1992: 86-93.

Gives a critical look at the professional techniques which have not proved helpful. Recalls the glorious fifities and sixties for the academic libraries and librarians, but now they are in crisis. Discusses the environmental deterioration and the crisis are deepening as the authorities donot pay adequate atention to the library. Says that readership is falling so a plea for budget cuts is justified. States that librariand are the real criminal in the act. Laments on the quality of courses and the library science education. Suggests the humanistic content in librarianship. But the game of politics, has ruined the academic library. However, the environment is changing now.

GUPTA, O P 1863

Development of university libraries in India after Independence, New Delhi: Concept Publishing Company, 1992. 227 p.

Examines in detail the aims and objectives of higher education in the context of changing modern world. Traces historical development of universities and university libraries. Focuses on the role of the UGC in building up and modernising the university libraries detailing the quality improvement programme.

HAR SWAROOP SINGH 1864

Some thoughts on an ideal university library, *Univ News* 30 (35) Aug 31, 1992: 15-18.

Mentions role of library in a university. Laments on the serious resources crunch affecting collection development in our libraries. Explains that the modern technology and library systems warrant the need for resource sharing through computerised network, and thus promote research activities in universities. Mentions services a modern university library has to perform. Emphasises the role of professionals and much-needed orientation in new technology in the efficient management of resources.

ISSAC, K A 1865

University libraries in India, In *Papers*, 58th IFLA General Conference, New Delhi, 30 Aug-5 Sept 1992, pp 1.9-1.12

Provides history and structure of university education with 190 universities, 7121 colleges having libraries of their own. Points out disparity between the different university libraries in respect of budget, book resorces and services. Mentions that absence of a national funding policy has led to the haphazard development of libraries. Suggests that a centralised integrated system is desirable for each university with suitable library standards. Describes the need of resource sharing and implementation of INFLIBNET project. Concludes that library use should be made indispensable.

JAYASWAL, P K 1866

Ecology of the university library: An empirical assessment, *Univ News* 30 (35) Aug 31, 1992: 41-45; Also in *CLIS Observer* 9 (3-4) July-Dec 1992: 78-85.

Defines concepts like ecology, organisation, role relations. Discusses hierachical and colleaguial relationship, professional - client relationship, hierarchical relations, superior - subordinate relationship, delegation of authority. Describes these aspects of social system in relation to libraries and library professionals. Mentions some comments of client of actual role attributes of librarians.

KRISHAN KUMAR 1867

Development of university libraries during 1980s, *Univ News* 30 (35) Aug 31, 1992,: 53-56.

Discusses the large infrastructure of higher education with 189 universities and 7121 colleges. Describes the growth of univertisy libraries in India in terms of users, position of univertisy librarians, budget, collections, services, computerization, networking during the 1980s. Concludes that more services need to be provided within the given constraints.

KRISHAN KUMAR 1868

University libraries: Problems and solutions, *ALR*, 3-12.

Presents the current dismal situation of university libraries in India. Identifies major problems faced by these libraries. Describes in detail various suggestions given to solve the problems. These included improved access to resources, innovative practices, resource sharing, user education, user friendly library, management, exchange of publications, professionalisation, modernisation, application of IT, research, etc.

MANGLA, P B 1869

University libraries and librarians in India: An overview, *Univ News* 30 (35) Aug 31, 1992: 3-11; Also in *CLIS Observer* 9 (1-2) 1992: 57-70.

Describes the importance of university library. Traces the devlopment of university education and university libraries in India. Gives reasons for slow development. Discusses role of UGC and foreign assistance in the development of university libraries. Explains status of academic librarians. Brings forth the present scene of the libraries and librarians, their qualifications and positions filled. Discusses their research and other academic activities. Concludes that the trend is quite encouraging.

MITRA CHENOY, KAMAL A 1870

University libraries: A user's perspective, *Univ News* 30 (35) Aug 31, 1992: 31-32.

Compares the library facilities in India and abroad. Deals with the problems our university library system is currently facing. Describes such problems as storage, thefts, reserve section, etc. Points out remedies with the help of new technologies such as networking, security measures, bibliographical services, etc. Calls for change in attitude of administrators.

PADMANABAN, T 1871

Documentation and library services of Tamil University, *DAB*, 261-264.

Describes the library and information activities of Tamil University such as collevction development of Tamil books, periodicals, Mss, rare books, library building, etc. Discusses documentation services such as computerisation activities, doctoral dissertations on Tamiliana, catalogue of palm-leaf Mss. Also discusses special activities ad mobile library, photograph archives, Indian Office Library records, and Tamil folklore achieves.

RAM REDDY, G 1872

Foreword, *ALR*, ix-x.

Considers information as a basic resource for national development of which India has considerable stock. Highlights importance of university libraries in the acquisition of information, national planning, future development. States that university libraries have to face a new challange where cooperation among libraries is needed.

SRIVASTAVA, A P 1873

A university and its library; academic culture and work ethos, *Univ News* 30 (35) Aug 31, 1992: 63-67.

Points out the tragedy that many university and colleges in India will continue to operate even if their libraries cease to exist, reflecting lack of interest in studies both by students and teachers. Studies report that hardly 10% of teachers go beyond textbook reading, hence they require help from librarians.

SUDARSHAN RAO, S 1874

University libraries in India: Their role in academic research, *ALR*, 35-46.

Explains different functions of universities and role of university library in effective research. Points out use of libraries in various stages of research, while it helps in selecting and defining the research topic, initiating research, avoiding duplication of research, providing information of funding agencies, thesis/report writing. Deals also with university libraries services for effective research. Concludes that university libraries should urgently publicise their resources and services.

UNIVERSITY NEWS, New Delhi, Association of Indian Universities, 30 (35) Monday, August 31, 1992. Editor: Sutinder Singh 1875

Special Issue on university libraries, brought out on the occassion of IFLA 58th General Conference, New Delhi, 1992, and devoted to Padmashri S R Ranganathan as a Centennial tribute to the great master. Includes 33 articles contributed by eminent Indian scholars in the field of librarianship, and education.

027.7254 (1)UGC's Information Centres

GUPTA, O P 1876

University Grants Commission and centres for information resources, *Her Lib Sci* 31 (1-2) Jan-Apr 1992: 57-60.

Refers to the educational system and goals set out by various Commisions and Committees. Discusses situation of higher education and its development through UGC. Mentions growth of information activities and setting up of National Information Centres for Science Information at the IIS, Bangalore, and similar centres for social sciences and humanities. Describes the information resources and services rendered from these centres.

027.725413 University Libraries - Orissa

027.725413 (1) Behrampur University Library

PANDA, K C 1877

Behrampur University Central Library: A profile, *CLIS Observer* 10 (3-4) July-Dec 1993: 73-76.

Gives the establishment of Behrampur University in 1967. Discusses about the library building, reading material, library personnel, etc. Focuses on services being rendered by this University Library. Mentions its inadequacies and gives suggestions for the remedial measures. Describes resources, salary scales, and use of its resources. Concludes that it needs to be improved with better funding.

027.7254162 University Libraries - Assam

027.7254162 (1) Gauhati University Library

LAHKAR, BINA MEDHI 1878

Computerisation of Gauhati University Library, *LIT*, 86-91.

Mentions the establishment and development of Gauhati

University Library since 1948. Gives its staff structure, and library members. Discusses factors to be considered while introducing computerised library system. Describes the proposal for installing of computer in the University Library.

027.725482 University Libraries - Tamil Nadu

027.725482 (1) Annamalai University Library

KALIYAPERUMAL, R 1879

Annamalai University Library, In *Souvenir*, XV National IASLIC Conference, 26-29 Dec 1992, hosted by Annamalai University Library and Dept of Library & Information Science, Annamalai University, 1992, pp 61-64.

Traces the history and development of this University Library. Describes its collection of books, journals, rare books, and other reading materials. Explains its services, including interlibrary loan, being rendered to the users.

027.725482 (1) Tamilnadu Agricultural University Library

BORAIYAN, R 1880

Tamil Nadu Agricultural University Library: A profile, *IJALIS* 20, 1992: 7-13.

Describes the establishement, administration and financial position of T N Agricultural University Library. Explains physical layout of building and equipments needed. Mentions about the library collections as books and journals, rare books, reference collection, theses and dissertations, statistical sources, reports, bulletins, etc. Explains services of the library. Mentions its future programmes.

027.725483 University Libraries - Kerala

027.725483 (1) Kerala Agricultural University Library

RAJASEKHARAN, K 1881

Library scene in Kerala Agricultural University, *ALD*, 35-45.

Presents a profile of the Kerala Agricultural University Library giving its present status of the various libraries attached to it with data about membership, distribution of actual staff, availability of resources. Discusses need for coordination among the college libraries. Describes the need for a central library which can act as a clearing house of information and appointment of university librarian, library advisory committee for proper management, the services to be offered, etc. Explains need for computerisation of library activities and interlinking agricultural libraries.

027.725484 University Libraries - A P

SOMARAJU, P 1882

Library support to research in universities, *CRL*, 196-204.

Presents a state of university library system with reference to their documentary sources and information services offered to research community. Includes identification of strength and weakness of library sources, effectiveness of the information services offered in view of the research scholars' needs. Makes a case study of Andhra University.

027.725484 (1) Osmania University Library

ISAAC, DOROTHY 1883

Osamina University Library: A brief resume, *ILS*, 4 p.

Traces the history of Osmania University Library since 1918. Discusses about the finances, holdings, membership, reader services, extension and promotional activities, theses, government documents, UN Publications, gifts, Mss, and so on.

027.725484 (1) Dr B R Ambedkar Open University Library

CHANDRAIAH, I 1884

Library service of Dr B R Ambedkar Open University, *LID*, 262-264.

Explains role of library in distance education. Describes the library services offered by Dr B R Ambedkar Open University Library. Mentions also about its reading materials including non-book documents, and gives also its staff pattern.

CHANDRASEKHRA RAO, V and SUJATHA, G 1885

Open University Library and its relationship with the teaching/ learning programmes - a case study of Ambedkar Open University Library system, *LID*, 247-253.

Describes the Ambedkar Open University Library system and its role in the teaching/learning programmes of the University. Enumerates various problems faced by this Library system such as non-availability of suggested books, facilities to outside experts, bibliographic control of distance education materials, A V aids, library budget, services, etc.

027.725492 University Libraries - Bangladesh

ISLAM, M S 1886

Promotion and development of university libraries in Bangladesh: Report on the study visit in the United Kingdom, *Her Lib Sci* 31 (3-4) July-Oct 1992: 237-241.

Describes the study of university library development in the United Kingdon using modern amenities and their applicability to Dhaka University Library. Identifies present problems of Dhaka University Library and emphasises need for modernised library system.

027.8 SCHOOL LIBRARIES

APEJI, ADECHE 1887

Meaningful children's education: A programme of cooperation between the library and the teaching staff, *Int Lib Move* 15 (2) June 1993: 41-47.

Discusses how a collaborative effort on the part of the school library staff and the teaching staff, can lead to a meaningful children's education. Discusses ways to achieve this aim by way of constant dialogue, curriculum developmets, collection development, libray use and help to children.

BARUAH, APURBA 1888

Libraries nursing education, *LIN*, 65-66.

States that school libraries are the nurseries for sowing seeds of creativity. Points out the importance of school libraries. Describes the school libraries as discussed in the various Committees and Commissions reports in post-Independence India. Discusses their recommendations regarding furniture, personnel, class libraries, etc.

GORDON, CORRIE 1889

The school and the library, *LM*, 138-142.

Highlights the need for setting up school libraries for children. Mentions examples from Britain where they are developing elementary school libraries which can be started in India also. Suggests ways in which other public libraries also might cooperate with the schools.

KUNJU, M AHAMMED 1890

School library - a source for initiating and developing learning skills, *RDAL*, 16-21.

Explains the role of school libraries in educational programme. Mentions purposes of the school library as recommended by American Library Association. Descsribes reading programme, curriculum development, books, reference service, arrangements of library materials, initiation to users, etc. Concludes that existing facilities are far from satisfactory.

NAGARAJAN, M and SIVAKUMAR, R 1891

School libraries in Chidambaram town, In *Souvenir,* XV National IASLIC Conference, 26-29 Dec 1992, hosted by Annamalai University Library and Dept of Library & Information Science, Annamalai University, 1992, pp 69-74.

Mentions aims and objectives of a school library, Describes its educational use, responsibilities, etc. Gives data about the seven school libraries in Chidambaram town (TN), regarding their collection, readers, services, building, staff, etc.

SEN, BANDANA 1892

Meeting the needs of students at an international school, In *Papers,* 58th IFLA General Conference, New Delhi, 30 Aug - 5 Sept 1992: 3.16-3.17.

Describes the elementary school of the American Embassy in New Delhi and its elementary library program as the students have varied cultural and educational backgrounds. Discusses the library programs as reading club, teaching library skills such as Dewey Decimal Classification, and card catalogue, book writing contests, conducated interests surveys, etc. which they find interesting.

SUNIL KUMAR 1893

Changing role of school library in present scenario, *ILA Bull* 28 (3-4) Oct-Mar 1993: 124-127.

Discusses present position of school library in the light of changing trends in school education. Describes role of school library in teaching learning process as well as personality development of the pupils.

027.80954 School Libraries - India

LUTHRA, K L 1894

School library development in India, *CLIS Observer* 10 (1-2) Jan-June 1993: 4-16.

Mentions importance of school library. The NCERT survey of 1993 reveals that school libraries in India are not receiving the attention they deserve. States that their resources in terms of accommodation, reading material and staff are very inadequate in relation to the demand, and supports with tables. Suggests that school libraries can lend quality to education if they are adequately equipped.

RAMAIAH, L S 1895

School libraries in India: An investment for national development, *ALR*, 25-34.

Deals with need for school libraries in India and how these help in developing reading habits. Discusses about reading materials in school libraries. Suggests various norms and guidelines for school libraries. Gives a table providing state wise data about villages, schools, literacy ratio, etc.

027.809669 School Libraries - Nigeria

OMOTSO, R OLADELE 1896

Library services and the new 6-3-3-4 system of education in Nigeria, *Iaslic Bull* 38 (3) Sept 1003: 97-105.

Discusses main features of the new policy on education with more emphasis on science, technology and vocational subjects. Examines the role of school libraries in the new education system taking note of the emphasis on continuous assessment. Discusses the present state of library services in the primary and secondary schools. Mentions that despite unsatisfactory situation of education, functional and effective library services are still possible if educational policy makers are ready to accord libraries their rightful place in the educational process.

028.7 SOURCES OF INFORMATION

REFERENCE SOURCES

AGRAWAL, S P 1897

National social science information resources in developing countries with a slant to India, *LIS*, 183-189.

Defines information ressources. Points out the reasons for lagging behind in the use of information sources because of less use of IT, low priourity in information management programme, lack of information channels, and lack of information consciousness, hence we need national information policy.

AGRAWAL, S P 1898

Social science information resources in developing countries and their international dispersal, *Lib Prog (Int)* 13 (1-2) Jan-Dec 1993: 25-30.

Discusses about the social science information sources and their dispersal in developing countries, though social science information is of low priorty for governments. Makes emphasis on adequate or satisfactory use of inforamtion sources in developing countries. Describes all this in Indian experience.

AMARAKOON, LIONEL R 1899

Gaining access to health science literature, *ML*, 21-27.

States that output of information about health increased by the forms for its generation have produced a variety of information carriers. Examines the ways and means of accessing world's health literature and information using material resources such as periodicals, fugitive literature, commercial in formation services, computerised databases, etc. Evaluates new information storage and distribution technologies of microforms, online and offline searches of MEDLARS and MEDLARS on CD-ROM. Discusses also resource sharing.

AWOGBAMI, P A 1900

Communicative analysis of Annual Reports in Nigerian agricultural institutes/parastatals, *CLIS Observer* 10 (3-4) July-Dec 1993: 84-87.

Mentions aim of agriculture research. Explains the term Annual Report. Describes to look on the results the Annual Reports convey to those who will ultimately use them. Based on a survey on the basis of a questionnaire administered to 470 workers of the 21 research institutes/parastatals. Makes suggestions to improve the production of Annual Reports further so as to increase their use.

BORAIYAN, R 1901

Information sources in agricultural research and development: use of indexing services, *Her Lib Sci* 31 (1-2) Jan-Apr 1992: 16-22.

Describes agricultural literature and its characteristics. States the structure and uses of indexing services like AGRINDEX, Bibliography of Agriculture, Biology and Agricultural Index, Current Contents in Agriculture, Biology and environmental science, and Science Citation Index.

BURAGOHAIN (PHUKAN), ALKA 1902

Source material for South-Asian studies in the United Kingdom, *Her Lib Sci* 31 (1-2) Jan-Apr 1992: 3-9.

Explains the concept of area studies. Discusses Indological and South Asian studies and their areas in libraries in UK. Mentions the source materail available in some centres, and the oriental collection of the British Library, India Office Library, London. Mentions the bibliographical sources. Describes also the Asian collection in Indian Institute Library in Bodleian and other centres/libraries.

HEMALATHA, K, NAGABHUSHNAM, P and
PULLA REDDY, V 1903

An opinion survey of the readers of 'The Hindu' in Tirupati town, *Her Lib Sci* 31-(1-2) Jan-Apr 1992: 45-56.

States the objectives and methodology of collection of data conducted through a survey on the use of the national newspaper *The Hindu.* Gives analysis of data and its findings under various heads. Examines also other features of the newspaper like objectivity, credibility, use of supplements and physical production. Gives also conclusion and suggestions.

JASIMUDDIN, M 1904

The hospital record: A non-conventional reading material for a developing country like Bangladesh, *ML*, 193-199.

Points out health problems in Bangladesh. States that teaching in medical institutions is primarily dependent on experiences hence hospitals and knowledge from foreign books and periodicals is used. Mentions that bio-medical literature in Bangladesh is not enough and hence local hospital reocrds are used as reliable source of information. Explains that IPGMR Dhaka has organised the Hospital Record Centre for record management.

JONES, DOUGLAS E 1905

Sources of agricultural information, *LT*, 172-190.

Provides an overview of the types of agricultural information. The formats now being utilised for its storage and distribution, the organizations which play a role in its creation and dissemination, and where it may be found/accessed. Identifies important questions of limited resources, what to collect, how to improve bibliographic control of library materials, and impact of computers on agricultural sources.

KARISIDDAPPA, C R 1906

Development of reference sources in Kannada: A methodological analysis, *CRL*, 103-119.

Defines a reference book. Attempts to present a methodological analysis for the development of Kannada reference sources, by identifying typology for refernce work in Kannada; and by development of methodology for compilation of reference works in Kannada. Studies the tools from the points of view of library services.

KARISIDDAPPA, C R 1907

Development of reference sources in Kannada; A methodological analysis, *DAB*, 209-222.

Defines a reference work. Gives types of reference books and their importance in the library. Makes an attempt to identify/ formulate a compilation of reference works in Kannada. Concludes that to provide socio-economic benefit to the information generated, it is necessary to build up good reference collection.

LAHIRI, A 1908

Initiatives to facilitate access to S & T information in India, In *Papers,* 58th IFLA General Conference, New Delhi, 30 Aug-5 Sept 1992, pp 2.11-2.14.

Presents the S & T scenario in India. Gives picture of STI market which has to coexist with business and financial information. Describes the role of promotional and executive institution such as government, non-profit and profit organisations. Discusses the strategies for STI market development including use of technologies for access, safeguarding access, contribution to knowledge base, generation of database, etc. Concludes that it should facilitate Indian users to access international sources of information and foreign users of the Indian sources of information.

MAHESHWARI, S 1909

Information sources in law; their role for the legal profession, *Her Lib Sci* 31-(1-2) Jan-Apr 1992: 22-26.

Describes the kinds of information sources available in the field of law and their help to the practicing legal professional. Descrbies the collection. of legal materials in the Mysore Bar Association Library.

MISHRA, B N 1910

Importance of information on wildlife literature, *LIT*, 312-313.

States that in view of the importance of plants and animals, wildlife literature sources of information be developed. Mentions that in this context ENVIS has an important role to play.

MURTHY, S S 1911

Indian science and technology - infromation source, *CS*, 339-351.

Discusses briefly the various sources of S & T information in India, including libraries, technical information centres, data centres, etc. States that most of the information sources function under the central government organisations/departments. Lists information sources Ministry/Dept-wise to give an idea of their hierarchical status.

RAJAM, V 1912

Malayalam reference books in humanities, *DAB,* 223-233.

Attempts to discuss the available reference sources, general as well as specialised, in the field of humanities published Malayalam language. Points out notable scarcity in the production of reference sources in this area.

ROURONEN, KYLLIKI and MANOHAR LAL 1913

Indian information sources : Economics and business, New Delhi: Concept Publishing Company, 1992. 232 p.

Documents various sources - books, journals, government publications reports, doctoral dissertations, institutions, etc in the field of Economics, Commerce and related areas. Maps out reference sources for the researchers to locate and contact right sources without wasting time and energy.

SEN, B K and PRASAD, K V S 1914

Individuals as sources of information: A holistic view, *Iaslic Bull* 37 (1) Mar 1992: 23-30.

Alludes the important role played by individuals as nondocumentary sources of informattion. Points out various situations and contexts in which individuals becoms more important sources in various sectors of activity, such as research, academic, agriculture, industrial, business, social, rural, etc. Points out ways and means of contacting and consulting individuals. Discusses limitations also.

SHAH, P C 1915

TEXICON: Production and publication, *STIM*, 101-106.

Describes the production and publication of TEXICON, quarterly secondary periodical organised and published by NICTAS at ATIRA, Ahmedabad. Points out need, coverage, scope and users of TEXICON. Explains the sequence followed in production and publication of TEXICON. Describes the marketing and publicity of this service.

SUKHBIR SINGH 1916

Reference sources on Punjab: An evaluation-II *Int Lib Move* 15 (2) June 1993: 53-64.

Makes an evaluative study of some of the more reference sources available on Punjab which include such categories as Who's who, handbooks, directories, atlases, gazetteers, indexes and abstracts, union catalogue of social science periodicals. Indentifies materials which are lacking on Punjab.

VYAS, ANJU and SINGH, SUNITA 1917

Women's studies in India, New Delhi: Sage Publications, 1993. 257p.

Includes a variety of reference and information sources on the various aspects of women's studies in India designed to be used by researchers in the subject.

VYAS, S D 1918

What ails Indian social science information sources, *ALR*, 99-104.

Deals with such problems of Indian bibliographical tools as they suffer from finance, staff, lack of cooperation and coordination, lack of user-oriented tools, library networks, computer appplication.

Offers useful suggestions at two levels-discover new techniques, more user surveys should be conducted. Concludes that latest IT should be used to improve bibliographical tools.

028.9 READING INTERESTS AND HABITS

ARVIND KUMAR 1919

Let the books and readers come near each other, *Fortnight* 6 (4) 28 Feb 1993: 1.

Explains that the reading habits are growing these days not only in the adults but in children also. States that it is quite clear from the various book fairs and the sales therof. Mentions that the obstacle rather is the non-availability of books in a variety of subjects people want to read.

CHANDRASEKHARAN, K 1920

The book habit, *LM*, 102-105.

Highlights the value of books in one's life. Brings forth the value of libraries which for its growth and influence, depends on the quality and variety of books it has in its stock.

PANANDIKER, SUREKHA 1921

Promotion of reading habits through home libraries, In *Papers*, 58th IFLA Genral Conference, New Delhi, 30 Aug-5 Sept 1992, pp 3.9-3.11.

States that a personal touch is required to introduce children to books and literature. Describes that the Association of Writers and Illustrators for Children (AWIC) have set up home libraries through member volunteers who keep the library open in her home twice weekly for two hours. This is a unique project that won the 1990 IBBY Asahi Reading Promotion Award.

SASTRI, P P S and SASTRI, S S 1922

The use of librares, *LM*, 163-166.

Survey of promoting childern's education in Malaysia, Thailand and Japan, *Lib Prog (Int)* 11 (2-2) Jan-Dec 1991: 5-8.

Discusses the role of books in education and development of children. Desbribes the need to create a reading culture among childern of Malaysia, Thailand, and Japan as they all are trying to eradicale illiteracy through education. Mentions various efforts being made by these countries in this direction.

SWAMINATHAN, K 1924

Books and life, *LM*, 50-53.

Talks of illiteracy of masses and that of educated people as there is decline of reading habit since the turn of the century. Lays emphasis on the importance and role of books with which we recreate and rediscover. Says that library classes in colleges be started to develop reading.

WEINGAND, DARLENS E 1925

Literacy and reading in Iceland, *Jl Lib & Inf. Sci* 16 (2) Dec 1991: 144-159.

Examines very high literacy rate in Iceland. Presents secondary data concerning publishing, library scene, etc. Analyses data got on the basis of a survey of citizens, series of interview, sponsored by the Spencer Foundation.

PART III

PUBLISHING, SOCIAL SCIENCES, LIBRARY LEGISLATION, AND OTHER RELATED SUBJECTS

PART III

PUBLISHING, SOCIAL SCIENCES, LIBRARY LEGISLATION, AND OTHER RELATED SUBJECTS

030 ENCYCLOPAEDIA BRITANNICA, ENCYCLOPAEDIAS

PARAMESWARAN, M 1926

Propaedia of Encyclopaedia Britannica : A conceptual model of knowledge organisation, *COP*, 260-268.

Gives introduction of the Encyclopaedia Britannica (EB) and its parts. States that *EB* is the best example of general encyclopedias and the most comprehensive survey of knowledge. Describes that the nine parts of knowledge are represented as segments of the circle of knowledge and arranged like petals around the tenth part, namely the study of knowledge. The parts are further divided into divisions, sections and subsection. Explains that each of the ten segments corresponds to either one or more academic disciplines. Establishes some similarity between ten segments of knowledge in the *Propaedia* and the ten (Main Classes) in DDC. Concludes that it is a good example of cognitive library classification scheme.

039. 9145 Encyclopaedia in Oriya

PADHI, PITAMBARA 1927

Encyclopaedia making in the Oriya language : Its genesis and development, *CLIS Observer* 10 (1-2) Jan-June 1993: 17-25.

Aims at making an objective assessment of the growth of Oriya reference sources particularly of encyclopaedias from 1807. Excludes reference sources in English. Study based on author's doctoral thesis. Suggests methods for encyclopaedia compilation, editing, evaluation, etc.

050 PERIODICALS. JOURNALS . SERIALS

GUPTA, PAWAN K 1928

Serial publications in India, In *Papers*, 58th IFLA General Conference, New Delhi, 30 Aug - 5 Sept 1992, pp 5.12-5.14.

Deals with the history and development of serial publications in India. Describes the present status of serials with examples and statistical data. Seems to be an introduction to the provision of legal deposit, guides and union catalogue of serials, indexing and abstracting services, etc. Points towards a bright future.

MARICIC, SINISA 1929

Evaluating periodicals at the scientific periphery, *Iaslic Bull* 38 (1) Mar 1993 : 1-16.

Defines in this review article, scientific periphery giving its characteristics. Studies 531 journals from the period 1945-89 using two types of variables. Suggests sharp dichotomy between science and social science plus humanities with journals longevity. Evaluates journals on terminology, approach, internal evaluation, editing-and publishing quality. Mentions about indicator correlations. Discusses few basic questions in view of the methodology described.

070.5 PUBLISHING

BEDI, D S and AGGARWAL, K R 1930

Colour printing-today and tomorrow, *Desi Bull Inf Tech* 12 (2) Mar 1992: 3-10.

Mentions how various R & D activities led to the advent of colour printing-an exciting trend in printing technology. Discusses about various challenges and problems in colour printing. Elaborates the basic colour printing technologies, viz. dot matrix, ink-jet, thermal transfer and laser, some of which can increase quality with lower cost. Predicts the predominance of true colour laser printers and other technologies, giving photographic quality printing at desktop.

COLAIANNI, LOIS ANN 1931

Medical librarians as more active consumers of the published literature, *ML*, 89-91.

States that for years the relationship between medical librarians and editors and publishers has been one where librarians purchase the publishing output. Mentions that it is apparent that medical librarians should assume a more active role to encourage publishers to use permanent paper, to adhere to standards, to publish errata in a citable format, to consider the effect prior to changing titles, to improve article titles and abstracts to ensure retrieval, and so on.

070.5 (1) Multimedia Publishing

FELDMAN, TONY 1932

Turn of the tide- a new age in multimedia publishing, *Ann Lib Sci & Docum* 39 (3) Sept 1992: 86-88.

Mentions about growth in electronic information. Stresses the role of CD-ROM technology creating the concept of digital multimedia. Explains the spread of multimedia and its relation with the publisher.

070.5 (1) DTP

ARUNA, A 1933

Role of desk top publishing (DTP) in information centres, *CRL*, 164-176.

Traces the history of DTP. Discusses its major advantages and disadvantages. Assesses some of the software packages available in India. Highlights the role of DTP in information centres.

GAUR, R C, GAUR, KAVITA, BOSE, SANGEETA and SINGHAL, SEEMA 1934

The use of Desk Top Publishing for in house publishing & printing, *ITAH*, 93-104.

Outlines the importance of DTP technology-just 10 years old - in the production of in-house publications. Explains the need for in-house publishing in libraries to save time, and effort, improve quality, for effective communication, etc. Describes various components of DTP as computer and computer softwares. Gives benefits of using DTP system. Provides case studies of CRRI, Tata Unisys Ltd, etc.

KRISHAN KUMAR 1935

Desktop publishing : A revolutionary technology, *CTIT*, 73-88.

Traces the emergence of DTP. Discusses state-of-the-art of printing industry. Describes the pressure on publishing and printing industries. Describes DTP as a revolutionary technology as it brought 'what you see is what you get' environment. Discusses about advantages of DTP which made it popular. Mentions its components which make the system work. Illustrates it with flowcharts.

NATARAJAN, M 1936

Desktop publishing : Its impact on library and information centres, *CTIT*, 61-72.

Defines DTP. Discusses need for DTP. Mentions key elements, components, software of DTP. Describes as to why DTP is required in libraries as public service desks, displays materials, administrative applications, presentation support. Describes the available DTP softwares. Mentions about marketing, advantages and disadvantages, and maintenance of DTP computer.

RAMESH, D B , DAS, SUCHITRA and SAHU, J R 1937

Desktop publishing - its elements, economics and applications, *Luck Libn* 24 (2) Apr-Jun 1992 : 58-62.

Presents a comparative flowsheet on various steps involved in the DTP and Traditional Publishing Technique (TPT). Describes the DTP system, its elements, economics, applications, advantages, software available in the market.

RAVINDRA KUMAR, NAGAR, B R and
SRIVASTAVA, MANJU 1938

Indian Science Abstracts : The role of DTP using Xerox Ventura Publisher Ver. 2.0. *CTIT*, 89-94.

Describes processing of Indian Science Abstracts (ISA) through conventional methods during 1965-89, followed by its processing with DTP for ISA giving its layout. Mentions the future trends in ISA. Concludes that processing time is reduced to one third as compared to the output through conventional methods.

070.50954 Publishing - India

KAR, DEBJANI 1939

Printing : Its origin and development with particular reference to preindependent India, *Coll Lib* 9 (1-4) 1993: 14-20.

Traces origin and spread of printing from ancient times. Discusses advent or invention of printing in Europe. Explains Gutenberg and his role in typographic printing. Describes development of processes and presses, early printing in India. Mentions role of William Carey in the history of Indian printing.

NARENDER KUMAR 1940

Book publishing : Problems and prospects, *Granthana* 3 (1) Jan 1992: 7-28.

Assesses the status of various types of books published in India including text books and children's books. Examines various variables that influence production and sales of books. Explains also role of few agencies, training facilities available and prospects of book publishing in India.

300.3 Social Sciences - Dictionaries

PURKAYASTHA, PRADIPTO DAS 1941

Dictionaries in the social science, *Int Lib Move* 15 (2) June 1993 : 65-70.

Provides a brief overview of some of the randomly selected dictionaries in the social sciences. The account is neither exhaustive, not representative.

302.2 Communication

EFFECTIVE technical presentation, *Desi Bull Inf Tech* 1942 13 (4) July 1993 : 3-7.

Discusses how to present technically your paper at the seminars, conferences, and help in improving your participation at such meetings and to become a more effective presenter and communicator. Gives general tips for planning the presentation, delivering the talk, use of visuals. Outlines reasons for failure of a presentation.

GUPTA, O P 1943

Audiovisual media for educational communication, *ALR*, 259-265.

Discusses role of IT and education and information communication. Mentions need for effective communication system for the overall development of society. Explains modern AV communication methods, and impact of AV communication which is yet to gain popularity. Points out major impediments in effective communications. Highlights role of UGC in initiating 'Countrywide Classroom' programme for higher education on Doordarshan National Network. Mentions future programmes also.

GUPTA, R C 1944

Communications among structural engineers, *ALIS*, v 4, 21-30.

Gives importance of land among basic human needs. Feels that AVs play important role in providing such information to its users. Puts forward the bottlenecks faced by its clientele in way of proper communications. Concludes that information communication is a regular process among experts in their work and study.

PANDEY, R D 1945

Study of information theory of Shannon and Weaver, *INICAE* 11 (1) Mar 1992 : 64-72.

Explains the concept of Information Theory. Describes some of the fundamental elements of the theory and processes that enter into communication model. Analyses human communication in general and mathematical theory of communication of Shannon and Weaver. Defines areas where communications breakdowns occur. Suggests reasons and remedies for failures to communicate.

RANGRA, V K and AJITH, P M 1946

Audio-visual communication techniques and technologies for information presentation, *ALIS*, v 4, 65-73.

Gives briefly the role of AVs in the perception of information. Describes AV communication technologies such as OHP, transparencies, 35 MM slides, audio tape recording, tape slide projection, motion picture film and video, computer system, video/TV projection, giving nomenclature and cost of the projecting equipment for acquisition. Covers also the multi-image/multivision and multimedia projection techniques.

SATIJA, M P 1947

Communication and Ranganathan, *Int Lib Move* 14 (2) June 1992 : 73-78.

Stresses the need of communication. Describes Ranganathan's contribution in communication of ideas through his various writings divided in four kinds : Seminal standard, research standard, non-specialist standards, and elementary standards. Mentions his contribution to LIS journals, series, etc.

TECHNICAL communication training course evokes keen participation, *NISSAT News* 11 (2) Apr-June 1992 : 5-6. 1948

Discusses about the fifth NISSAT-sponsored training course in technical communication organised by the SIS at NISTADS, New Delhi during 26-29 Feb 1992. Mentions the topics covered under five broad categories as general aspects editorial practice, storage and retirieval of information, communication of S & T information through mass media, and printing and production.

306.46 Technologies

A CHRONOLOGY of future technologies, *NISSAT News* 12 (4) Oct-Dec 1993: 19-21. 1949

Gives a chronology of future technologies compiled by Japanese researchers and is reprinted from STA TODAY, the monthly newsletter of the Science and Technology Agency, Japan. Mentions about the new technological developments starting with the year 2001 upto 2020.

331.544 Migration of Labour

PANDEY, HIMANSHU 1950

A probability model for migration from rural areas, *Jl Inf Sci* 3 (4) Apr-June 1993 : 195-199.

Attempts to study the pattern of migration from households through probability models, using rural households data on migration.

344.092 LIBRARY LEGISLATION

344.09254 LIBRARY LEGISLATION - INDIA

BARUA, B P 1951

Model public library bills : A critics view, *PLD*, 31-41.

Points out the four model public library bills in existence of 1930, 1963, 1966, and 1990. Makes a comparative analysis of the essential features of the four model bills. These features include the preamble, definition, state library authority, state library committee, Directorate of libraries. Public library finance, etc. Discusses the impact of model bills. Proposes alternative models. Gives reasons of library legislation as the providion of finances for their development. Suggests that there should be option to choose the model.

BISWAS, ASIT RANJAN and BALAKUMARI, N 1952

Ranganathan's influence on library legislation in India, *RAT*, 21-29.

Discusses need for and objectives of library legislation. Describes various efforts made by Ranganathan for framing of bills in the states. Explains library legislation in the states which have enacted them like Tamil Nadu, Andhra Pradesh, Karnataka, Maharashtra, West Bengal, Kerala, Haryana, and Manipur. Discusses the present position of the states which have yet to enact library legislation.

KAULA, P N 1953

Library legislation in India, In : *Trends in international librarianship* : A festschrift honouring Anis Khurshid, edited by Naimuddin Qureshi and Zahuruddin Khurshid, Karachi : Royal Book Company, 1991.

Deals with the state of affairs of library legislation in India. Describes the various efforts made in this direction by individuals and government, and the states in which library acts have been enacted and implemented. Mentions the need to have library legislation in all the states.

MAJEED KHAN, M A 1954

Structure of integrated public library system with a base, *SPLS*, 4.1-4.5.

Defines integrated library systems. Explains the main features of library legislation in India. Describes in detail the factors to be kept in view while enacting a public library law. Concludes that library law is essential for organisation and development of public library system and the Govt. of India should appoint a committee or commission for this purpose.

NARASIMHA RAJU, G V S L 1955

Persisted issues of public library legislation, *Granthana*, 3 (1) Jan 1992: 29-39.

Examines conceptual problems related to library legislation. Explains salient features to be incorporated in a model Act and puts forward some suggestions. Evaluates cess system. Dwells on the need for a specific legislation on public libraries. Draws elaborately on 22 principles as expounded by F M Gardner for consideration before library legislation is contemplated.

NAVALANI, K 1956

The tallest torch bearer, *PP*, 117-122.

Explains about Ranganathan's interest in library movement and library legislation almost from the late 1920s. Describes about his efforts from 1933 which were largely unsuccessful, but he continued relentlessly to succeed in 1948. Discusses his passion for public library legislation, and organised All India Seminar on Public Libraries in 1972 where he pleaded for National Grid of Public Library System for India.

RAMAN NAIR, R 1957

Principles for framing public library acts, *Luck Libn* 24 (2) July-Sept 1992: 118-125.

Traces the development of library legislation through the law meant for independent library units to that for library systems that provide for networking and resource sharing. Emphasises the importance legal provisions required in library acts. Points out the aspects that need special attention in countries like India.

VENKATAPPAIAH, V 1958

Model Public Libraries Acts - a comparative study, *Granthana* 4 (1-2) Jan-July 1993 : 19-28.

Attempts to compare five Acts/Bills for public libraries prepared during the last 60 years. Coves 9 aspects for study such as preamble, state level authority, national level authority, information executive at state level, city/district level authority, chairman of city/district authority, library fund, library cess.

VENKATAPPAIAH, V 1959

Model Public Libraries Act of ILA : Pleas for enactment, *Her Lib Sci* 31 (1-2) Jan-Apr 1992 : 94-95.

States that so far only eight states have enacted the Public Libraries Act and the remaining states and UTs have yet to pass the Libraries Act for effective and systematic service with regular funds. Mentions that the ILA's model public libraries act was published in its Bulletin in Oct-Dec 1990 which may be passed.

VENKATAPPAIAH, V 1960

State Library Authority; a missing live wire in the Madras Act, *Rilisar Bull* 8 (1) Jan-Mar 1993: 42-48.

Describes the State Library Authority in various library Acts. Discusses about the Head of the Authority. Mentions objectives of the State Library Authority (SLA). Explains SLA in context with Madras Libraries Act which is rather under revision. Mentions few features of ILA's Model Act.

VENKATAPPAIAH, V 1961

State Library Authority : Missing live wire in our library Acts, *PLD*, 133-140.

Mentions the states which have passed library legislation. Explains the role of State Library Authority (SLA). Discusses its duties. Mentions its status. Makes a comparison of SLA in all the states with library Acts as also the provision for Minister for Libraries. Points out the framing of Model Public Libraries Act in 1989 on request of the ILA.

344.0925413 Library Legislation - Orissa

MISHRA, SANJAY 1962

Orissa marches towards library legislation, *IJILIS* 5 (3-4) July-Dec 1992 : 221-234.

Discusses the need of public library and its role in promotion of literacy as well as information and public relation. Stresses the ceaseless efforts of last two decades that Dr B B Shukla has taken up for implementation of library legislation in Orissa and the High Power Committee's decision to implement the Act in March 1993.

SHUKLA, B B 1963

Enactment of public library legislation for Orissa, *Her Lib Sci* 31 (3-4) July-Oct 1992: 253-255.

Discusses about the efforts made by the author to get the Library Bill enacted in Orissa since 1974 by organising meetings, seminars, conferences, and urging upon the Government of Orissa to enact the Bill into Act. Gives the Appeal he has made to the Chief Minister of Orissa on 27 January 1992 in this regard.

SHUKLA, B B 1964

State Conference on Library Legislattion for Orissa, *Her Lib Sci* 31 (1-2) Jan-Apr 1992: 69-73.

Reports about the Third State Conference on Library

Legislation for Orissa and the UGC Payscales for College and University Librarians was held on 2 October 1991 at Utkal University, Bhubaneswar, and was organised by the *IJILIS*. Discusses the Welcome, Inauguration, Keynote Address by P N Kaula, and the two technical sessions.

VENKATAPPAIAH, V 1965

Orissa needs a comprehensive library act, *IJILIS* 6 (1-2) Jan-June 1993: 101-124.

Deals comprehensiviely with the need for library legisalation in all the states. Discusses briefly the attempts of ILA, ULA, OAAPL in this direction, and the submission of Model Public Library Bill by the author to the Chief Minister, Orissa in 1991. Discusses constant efforts of Dr. B B Shukla for overall library movement in the state since 1973, and particularly awaring people for library consciousness and promulgation of Library Acts for Orissa. Elucidates guidelines for legislation, salient features of Model Library Act, State Library Authority, and the structure of the state library system.

344.092542 Library Legislation - UP

VENKATAPPAIAH, V 1966

Library legislation in Uttar Pradesh : An immediate need, *Luck Libn* 24 (4) Oct-Dec 1992: 159-164.

Stresses the need for the enactment of UP Library Act in Uttar Pradesh. Describes the efforts made by the professional associations and persons to achieve this end. Suggests that the UP Public Library Bill drafted by the Viswanathan Committee needs revision to incorporate a few more useful provisions.

344.09254558 Library Legislation - Haryana

MAHAWAR, K L 1967

Haryana Public Libraries Act, *PLD*, 141-148.

Explains the provisions of the Haryana Public Libraries Act. Gives its background and objectives. Discusses State Library Authority, Directorate of Public Libraries, Director of Libraries, State Librarian, creation of public library fund, library cess. Gives an overall assessment.

344.0925483 Library Legislation - Kerala

NASIRUDEEEN, T P O 1968

History of library legislation in Kerala : An overview, *CS*, 39-46.

Traces the role of Kerala Granthasala Sangham in library movement and provides a bird's eyeview of the attempts at library legislation in Kerala and passing of the Kerala Public Libraries Act.

RAMAN NAIR, R 1969

Reforms required in Kerala Public Library Act, 1989, *ILA Bull* 28 (1-2) Apr-Sept 1992: 35-42.

Argues that public library system in federal countries will be effective only if they are planned as national systems. Suggests the reforms that are essential to be made in the Kerala Public Library Act to achieve its aims and objectives.

SUKUMARAN NAIR, N 1970

Library legislation in Kerala, *TDF*, 70-77.

Dicusses the need for library legislation. Describes earlier attempts made in this respect in Kerala. Gives the present public library set up in Kerala. Outlines the Kerala Public Libraries Act 1989 spreading over ten chapters. Mentions the provision of finance. Gives features of the model bill. Concludes with an opromistic note.

344.0925484 Library Legislation - A P

RAGHAVAIAH, A 1971

Library legislation in India with special reference to Andhra Pradesh, *SPLS*, 3.1-3.4.

States the importance of library legislation Traces the history of A P Public Libraries Act of 1960 Mentions difficulties in depositing library cess and delay in remittance. Describes the penal clause. Discusses the aims and object of A P Grandhalaya Parishad set up in the place of the State Library Committee.

346.0482 COPYRIGHT LAW

NYEREMBE, M P 1972

Legal problems arising from data protection and the use of online information sources : A challenge to Third World countries, *Int Lib Move* 14 (2) June 1992 : 96-105.

Attempts to point out present and possible future problems and the policies which should be considered in any proposed solution for protection of programs and data.

346.04820954 Copyright Law - India

GOEL, PREETI 1973

Copyright in India, *Univ News* 31 (24) June 14, 1993: 9-10.

Defines copyright. Discusses need for copyright and the provision of the international copyright describing them in historical perspective. Explains the Indian scenario since 1914 and the Copyright Act of 1957.

346.0486 PATENTS LAW

HIRWADE, ANIL W and HIRWADE, MANGLA 1974

Patenting activity during 1991: Indian scenario, *ILA Bull* 27 (4) Jan-Mar 1992: 182-193.

Analyses trends in patenting of inventions, the patents accepted and notified during 1991, with reference to the country of origin and subject. Gives major patents of Indian origin patents and subjectwise breakup of major countries filing patents in India.

374.4 DISTANCE EDUCATION

MUTTHIRULANDI, RAJA 1975

Distance education : Are we on the right path ? *IPLA Souvenir*, 3p.

Deals with the spread of correspondence courses started by many university/colleges in India to relieve the pressure on the regular system. Suggests the use of some major needs in the field of education using appropriate technology and strategies.

384.5 (1) Technical Communication

SHARMA, R N and TANEJA, RAM D 1976

Technical communication: SIS training course, Chandigarh, *NISSAT News* 12 (1) Jan-Mar 1993: 14-16.

Reports about the Sixth Course in the series of courses in technical communication organised by the Society for Information Science and the DSIR under the NISSAT Programme, held at the Institute of Microbial Technology, Chandigarh, during 3-6 Nov 1992. Gives the features of the course, the inaugural function, the valedictory, and the participants' response. Mentions the topics dealt with in the lectures and tutorials. Makes suggestions for improving the usefulness of future courses.

418.02 TRANSLATION. SCIENTIFIC TRANSLATION TECHNICAL TRANSLATION

CHAWLA, ASHOK K 1977

Scientific translation : Current perceptions, *NISSAT News* 12 (1) Jan-Mar 1993: 12-13.

Reports about the one-day colloquium organised by the Indian Scientific Translators Association on the occasion of the International Translation Day on 30 Sept 1992 in which 40 experts from various institutions participated to discuss about the current perceptions of the scientific translation. Mentions to promote translation activities, to improve the status of translators, and to set up a databank for terminology.

DESHPANDE, A L 1978

Translation as a literary discipline : Rewards of being a translator, *Univ News* 31 (19) May 10, 1993 : 7-8.

Deals with translation as a literary discipline, and very close to creativity. Mentious about the rewards of being a translator.

MAHESWARAPPA, BS, KARISIDDAPPA, CR and SANGAM, SL 1979

The foreign language barrier among the Indian statisticians, *ALR*, 223-235.

Makes a study to know foreign language knowledge, methods of keeping abreast, steps to overcome language barrier, usefulness of translation services. Suggests some remedial measures. Analyses data collected in statistics through questionnaire.

NEGERI, BEKLE 1980

Need for technical translation service for the manufacturing sector in Ethiopia, *Ann Lib Sci & Docum* 40 (2) June 1993: 56-58.

Discusses technical translation activities in the public manufacturing sector based on a questionnaire survey conducted with 40 representative enterprises drawn from seven industry groups in Ethiopia. Recommends for setting up technical translation service at national level.

418.02 (1) MACHINE TRANSLATION

A MULTILINGUAL computer aided translating system 1981

will handle nine languages, NISSAT News 12 (3) July-Sept 1993: 24-25.

Describes Eurotra, a computer aided translating system will, in a few years, make it possible to juggle with the nine official languages of the European Community. States that it will speed up translation process and reduce the enormous costs work on which is being done since 1982.

UNESCO/NISSAT/NISTADS Regional Workshop on New 1982

Information Technologies : Machine translation, NISSAT News 11 (1) Jan-Mar 1992: 7-8.

Discusses about the Regional Workshop held on machine translation at New Delhi held during 16-20 Dec 1991. Lists its main objectives. Gives the recommendations that emerged from the discussion at the Workshop relating to machine translation, terminology and training. There were in all 20 participants from ASTINFO countries.

494.82703 Telugu Dictionary

CHETTY, P RAJARATNAM, ANKI REDDY, D C and PRATAPA REDDY, B 1983

Subject dictionaries in Telugu language : A study, *Iaslic Bull* 38 (1) Mar 1993: 45-48.

Defines a dictionary. Differentiates general and subject dictionaries. Narrates subject dictionaries in Telugu language including contribution of the great Telugu lexicographers. Observes the trend in the subject. Suggests for further development in this field.

VENUGOPAL, M V and SANKARA REDDY, M 1984

Concordance as tool for research in language: An appraisal of padaprayoga kosas in Telugu, *Iaslic Bull* 38 (1) Mar 1993 : 39-43.

Explains the meaning, method and scope of concordance as a tool of lexicographic research. Examines its status in Telugu. Points out need for extending its scope and coverage in the light of resurgence of activities in India aimed at modernization and development of all languages including Telugu. Suggests necessity and possibility of using computer as a means to eliminate the tedium and ensure speed and accuracy as well as cost-effectiveness.

610.5 Medical Journals

ADDO, D B 1985

Viability and stability of African medical journals, *ML,* 1-6.

Identifies communication as one of the serious impediments in the practice of science in developing countries and often research findings of scientists in developing countries are rejected by established journals for insignificance of results. Reviews the efforts, pattern of growth and characteristics of these journals. Considers orientations and measures, including the possible role of librarians needed to ensure sustained growth.

BHAT, M K 1986

Physical elements in the make-up of select Indian health science serials : Their role in information delivery, *ML*, 47-53.

Examines through the sample study of 32 Indian health science serials various physical elements in their make up that impact the users and information processing. Mentions these elements relate to cover, content pages, layout of first page of article, information about subscription and ad rates, instruction to authors, ISSN and RIN number, coverage by indexing/ abstracting services, numbering of volume/issue, volume indexes for subject. Reveals wide variations in the inclusion of these elements by different journals.

STEPHEN, L 1987

Medical journals in the West and in India, *Nat Medi Jl India* 5, 1992.

Discusses about the status, publications, use, etc of the medical journals in the Western countries as compared to India.

TONOSAKI, MASAAKI 1988

Categorization of tertiary medical journals by their bibliographic structures' point of views, *ML*, 479-485.

Discusses for the bibliographic structure of tertiary medical journals systematically by using 36 review medical journals, the relationships between the number of columns and total pages in one volume, average page number per article, total number of pages, publication countires, frequencey and column structure, etc. Shows that tertiary medical journals can be mostly categorised in three groups.

808.899282 Children' Literature

APEJI, ADECHE 1989

Macmillan's children's literature : An appraisal, *Int Lib Move* 14 (1) Mar 1992: 1-11.

Defines children's literature. Describes in detail the children's literature produced by Macmillan Publisher for which a survey was conducted from the Publishers at Ibadan, National Library Lagos, some bookshops, etc.

891.1 (1) Katha

DHARMAJARAN, GEETA 1990

Katha and its literacy projects, In *Papers*, 58th IFLA General Conference, New Delhi, 30 Aug - 5 Sept 1992.

Describes in detail about the Katha and its literary projects which will be helpful in furthering the cause of literature in India.

920.3 Rammohun Roy - Biography

BOSE, NEMAI SADAN 1991

Rammohun Roy : Pioneer of political protest movement in India, *Granthana* 3 (2) July 1992: 105-113.

Identifies three broad trends in the general conclusions of historical writings and research works on Rammohun Roy which differ sharply in their assessment and conclusions. Concludes that it was Roy who gave the idea of launching political protest movement in India. Gives its techniques followed be earlier political associations and the INC till the end of the 19th century.

954.03 History of India - Early 19th Century

DAS GUPTA, ASHIN 1992

Calcutta and the Indian Ocean in the days of Rammohun Roy, *Granthana* 4 (1-2) Jan-July 1993: 1-7

States that a fuller understanding of Rammohun Roy's thoughts be considered against other alternatives that existed in his times. Considers three alternatives as the King Alungpaya of Burma, Prince Dipanagara of Central Java, and Rammohun Roy, and critically explores the alternatives offered by these conditions that prevailed in the early 19th century colonial Indian Ocean areas.

PART - IV

SUPPLEMENT

020.3 LIS-Dictionaries

KAWATRA, P S 1993

Dictionary of library science, New Delhi : Castle Books, 1992 267 p.

Includes hundreds of LIS terms arranged in alphabetical order. Gives standard definitions in clear, simple and lucid style. Also gives synonyms, acronyms and abbreviations with definitions so as to make it useful for all.

023

MANPOWER DEVELOPMENT STAFF DEVELOPMENT

SURIYA, M and SELVAM 1993-A

A study of career development among library professionals with special reference to Annamalai University, *LIM* , D2.

Analyses the personal and professional characteristics of the staff members of the Annamalai University Library and the effect of these variables on their respective carrier development, and impact of personal and family characteristics on career development.

023.8 In service Training

SHAH, A A 1994

In-house training as a method of enhancing the efficiency of professionally trained and untrained staff in CSMCRI - Bhavnagar Library -a case study, *LIM*, D 1.

Discusses the problems encountered by the library due to lack of adequate staff, and the measures taken at the CSMCRI Library for enhancing the capacity and capability of the existing professional and non-professional staff.

025.0285 Library Computerisation

PATWARDHAN, D V 1995

A case study of computerisation activities in Technical Information Centre of KEC, *LIM* F2.

Explains the need for computerisation of in house functions

of Technical Information centre. Reviews steps involved in automation. Explains factors involved in choosing the functions which are to be computerised on priority. Discuss databases activities of TIC and their benefits to users.

VAGISWARI, A, LOUIS, CHRISTINA and MANJUNATH, H N 1996

Indian Institute of Astrophysics library automation: A case study, *LIM*, F3.

Mentions about IIA library. Explains about the experience of automation at this library and creating the database of books with CDS/ISIS Ver 2.3. Lists the features of the system. Mentions also the limitations. Discusses about the circulation, serial control, ordering, and so on.

VENUGOPAL, S and SEETHARAMAN, P 1997

Case study on automation at Bharathidasan University Library, *LIM*, F 1

Describes the bibliographical databases design,and outlines the contents and formats of the record. Records merits of bifurcating the Master Database. Proposes practical steps to be followed for retrospective conversion of bibliographical records. Presents the problems encountered while translating the whole spectrum of pragmatic techniques towards achieving an integrated library management system.

025.1 LIBRARY MANAGEMENT

JANAKI, A 1998

Quality concepts in library management: A case study of HMT's Central Technical Information Centre, *LIM*, E 2.

States what is quality and how to manage it. Discusses the adoption of '5 S' Principles, participative management, just in-time techniques of CTIC to improve the quality of its services. Concludes that quality has gained utmost importance.

PANIGRAHI, PIJUSHKANTI and PRASAD, A R D 1999

Computer simulation: An alternative to case study, *LIM*, A I.

Discusses case study and its applications. Discusses computer simulation and its uses in library management. Explains how computer simulation can help library managers to understand real-world-systems. Demonstrates in detail a simulated circulation system. Concludes that for effective management of information systems, case study complements simulation as a method of evaluation.

PRASAD, K M 2000

Time management in HMT's Central Technical Information Centre: A case study, *LIM*, 1.

Defines time management. Discusses the methodologies followed in CTIC in the efficient management of time in rendering information service to its users.

SEETHARAMA, S, ED 2001

Workshop on library and information management, August 7-9, 1992, Bangalore: Documentation Reseearch and Training Centre, 1992, various pagings.

Includes 23 papers presented at the DRTC Workshop organised in the Ranganathan Centenary Year at DRTC, Bangalore during August 7-9, 1992. Discusses various aspects of library and information management, grouped into eight parts numbered A to H.

SEETHARAMA, S and PAUL PANDIAN, M 2002

PLANNER: An automated decision support system for planning of libraries and information centres, *LIM*, A 2.

Discusses the need for planning and highlights the elements of library planning. Provides details regarding PLANNER which is an automated decision support system for planning of libraries and information centres. Mentions also its limitations.

SURYANARAYANA, Y V 2003

Problems in the management of libraries: A case study, *LIM*, B 4.

Introduces library of the Central Tobacco Research Institute, Rajamundry. Discusses some problems encountered in the area of financial management regarding budget details, stock verification, and manpower utilisation in this special library and information centre.

025.11 (1) Cost-Benefit Analysis

VAISHNAV, A A and BASOLE, MEDHA 2004

Cost-benefit analysis in relation to the reading room section of Marathawada University Library, *LIM*, G 1.

Analyses the cost of running the Reading Room Section of

Marathawada University Library considering book use as a criteria for measuring benefits, total transactions during 1990 were considered. The imputed cost and depreciation was calculated on fixed investment. Calculates total cost and benefits by using various models. Mentions the average benefits per book.

025.1794 Microforms

KAPOOR, S K 2005

Integrated micrographic information storage and retrieval system in GSI: A case study, *LIM*, H 1.

Discusses the planning and implementation of an integrated micrographic information storage and retrieval system at Geological Survey of India, Calcutta. Suggests also the use of optical storage system alongwith micro-graphic systems for effective management of information resources. Concludes that it has served to provide micro publishing of GSI's own serial documents.

025.48(1) Bibliometrics

NAVANEETHAN, R 2006

Having live periodicals in a technical library-why and how? A case study, *LIM*, B2.

Applies quantification technique for deciding the usefulness of currently subscribed journals in the technical libraries. Considers two factors-unit cost of useful item published by each periodical and percentage of useful productivity of each periodical -as deciding factors which resulted in maintaining a live collection of periodicals. Gives data in Appendices.

RAVICHANDRA RAO, I K 2007

Bibliometric approach for evaluation of library collection : A case study, *LIM*, B 1.

Analyses circulation transaction record to study the concentration of uses in relation to documents in specialist library. Observes that hardly 40 per cent of the documents were used. Works out median time lag and idle time of books as 34.7 and 26.7 months respectively. Discusses application of bibliometric techniques for library operations.

025.2 COLLECTION DEVELOPMENT

SURIYA AM and VENKATAKESAVAN, R 2008

Collection management in the Rajah Muthiah Institute of Health Science Library: A case study, *LIM*, B 5.

Explains collection management in collection development and collection evaluation. Mentions the objectives. Analyses data related to library expenditure, number of users, collection size, circulation procedures for the period 1980-81 to 1991-92. Examines the utility of the libraries regarding its growth, cost per volume, volume per user, cost per circulation, etc.

025.52 REFERENCE AND INFORMATION SERVICES

GOPINATH, M A 2009

Reference service in action, *LIM*, C.1

Presents case studies on reference service. Analyses them in the context of user's expression of his need, the search, and the feedback. Identifies the all pervasive role of the librarian and delineates the knowledge and skill required for providing reference service. Highlights Ranganathan's approach in organising reference section/system/services.

025.5276 Reference and Information Services-Special Libraries

RAMANANDA, B S 2010

Technical information services at Titan Watches Ltd: Case studies, *LIM*, C2.

Discusses five case studies pertaining to technical information services to the different clientele, viz, purchase, top management, R & D and design, marketing, and users at all levels. Concludes that information professionals should have high qualifications in appropriate subject field and LIS.

025.52781 Reference and Information Services-Medical Libraries

MURTHY, SUDHA S 2011

Case studies in a specialised health science library, *LIM*, C 4.

Mentions about information service units and the National Tuberculosis Institute. Presents case studies involving medical and para-medical professionals, and health administrators for whom information is vital for decision-making and also for updating their knowledge.

025.58772 User studies - University Libraries

SATYANARAYANA, M 2012

Utility of periodicals in the Andhra University Library: Case study, *LIM*, B 3.

Mentions importance of periodicals as sources of information. Explains the methodology. Studies the use made of periodicals by the faculty of Andhra University who visited the library during the period of survey. Analyses the data by users, periodicals consulted in different subjects, borrowed periodicals. Mentions reasons for poor utility of periodicals. Makes suggestions to enhance their use.

025.82 (1) Stock Verification and Computer

ASUNDI, A Y 2013

Computerised collection inventory: A case study of City Central Library of Bangalore, *LIM*, B 6.

States collection management in libraries is a ongoing problem. Discusses about City Central Library, Bangalore. Describes a computerised procedure named INVENTORY which could be used for stock verification of both small and big libraries. Mentions the steps to be taken in stock verification operation.

025.84 (1) Weeding

RAMAKRISHNA REDDY, K 2014

Weeding-out of documents: A case study, *LIM*, B 7.

Explains what is weeding. Discusses need for weeding-out. Presents the methodology evolved and adopted in NICMAP Library for weeding-out of various types of documents, based on data collected from 1989-90 to 1991-92. Describes about the disposal of weeded -out documents. Gives data regarding the case study in Annextures.

028.7 Sources of Information

SHAH, P C 2015

Production and publications of a secondary periodical: A case study, *LIM*, C 3.

States the setting up of ATIRA and NICTAS in Ahmedabad. Discusses the steps involved in the production and publication of TEXICON, a secondary periodical from NICTAS. Describes the marketing efforts undertaken and provides information on the cost of production of TEXICON.

070.5 (1) DTP

ARUNA, A 2016

Usefulness of desk top publishing in documentation centres: A cost benefit study, *LIM*, G 2.

Mentions about DTP. Gives its need in research organisations. States its advantages. Makes a case study of the cost-benefit analysis of the DTP and phototype setting. Discusses problems in DTP operations. Gives their solutions. Concludes that DTP is the best alternative to traditional printing for any organisation.

PART V
INDEXES

PART -V
SUBJECT INDEX

AUTHOR INDEX